Stalin's Soviet Justice

Stalin's Soviet Justice

"Show" Trials, War Crimes Trials, and Nuremberg

Edited by David M. Crowe

BLOOMSBURY ACADEMIC
LONDON • NEW YORK • OXFORD • NEW DELHI • SYDNEY

BLOOMSBURY ACADEMIC
Bloomsbury Publishing Plc
50 Bedford Square, London, WC1B 3DP, UK
1385 Broadway, New York, NY 10018, USA

BLOOMSBURY, BLOOMSBURY ACADEMIC and the Diana logo are trademarks
of Bloomsbury Publishing Plc

First published in Great Britain 2019
This paperback edition published in 2021

Copyright © David M. Crowe, 2019

David M. Crowe has asserted his right under the Copyright, Designs and Patents Act, 1988, to be identified as Editor of this work.

Cover image © Members of the Soviet delegation during the Potsdam Conference between the USSR, US and UK, Berlin, 1945. (© SPUTNIK / Alamy Stock Photo)

All rights reserved. No part of this publication may be reproduced or transmitted in any form or by any means, electronic or mechanical, including photocopying, recording, or any information storage or retrieval system, without prior permission in writing from the publishers.

Bloomsbury Publishing Plc does not have any control over, or responsibility for, any third-party websites referred to or in this book. All internet addresses given in this book were correct at the time of going to press. The author and publisher regret any inconvenience caused if addresses have changed or sites have ceased to exist, but can accept no responsibility for any such changes.

A catalogue record for this book is available from the British Library.

A catalog record for this book is available from the Library of Congress.

ISBN: HB: 978-1-3500-8334-9
PB: 978-1-3501-9691-9
ePDF: 978-1-3500-8335-6
eBook: 978-1-3500-8336-3

Typeset by Deanta Global Publishing Services, Chennai, India

To find out more about our authors and books visit www.bloomsbury.com and sign up for our newsletters.

Alexander Victor Prusin
(1955–2018)
'Of Blessed Memory'

Contents

List of Contributors		viii
Introduction *David M. Crowe*		1
1	Late Imperial and Soviet "Show" Trials, 1878–1938 *David M. Crowe*	31
2	Traitors or War Criminals: Collaboration on Trial in Soviet Courts in the 1940s *Alexander V. Prusin*	79
3	*Nikto ne zabyt*: The Politicization of Soviet War Dead *Thomas Earl Porter*	105
4	The Human Face of Soviet Justice? Aron Trainin and the Origins of the Soviet Doctrine of International Criminal Law *Valentyna Polunina*	127
5	"May Justice Be Done!" The Soviet Union and the London Conference (1945) *Irina Schulmeister-André and David M. Crowe*	145
6	The Soviet Union at the Palace of Justice: Law, Intrigue, and International Rivalry in the Nuremberg Trials *Francine Hirsch*	171
7	Soviet Journalists at Nuremberg: Establishing the Soviet War Narrative *Jeremy Hicks*	199
8	From Geneva to Nuremberg to New York: Andrey Vyshinsky, Raphaël Lemkin, and the Struggle to Outlaw Revolutionary Violence, State Terror, and Genocide *Douglas Irvin-Erickson*	217
Bibliography		233
Index		240

List of Contributors

David M. Crowe is a presidential fellow at Chapman University and Professor Emeritus of History and Law at Elon University, where he held a joint appointment at the School of Law and the Department of History. His most recent books include *Da tu-sha gen-yuan li-shi yu yubo* (The Holocaust: Roots, History and Aftermath) (2015), *Germany and China: Transcultural Encounters since the Eighteenth Century* (with Joanne Cho; 2014), *War Crimes, Genocide, and Justice: A Global History* (2014); and *The Holocaust: Roots, History, and Aftermath* (2008). His books have been translated and published in Chinese, Dutch, German, Japanese, Polish, and Ukrainian.

Jeremy Hicks is Professor of Russian Culture and Film at Queen Mary University of London, UK. He is the author of *Mikhail Zoshchenko and the Poetics of Skaz* (2000), *Dziga Vertov: Defining Documentary Film* (2007), and *First Films of the Holocaust: Soviet Cinema and the Genocide of the Jews, 1938–1946* (2012), which won the ASEEES's 2013 Wayne C. Vucinich Prize for the most important contribution to the field of Slavic, East European, and Eurasian studies.

Francine Hirsch is Professor of History at the University of Wisconsin-Madison, USA. Her first book, *Empire of Nations: Ethnographic Knowledge and the Making of the Soviet Union* (2005), received the 2007 Herbert Baxter Adams Prize of the American Historical Association, the Council for European Studies 2006 Book Award, and the 2006 Wayne S. Vucinich Prize of the ASEEES for the most important contribution to Russian, Eurasian, and East European studies. Her forthcoming book, *Soviet Judgment at Nuremberg*, will be published in 2019.

Douglas Irvin-Erickson is Assistant Professor of Conflict Analysis and Resolution, Director of the Genocide Prevention Program, and Fellow at the Center for Peacemaking at the School for Conflict Analysis and Resolution at George Mason University, USA. He is the author of *Raphaël Lemkin and the Concept of Genocide* (2016) and the editor of *Genocide Studies and Prevention: An International Journal*, the official publication of the International Association of Genocide Scholars.

Valentyna Polunina is an affiliate member of the University of Heidelberg's Cluster of Excellence "Asia and Europe in a Global Context" program, Germany. She received her doctorate from the University of Heidelberg. Her dissertation deals with the trial of Japanese war criminals and Japan's biological warfare program at Khabarovsk in 1949. Prior to her current position with Germany's *Der Spiegel* in Washington, D.C., she taught in the Russia-Asia department at the Ludwig Maximilian University of Munich, Germany.

Thomas Earl Porter is Professor of Modern European History at North Carolina Agricultural and Technical State University in Greensboro, NC, USA. He has written extensively on the government and politics of late imperial Russia, the role of Russian public organizations during the First World War, the failure of Russian liberalism, and the fate of Soviet POWS during the Second World War. His most recent work is *Prince George L. L'vov: The Zemstvo, Civil Society, and Liberalism in Late Imperial Society* (2017).

Alexander Victor Prusin is Professor of History in the Humanities Department of the New Mexico Institute of Mining and Technology, Socorro, USA. He has authored a number of articles and three books: *Nationalizing a Borderland: War, Ethnicity, and Anti-Jewish Violence in East Galicia, 1914–1920* (2005); *The 'Lands Between': Conflict in the East European Borderlands, 1870–1992* (2010); and *Serbia under the Swastika: A World War II Occupation* (2017).

Irina Schulmeister-André is a judge of the District Court Gießen, Germany. She was a scholar at the Max Planck Institute for Legal History in Frankfurt am Main, where she began her research for her doctoral thesis on the role of the Soviet Union in the Nuremberg IMT trial.

Introduction

David M. Crowe

War has had a dramatic, and at times, devastating impact on Russia over the past few centuries. After the Napoleonic invasion in 1812, Alexander I, who once toyed with the idea of modest Enlightenment-era reforms, reverted to what would become standard political behavior for many of the tsars in the late imperial period—a rigid autocracy designed to protect the imperial system from real and imagined forces that threatened its power and stability. But what Alexander I, Nicholas I, Alexander III, and Nicholas II could never do was to halt the revolutionary fervor that was sweeping into Russia from Europe in the nineteenth and early twentieth centuries. In some ways, one could argue that Lenin and Stalin, who dominated Soviet Russia from 1917 to 1953, faced similar challenges, though the nature of the threats to their power and stability were driven, at least during the first decade of Bolshevik rule, by power struggles within the upper echelons of the Communist Party about the ideological and practical direction of Soviet rule.

Once Stalin won his power struggle against his principal rival, Leon Trotsky, he adopted new campaigns to collectivize Russian agriculture and dramatically increase industrial production. He decided in the late 1920s to use "show" trials as one of the ways to respond to growing domestic opposition to both programs. The "show" trials, extralegal proceedings that bore modest resemblance to more traditional Western-style trials, were carefully orchestrated to convince the public of the dire nature of such threats. Thematically, Stalin used them to highlight his fears about an ongoing threat of domestic and international forces determined to destroy the Soviet state. Wrapped in a façade of legality, the "show" trials were well-crafted propaganda exercises designed partially to rally a nation to support Stalin's goals.

"Show" trials in Russia can be traced back to that one bright spot in late imperial history—the reign of Alexander II, the "tsar liberator." Alexander II was not a visionary liberal but a pragmatist who realized that Russia's defeat in the Crimean War (1853–1856) was based on its economic and military backwardness vis-á-vis its principal opponents—England and France. Soon after he came to power, Alexander II initiated a series of reforms that addressed not only the single biggest factor for such backwardness—serfdom—but also the military, law, and the structure of civil society.[1]

As his reform program unfolded, it spurred new discussions among enlightened Russian thinkers such as Alexander Herzen and Boris Chicherin about different approaches to the transformation of Russian society. Some, like Mikhail Bakunin and Serge Nechaev, called for more radical, violent approaches to change that, according to

Vera Broido, advocated a "passion to destroy" that would result in "a new Russia based on free associations and the equally vague society forms."[2]

Chapter 1

David M. Crowe notes in "Late Imperial and Soviet 'Show' Trials, 1878–1938" that this included plans to assassinate prominent government officials to create uncertainty and instability throughout the country. By the 1870s, a new generation of revolutionaries decided to act more boldly, even if such actions led to their executions. One of them, Vera Zasulich, a young revolutionary with strong ties to Nechaev, was motivated not only by a series of government trials of several hundred revolutionaries in 1877 and 1878 but also by stories about the public flogging of another revolutionary, Alexei Bogolyubov, in St. Petersburg's Kresty prison. The beating had been ordered by Dmitri Trepov, the governor general of the city, who was offended when Bogolyubov refused to tip his hat when Trepov walked by during an inspection of the prison.[3]

Zasulich's plan was to assassinate Trepov in his office and then stand trial for his murder. But since she only wounded him, she was charged with attempted murder. And even though she confessed to her crime, the government decided a public trial and conviction by a jury, one of the centerpieces of the 1864 judicial reform program would "show the loyalty of Russia's people to their tsar."[4] But the government's plan backfired in large part because the judge, Anatony Koni, and Zasulich's attorney, P. A. Aleksandrov, were able to manipulate the proceedings in such a way that convinced the jury and much of the public of her innocence. This miscalculation led to what Julie A. Cassiday considers

> the validation of terrorism as a political act and was seen by many, including L.N. Tolstoi, as a "harbinger of" revolution. The moral ruling handed down by the Zasulich jury, as well as the popular support this verdict received, illustrated to other Russian radicals how the tsarist court could function as a tool for the cause of social change.[5]

This was certainly the case when it came to the ideas of radicals like Sophia Perovskaya, and the brother of Lenin, Alexander Ulyanov.[6]

The trials of Perovskaya in 1881 for her role in the assassination of Alexander II and Ulyanov six years later for the attempted murder of Alexander III lacked some of the theatrics of the Zasulich proceedings but did engender considerable public interest in their ideas and fate. This was particularly the case with Perovskaya and her co-conspirators. Though she was spared execution until she gave birth to her child, the government staged a large, theatrical execution for her accomplices that drew a crowd of about 100,000 people.[7]

Alexander III personally orchestrated the trial of Ulyanov and his co-conspirators, and wanted to avoid any hint of a "show" or public spectacle. But efforts to conduct it in semi-secrecy failed when news of its sessions appeared in European Russian newspapers. The body of evidence against Ulyanov was overwhelming, and he openly admitted that he played a key role in the construction of the bombs that were to be used to kill the tsar. He also told the court that he "acted out of his own free will and rational mind."[8]

Robert Service and Elizabeth Wood argue that his execution gradually transformed his younger brother, Lenin, into a committed radical who encouraged young revolutionaries to use imperial trials to promote their radical ideals.[9] However, Crowe argues that it is important to differentiate between the "show" trials of the late imperial period from those conducted in the first two decades of Soviet power. Though the governments of Alexander III and Nicholas II did what they could to prevent radicals from using their trials for propaganda purposes, the trials themselves were conducted with a modicum of justice that would be absent in Soviet "show" trials.

But one must be careful with this idea because, as George F. Kennan has noted, over time tsarist officials developed a sinister program involving the secret police, the courts, and the exile system to strengthen their hands in their fight against terrorism. It rested on what he called "three classes of facts."

> Making indiscriminate arrests a means of inspiring terror and with the hope of obtaining clews to secret revolutionary activity; second, the use of imprisonment as a species of torture to extort confession or compel the prisoner to betray friends; and, third, the illegal detention of political "suspects" in solitary confinement for months and years while the police scour the empire in search of incriminating evidence upon which to base indictments.[10]

The Soviets adopted similar tactics on a much broader scale and used "show" trials as part of their campaign against those that threatened the sanctity of Soviet power. In an article in *Pravda* in 1918, Lenin wrote that the only way for the Bolshevik-led socialist revolution to succeed was through "iron rule" that was "revolutionary, bold, swift, and ruthless."[11] During the civil war (1918–1921), the Bolsheviks created revolutionary tribunals that were nothing more than "kangaroo courts" that dispensed field justice for anyone deemed a threat to Soviet power. Some used what Cassidy calls the "unsophisticated theatricality" of late imperial "show" trials, with some judges reaching their decisions based on their "revolutionary conscience."[12]

Once the civil war ended, Lenin decided that he wanted to move away from this more superficial form of justice and began to use what Mark Jensen notes were more "noisy, *educative* model trials" throughout the country.[13] Crowe writes that what followed, the trial of thirty-four Socialist Revolutionaries (SRs) in 1922, marked a whole new direction in Soviet criminal law based on a new penal code adopted on the eve of the trial. Before it opened, Lenin ordered a press campaign that encouraged nationwide demonstrations during the trial.

The SRs, once one of the most prominent revolutionary parties in Russia, was now a mere shadow of itself. The purpose of the trial was to destroy any hint of the party's heralded past and strengthen the Bolshevik's hold on power during the early phases of a new controversial program—the NEP (*Novaya Ekonomicheskaya Politika*; New Economic Policy). The thirty-four defendants were charged with opposing the Bolsheviks during the civil war, mass terror, and involvement in plans to assassinate Lenin in 1918. The court found two-thirds of the defendants guilty of counterrevolutionary crimes and sentenced them to death, but soon reduced them to life in prison. The rest of those convicted received much shorter sentences.[14]

What followed was an effort to codify criminal and civil law though, as Lenin reminded Dmitri Kursky, his commissar of justice, it was important not to "remove the terror" from the new criminal code. Crime was now viewed a "socially dangerous" act while justice itself was to be guided by the principles of retroactivity and analogy, which gave judges wide latitude to decide what was and what was not a crime. Moreover, they were to be guided in their decisions by their "socialist legal consciousness." According to Peter Solomon, the core Bolshevik ideas about criminal law at this time were "analogy, judicial discretion, and class favoritism."[15]

Crowe argues that the practice of criminal law during the NEP was very unsophisticated and ultimately led to calls for its revision, particularly after Stalin successfully defeated Trotsky in their struggle for power in 1927–1928. According to Harold J. Berman, the new criminal code further strengthened "analogy as a key principle of Soviet criminal law."[16] These changes took place in the midst of Stalin's early plans to dramatically increase agricultural and industrial production as part of a larger goal of making the Soviet Union a nation that could defend itself from countries like Britain, France, and Japan. This led to a campaign that Robert Service calls "terror economics" that resulted in widespread chaos, economic disruption, and the deaths of millions, particularly in Ukraine.[17]

Stalin responded to growing criticism of these policies with a series of "show" trials in the late 1920s and early 1930s that were meant to send a message to anyone, real or imagined, who criticized or resisted his efforts to transform Soviet Russia. Each of these proceedings—the Shakhty trial (1928), the Industrial Trial (1930), the Menshevik trial (1931), and the Metro-Vickers trial (1933)—were far better orchestrated than the SR trial. The secret police (OGPU; *Gosudarstvennoe politicheskoe upravlenie*), for example, used harsh interrogation methods to exact confessions from the defendants, and worked closely with Nikolai Krylenko, the chief prosecutor in all three trials, and Andrei Vyshinsky, the chief judge in the first two trials and chief prosecutor in the Metro-Vickers trial.

Krylenko and Vyshinsky worked closely with Stalin and Viacheslav Menshinsky, the head of the OGPU, to make certain that the dictated testimony of the Russian defendants fit comfortably with the charges in each trial's indictments. Any defendant who strayed from the legal script was verbally challenged by Krylenko or Vyshinsky in court and subjected to harsh interrogation methods soon after he gave his testimony. This would not be the case with the German and British defendants in the Shakhty and Metro-Vickers trials who, for the most part, proved uncooperative.

These legal spectacles were widely covered in the domestic and international press, which helped convince some of the foreign observers, who had doubts about the fairness of the proceedings, that many of the defendants were guilty of charges of "wrecking" the economy and working with Germany, Japan, or Poland to overthrow the Soviet government and introduce a capitalist system in Russia.

Vyshinsky's role in these early "show" trials greatly enhanced his reputation, at least in Stalin's eyes. He was appointed First Deputy Procurator General in 1933, Prosecutor

General in 1935, and chief prosecutor in Stalin's Moscow "show" trials from 1936 to 1938. Now the country's foremost legal theorist, he explained in *The Law of the Soviet State* that the role of justice in the Soviet Union was to ensure that all "institutions, organizations, officials, and citizens" abided fully by the country's laws.[18]

Planning for the three Moscow "show" trials began slowly after the assassination of Sergei Kirov in late 1934. They were driven by Stalin's paranoia about what he perceived to be disloyal, pro-Trotskyite elements in the upper echelons of the Soviet elite. A brief "Leningrad/Moscow Centre" trial in early 1935 served as a prelude for the Moscow trials, which Nikita Krushchev later charged centered on prominent Soviet leaders who had nothing more than ideological differences with Stalin.[19]

The transcripts[20] of the three trials—the "Trotskyite-Zinovievite Terrorist Centre" (August 1936), the "Anti-Soviet Trotskyite Centre" (January 1937), and the "Anti-Soviet Bloc of Rights and Trotskyites" (March 1938)—highlight the abhorrent cruelty of the proceedings which were based on a large body of fabricated evidence carefully put together by the architects of the trials—Stalin, Vyshinsky, Vasili Ulrikh, the head of the Military Collegium of the Supreme Soviet of the USSR (*Voennaya kollegiya verkhovnogo suda SSSR*), which conducted the trials, and the heads of the new secret police commissariat, the NKVD (*Narodnyy Komissariat Vnutrennikh Del*; People's Commissariat of Internal Affairs), Genrikh Yagoda, and Nikolai Yezhov. The challenge for Vyshinsky, Ulrikh, Yagoda, and Yezhov was to create a detailed, mostly fabricated body of evidence and then force the defendants to memorize a legal script that proved not only their guilt but also that of some of their co-defendants.

But, as Crowe points out, Ulrikh and Vyshinsky were not always able to control the testimony of some of the defendants, who refused to admit to the most treasonous charge— espionage. During the last Moscow "show" trial, Nikolai Krestinsky, a close associate of Lenin and former member of the Politburo and Central Committee, testified that he had never been a Trotskyite and a German spy. That evening, he was beaten and forced to recant his testimony. The same happened to Nikolai Bukharin, an Old Bolshevik and one of the party's most prominent members. He refused to bend completely to Vyshinsky's will and sparred with him throughout the trial.

The outcomes of the trials were foregone conclusions, though Stalin met with Vyshinsky and Ulrikh at the end of each of them to decide the fate of the defendants. Once the last of the Moscow trials ended, Stalin decided to forego future open trials, and initiated a new purge against alleged centers of opposition in the secret police, the foreign office, the party, and the military. He had already wiped out the middle and senior leadership of the Soviet military after the secret trial of Marshal Mikhail Tukachevsky and seven other generals on June 11, 1937. Crowe concludes that Stalin slowly became concerned about the damage that the purges had done to the political and military fabric of the Soviet state, which helped temper his desire for further assaults against his real and imagined enemies.

Chapter 2

But, as Alexander Prusin notes in "Traitors or War Criminals: Collaboration on Trial in Soviet Courts in the 1940s," tensions with Nazi Germany and Japan after the outbreak of war in 1939 prompted the Central Committee to call for the "intensification of struggle against traitors of the Motherland." It ordered the use of military tribunals under the control of the Military Collegium to expedite trials against escapees from the Soviet Union.[21] This was followed by Stalin's decision after the German invasion of the Soviet Union in 1941 to begin to arrest and try those suspected of collaboration with the enemy. Prusin estimates that by 1943 about 70 million Soviet citizens found themselves under Axis occupation. Of this number, about a million collaborated with the enemy. The Kremlin decreed in the summer of 1942 that anyone in the Red Army could sit on tribunals that dealt with individuals suspected of collaboration or high treason. A few months earlier, the military's chief prosecutor, Viktor Bochkov, ordered the tribunals to charge deserters with Article 58-1a (high treason) instead of "complicity" under Articles 58-3 and 58-4 of the Soviet criminal code, since rulings under the latter articles had resulted in milder prison terms.[22]

That fall, the government created a special investigative commission, the ChGK (Extraordinary State Commission), to begin to gather evidence for war crimes committed in the Soviet Union. Stalin created the commission in response to the Allied creation of the United Nations War Crimes Commission, which he refused to join. This was followed in the spring of 1943 by Decree 39, which stated that Axis troops and their Soviet accomplices who were guilty of atrocities against Soviet civilians and POWs would be hanged, while locals who assisted in such crimes could be sentenced to hard labor for fifteen to twenty years. The trials of those accused of committing these atrocities would be handled by field courts-martials who would try suspected culprits on the spot, followed by immediate punishment. Efforts by the military to clarify the nature of such atrocities and those it deemed traitors (*izmenniki*) and "turncoats" (*predateli*) clouded the meaning of such crimes, though both charges were used interchangeably by the courts-martials and tribunals.[23] This led to a series of military "show" trials and public hangings that, at least in one instance, Prusin notes, resulted in the post-execution mutilation of a convicted Soviet collaborator.

After the victory in Stalingrad in early 1943, Stalin conducted several major "show" trials in Krasdonar, Krasnodon, and Kharkov. Prusin argues that these highly publicized trials "clearly underscored the ideological and retributive nature of the Soviet legal system and the state's unrelenting will to punish political offenders." Simultaneously, as the Soviets began to retake territory earlier lost to the Germans, the NKVD intensified its search for collaborators. By the end of 1943, they had arrested almost 81,000 suspects, and used fabricated evidence to force individuals to admit their guilt.[24]

In late 1943, the Supreme Court clarified differences between "traitors" and "accomplices" and considered those in the former category to be individuals who went beyond compliance with German orders and aided or abetted in mass murder, violence, destruction of property, persecution, and espionage. Traitors were to be tried under Articles 58-1a and 1b of the criminal code, while "accomplices"—those forced to work for the German military or in agriculture, transport, or industry—were to be tried under article 58-3 or Part 2 of Decree 39. Unfortunately, the courts-martials and tribunals had little respect for such legal differences, which led the Supreme Soviet and the Supreme Court to issue new guidelines in the spring of 1944 to better clarify differences between "traitors" and "accomplices." In the end, Prusin argues, these changes replicated the terminology of the early Soviet era which emphasized the ideological roots of Soviet justice.[25]

Prusin also discusses the impact of such policies on some minority groups, particularly the Crimean Tatars, who were forcibly deported to other parts of the Soviet Union in the spring of 1944.[26] The plight of the Tatars is important because it underscores part of what Prusin terms the retributive nature of Stalin's policies after the war as he sought to reestablish firm control over the country after four years of more relaxed, open wartime rule.

The secret police also targeted suspected Georgian, Ukrainian, and Latvian collaborators who had worked with the Germans and were involved in some of the mass murders of Jews, Roma, and others. They also investigated individuals in Soviet republics who had suspicious bourgeois backgrounds or lived in areas occupied by the Axis. They used the same investigative methods used by the secret police during the prewar purge trials to force individuals to name real or imagined accomplices. But Prusin reminds us that some of those who were tried for treason or collaboration by Soviet courts during the war were guilty of playing key roles in the mass murder of Jews, Roma, and other victims of Nazi genocide.

Chapter 3

Such legitimacy is important to remember since it played an important role in Stalin's efforts throughout the war to hold those accountable for crimes committed in the Soviet Union. Thomas Earl Porter's chapter, "*Nikto ne zabyt*'[27]: The Politicization of Soviet War Dead," begins by looking at the failure of the international community after the First World War to make aggressive war a crime, something Aron Trainin, Vyshinsky's protégé, discussed in his *The Defense of Peace and Criminal Law* (1937). Porter correctly points out that Trainin was not the first to suggest this. Mark Lewis notes in *The Birth of the New Justice* (2014) that the *Association Internationale de Droit Pénal*, for example, advocated the creation of an international criminal court that would have the powers to prosecute national leaders and generals for waging aggressive war.[28]

But it was Trainin's most important study, *On the Criminal Responsibility of the Hitlerites*, Porter argues, that helped lay the groundwork for the development of conspiracy as the overarching charge at the Nuremberg International Military Tribunal (IMT) trial in 1945–1946. Crowe noted in Chapter 1 that Vyshinsky first raised the issue of conspiracy and complicity in the trial of Nikolai Bukharin et al. in 1938. He told the court that complicity went beyond the narrow legal confines of conspiracy and allowed prosecutors to establish "a common line uniting the accomplices in a given crime, that there is a common criminal design." It was up to prosecutors, Vyshinsky added, to "establish the existence of a united will directed towards a single object common to all the participants in the crime."[29] But it should be remembered that the idea behind the use of the complicity in the Moscow trials was to allow Vyshinsky to use a charge far easier to prove than conspiracy.

Traditionally, conspiracy is a difficult charge to prove because it involves more than one individual. Neal K. Katyal argues in his article, "Conspiracy Theory," that one of the reasons for this is that conspiratorial crimes involving groups are "far more dangerous" to society "than their individual activity."[30] This idea was certainly borne out during the Second World War, when a number of special German killing squads such as the *Einsatzgruppen* and Wehrmacht units were involved in the mass murder of groups deemed racially inferior by the Nazi leadership.

Francine Hirsch and George Ginsburgs point out that the Soviets were the first to recognize that conspiracy, with its deep roots in Anglo-American law, was a useful tool when it came to the prosecution of Nazi war criminals.[31] Consequently, the question of holding Germany's military and civilian leadership responsible for the crimes they committed in the Soviet Union during the Great Fatherland War was a constant domestic and international theme in Soviet propaganda. This dovetailed with the Allied St. James declaration of January 13, 1942, that called for the "punishment, through organized justice" of those responsible for war crimes.[32]

Over the next three years, Porter argues, the Soviets played a leading role in demanding that an international tribunal deal with Nazi criminality, anchored in part by the large body of evidence being gathered by Stalin's war crimes commission—the ChGK. Part of its function was to gather evidence for use in future war crimes trials and document the widespread suffering of the Soviet people during the war. The ChGK also gathered detailed information about the widespread damage done to the Soviet economy, which could later be used to support Soviet reparations claims.

But Stalin was not going to wait until war's end to begin to exact justice, first against collaborators and later POWs responsible for war crimes. Consequently, in the months after the victory at Stalingrad, the Kremlin began to prosecute Germans and their allies for alleged war crimes. In an article in the *Soviet Monitor* in August 1943, Trainin reiterated his ideas about the German elite and criminal conspiracy. Arieh J. Kochavi adds in his *Prelude to Nuremberg* (1998) that Trainin, in response to international criticism of the Kharkov trial in late 1943, reminded the Allies that the defendants argued that they were only following orders to evade responsibility for their crimes. Those found guilty, he pointed out, were only convicted for the crimes they committed personally, and not allowed to use superior orders as a defense.[33]

Porter adds that the Soviet effort to bring collaborators and German war criminals to justice was based not only on the devastating war taking place in the Soviet Union but also on the vast body of evidence being collected by the ChGK. Headed by Nikolai Shvernik and prominent political figures Vyshinsky and Andrei Zhdanov, it had a large staff with ample funding that enabled its investigative staff and Red Army intelligence units to travel to recently liberated Soviet territories to investigate the atrocities committed by the Germans and their allies. They gathered over 250,000 statements and estimated the damage in the newly liberated areas to be about 700 billion rubles ($1.17 billion).[34]

But, as Yitzhak Arad has noted in *The Holocaust in the Soviet Union* (2009), once the ChGK began its work, Stalin insisted that investigators refer to all victims as "Soviet citizens," even though Soviet leaders were aware of the mass murder of Jews.[35] Porter notes, for example, that Vyacheslav Molotov (Stalin's foreign minister), whose wife was Jewish, documented Nazi policies toward Soviet Jews in his private papers. He also noted Lenin's comment that anti-Semitism evoked "disgust from the entire civilized world."[36] And in late 1942, *Pravda* published an article on the Allied declaration of December 17, 1942, that stated that after the war they would prosecute those responsible for crimes against the Jews of Europe.[37] Stalin fulfilled this pledge at Nuremberg, where Soviet prosecutors presented ample evidence documenting the heinous nature of German crimes against Soviet Jews.

Chapter 4

Valentyna Polunina writes in "The Human Face of Soviet Justice: Aron Trainin and the Origins of the Soviet Doctrine of International Criminal Law" that Trainin, who was Jewish, was well aware of the genocidal nature of Nazi crimes. He studied law at Moscow State University and later taught there during Vyshinsky's tenure as the university's rector. He taught courses on Soviet criminal law and criminal ethnology, while his early publications focused on economic crimes as well as analyses of the new Czech, German, and Polish criminal codes.[38] He was also interested in questions about aggression in international law, particularly the ideas of Vespasian Pella and Emil Rappaport, prominent members of the *Association Internationale de Droit Pénale*, which advocated the creation of an international criminal court to prevent aggression and "solve jurisdictional conflict between states."[39]

In 1935, Trainin published *Criminal Internvention: The Movement towards the Unification of Criminal Law in Capitalist Countries* (*Ugolovnaya interventsiya: dvizhenie po unifikatsii ugolovnogo zakonodatel'stva kapitalisticheskikh stran*), with an introduction by Vyshinsky. Both criticized Raphaël Lemkin's "grouping of 'barbarism' and 'vandalism,' together with laws against state terrorism."[40] Michelle Jean Penn argues that Vyshinsky criticized Lemkin's ideas as an attempt "to promote 'liberal-legal prejudice' as 'sharp weapons' to 'attack the most vital interests of the working masses.'"[41] Polunina adds that Trainin was equally concerned about the question of aggression in international law and agreed with Pella and Lemkin that it should be considered an international crime.

Two years later, Trainin published an equally important work, *The Defense of Peace and Criminal Law* (*Zashchita mira I ugolovnyi zakon*), at a time when Stalin saw the Soviet Union threatened by Germany and Japan. Trainin argued that criminal law should be used as a weapon against war and fascism while bemoaning the ineffectiveness of the League of Nations in preventing wars of aggression. He also discussed different crimes against peace, particularly "hostile actions," which, in recent years, had resulted in the development of methods "for the extermination [*istrebliniia*] of humanity." The core persecuted groups, Trainin went on, were "victimized by capitalist aggression." Such crimes should come before an International Criminal Court to "combat crimes encroaching on the peaceful coexistence of peoples."[42]

Vyshinsky rewarded Trainin for his work with a doctorate in legal sciences in 1938, followed by an appointment to the country's most prominent legal institution—the Institute of Law of the Soviet Academy of Sciences. He was also behind Trainin's new book, *The Doctrine of Complicity* (*Uchenie o souchastii*), which was published in 1941. Trainin drew heavily on Vyshinsky's definition of complicity from the Bukharin trial, and discussed four types of conspirators—instigators, organizers, agents, and perpetrators. The most dangerous were the organizers who created the criminal group, developed its plan of action, and controlled its criminal act. Trainin added that there were three types of complicity and that the most important was "special complicity *sui generis*" because it involved participants who, knowing one another, were united in their conspiratorial goals.[43] This, of course, buffets Kaytal's argument about the greater danger of the conspiratorial group to society vis-à-vis the individual criminal.

Trainin also discussed complicity in his seminal work, *On the Criminal Responsibility of the Hitlerites*, which Vyshinsky edited. Published in the midst of serious Allied discussions about the conduct of trials of German war criminals in 1944, Trainin called for the creation of a set of international legal principles to help guide such talks. His chapter on complicity, Polunina argues, emphasized that Hitler, his ministers, Nazi Party leaders, top Wehrmacht commanders, heads of industry and finance, and members of Hitler's inner circle were the ones most responsible for Nazi crimes.[44] She adds that his most unique proposal in *Criminal Responsibility* was the idea that aggressive war should be a criminal offense in international law. In other words, war criminals should be tried not only for their individual crimes but also for waging a war of aggression, a fundamental crime against peace. To Trainin, this was the "crime of crimes."[45]

Trainin's book was translated into English and widely distributed in Washington, London, and Paris in late 1944 and 1945 as the Allies began to discuss the creation of an international tribunal to try Nazi war criminals. And while his book certainly planted the seed for some of the core legal concepts under discussion by the Allies, it was his presence as a member of the Soviet delegation at the London Conference in the summer of 1945 that was key in terms of his influence on Allied thinking about German criminality.

Polunina notes that Robert Jackson, the chief American negotiator in London, was deeply affected by Trainin's ideas about aggressive war. The US Supreme Court justice was also impressed by Trainin's emphasis on the importance of a fair trial, something that Jackson strongly emphasized at the conference. She writes that *Criminal Responsibility* also affected a number of lawyers working with the UNWCC (United Nations War Crimes Commission) and Justice Radhabinod Pal, the Indian judge at the International Criminal Tribunal for the Far East (1946–1948). Pal wrote a separate judgment at the end of the trial and devoted a number of pages to *Criminal Responsibility*.[46] He agreed that the charge of crimes against peace (aggressive war) was a new concept in international law but did not accept Trainin's argument that the Moscow Declaration of 1943 introduced a new epoch in international law.[47]

Trainin continued his work on the evolution of international criminal law after the war, with a focus on the question of "crimes against mankind" vis-à-vis "crimes against humanity."[48] He wrote that "crimes against mankind" were "encroachments on the foundations of the existence and progressive development of nations" in *Protection of Peace and the Fights against Crimes against Mankind* (*Zashchita mira i bor'ba s prestupleniyami protiv chelovechestva*, 1956).[49] On the other hand, he now differentiated between illegal aggressive wars and what he considered just wars of liberation, which underscored Soviet support of the anti-colonial civil wars being fought around the globe. He also discussed the concept of genocide that was legally enshrined in the 1948 Genocide Convention.[50] Unfortunately, Polunina concludes, he came under attack in 1952 as part of Stalin's anti-cosmopolitan campaign against Jews that called for their removal from jobs in the arts, medicine science, education, and journalism because of their questioned loyalty to the Soviet Union.[51] He was dismissed as head of the department of criminal law at Moscow State University though he continued to teach there until his death in 1957. But nothing could take away from the fact that he was one of Russia's foremost legal minds during one of the most significant periods in Soviet legal history

Chapter 5

Trainin's principal contributions to international criminal law were made between 1944 and 1946, when he published *Criminal Responsibility* and served as a key Soviet delegate to the London Conference and legal adviser during the Nuremberg IMT trial.[52] According to Francine Hirsch, scholars traditionally viewed the role of the Soviets at the London Conference and Nuremberg Trial as weak and ineffective. But a new generation of scholars such as Hirsch and George Ginsburgs have reevaluated the Soviet role in the trial and cast it in a more nuanced, contributory light.[53]

Irina Schulmeister-André[54] and David Crowe argue in their chapter, "'May Justice Be Done!' The Soviet Union and the London Conference (1945)," that almost from the moment that Big Four[55] delegates decided to conduct trials of major German war criminals at the San Francisco conference in early May 1945, questions arose about the willingness of the Soviets to take part in planning for such a trial. Over the next six weeks, the Kremlin refused repeated requests to appoint a delegation to meet with American, British, and French representatives in London. When the Soviets finally responded, they requested a delay in the opening of the London Conference until June 26. Their principal delegates were Iona Nikitchenko, the deputy chairman of the Supreme Court and one of the judges at the first of the three Moscow "show" trials in 1936, Trainin, and Oleg Troyanovsky, Nikitchenko's major domo.

The American and British delegations were much larger than the Soviet delegation which, along with the long Soviet delay in accepting the invitation to the conference, raised questions about Moscow's seriousness about the talks and an international trial. But these delays, Schulmeister-André and Crowe argue, had more to do with not knowing how to cooperate in such discussions and participation in an international trial. Consequently, Vyshinsky, Molotov, and Stalin fell back on the micro-managed decision-making process that had served them well during the earlier "show" trials. They issued, for example, eight directives for the top Soviet delegates that robbed them of any autonomy when it came to major and minor decisions at the London Conference. They also required Nikitchenko and his team to send the Kremlin copies of all major and minor proposals made by the other delegations. And though they were allowed to give their opinions about such proposals, it was the "big three" in the Kremlin that made the final decisions for the London delegation.

Building off of the American draft from the San Francisco conference, the British, French, and Soviets responded with numerous counter proposals about the mechanical and legal conduct of the trial, its location, and the role of the Allied Control Council. They included different views and interpretations about certain legal concepts and practices that confused the Soviet jurists. Nikitchenko and his team were concerned about the ability of a prosecutor to issue indictments and the idea of trying organizations before trying individuals. As Crowe notes in his *War Crimes, Genocide, and Justice: A Global History* (2014), this concerned Robert Jackson, the head of the US delegation, who considered the conspiratorial role of Nazi Party, military, and related organizations important in laying the groundwork for trying individual members of such organizations found guilty of criminal activity.[56]

Telford Taylor noted in his memoir on the trial, *The Anatomy of the Nuremberg Trials* (1992), that Jackson was determined to "make a show" of force during the conference to underscore his discomfort in working with the Soviets.[57] While some of the delegates were uneasy with his approach, it was understandable, given Stalin's past crimes, particularly during the first two years of the war when he was an active ally of the Nazis. Jackson was also worried about the ability of the Soviet delegation to agree to anything, given earlier delays.

Schulmesister-André and Crowe, using American and Soviet documents, point out that what kept the talks alive was the willingness of the delegates to compromise when it came to sticky issues. While there were some points that could easily be dealt with, there were also highly controversial issues that were much harder to resolve. The question of crimes against peace was at the heart of the American proposals and rested on the idea that aggressive war was already an accepted international crime. The Soviets objected to the general wording of Article 6, which dealt with jurisdictional and general principles of the proposed charters, and wanted to make certain that it was used just to indict major Nazi war criminals. They were fearful that if the idea of crimes against peace was applied too liberally, it could entrap Soviet leaders who had overseen Moscow's occupation of parts of Poland in the fall of 1939, the Katyn massacre, and the invasion of the Baltic states in the summer of 1940.

The Soviet delegation also opposed the idea of prosecuting Nazi organizations. This was driven principally by Nikitchenko and Trainin's difficulty in understanding American ideas on this question. Nikitchenko explained that while Soviet law held gangs, organizations, and their members accountable for individual criminal acts, it did not recognize the "criminal responsibility of non-physical bodies."[58] This matter was resolved when Jackson agreed to accept Nikitchenko's suggestion that the key to resolution was reaching "the organization through proof of what individuals did."[59]

There were also differences about the rules of procedure for the judges and the prosecutors. The United States wanted broadly defined rules which the tribunal could develop during the trial. The British and the Soviets disagreed, and wanted basic rules of procedure in the charter, while the French and the Soviets argued that such rules should be reserved for the tribunal and not the prosecution. In the end, the delegations accepted an Anglo-American compromise in Article 13 that allowed the tribunal to draw up its own rules of procedure while the Chief Prosecutors' Committee could present draft rules of procedure that the tribunal could accept, alter, or reject.[60]

The Soviets were never satisfied with the idea of prosecutorial independence spelled out in Articles 14 and 15, particularly given that eighteen of the twenty-four

Germans to be tried were in British or American custody. These articles stated that each prosecution team could propose to indict an individual and submit the idea to the Prosecution Committee. In case of a tie, the committee would side with the party that selected the indictee. The Soviets were also concerned that Article 15, which prevented witnesses or defendants from being "taken out of the possession of the country that proposed his indictment" without that country's assent, would limit access to said individuals. In such instances, the British promised the Soviets access "at a convenient spot."[61]

There were also differences of opinion when it came to questions about the right of the court and the prosecutors to question a defendant in court under Articles 17 and 24. Jackson thought that this could result in "compulsory self-incrimination," while Trainin argued that while judges and prosecutors should be able to do this, they could not "compel a defendant to answer." In the end, it was decided not to put anything in the charter about this matter because it might encourage defendants not to respond to any questioning in court.[62]

There were also some serious differences about the right of the tribunal to appoint "special officers" under Article 17 to gather evidence outside of court. Trainin opposed this idea while Jackson thought it would be a mistake not to include such a provision in the charter because it could affect the functioning of the court. Sir David Maxwell Fyfe, the top British representative at the conference, intervened and explained that since such rights were inherent in the authority of the tribunal, Trainin was not objecting to such rights, just their stated inclusion in the charter. Trainin then offered a compromise that Fyfe and Robert Falco, the French delegate, supported, which allowed the court in certain cases to appoint special interrogators to obtain such evidence. Jackson strongly objected, which underscored the vast differences between the US and the Soviet perspective on the trial.[63]

What was at play here were the realities of the significant differences between the US and the Soviet visions of the trial. The American system was based on centuries-old Anglo-American practices and precedents, while the Soviet model was developed to ensure the judges and the prosecution wielded absolute control over a trial and its outcome. Jackson was well aware of this and finally decided that it was time to discuss the significant differences between the two systems.

By the end of July, he had become so frustrated with the Soviets, particularly when it came to decisions about aggression, conspiracy or the common plan, and crime itself, that he wondered if the delegates would be able to conclude an agreement. Fyfe and Nikitchenko were more positive and argued that they were close to an agreement on the stickiest points of the charter.[64]

On July 26, Jackson flew to Potsdam to discuss these problems with Secretary of State James Byrnes, who told him not to deviate from any core principles of American foreign policy when it came to any agreement on the trial. On the other hand, Byrnes added, Jackson should do everything possible to reach an agreement that included the Soviets but on a "sound basis." In the end, Byrnes left the decision up to Jackson.[65]

In the meantime, a new round of British and Soviet proposals sought further to find middle ground.[66] The Soviets felt strongly that the Moscow Declaration of October 30, 1943, should be the basis for trying German war criminals, and provided a list of those members of the "Hitler clique" who should be placed on trial. At this point, the discussions followed two tracks—talks in Potsdam among the Big Three[67] and four-power delegation talks sponsored by Britain's new Lord Chancellor, Sir William Jowitt. On August 1, in London, the Big Three issued the Potsdam Protocol or Agreement which, among other things, announced the results of the talks in London to date.[68]

The same day, Jowitt met with Jackson to discuss American perspectives on the charter, and the following day met with all four delegations. Jowitt emphasized the importance of fulfilling the Moscow Declaration by jointly bringing to trial Germany's major war criminals. He then carefully led the discussion of each article of the charter. It is apparent from reading the transcripts that all of the delegations were now willing to compromise and, by the end of the day, reached a general consensus on the terms in the agreement and charter, which the head of each delegation signed on August 8. On October 6, the trial's chief prosecutors signed a separate protocol that dealt with some translation discrepancies in Article 6.[69]

Schulmeister-André and Crowe argue that the role of the Soviets at the London Conference should be seen in a positive light. Though handicapped by the need to consult frequently with Stalin and Vyshinsky, their concerns about various aspects of the agreement and charter not only reflected their own interpretation and perspectives on Soviet criminal law but often those voiced by the French delegation. This, coupled with Russia's wartime experiences, played a key role when it came to questions related to crimes against peace and war of aggression. Nikitchenko and Trainin were particularly stubborn when it came to questions about this issue as well as the site of the trial and the headquarters of the tribunal. But they were never intransigent and proved to be willing to compromise. Moreover, according to Sidney Alderman, Jackson's "first assistant,"[70] the Soviet delegates "were second to none in politeness and tact."[71]

They asked very detailed questions, while their influence can be clearly seen in the agreement and charter. This was particularly the case when it came to questions about the tribunal's presidency, its votes on court decisions, procedural rules, the committee of chief prosecutors, the tribunal's permanent seat in Berlin, and the right of the judges to question witnesses and defendants. In the end, the Soviets played a very important role in the London Conference though they would find it far more difficult to play a similar role in the Nuremberg Trial because of their lack of knowledge and skills about the operation of Western-style criminal trials.

Regardless, the legal principles in the charter and the 1946 IMT trial judgment were later considered by the United Nations to be core principles of international law. This was particularly the case when it came to the four crimes defined and later adjudicated in Article 6—crimes against peace, war crimes, crimes against humanity, and conspiracy to commit such crimes. Later, the UN added complicity as a crime under the Nuremberg principles. Such precedents also meant that heads of state who committed such crimes were to be held liable for any criminal actions under international law. Nor could one argue that they were simply following superior orders when it came to criminal acts. On the other hand, all accused of such crimes had the right to a fair trial.[72]

Chapter 6

Yet, as Francine Hirsch notes in her chapter, "The Soviet Union at the Palace of Justice: Law, Intrigue, and International Rivalry in the Nuremberg Trials," these precedents have done little to convince scholars of the important role played by the Soviet Union in the shaping and conduct of the Nuremberg Trial. She blames this not only on the fact that Soviet documents on the trial were inaccessible during the Cold War but also on the writings of Western judges and prosecutors who took part in the trial. They saw any significant discussion about the Soviet role as a threat to the legacy of postwar justice. Hirsch adds that there is a contradiction in all of this that lies at the heart of what she calls "the Nuremberg moment." The Soviets' faith in political trials and their innovative ideas about international law were critical to the trial's success. At the same time, given the horrific nature of German crimes in Russia, Stalin hoped the trial would give a full public accounting of Nazi crimes which, in turn, would validate the country's political system, and lay the groundwork for significant postwar reparations. He also hoped the trial would underscore the importance of the Soviet Union's role in defeating the Germans and liberating Europe, which would allow his country to take its place among the great postwar global powers. Instead, by trial's end, many saw the Soviet Union as one of Nazi Germany's co-conspirators.

Hirsch draws most of her material from a number of archives in Russia—the State Archive of the Russians Federation (GARF), the Russian State Archive of Socio-Political History (RGASPI), the Russian State Archive of Literature and Art (RGALI), the Archive of the Foreign Policy of the Russian Federation (AVPRF), and the Archives of the Russian Academy of Sciences (ARAN),[73] which provide new insight into the Soviet Union's role in the planning and operation of the Nuremberg IMT trial. As noted in earlier chapters, Soviet jurists, particularly Aron Trainin, played an important role in promoting the idea that aggressive war was a crime in international law. The same was true when it came to the idea of complicity, though Western jurists initially dismissed these concepts as ex post facto law.

Once plans for the trial began in earnest after the London Conference, Soviet leaders, who initially believed its outcome would be a fait accompli, began to have doubts about their decision to support it. They now thought that holding it in Nuremberg in the US zone gave the Americans control over the proceedings, while the decision to allow the defendants to have German lawyers and German witnesses put them at a considerable disadvantage, given that their judges and prosecutors had little or no experience with this aspect of an open trial.

Hirsch uncovered a classified report from Nikolai Ivanov, the Kremlin's ambassador to London, discussing some of these problems. In the midst of making plans for the trial in September, Jackson learned that Nikitchenko would not serve as Soviet chief prosecutor. Instead, he would be replaced by Gen. Roman A. Rudenko. Ivanov, concerned about Rudenko's ability to deal with the diplomatic intrigues of the 1930s, the causes for the outbreak of the war, the Soviet position on Moscow's ties with Nazi Germany from 1939 to 1941, and the translation of court documents into Russian, told the Kremlin that if Rudenko was not properly briefed on all of these and other serious matters before the trial, it was possible that the Soviet team could find itself "defenseless" during the proceedings.[74]

Rudenko and the rest of his team were further handicapped by the fact that the Moscow-based Nuremberg Commission rewrote the speeches of the prosecutors, selected evidence, and prepared witnesses for the Soviet prosecutors. Just before the trial began, Rudenko and Nikitchenko learned that there was a price to pay if they strayed from Stalin's game plan. They made the mistake of signing off on some organizational matters without getting the Kremlin's approval and were immediately called back to Moscow where they were severely reprimanded for their action.[75]

Since much of the history of the Nuremberg Trial has been written principally from a non-Soviet perspective, it is important, Hirsch writes, to understand some of the more subtle themes of the trial, particularly the national and ethnic narrative that would be told about the causes of the war, its victims, and the policies that led to the rise and international successes of Nazi Germany. What, for example, would be made of the French and British abandonment of Czechoslovakia and Soviet actions toward Poland? These and other issues came to the fore in the fall of 1945 as the prosecution teams began to put together the trial's indictment.

Soviet prosecutors felt that all four counts belittled the important role and sacrifices made by the Soviet people during the war, particularly when it came to their important role in destroying the Nazi war machine. Vyshinsky blamed Rudenko for this as well as the fact that the indictment mentioned Jews, Poles, and Roma (Gypsies) as victims of the Nazis but not the Slavic peoples. Molotov suggested that the list of victims include the Russians, Belorussians, Ukrainians, and Jews, and, in the end, Count 1 did mention the "annihilation of Belo-russians and Ukrainians." Count 3 discussed the destruction of various "races and classes of people and national, racial or religious groups, particularly Jews, Poles, and Gypsies."[76]

However, as Alexander Prusin and Thomas Porter note in Chapters 2 and 3, some of these problems can be traced back to the Soviet refusal to take part in the UNWCC's investigation of war crimes, and the creation of Stalin's secretive ChGK. Though it gathered a wealth of material on the crimes and destruction suffered during the German occupation, his paranoid failure to share much of this information with the Allies during and after the war undercut one of the principal reasons for the Soviet decision to take part in the Nuremberg Trial—letting the world know about the country's sacrifices, losses, and overall role in defeating Nazi Germany.

The Soviets also made a mistake when they tried to blame the Germans for the murder of over 20,000 Polish officers at Katyn and other areas in occupied Poland in the spring of 1940. By the time the trial began, most of the Allied prosecutors were aware that it was the Russians and not the Germans who had committed this atrocity. During the pretrial discussions, Rudenko insisted that Germany be charged with the crimes, something the other prosecutors opposed, since this would allow the defense to challenge it during the trial.[77] Rudenko refused to take their advice, and it was included in Count 3, section c, which charged the Germans with murdering 11,000 Polish officers in September 1941, not the spring of 1940.[78]

And when it came to the Molotov-Ribbentrop pact, Vyshinsky told Rudenko that "under no circumstances" was it to be interpreted as the "springboard for" Nazi actions,[79] particularly when it came to the Soviet invasion of Poland. Vyshinsky also insisted that more attention be given to the German invasion of Czechoslovakia in the spring of 1939. In the end, Hirsch writes, Vyshinsky won this argument and the secret accord between Hitler and Stalin was described in neutral terms in the indictment though it would continue to haunt the Soviets throughout the trial.[80]

But Soviet efforts to minimize their crimes during the early years of the war do nothing to diminish the significant Soviet losses suffered between 1941 and 1945. According to Col. Gen. G. F. Krivosheev, almost 27 million Soviet citizens died during this period, about two-thirds of them civilians.[81] And reports from the ChGK and Nikolai Voznesensky, who headed Gosplan (*Gosudarstvennyi Planovaya kommissiya; State Planning Commission*) in the fall of 1945, painted a grim picture of the economic destruction wrought by the Nazis—70,000 villages, 32,000 factories, and 65,000 kilometers of railroad tracks destroyed, 100,000 collective and state farms "laid waste," and 25 million homeless. The cost of the invasion was put at 700 billion rubles ($1.17 billion), while the country lost "30% of its national wealth."[82]

The figures in the indictment underscore these losses,[83] particularly Count 3(a), 2, "War Crimes," which included specific figures on Soviet population losses. But this section clouds over Jewish deaths, while those murdered by the Nazis were referred to as "persons, citizens of the USSR and other countries, and Soviet citizens." In fact, there is only one instance in the indictment where some victims are referred to as Jews. The same was true in Count 3(c), which focused on crimes against Soviet POWs.[84] On the other hand, Count 1, 3(d), estimated that 5.7 million Jews had been "deliberately put to death by the Nazi conspirators." Count 4 (a–b) went into slightly more detail on this question and provided examples of specific acts relating to the mass murder of Jews in the Soviet Union.[85]

The intense discussions during the preparation of the indictment were a foreshadowing of many of the problems the Soviets and the other delegations would face from defense lawyers when it came to the charge of waging aggressive war. Jackson warned the Allied prosecutors to be prepared for this. Vyshinsky was so concerned about this that he came to Nuremberg just after the trial opened in November to try to convince the other prosecution teams to reach a gentlemen's agreement that would avoid all mention of "questions that the USSR, USA, England, France, and other United Nations do not want to become subjects of criticism from the side of the accused."[86] Though he was successful, this did not stop the defense from trying to raise such questions throughout the trial.

The chief prosecutors divided the trial into four parts. It was begun by the United States, which handled the charge of waging aggressive war. The British dealt with crimes against humanity and joined the United States in its cases against individual defendants. The French were responsible for war crimes and crimes against humanity in Western Europe, while the Soviets dealt with crimes against humanity in Eastern Europe and the Soviet Union. Each of the prosecution teams also played roles in portions of the trial not specific to their larger area of coverage.[87]

The Soviets became increasingly frustrated with the pace of the trial and the fact that they were the last to present their case against the Germans. This was doubly so because the United States spent so much time discussing German crimes in the Soviet Union. To some extent, their frustration was understandable, given that they had liberated much of Eastern Europe, including most of the Nazi death camps in occupied Poland,

and had gathered a vast body of evidence on the German extermination campaign in Poland and western Russia.

This, coupled with news that the defense was going to use dozens of witnesses to testify about Soviet crimes in Poland and the Baltic states from 1939 to 1941, forced Stalin and Molotov to produce new witnesses and evidence to challenge what they saw as the defense's efforts to claim that the German invasion of the Soviet Union was in response to reports that Stalin was about to launch an invasion of Germany. The most prominent new witness was Field Marshal Friederich von Paulus, the defeated commander of German forces at Stalingrad, who stated that the German invasion of the Soviet Union was premediated.[88]

The Soviet prosecutors also presented gruesome evidence that underscored the brutality of Nazi barbarism, which included Soviet film footage about the depravity of such criminal acts. But their decision to use phony evidence to counter defense claims about Katyn, Hirsch argues, threatened to undercut the Soviet case as well as the legitimacy of entire trial.

The Soviets finished their presentation in early March, and the defense began their cases a few days later. In the interim, Winston Churchill gave voice to a growing concern throughout Europe about what the former prime minister called a Soviet "iron curtain" that was "descending over Central and Eastern Europe." His charge, that Stalin threatened postwar "peace and democracy,"[89] emboldened the defense, which led Jackson to remind the other prosecutors of the list of taboos that they promised not to bring up in response to defense attacks against Allied wartime policies. The Soviets sent Jackson this list and in mid-March Vyshinsky ordered Rudenko to tell the judges that defense efforts to raise the question of Katyn was in direct violation of Article 21 of the charter, which dealt partially with the validity of documents gathered by Allied investigative committees. He also ordered the creation of a new body of evidence if the judges turned down Rudenko's request.[90]

The lengthy defense cases underscored the vulnerability of Soviet prosecution efforts at Nuremberg, and their inexperience in dealing with a viable legal defense team of lawyers. Moreover, they were also unprepared for the court's determination to allow the defendants a fair trial, something anchored by Jackson's comments in a speech before the American Society of International Law in the spring of 1945.

> The ultimate principle is that you must put no man on trial under the forms of judicial proceedings if you are not willing to see him freed if not proven guilty. If you are determined to execute a man in any case, there is no occasion for a trial.[91]

But, as Jackson noted during the London Conference, this did not mean that the defense should be allowed to use "obstructive or dilatory tactics" during the trial.[92] He added that anything less than a fair trial could be criticized domestically and internationally and would rob such a trial of its educational and legal value historically.

Mikhail Kharlamov, an informant who was also the head of the large Soviet press contingent at the trial,[93] wrote to Moscow that the Soviet prosecutors were handicapped by such inexperience and the "international situation," and were now being subjected to attacks by German war criminals.[94]

Regardless, Nikitchenko was quite aggressive in response to defense efforts to have admitted into evidence the secret protocols of the Molotov-Ribbentrop agreement that had divided parts of Eastern Europe into Soviet and German spheres-of-influence.[95] He demanded that such evidence be disallowed, while his peers asked that the defense submit an original copy of the secret protocols for consideration by the tribunal. Dr. Alfred Seidl, one of the attorneys for Rudolf Hess and Hans Frank, did what he could to convince the court of the legitimacy of the contents of the secret protocol, and when that failed, he shared it with the press with the help of Thomas Dodd, one of the American prosecutors.

Seidl continued to raise the question of the secret protocols and Katyn, which led Vyshinsky to create a special sub-commission, led by Trainin, to go through all of the documentation on Katyn and identify files that could be used to expose German guilt. They were also to write a statement for Nikitchenko that denounced the tribunal's recent decision to reject his articles about the interpretation of Article 21.[96]

Rudenko, in desperation, asked the other prosecution teams to help out with the question about Article 21 and the secret protocols, which he thought the defense was using to divide the prosecution. In early June, he petitioned the court to reject Seidl's request about the secret protocols, noting that it was a tactic meant to divert attention away from the crimes of the defendants. The judges agreed though this did little to lessen the damage done to the Soviet case, particularly after the terms of the secret protocols had been made public. But the Allied prosecutors refused to help the Soviets when it came to German defense efforts to deal with Katyn.

From Hirsch's perspective, the Katyn question, regardless of who was thought to be guilty for the mass murders, proved to be costly for the Soviets because the court had allowed the defense to paint a picture of Soviet guilt in open court. This meant, she concludes, that the Soviets had visibly lost control over the war's narrative. This loss was really brought home at the end of the trial when the court found three of the defendants not guilty (Hans Fritsche, Franz von Papen, Hjalmar Schacht) and declared the Reich Cabinet, the General Staff, and the High Command not to be criminal organizations. In his lengthy dissenting opinion, Nikitcheko challenged each of these decisions as well as the decision to sentence Rudolf Hess to life imprisonment.[97]

Chapter 7

Jeremy Hicks discusses the question of who won and who lost at Nuremberg in his chapter "Soviet Journalists at Nuremberg: Establishing the Soviet War Narrative." Some scholars see the trial as a victory for the United States, and a "devastating propaganda failure" for the Soviets,[98] particularly in light of the fact that the Soviets thought the trial would give them the opportunity to promote the idea of "Russian exceptionalism, heroism, and victimization" and its unique role in defeating the Nazis.[99] This has led to the marginalization of the Soviet account of the war, its role in the creation of the trial, and the important evidence that Soviet prosecutors presented during the trial.

But this was not the case when it came to the important role played by Soviet journalists, who provided the Russian public with details about the trial and Nazi crimes. What made their accounts different from those of Western reporters was the fact that many of them had been eyewitnesses to the worst crimes of the Nazis. Each of these journalists, Hicks concludes, was able to write such accounts with their own distinct voices despite the constraints of traditional Soviet censorship.

About a third of the 147 reporters accredited at the trial came from the Soviet Union.[100] They immediately faced the challenge of how to be certain that when they wrote about the proceedings, they emphasized the importance of the country's role in the war's overall narrative. They were also forced to rethink their wartime caricatures of some of the important Nazi leaders in the dock. Artist Nikolai Zhukov later wrote that his sketches, for example, tried to capture what he saw as the moral corruption of some of the defendants in a more subtle, realistic way in an effort to capture what he saw as "their most unpleasant and negative character traits."[101]

Aron Trainin set the tone for the Soviet interpretation of the trial in several articles in *Pravda* in the summer and fall of 1945. Like some of the first journalistic reports about the trial, Trainin emphasized the importance of bringing to justice not only some of those individuals most responsible for Nazi crimes but also various party and military organizations. Proving the guilt of the latter, he argued, would also allow individual members of such organizations to later be tried by national courts.[102] Lev Sheinin, who had been involved in some of the "show" trial investigations in the 1930s, saw the trial as a "pathological-anatomical" clinical process that looked closely at how the "corpse of fascism functioned." The verdict, he argued, would help the Soviet people understand the reason for the "corpse's" behavior.[103]

Hicks adds that while reporters from Britain and the United States had a tendency to humanize the defendants, some of their Soviet colleagues condemned the practice, something that Leonid Trofimov wrote affected their overall experience during the trial.[104] This was particularly the case when it came to Hermann Göring, and what Leonid Leonov considered was the English-language press's obsession with the former Nazi air marshal.

On the other hand, the discussion of the role of Nazi Party as well as German civilian and military organizations during the trial enabled Soviet journalists to emphasize the important role played by the Wehrmacht not only in the invasion of the Soviet Union but also in the mass murder of Jews, Roma, and other religious and ethnic minorities during the Great Fatherland War. The OKW (*Oberkommando der Wehrmacht*; Wehrmacht High Command) directive of May 19, 1941, for example, called Bolshevism the deadly enemy of the German people, and ordered military commanders to remember that this "struggle requires ruthless and energetic action against Bolshevik agitators, guerillas, saboteurs, and Jews, and the total elimination of all active or passive resistance."[105] This directive set the tone for what would become the Nazis genocidal "race war" in the Soviet Union over the next four years.

One of the foci of the Soviet journalists during the trial was the core anti-communist ideology of the Nazis. In an article in *Pravda* a few weeks after the trial, Leonov wrote that Hitler's message to the German people was: "Our long-range artillery and SS angels in azure raiments will guard your slumber from the Mongolo-Slavic-Jewish designs of Moscow."[106]

This, coupled with the centrality of Soviet losses and contributions to the war effort, became the central theme of the Soviet journalists in Nuremberg. In the latter case, they emphasized testimony about the mistreatment of Soviet POWs at Dachau and Majdanek, which they compared to Auschwitz, the deadliest of the Nazi death camps.

They also played off of testimony and evidence presented in court by the other prosecution teams. Vsevolod Vishnevsky, the editor of the monthly *Znamy* and a war correspondent for *Pravda*, reported on the American film *The Nazi Plan* and compared its depiction of the German use of slave labor in Europe to the Nazi devastation and depopulation in the Soviet Union. This was personalized in stories by Boris Polevoi, a survivor of Auschwitz who wrote several articles for *Pravda* about his experiences in Germany's deadliest extermination camp. He was particularly interested in the testimony of Rudolf Höss, the commandant of Auschwitz and his boast that this was where the Germans perfected the technology of destruction.[107]

Soviet interest in the trial began to wane over time as more and more journalists returned home at the end of 1945. Those who remained tried to renew interest in the trial once Soviet prosecutors began their phase of the trial in early February. In an article in *Pravda* on February 9, Polevoi wrote that Rudenko's opening statement about the image of fascism gave birth to its "blood-drenched designs" in a way not seen earlier in the trial. Until this moment, he added, "the trial never yet grasped with such strength of conviction the mortal danger from which the Red Army and our Soviet state had saved humanity."[108]

The journalists also went to great lengths to report on the testimony of Rudenko's witnesses. Their intentions were to highlight the emotional content of such testimony and Sovietize these narratives. This created a problem when it came to a discussion of Jewish victimization during the war. Journalists like Ilya Ehrenburg and Vishnevsky mentioned the 6 million Jews murdered by the Nazis in some of their articles in *Izvestia* and *Pravda* in 1946, while other journalists downplayed such losses or Sovietized them.[109]

Soviet journalists also wrote about of the gruesome films presented in court by Russian prosecutors, which received far less attention than US films presented earlier in the trial. Hicks attributes this to waning journalistic interest in the trial in the Soviet press. But this did not deter Roman Karmen, who wrote the script for the Soviets' most prominent film—*Film Documents of Atrocities Committed by the German-Fascist Invaders* (*Kinodokumenty o zverstvakh nemetsko-fashistskikh zakhvatchikov*)—from calling the gruesome images, particularly of corpses, as "mute witnesses" to Nazi crimes in an article in *Izvestia* in early 1946. The film, he added, shocked everyone in the courtroom.[110] Ann and John Tusa concurred, and said it "surpassed in horror anything yet shown, anything envisaged from the evidence which had yet been heard."[111] Other Soviet films centered on Nazi efforts to destroy the cultural heritage of its towns and villages, though they never got the same attention as earlier American films.

Hicks, like Hirsch, emphasizes the changing dynamics of the trial after Winston Churchill made his "Iron Curtain" speech in Missouri in early March 1946. It enflamed growing Soviet frustration with the trial and led to a decline in coverage in the press. This changed toward the end of the trial when Rudenko made his closing arguments and later, his final statement. Both got full press coverage, as did lengthy criticism of the verdict and the Soviet dissenting opinion.

Such failures, Hicks argues, do nothing to diminish efforts by Soviet journalists to detail, sometimes through personal experiences, the horrors faced by the Russian people during the Great Fatherland War. This was done with some success while trying to deal with the demands of Soviet propagandists and censors. Their failure to convey these stories to a wider audience can be traced to the inability of the machinery of Soviet propaganda to adapt to the needs of Western media. In the end, of course, the real judges of such successes and failures, Polevoi argued, was posterity.[112]

Chapter 8

Equally important, of course, is that despite the flawed Soviet approach to the trial and Stalin's disappointment with its outcome, Rudenko, Nikitchenko, Vyshinsky, Trainin, and others played important roles in one of the most important legal undertakings in modern international legal history. The Nuremberg Trial gave birth to a number of new legal concepts and precedents that remain an integral part of international criminal law. It also gave voice to an entirely new concept in international criminal justice—genocide—which would lay the groundwork for the 1948 Genocide Convention. Douglas Irvin-Erickson discusses the evolution of this concept in "From Geneva to Nuremberg to New York: Andrei Vyshinsky, Raphaël Lemkin and the Struggle to Outlaw Revolutionary Violence, State Terror, and Genocide."

Irvin-Erickson argues that a look at the personal disputes between Lemkin and Vyshinsky in the 1930s and 1940s provides us with a new perspective on the evolution of international criminal law during this period. Vyshinsky, he notes, saw law as a coercive instrument that could be used to regulate behavior, while Lemkin saw it a normative instrument enshrined in law through bottom-up social movements, which could be used to regulate state and human behavior.[113] Vyshinsky first learned about Lemkin after the latter published a paper "Akte der Barbarei und des Vandalismus als Delicta Juris Gentium" (Acts of Barbarity and Vandalism as Offenses Against the Law of Nations) that discussed five new types of crimes under the law of nations that threatened the existence of national, racial, and ethnic groups—barbarity, vandalism, provoked catastrophes, the disruption of international human communication, and the deliberate spread of human, animal, or vegetable contagion.[114]

Vespasian Pella and de Vabres, later one of the French judges at Nuremberg, first used these terms in the context of international counterfeiting. Lemkin looked at them in a more theoretical context in response to the growing violence in Nazi Germany against Jews and state terror in the Soviet Union.[115] He defined barbarity as an attempt to destroy ethnic, religious, national, or other social collectives, and vandalism as similar efforts to destroy a group's cultural works, rituals, ceremonies, and beliefs.[116] Lemkin, who had written several books critical of early Soviet criminal codes, found a ready critic in Vyshinsky, who argued in his introduction to Trainin's *Criminal Intervention* (1935) that Lemkin was proposing unified anti-Soviet penal laws that focused on abstract ideas like terrorism. These laws were meant to limit state sovereignty and remove "the state from its pedestal." Vyshinsky saw this as counterrevolutionary bourgeoisie attempts to legalize the right to intervene in the affairs of any country under the pretext that they are concerned about the "fate of 'culture and civilization.'"[117] Irvin-Erickson adds that Vyshinsky saw this as part of an international political struggle against the

Soviet Union designed to protect a capitalist, imperialist international system from a Soviet-style socialist revolution globally.

Trainin went even further in *Criminal Intervention* and claimed that Lemkin also meant for barbarity to refer to the destruction and capture of railways, telegraphs, and state infrastructures, which were tactics used during revolutions. The same was true for vandalism, which targeted cultural artifacts. In doing so, Trainin argued, Lemkin was using these terms to try to promote the idea of outlawing revolutionary violence as acts of terrorism. This, he went on, was laying the groundwork for imperialist intervention in revolutionary situations that threatened their interests.[118]

Vyshinsky thought that international law was meant to serve the interests of the state and should be an instrument of state policy. That was certainly apparent during the Nuremberg Trial and underscores Soviet disappointment with its outcome. His perspective would also shape the Soviet response to the debate about the adoption of the Genocide Convention in the United Nations in 1947–1948. The fact that the idea for such an international accord was the brainchild of Lemkin ensured that the debate between Vyshinsky, the deputy foreign minister and Stalin's representative to the UN, would be revisited during the contentious struggle over the adoption of the convention.

While the seeds for Lemkin's ideas about genocide as an international crime can be traced back to his works in the 1930s, he gave them substance in his seminal work, *Axis Rule in Occupied Europe*, that was published in late 1944. He defined genocide as a "coordinated plan of different actions aimed at the destruction of the essential foundation of the life of national groups, with the aim of annihilating the groups themselves." He then described the eight techniques used by the Nazis during the war against "all elements of nationhood"—political, social, cultural, economic, biological, physical, religious, and moral. Lemkin added that genocide was not just a problem during times of wars but also peace. Consequently, he argued that national and international codes should be adopted to protect minorities from "oppression because of their nationhood, religion, or race."[119]

Lemkin hoped that the Nuremberg prosecutors would adopt genocide as one of its core charges, and when they did not, he looked to the United Nations to address what he considered an important void in international criminal law. In 1947, the United Nations asked Lemkin, Pella, and de Vabres to prepare a draft of a Genocide Convention, which, after considerable debate, began to wind its way slowly through various United Nations committees. Initially, the Soviets were quite supportive of the general spirit of the convention though, as time went on, their opposition intensified like that of the British and other delegations.

The staunchest criticism of the convention arose after the meeting of the Sixth (or Legal) Committee on April 30, 1948, when the Soviets voted against the adoption of the draft genocide Convention. Afterward, Platon D. Morozov, the Soviet delegate and vice chairman of the committee, issued a lengthy statement that declared that it was "not a sufficiently effective instrument for the suppression of genocide and does not therefore respond to the aim which was set forth before the Committee by the General Assembly and then by the Economic and Social Council." His principle arguments were that its definition of genocide did not link such crimes organically to Nazi-fascist racial crimes, included political groups as potential objects of genocide, and failed to "establish punishability [sic] of a number of dangerous crimes of genocide."[120]

Lemkin, Irvin-Erickson observes, thought that the British, the French, the Americans, and others had their own reasons to oppose the convention because they feared that they could be caught up in charges about their own mistreatment of minorities at home or in their colonies. The paradox, he argues, is that while all United Nations members thought genocide should be outlawed, they wanted a law that could not be applicable to their own grave actions but could be applied to any mass murder that hurt their own national interests. In the end, Irvin-Erickson concludes, Vyshinsky was correct when he argued that international law was not moral or neutral since it served the interests of the state. Lemkin agreed and understood that even though many countries had voted to approve its adoption, its ratification into law was to be decided by politicians in the individual member states. In the end, both of these legal giants agreed that politics was the guiding principle in all law.

But, as the authors in this book have shown, their views on the interpretation of politics, the state, and law were quite different. In *Axis Rule in Occupied Europe*, Lemkin wrote that "the idea of a nation signifies constructive cooperation and original contributions, based upon genuine traditions, genuine culture, and a well-developed national psychology."[121] These attributes, of course, can only be found in open, democratic societies. In 1947, Lemkin asked Pearl S. Buck, the recipient of the Pulitzer Prize and the Nobel Prize in Literature, to write a manifesto urging the United Nations to adopt a Genocide Convention. She gave voice to Lemkin's ideas about the enriching diversity of culture and called "free human groups, united by ethnical, religious, and cultural ties a great living force in civilization."[122]

Joseph Stalin, and his legal mouthpiece, Andrei Vyshinsky, could not have disagreed more though both periodically gave lip service to such ideas. What Lemkin and Buck described were tolerant ideals practiced and lived in a mature political environment that valued diversity in its many forms. Such diversity was anathema in the Soviet Union if it in any way challenged the power and authority of the state under the absolute control of Stalin. If we take nothing else away from our study of the Soviet "show" trials, Nuremberg, and United Nations efforts to adopt a Genocide Convention, it is the singular nature of Soviet politics under Stalin. Any perceived threat to his power and control over the vast Soviet Union was met with unparalleled harshness and brutality, often masked in the niceties of legal fiction.

Notes

1 *The Politics of Autocracy: Letters of Alexander II to Prince A.I. Bariantinskii, 1957-1864*, ed. Alfred J. Rieber (Paris: Mouton, 1966), 57.
2 Vera Broido, *Apostles into Terrorists: Women and the Revolutionary Movement in the Russia of Alexander II* (New York: Viking, 1977), 68, 75.
3 Julie Cassidy, *The Enemy on Trial: Early Soviet Courts on Stage and Screen* (DeKalb, IL: Northern Illinois University, 2000), 30.
4 Ibid., 31.

5 Ibid., 36-37.
6 Ibid., 31-36.
7 Walter G. Moss, *Russia in the Age of Alexander II, Tolstoy, and Dostoevsky* (London: Anthem Press, 2002), 251-252.
8 Philip Pomper, *Lenin's Brother: The Origins of the October Revolution* (New York: W.W. Norton, 2010), 169.
9 Robert Service, *Lenin: A Biography* (Cambridge, MA: Belknap Press, 2000), 60; Elizabeth Wood, *Performing Justice: Agitation Trials in Early Soviet Russia* (Ithaca: Cornell University Press, 2005), 23.
10 George Kennan, "Prison Life of the Russian Revolutionists," I. *The Century Magazine*, 35, New Series XIII (November 1887-April 1888), 285.
11 *Lenin on Politics and Revolution: Selected Writings*, ed. James E. Connor (New York: Pegasus, 1968,), 248-49, 264-65.
12 Cassidy, *Enemy on Trial*, 37-38.
13 Mark Jensen, *A Show Trial under Lenin: The Trial of the Socialist Revolutionaries, Moscow 1922*, trans. Jean Sanders (The Hague: Martinus Nijhoff, 1982), 27-28.
14 Ibid., 85-91.
15 Peter H. Solomon, *Soviet Criminal Justice under Stalin* (Cambridge: Cambridge University Press, 1996), 31.
16 Harold J. Berman, *Soviet Criminal Law and Procedure: The RSFSR Codes* (Cambridge, MA: Harvard University Press, 1972), 28.
17 Robert Service, *Stalin: A Biography* (Cambridge, MA: Belknap Press, 2004), 274-75.
18 Andrei Vyshinsky, *The Law of the Soviet State*, trans. Hugh W. Babb (New York: Macmillan, 1948), 45-46.
19 Nikita Khrushchev, *The Crimes of the Stalin Era: Special Report to the 20th Congress of the Communist Party of the Soviet Union*, annotated by Boris I. Nicolaevsky (New York: The New Leader, 1956), 14.
20 *Report of Court Proceedings: The Case of the "Trotskyite-Zinovievite Terrorist Centre."* Heard before the Military Collegium of the Supreme Court of the U.S.S.R., Moscow, August 19-24, 1936 (New York: Howard Fertig, 1967); *Report of Court Proceedings in the Case of the "Anti-Soviet Trotskyite Centre."* Heard before the Military Collegium of the Supreme Court of the U.S.S.R., Moscow, January 23-30, 1937. Verbatim Report (New York; Howard Fertig, 1967); *Report of the Court Proceedings in the Case of the Anti-Soviet "Bloc of Rights and Trotskyites."* Heard before the Military Collegium of the Supreme Court of the U.S.S.R., March 2-13, 1938 (Moscow: People's Commissariat of Justice of the U.S.S.R., 1938).
21 Directives of the Politburo, August 17, 1940; December 7, 1940, in V. N. Khaustov, V. P. Naumov, and N. S. Polotnikova, eds., *Lubianka: Stalin I NKVD-NKGB-GUKR "Smersh" 1939-March 1946* [Lubianka: Stalin and NKVD-NKVGB-GUKR "Smersh" 1939-March 1946] (Moscow: Mezhdunarodnyi fond "Demokratiia," 2006), 184, 201-04; Viacheslav Zviagntsev, *Voina na vesakh Femidy: voina 1941-1945 gg. v materialakh sudebnosledstvennykh del* [War on the Scale of Lady Justice: The War of 1941-1945 in the Judicial-Investigative Cases] (Moscow: Terra, 2006), 549; Yakov Aisenshtat, *Zapiski sekretaria voennogo tribunal* [Notes of a Military Tribunal's Secretary] (London: Oversees Publications Interchange, Ltd., 1991), 5-6; "Voennye tribunaly v usloviiakh Otechestvennoi voiny [The Military Tribunals in the Conditions of the Great Patriotic War]," *Sotsialisticheskaia zakonnost'*, 7 (1942), 1-3; M. Groszinskii, "Osobennosti ugolovnogo sudoproizvodstva v usloviiakh vonennogo vremeni [The Peculiarities of Criminal Proceedings in Wartime Conditions],"

Sotsialisticheskaia zakonnost', 13–14 (1942), 10–11; I. T. Goliakov, *Sovetskoe pravo v period Velikoi Otechestvennoi voiny* [Soviet Law during the Great Patriotic War] (Moscow: Iuridicheskoe izdatel'stvo Ministerstva Iustitsii, 1948), 2, 203.

22 V. S. Khristoforov, *Organy bezopasnosti SSSR v 1941-1945 gg* [The Soviet Security Services in 1941–1945] (Moscow: Izdatel'stvo Glavnogo arkhivnogo upravleniia Moskvy, 2011), 174–75; A. E. Epifanov, *Otvestvennost' za voennye prestupleniia, sovershennye na territory SSSR v gody Velikoi Otechstvennoi* [Responsibility for War Crimes Committed on the Territory of the USSR during the Great Patriotic War] (Volgograd: Volgogradskaia akademiia MVD Rossii, 2005), 39; David M. Crowe, *War Crimes, Genocide, and Justice: A Global History* (New York: Palgrave Macmillan, 2014), 153.

23 *Velikaia Otchestvennaia* [The Great Patriotic War] 2/3 (Moscow: "Terra-Terra, 1993–1999)," 130–31; Zviagntsev, *Voina na vesakh Femidy*, 624; Goliakov, *Sovetskoe pravo*, 2, 51; Epifanov, *Otvetstvennost'*, 22–23, 25, 29, 40, 69.

24 A. M. Beliaev, *Kuban v gody Velikoĭm Otechestvennoĭ Voĭny, 1941-1945: khronika sobyĭi* [Kuban during the Great Patriotic War 1941–1945: The Chronicle of Events] (Krasnodar: Sov. Kuban': 2000–2003), 2, 354–55, 418; Vanessa Voisin, *L'URSS contre ses traïtres L'Épuration soviétique (1941-1945)* (Paris: Publications de la Sorbonne, 2015), 259; Ilya Bourtman, "Blood for Blood, Death for Death: The Soviet Military Tribunal in Krasnodar, 1943," *Holocaust and Genocide Studies*, 22/2 (2008), 250–56; Aisenshtat, *Zapiski sekretaria*, 75; Khaustov, Naumov, and Polotnikova, *Lubianka*, 407; V.P. Iampol'skii, *Organy gosudarstvennoi bezopasnosti SSSR v Velikoi Otechestvennoi voinie: sbornik dokumentov* [The Soviet Security Services in the Great Patriotic War: Collection of Documents] (Moscow: Izdatel'stvo "Rus," 2008), 4/2: 205–14, 337; Epifanov, *Otvetstvennost'*, 39; Oleg Borisovich Mozokhin, "Statistika repressivnoi deiatel'nosti organov bezopasnosti SSSR," [Statistics of the Repressive Activities of the Soviet Security Services] http://istmat.info/node/255 [accessed August 25, 2012].

25 Iampol'skii, *Organy gosurdarstvennoi bezopasnodsti SSSR*, 4/2, 572–73; Epifanov, *Osvetstvennosti'*, 19, 49; A. A. Gertsenzon, Sh. S. Gringauz, N. D. Durmanov, M. M. Isaev, and B. S. Utievskii, *Istoriia sovetskogo ugolovnogo prava* [History of Soviet Criminal Law] (Moscow: Iuridicheskoe izdaetl'stvo Ministerstva Iustitsii SSSR, 1948), 454.

26 United States Holocaust Memorial Museum (USHMM), "Post-war Crimes Trials Related to the Holocaust, 1937-1943," from the Archives of the Security Service of Ukraine, Reel 56, Case 19376, Frames 1203–1206; Ibid., Reel 57, Case13135, Frames 923-27, 936-39, 957, 983, 1013–14, 1266, 1274, 1302–05; Ibid., 77, Case 20347, Frames 1371–73, 1460–61.

27 "*Nikto ne zabyt, nichto ne zabyto*" [No One Will be Forgotten, and Nothing Will be Forgotten], Porter notes, was emblazoned on almost every war memorial in the Soviet Union.

28 Mark Lewis, *The Birth of the New Justice: The Internationalization of Crimes & Punishment, 1919-1950* (Oxford: Oxford University Press, 2014), 79.

29 *Report of the Court Proceedings in the Case of the Anti-Soviet Bloc of Rights and Trotskyites*. Heard before the Military Collegium of the Supreme Court of the U.S.S.R., March 2–13, 1938 (Moscow: People's Commissariat of Justice of the U.S.S.R., 1938), 695.

30 Neal K. Katyal, "Conspiracy Theory," *The Yale Law Journal*, 112/1307 (2002-2003), 1370. [1314–98]

31 Francine Hirsch, "The Soviets at Nuremberg: International Law, Propaganda, and the Making of the Postwar Order," *American Historical Review*, 113/3 (2008), 707; George Ginsburgs, *Moscow's Road to Nuremberg: The Soviet Background to the Trial* (The Hague: Martinus Nijhoff, 1996), 31–32.
32 Crowe, *War Crimes*, 152.
33 *The Spectator*, December 23, 1943, 1; Arieh J. Kochavi, *Prelude to Nuremberg: Allied War Crimes and the Question of Punishment* (Chapel Hill: University of North Carolina Press, 2005), 69.
34 Edgar Snow, *The Pattern of Soviet Power* (New York: Random House, 1945), 18, 97.
35 Yitzhak Arad, *The Holocaust in the Soviet Union* (Lincoln: University of Nebraska Press, 2009), 539–40.
36 John P. Fox, "The Jewish Factor in British War Crimes Policy in 1942," *The English Historical Review*, 92/362 (January 1977), 82, 101–106 [82–106]
37 USHMM, RG22.009.01.04, 39–40.
38 Michelle Jean Penn, *The Extermination of Peaceful Soviet Citizens: Aron Trainin and International Law* (Boulder: Dissertation, Department of History, University of Colorado, 1917), 51–52.
39 Lewis, *Birth of the New Justice*, 11.
40 Douglas Irvin-Erickson, *Raphaël Lemkin and the Concept of Genocide* (Philadelphia: University of Pennsylvania Press, 2017), 48.
41 Penn, *Extermination of Peaceful Soviet Citizens*, 77.
42 Ibid., 101, 103, 108.
43 A. Trainin, "Uchenie o souchastii," in N. F. Kuznetsova, *Trainin, Izbrannie proizvedenia ed.* (St. Petersburg: Yuridichesky Center Press, 2004), 267, 270, 285–86, 293.
44 A. Trainin, *Ugolovnaia otvetstvennost' gitlerovtsev*, ed. A. Vyshinsky (Moscow, 1944), 87. See also the English translation of his work, *Criminal Responsibility of the Hitlerites*, Vols 1 & 2, ed. A.Y. Vyshinsky (Moscow: Legal Publishing House NKU, USSR, 1944).
45 Ibid., 35–36.
46 *Documents on the Tokyo International Military Tribunal: Charter, Indictment and Judgments*, ed. Neil Boister and Robert Cryer (Oxford: Oxford University Press, 2008), 885.
47 Ibid., 893–904.
48 Crowe, *War Crimes*, 110.
49 A. Trainin, *Zashchita mire i bor'ba s prestupleniyami protiv chelovechestva*, in Kuznetsova, *Trainin*, 706.
50 Ibid., 713.
51 Jonathan Brent and Vladimir P. Naumov, *Stalin's Last Crime: The Plot against the Jewish Doctors, 1948–1953* (New York: HarperCollins, 2003), 256.
52 Hirsch, "The Soviets at Nuremberg," 708.
53 See above plus George Ginsburgs and V. N. Kudriavtsev, eds., *The Nuremberg Trial and International Law* (Dordrecht: Martinus Nijhhoff, 1990) and Ginsburgs, *Moscow's Road to Nuremberg*, 1996.
54 For a detailed study of the evolution Soviet thinking, legally and politically, on the question of German war criminality and Nuremberg, see Irina Schulmeister-André's recent *Internationale Strafgerichtsbarkeit unter sowjetischem Einflusss: Der Beitrag der UdSSR zum Nürnberger Hauptkriegsverbrechersprozess* (Berlin: Duncker & Humblot, 2016).
55 Great Britain, France, the Soviet Union, and the United States.

56 Crowe, *War Crimes*, 162.
57 Telford Taylor, *The Anatomy of the Nuremberg Trials: A Personal Memoir* (Boston: Little, Brown, 1992), 62–63.
58 *Report of Robert H. Jackson, United States Representative to the International Conference on Military Trials* (London: Department of State, 1945), June 26, 1945, Doc. XIII, 72.
59 Ibid., 137–42.
60 Ibid., 424–25.
61 Ibid., 255.
62 Ibid., 257–58, 264.
63 Ibid., 264–66.
64 Ibid., 319, 343–46, 348–58, 362, 377; Crowe, *War Crimes*, 162.
65 Taylor, *Anatomy of the Nuremberg Trials*, 68–70
66 Ibid., 70.
67 Clement Atlee, the new British prime minister, Stalin, and Harry Truman, the new US president.
68 Crowe, *War Crimes*, 163.
69 *Jackson Report*, 399–429. Nikitchenko and Trainin signed the August 8 accord for the Soviets.
70 Taylor, *Anatomy of the Nuremberg Trials*, 46.
71 Sidney Alderman, "Negotiating the Nuremberg Trial Agreements, 1945," in Raymond Dennett and Joseph E. Johnson, eds., *Negotiating with the Russians* (Boston: World Peace Foundation, 1951), 53.
72 *Principles of International Law Recognized in the Charter of the Nürnberg Tribunal and in the Judgement of the Tribunal (1950)* (New York: United Nations, 2005), 1–3; Yves Beigbeder, *Judging War Criminals: The Politics of International Justice* (New York: Palgrave, 1999), 12–13.
73 ARAN (*Arkhiv Rossiiskoi Akademii nauk*); GARF (*Gosudarstvennyi arkhiv Rossiiskoi Federdatsii*); AVPRF (*Arkhiv vneshnei politiki Rossiiskoi Federatsii*); RGALI (*Rossiiskii gosudarstvennyi arkhiv literatury I iskusstva*); RGASPI (*Rossiiskii gosudarstvennyi arkhiv sotsial'no-politicheskoi istorii*).
74 AVPRF f. 082, op. 27, 122, d. 23,ll, 16–18; Taylor, *Anatomy of the Nuremberg Trials*, 99.
75 AVPRF f.06, op7, 0d. 208, I.21; GARF f.81, op. 38, d. 238, II.17–21.
76 Office of United States Chief of Counsel for Prosecution of Axis Criminality, *Nazi Conspiracy and Aggression*, I (Washington: United States Government Printing Office, 1946), 28, 32.
77 Jackson, *Anatomy of the Nuremberg Trials*, 177; Ann Tusa and John Tusa, *The Nuremberg Trial* (New York: Skyhorse Publishing, 2010), 113.
78 *Nazi Conspiracy and Aggression*, I, 42.
79 AVPRF f. 07, op. 13, 41, d. 10, II, 40–68; AVPRF f. 06, op. 7, 20, d. 208, I. 22.
80 For the sections on Czechoslovakia and the Molotov-Ribbentrop Pact, see *Nazi Conspiracy and Aggression*, I, 25–26, 27.
81 Colonel-General G. F. Krivosheev, ed., *Soviet Casualties and Combat Losses in the Twentieth Century* (London: Greenhill Books, 1997), 83–84; Max Hastings agrees with this estimate in his *Inferno; The World at War, 1939–1945* (New York: Alfred A. Knopf, 2011), 646, as does Gerhard L. Weinberg in his *A World at Arms; A Global History of World War II* (Cambridge: Cambridge University Press, 1994), 894. He also thinks that the figure could be 25 million or more.

82 Dmitri Volkogonov, *Stalin: Triumph & Tragedy*, ed. and trans. Harold Shukman (New York: Grove Weidenfeld, 1988), 504; Soviet industrial output declined significantly between 1940 and 1945. Mark Harrison, *Soviet Planning in Peace and War, 1938–1945* (Cambridge: Cambridge University Press, 1985), 253; for more on peasant and agricultural losses, see Alec Nove, "Soviet Peasantry in World War II," in Susan J. Linz, ed., *The Impact of World War II on the Soviet Union* (Totowa, NJ: Rowan and Allanheld, 1985), 77–90.
83 *Nazi Conspiracy and Aggression*, I, 46–48.
84 Ibid., 35–38, 41–42.
85 Ibid., 20–21, 53–56.
86 GARF f. 7445, op. 2, d. 391, LL. 45–46.
87 Crowe, *War Crimes*, 168.
88 Jackson, *Anatomy of the Nuremberg Trials*, 310.
89 Roy Jenkins, *Churchill: A Biography* (New York: Farrar, Strauss and Giroux, 2001), 810.
90 GARF f. 7445, op. 2, d. 391, II, 61–63.
91 Crowe, *War Crimes*, 161.
92 Ibid., 161.
93 Leonid Trofimov, "Soviet Reporters at the Nuremberg Trial: Agenda, Attitudes, and Encounters, 1945–1946," *Cahiers d' Histoire*, XXVIII/2 (2010), 55.
94 AVPRF f. 07, op. 13, 41, d. 9, II. 112–16.
95 *Soviet Documents on Foreign Policy*, III: 1933–1941, ed. Jane Degras (Oxford: Oxford University Press, 1953), 359–61.
96 GARF, f. 7445, op. 2, d. 391, ll, 50–51.
97 *Nazi Conspiracy and Aggression; Opinion and Judgment*, 166–88.
98 Hirsch, "The Soviets at Nuremberg," 701, 703.
99 James V. Wertsch, *Voices of Collective Remembering* (Cambridge: Cambridge University Press, 2002), 106.
100 Trofimov, *Soviet Reporters at the Nuremberg Trial*, 55.
101 Nikolai Zhukov, "Niurbergskii protsess. Reportazh khudozhnika N. Zhukova," in Boris Polevoi, ed., *V kontse kontsov. Niurnbergskie dneviki. Zarisovki Nikolaia Zhukova*, 2nd ed. (Moscow: Sovetskaia Rossiia, 1972), 247.
102 Aron Trainin, "Mezhdunarodnyi voennyi tribunal," *Pravda*, August 11, 1945, 4; Aron Trainin, "Prestupnye organizatsii gitlerizma," *Pravda*, December 23, 1945, 4.
103 Lev Sheinin, "Nemye svideteli," *Izvestiia*, December 2, 1945, 3.
104 Trofimov, *Soviet Reporters at the Nuremberg Trial*, 51.
105 David M. Crowe, *The Holocaust: Roots, History, and Aftermath* (Boulder: Westview, 2012), 197.
106 Leonov, "Liudoed gotovit pishchu," 180–81.
107 Boris Polrevoi, *Sobranie sochinenii* (Moscow: Khudozhestvennaia literatura, 1981), 130–31, 394.
108 Boris Polevoi, "Pomni ob etom, izbiratel," *Pravda*, February 9, 1946, 5.
109 Il'ia Ehrenburg, "Kontrataka nochi," *Izvestiia*, March 30, 1946, 3; Vsevolod Vishnevsky, "Posudimye I svideteli," *Pravda*, January 7, 1946, 3; Polevoi, *Sobranie sochinenii*, 8, 346.
110 Roman Karmen, "Mertvye obviniaiut," *Izvestiia*, February 20, 1946, 3; Joseph E. Persico, *Nuremberg: Infamy on Trial* (London: Penguin, 1995), 244–48.
111 Ann Tusa and John Tusa, *The Nuremberg Trial* (London: Macmillan, 1983), 198.
112 Polevoi, *Sobranie sochineii*, 8, 523.

113 Irvin-Erickson, *Raphaël Lemkin and the Concept of Genocide*.
114 Raphaël Lemkin, "Les Actes Constituant un Danger (Intere'taitque) Considere's Comme Delits du Droit des Gens," in Jiminez de Asua, Vespasien Pella, and Manuel Lo'pez Rey, eds., *Actes de la V'eme Conf'erence Internationale Pour l'Unification du Droit P'enal, Madrid 14–20 Octobre 1933* (Paris: A. Pedone, 1935), 48–56.
115 Claudia Kraft, "Nationalisierende Transnatioinalisierung: Internationale Strafrechtswissenschaft in der Zweishcenkriegszeit," in Dietmar Müller abd Adamantios Skorodos, eds. *Leipziger Zugänge zur Rechtlichen, Politischen und Kulturellen Verflechtungsgeschichte Ostmillteeuropas* (Leipzig: Leipziger Universitätsverlag, 2015), 15–26.
116 Irvin-Erickson, *Raphaël Lemkin*, 46–47.
117 Andrey Vyshinsky, "Introduction," in Aron Trainin, ed., *Criminal Intervention: The Movement for the Unification of Criminal Law of the Capitalist Countries* (Moscow: State Publishing House OGIZ, 1935), 3–6.
118 Anton Weiss-Wendt, *The Soviet Union and the Gutting of the UN Genocide Convention* (Madison: University of Wisconsin Press, 2017), 13–14.
119 Raphaël Lemkin, *Axis Rule in Occupied Europe: Laws of Occupation, Analysis of Government Proposals for Redress*, 2nd ed. (Clark, NJ: The Lawbook Exchange, 2008), 79–95.
120 *The Genocide Convention: The Travaux Préparatories*, ed. Hirad Abtahi and Philippa Webb, II (Leiden: Martinus Nijhoff, 2008), 1152–54.
121 Lemkin, *Axis Rule*, 91.
122 Theodore F. Harris, in consultation with Pearl S. Buck. *Pearl S. Buck: A Biography*, II: *Her Philosophy as Expressed in her Letters* (New York: John Day, 1971), 84–85.

1

Late Imperial and Soviet "Show" Trials, 1878–1938

David M. Crowe

In 1864, Alexander II issued a series of legal reforms that unwittingly set the stage for a number of trials over the next half century that Julie A. Cassidy argues were "highly publicized" legal spectacles that radicals used to promote their revolutionary ideas and garner the support of "the peasant and working masses in whose name they acted."[1] The early imperial "show" trials were meant to promote one of the central ideas of the 1864 reforms—trial by jury. Alexander II also hoped the reforms would

> install in Russia fast, just, and merciful courts, equal for all Our subjects, to heighten judicial power, to give it the necessary independence, and in general, to strengthen in Our people the respect for law without which public prosperity is impossible, and which must serve as a permanent guide for the actions of all and everybody, from the person of the highest to that of the lowest rank.[2]

The new reforms provided for the separation of the court system from the administrative and legislative elements of the government, greater independence and protections for judges, a stronger adversarial system with open courtroom proceedings, and jury trials for "serious criminal offenses."[3]

According to Cassidy, the imperial "show" trials, which began in the 1870s, were a series of "highly publicized public spectacles that spread the ideas of Russian radicalism even as they condemned the radicals themselves to imprisonment, exile, hard labor, civil death, or execution."[4] They also became a source of "popular entertainment" that drew large audiences and helped, according to Elizabeth A. Wood, create a link in the public imagination between "revolution and trials." Georgii Plekhanov, one of Russia's foremost Marxists, saw the "revolutionary trials in the 1870s and 1880s" as "the greatest historical drama which is called the trial of the government by the people."[5]

The trial of Vera Zasulich in 1878 was the most important of these legal "spectacles." Zasulich was a prominent member of a radical revolutionary group, the Southern Mutineers (*Yuzhnye buntari*). In 1877, one of her friends told her about the savage beating of Alexei Bogolyubov, a young revolutionary in Kresty prison in St. Petersburg who had failed to tip his hat when Dmitri Trepov, the Governor-General of

St. Petersburg, walked by while inspecting the prison. When she heard news of the beating, Zasulich decided to try to assassinate Trepov. Though she only wounded him, her trial a few months later allowed her to use it to draw attention to her revolutionary ideals.[6]

Anatoly Koni, the presiding judge, openly discussed the propagandistic and theatrical dimensions of the Zasulich's "show" (*pokazatel'nyi*) trial in his memoirs. As the presiding judge, he chose the jury and gave it instructions on what to consider when making a decision on Zasulich's fate. His approach was criticized by the prosecutor, Konstantin Kessel, who pointed out numerous procedural missteps during the trial and theatrical outbursts from those in attendance.[7]

Before the trial began, the minister of justice Count Konstantin Palen told Koni that he should do everything possible to emphasize the political nature of Zasulich's crime. This would ensure that the jury saw it as an act of revenge committed by a spoiled youth. Her conviction, he added, would also underscore the credibility of a jury trial, something that had been criticized by opponents of the 1864 judicial reform program. Koni disagreed with Palen's suggestions and told him that his role as judge was simply to allow the jurors to make their own decision about Zasulich's guilt or innocence.[8]

Palen, however, was determined to have Zasulich tried and convicted as a common criminal without considering the political implications of this approach. He also chose to do it publicly, somehow thinking a jury would agree with the prosecution and reach a decision that would "show the loyalty of Russia's people to their tsar." He was confident that a jury would convict her because she had already confessed to the charge of attempted murder.[9] Unfortunately, his choice of Kessel as the chief prosecutor, and his efforts to try to convince Koni to guarantee a guilty verdict, backfired. This, coupled with the fact that Zasulich's attorney, P. A. Aleksandrov, was a "gifted orator" who was able to sway not only public opinion about the case but also the jury, resulted in her acquittal.[10]

The trial was held in a highly charged atmosphere that was open to the public.[11] Kessel proved no match for Aleksandrov, and Koni let him play out his theatrical approach to the case. He was able to transform the victim, Trepov, into a villain and argued that the vicious beating of Bogolyubov was a disgrace to public authority, which underscored Russian society's distaste for the "tyranny of the whip." His also argued that Trepov's order to have Bogolyubov flogged was illegal. In his memoirs, Koni wrote:

> Since the jury recognized the fact that the violence on one side (the public authorities) did not authorize violence on the other side (the subjects), the court had every reason to emphasize the first act of violence, to underscore its moral effects, as opposed to focusing on the circumstances of the defendant's life and thus presenting a petition to the tsar for mitigation of the sentence and mercy. . . . The court's verdict—firm and detailed—would have demonstrated to our sovereign how shamelessly the tsar's official had been in exceeding the limits of legality and trampling personal dignity.[12]

Aleksandrov also depicted Zasulich as a martyr whose impoverished childhood had been instrumental in forming some of her radical ideas. Her plan to shoot Trepov, he argued, was driven by her desire "to protect her fellow citizens and to ameliorate their social lot—'What was considered a state crime yesterday becomes a highly esteemed feat of civic valor today or tomorrow.'"[13]

According to Cassidy, Koni was determined to conduct a fair trial and refused to show "any bias during the trial." He also did "a remarkable job . . . of giving both prosecution and defense a fair hearing."[14] He responded to one of numerous public outbursts, for example, with the warning—"A court is not a theater; approval or disapproval is forbidden here. If this is repeated again I will be forced to clear the room."[15]

But Koni also knew that Russian juries were more inclined to base their decisions on the "moral and circumstantial issues, such as the moral character of the defendant, the defendant's past behavior, evidence of contrition, and the commensurability of the sentence and the indicted behavior" than the interpretation of the law itself. Consequently, he told the jury before they began their deliberations that their decision should be based on "your deepest conviction, based on all that you have seen and heard, and constrained by nothing beyond the voice of conscience [*krome golosa vashei sovesti*]."[16]

In the end, Alexandrov's strategy worked, and after only ten minutes, the jury declared Zasulich's innocence. Koni described what followed in his memoirs:

> It is impossible for one who was not present to imagine the outbursts that drowned out the foremen's voice and the movement that like an electric shock sped through the entire room. The cries of unrestrained joy, hysterical sobbing, desperate applause, the tread of feet, cries of "Bravo! Hurrah! Good Girl [*modoltsy*]! Vera! Verochka! Verochka!" merged in one roar both moan and howl. Many crossed themselves; in the upper, more democratic sections for the public people embraced; even in the places for the judges there was enthusiastic applause [*userd—neishim obrazom khlopali*].[17]

According to Gregoriy Gradovskii, a journalist who attended the trial, the impact of the decision was that "it is not she who has been brought to trial but me and all of us—all of society."[18]

The government refused to accept the verdict and planned to retry her. She fled to Switzerland and later became close friends with a budding young lawyer and revolutionary, Vladimir Ilyich Ulyanov—Lenin. She also co-founded the first Russian Marxist group, Emancipation of Labour, and Lenin's first journal—*Iskra*. Over time, they parted ways politically, particularly when she returned to Russia after the 1905 Revolution.[19]

This marriage of shared feelings and the use of media during the Zasulich trial created a model later used in Soviet "show" trials. The same was true when it came to the theatrical staging of a trial and efforts to manipulate public attitudes both in and outside of the courtroom, hallmarks of Soviet "show" trials in the 1920s and 1930s. The goal of such trials was to showcase the power of authority in a courtroom over the rule of law. But such trials during the late imperial period were only part of what George Kennan calls the three dimensions of government policies when dealing with political prisoners.

> First, the custom of making indiscriminate arrests as a means of inspiring terror and with the hope of obtaining clews to secret revolutionary activity; second, the

use of imprisonment as a species of torture to extort confession or compel the prisoner to betray friends; and third, the illegal detention of political "suspects" in solitary confinement for months and years while the police scour the empire in search of criminating evidence upon which to base indictments.[20]

This was certainly the case when it came to the cases of Sophia Perovskaya and her five co-defendants in 1881, who were charged with the murder of Tsar Alexander II on March 1, 1881 (the *Pervomartovtsy*; those of March 1). Perovskaya, who was in charge of the bomb squad that assassinated him, came from an extremely well-to-do family. Radicalized at an early age and imprisoned in 1874, she became involved with the People's Will Party (*Narodnaya volya*), which advocated the assassination of prominent officials. This, Perovskaya argued, would lead to a popular uprising that would destroy the alliance between the imperial and capitalist systems, and pave the way for a popularly elected government.[21]

The trial, which was held in the same courtroom as the Zasulich trial, was open only to top government officials, "some ladies of society," and members of the Russian and foreign press. It was conducted before a Special Session of the Ruling Senate for the Adjudication of Matters Pertaining to State Crimes.[22] The government chose Nicholai Muraviev, a law professor and member of one of Russia's most storied noble families, as chief prosecutor. The indictment charged each of the defendants with "evil designs" against the "Sacred Person of the Gossudar [*Gosudar*, sovereign] the Emperor," crimes that could result in a sentence of *katorga* (hard labor in prison or exile) or execution.[23]

The trial opened on March 26, and each of the defendants was allowed to make a statement after declaring their guilt or innocence. Perovskaya admitted to several attempts to assassinate the tsar and her continued belief in the ideals of the People's Will.[24] One of her co-defendants, Andrei Zhelyabov, went much further and tried to use the trial as a platform to give a more detailed voice to the ideals and goals of People's Will. He also filed a pretrial motion that challenged the Senate's right to try him and demanded a public trial by jury.[25] A *Times* reporter wrote that Zhelyabov was the "wiry type of the fierce and unyielding demagogue."[26]

Muraviev challenged all of this and in his closing summary of the prosecution's case described a "saintly, heroic Tsar struck down by beastly assassins" who gave up his life "for God, for Russia . . . in mortal combat with the enemies of justice, of order, of morality, of family life." He found it strange that People's Will could not find a "stronger hand, a stronger mind, a more experienced revolutionary than Sophia Perovskaya." He also wondered why a woman would be "acting in such a beastly role."[27]

Perovskaya's attorney admitted that though she had "gone astray," she had "noble character," which he hoped would be a mitigating factor. In her statement, Perovskaya expressed her deep commitment to the ideals and goals of People's Will and challenged Muraviev's claim that the assassins were "immoral and brutal." Anyone who knew us, she told the court, and understood the harsh conditions we worked under to achieve our goals would never accuse us of being immoral or brutal.[28]

Given the nature of their crimes, all of the defendants were found guilty and sentenced to be hanged. Any appeals would be heard by Alexander II's bereaved son, the future Alexander III. He ultimately decided to approve all of the sentences except one—that of Gesi Gel'fman, who was pregnant. Her sentence was delayed until she gave birth and she remained imprisoned in harsh conditions in the Peter and Paul fortress. She became ill after the child was born in early 1882 and died, while the child was given up for adoption.[29]

While the government did everything it could to prevent the outbursts that took place during the Zasulich trial, it could do little to stop a groundswell of support in some quarters for mercy for the defendants. Vladimir Soloviev, a prominent docent at St. Petersburg University, considered "capital punishment" to be "wrong and unchristian," and asked the tsar not to execute the defendants.[30] Leo Tolstoy did the same and told Alexander that if he pardoned his "father's assassins he could only strengthen his authority." One of the tsar's closest advisers wrote to the famed writer that "your faith is one thing, and mine and the church's another. . . . Our Christ is not your Christ. Ours I know as a man of strength and truth . . . but yours appears to me to possess traits of weakness."[31]

These appeals fell on deaf ears and the government decided to transform the executions into a spectacle. On April 3, those condemned to death were dressed in black, shackled, and paraded through the streets of St. Petersburg in separate, elevated wagons with large placards across their chests that read "tsaricide." Thousands of troops and police lined the streets as the procession moved to the sound of drumbeats to Semenovskaya Square where they were to be hanged. They were met there by a crowd of about 100,000 people. A large number of public officials, diplomats, and the press surrounded the gallows.[32] Some had acquired tickets to the hanging so they could "take away pieces of the hanging ropes—considered good luck souvenirs" after the executions.[33]

Russian intellectuals and writers such as Fyodor Dostoevsky were fascinated by such trials, while the Bolsheviks did everything they could to publicize trials that workers and others could use as soapboxes to promote their ideas. Dostoevsky attended the Zasulich trial and considered it a turning point for him when it came to the value of juries in Russian trials. Gary Rosenshield also thinks it influenced his decision to put a jury trial at the end of *The Brothers Karamazov* as a way of "advancing his moral, religious, and political ideas."[34]

Vladimir Ilyich Ulyanov—Lenin—was only seventeen years old when the second *Pervomartovtsy* trial took place in 1887. One of the defendants was his brother, Alexander, who was tried for his role as a bomb maker in an assassination attempt against Alexander III on March 1, 1887. Lenin's sister, Anna, was also arrested for her role in the plot. Alexander initially denied making the bombs but did admit that he had gathered the material to make them. But once he learned that several of his co-conspirators named him as a key figure in the plot, he became more open about the group's plans and his role in planning the assassination.[35]

The four-day trial, which began on April 15, was carefully orchestrated by Alexander III, who was well aware of the dangers of "show" trials and spectacle-like public executions. He preferred "without any fanfare [to] dispatch them [the defendants] to Schlüsselburg (Shlisselburg) Fortress. That would be the most severe and unpleasant punishment." Vera Figner, one of the leaders of the assassination of

Alexander II, spent twenty years in Schlüsselburg Fortress. Prisoners there, she wrote in her memoirs,

> were like people shipwrecked on an uninhabited island. We had nothing and no one in all the world save each other. Not only people, but nature, colors, sounds, were gone, all of them. And instead there was left a gloomy vault with a row of mysterious, wall-in cells, in which invisible captives were pining; an ominous silence, and the atmosphere of violence, madness and death.[36]

The tsar was ultimately convinced that it would be best to hold a closed trial before a special Senate tribunal. Alexander III kept close tabs on the trial and was given ample briefings about its progress as well as copies of the depositions of each of the defendants. He made notes in the margins of the interrogation transcripts that were "notable for their expressions of disgust and disdain."[37]

Though authorities tried to create a "virtual wall of secrecy around the trial,"[38] accounts soon appeared in the Russian émigré press and then in Russia itself. The body of evidence against Alexander Ulyanov was overwhelming, and he admitted that he played a key role in the construction of the bombs and "acted out of his own free will and rational mind."[39] And unlike some of his fellow conspirators, he tried to protect others involved in the plot and at one point during the trial took responsibility for someone else's role in the assassination attempt.[40]

On April 18, Alexander, aware that his mother, Maria, was in the courtroom, explained in detail "the scientific rationale for Russian terrorism." In testimony similar to that of Nikolai Bukharin during his "show" trial in 1938, Alexander carefully intellectualized the core ideals of many of his revolutionary contemporaries. According to Philip Pomper, "Sasha's (Alexander's) speech was the transcendent moment of the trial."[41] The next day, the judges found all of them guilty of all charges but only sentenced seven to death, including Alexander Ulyanov. The rest received prisons terms of two to twenty years of hard labor.[42]

Traditional Soviet biographies of Lenin consider Alexander's execution "the turning point in Lenin's life. In that year he irrevocably took the path of revolution."[43] Robert Service says that Lenin told the family's tutor after the execution that his brother acted the way he did because "he couldn't act in any other way."[44] Over time, Lenin would become just as radical and encouraged Bolsheviks to do everything possible to publicize any trials used by workers to promote their radical ideas. Lenin, himself a lawyer, wrote in the years just before the 1905 Revolution that the courtroom was "an organ of power." Liberals, he added, "sometimes forget this, but it is a sin for a Marxist to do so." He also advised young radicals and members of the new Duma who were arrested and put on trial to make certain that they transformed each one "into a political trial by the accused themselves, so that the government would no longer dare to cover its political revenge with the comedy of criminality!" Most importantly, they were "to use the court as a means of agitation."[45]

Michael Florinsky saw the "show" trials in the late imperial period as a "powerful impetus to political terror; the verdict, interpreted as public endorsement of terroristic methods swayed many terrorists who had formerly opposed political murders" to embrace such murders in the immediate years after the Zasulich trial.[46] Political terror became one of the primary tools that Lenin and the Bolsheviks used in their struggle against the real and imagined enemies of the young Soviet state. In the spring of 1918, Lenin wrote in an article in *Pravda*, "The Immediate Tasks of the Soviet Government," that stated that unlike previous bourgeois revolutions, the Bolshevik-led socialist revolution in Russia was driven not by class interests but by the desire to create a state where the "working and oppressed people" have a "chance to take an active part in the independent building up of a new society." Consequently, his government needed to embrace dictatorship ruthlessly to suppress and eradicate capitalism and win the coming civil war. True dictatorship, he added, "is iron rule, government that is revolutionary, bold, swift, and ruthless in suppressing both exploiters and hooligans."[47]

Such ruthlessness became the hallmark of Soviet rule during the long Russian civil war (1918-1921). Bolshevik economic and political policies, particularly "war communism" and the "red terror,"[48] had a devastating impact on the country, and set the stage for what Isaac Steinberg, a Left Socialist Revolutionary who served briefly as Lenin's commissar of justice, feared would become an "intrinsic feature of the regime" once the civil war was over.[49] Lenin planted the seed for the Bolshevik reign of terror in his February 21, 1918, decree "The Socialist Fatherland is in Danger!" which gave Bolshevik authorities the right to shoot "on the spot" a wide category of individuals deemed enemies of the regime.[50]

Steinberg voiced strong opposition to the decree, particularly when it came to the use of the death penalty, which he said "killed the whole pathos of the manifesto." Lenin responded that there was no way his party could be "victorious without the very cruelest revolutionary terror."[51] He added that such actions were necessary "in the name of revolutionary justice." If that was the case, Steinberg noted, then we should call it

> the Commissariat for Social Extermination and be done with it! Lenin's face suddenly brightened and he replied, "well put . . . that's exactly what it should be . . . but we can't say that."[52]

Piotr Stuchka, a deputy people's commissar of justice and one of Soviet Russia's most prominent jurists, supported Lenin's policies, and pointed out in an article on "revolutionary legality" in the *Encyclopedia of State and Law* (*Entsiklopedita gosudarstva I prava*; 1925)[53] that during the civil war the Bolsheviks were forced to adopt "extraordinary measures" that were "proclaimed as the general rule when in it came to questions about the conceptualization of 'revolutionary legality' and practices."[54] The adoption of the NEP (*Novaya Ekonomicheskaya Politika*; New Economic Policy), he added, which some saw as a retreat from earlier revolutionary ideals, led to the creation of a new forward looking "revolutionary legality" that focused on "class interests and the protection of its workers' and peasants' state authority."[55]

Soon after they seized power, the Bolsheviks created revolutionary tribunals to deal with those they deemed a threat to Soviet power. These, coupled with Peoples' Courts, which would deal with ordinary crimes, were to adjudicate vaguely defined "counterrevolutionary" crimes that gave these "kangaroo courts" extreme powers to deal with a wide range of crimes. Working hand in hand with the Cheka (*Vsrossiiskaya chrezvychainaya komisssiya*; All Russian Extraordinary Commission), the secret police, the tribunals handled "tens of thousands of cases before being disbanded in 1922."⁵⁶ Some of these early trials embraced the "unsophisticated theatricality" of the Zasulich trial and emphasized the importance of "revolutionary conscience" in determining the guilt or innocence of those accused of anti-Bolshevik crimes. Judges and prosecutors denounced "all claims to objectivity" as "bourgeois falsification."⁵⁷

This was certainly the case during the trial of Countess Sophie Panina, one of Russia's wealthiest women who held several ministerial posts in Alexander Kerensky's Provisional Government. Just weeks after the Bolsheviks took control of Petrograd (formerly St. Petersburg), Panina was put on trial for refusing to turn over funds from the ministry of education to Lenin's new government. From the Soviet perspective, the trial was an opportunity to showcase Bolshevik proletarian power vis-á-vis the power of a wealthy representative of everything they despised in Russian society. The public trial took place in the Grand Palace of Grand Duke Nikolai Nikolaevich, the tsar's cousin and former commander of Russian troops on the eastern front. While there was some effort to follow normal trial procedures, the decision to allow comments from the floor, as well as emotional appeals from her attorney, Ia. Ia. Gurevich, led to outbursts that created a circus-like atmosphere. Panina later wrote that, for her, the high point of the trial was the testimony of N. I. Ivanov, a factory worker who testified in her defense. He spoke emotionally about her years of educational and cultural work with "the common working people." His speech "produced in the hall the effect of an exploding bomb, and provoked unusual agitation among the judges." In the end, the judges decided simply to censure Panina.⁵⁸

Soviet leaders also encouraged the use of agitation trials to create enthusiasm for Bolshevik values during the civil war.⁵⁹ The first agitation trials were meant to help political instructors transform soldiers into "conscious" warriors and better understand what they were fighting for. At the end of the civil war, the military and the party used agitation trials to promote the idea among the troops that they were now the "true bearers of communist culture among the peaceful civilian population."⁶⁰ In the fall of 1921, the party sent out information about how to organize "political trials, political dialogues with women workers, and revolutionary plays," and over the next two years, it intensified efforts to promote agitation plays throughout the military to stimulate discussion about problems in Soviet society and ways to respond to "healthy phenomena, desertion, pillage, instability."⁶¹

In 1922, Lenin wrote Dmitrii Kursky, the commissar of justice, that

> a series of "noisy, *educative* model trials" must be held in various centres, and must be accompanied by plenty of "tumult" in the press. After all, trials had an "enormous educational significance."⁶²

What followed was the trial of thirty-four Socialist Revolutionaries who were accused of opposing the Bolsheviks during the civil war, which included plans to topple the Soviet regime, various acts of terror, and involvement in Fania Kaplan's attempt to assassinate Lenin in 1918. These became key charges in the 1922 trial but also in some of the "show" trials in the 1930s.⁶³

In early 1922, the Berlin-based Russian newspaper *Novyi mir* published a pamphlet that accused the SR leadership of anti-Soviet activities in 1917–1918, and the attack on Lenin. This was followed a few days later by similar accusations in *Izvestia*. The indictment mirrored these accusations, which centered around charges that the leadership of the SR Party was engaged in an "armed struggle against the Soviet regime, of having organized murderous assaults and raids, and of having maintained treasonable contacts with foreign states."[64]

Before the trial began, Lenin ordered that it should "be surrounded by an extra vehement campaign against the Socialist revolutionaries." Nikolai Krylenko, the chief prosecutor, Nikolai Bukharin, a leading party theorist, and Anatoly Lunacharskii, the head of the People's Commissariat of Enlightenment (*Narodnyi kommissariat prosveshcheniia*), sent guidelines to provincial party leaders to help foment this nationwide campaign in the press and in party propaganda. This included pamphlets that proclaimed "Into the streets! To the graves of the murdered leaders."[65] What followed were demonstrations nationwide that called for the brutal punishment of those in the dock.[66]

The trial, which began on June 8, was held in the House of the Unions in Moscow. Krylenko served as chief prosecutor with Georigii Pyatakov as the presiding judge. There was no applicable penal code at the time the alleged crimes took place nor when the indictment was written. Consequently, Soviet jurists rushed to finish a draft criminal code that had been in the works for some time. Lenin insisted that it include language that would allow a court to "punish any oppositional political activity with the death penalty by linking the activity in question with 'the international bourgeoisie and its fight against us.'" Articles 58–60 of the new code, which went into force a week before the SR trial began, addressed his concerns.[67]

The prosecution focused principally on the alleged crimes of twelve of the thirty-four defendants who had been prominent SR leaders.[68] The principal goal of the prosecution was to prove that the SRs were behind "almost all opposition against the Bolsheviks." On the other hand, they were depicted throughout the trial as "nothing but a paltry handful of indecisive cowards, of absolutely no significance."[69] An international defense team tried to counter what they considered the prosecution's distorted, untruthful Bolshevik claim that the SR leadership had been involved in an ongoing terrorist campaign to undermine Soviet power from 1918 to 1921. While there is no question that the SRs, once one of the most powerful revolutionary groups in Russia, were staunch opponents of the Bolsheviks, their power had waned considerably during the civil war. By 1921, most of its leaders were in jail or living in exile.[70]

But, like all future Soviet "show" trials, the SR trial had nothing to do with justice or truth. Its principal goal was the removal from the political landscape of any group or individual who presented a real or fictitious threat to Lenin, and later, Stalin. Consequently, the outcome of the trial was a foregone conclusion. On August 7, the court found twenty-two of the defendants guilty of various crimes including "counter-revolutionary intentions ... armed interference [or] a 'declaration of war' against the Republic," and membership in an organization with such aims, and sentenced them to death. The other defendants received prisons terms of two to ten years. But within days, party leaders commuted the death sentences to life in prison in return for a promise that the convicted leaders would cease their illegal activities against the Soviet state. The rest had their sentences reduced to time served.[71]

The adoption of the 1922 penal code just days before the SR trial began reflected new changes taking place in the Soviet legal system, driven in large part by the NEP. A year earlier, widespread post–civil war famine in the countryside triggered peasant rebellions that spread to the cities, culminating in the Kronstadt naval rebellion.[72] After Trotsky brutally put it down, Lenin ordered a "campaign of mass terror" against those villages that had risen up against the Soviets. Crack Soviet troops used poison gas, heavy weapons, and armored cars to arrest, murder, and in some instances, deport thousands of peasants to Soviet concentration camps to put the widespread uprising down.[73]

In the spring of 1921, Lenin introduced plans for the NEP to alleviate widespread food shortages and appease the peasants. The idea was to use capitalist incentives to revive the economy with the government maintaining control over the "commanding heights" of the economy—heavy industry, transportation, banking, and foreign trade.

He also decided to rein in the Cheka and allow "judicial organs" to "assume the duty of dealing with infractions of Soviet law." In a speech to the Ninth All-Russian Congress of Soviets, on December 21, 1921, Lenin argued that though the Cheka was viewed abroad as "an example of Russian barbarism," it had been an "effective weapon" against efforts to destroy the young Soviet republic. But it was now time, he went on, to begin to limit its authority to "the purely political field."[74] But Lenin was not doing away with the secret police, and replaced the Cheka with the GPU (*Gosudarstvennoe Politicheskoe Upravlenie*; State Political Administration). The Treaty on the Creation of the USSR (December 30, 1922) stated that GPU's "mission was to coordinate the revolutionary efforts of the union republics in the struggle against political and economic counterrevolution, espionage, and banditry."[75]

This was followed by plans to codify Soviet criminal and civil law as part of the "fostering revolutionary legality" campaign in the early years of the NEP. With the end of the civil war and "war communism," Lenin and others in the top leadership saw the need to create a more sophisticated legal system that reflected a new postwar era of peace and stability. Dmitrii I. Kursky, a graduate of the Juridical Faculty of Imperial Moscow University and commissar of justice from 1918 to 1928, stated in early 1922 that

> the old rule that a court shall decide by itself what is criminal and not criminal requires change. We have already worked out a criminal code. The same is true of procedural law. . . . Every citizen must know by what court and for what offense he is being tried and what punishment is possible. . . . We are leaving behind the short slogans in the field of law and are going on to a complicated system of law in an exceptionally difficult economic and political atmosphere.[76]

Lenin reminded Kursky, though, that

> justice ought not to remove the terror; to promise this would be self-deception or deception. It ought to establish and legalise it by principles, clearly and honestly.[77]

From Lenin's perspective, the new proposed criminal code was to reflect the general ideas of the civil war era's directive, *Leading Principles of the Criminal Law of the R.S.F.S.R.*, which had been issued at the end of 1919 to guide local courts. Set up by decrees in 1917 and 1918, the local courts, made up of a chief judge and two assessors, were meant to provide local justice throughout areas controlled by the Bolsheviks. The tribunals could still use tsarist and provisional government laws as long as they were not in conflict with basic Bolshevik concepts of law and justice.[78]

Leading Principles noted that during revolutions "old law" disappeared with the "old states," while "new law emerged in the aftermath of the victory of the working classes." Criminal law, it explained, was the body of law meant to defend "the social structure of the existing society against violations, called crimes, by repressive measures, called 'penalties.'" Article 5 of the *Leading Principles* defined crime as a "violation of the order of social relations which is protected by Criminal Law," while Article 7 stated that it was left up to the judge to decide whether a "certain action was dangerous to a society" and if it warranted a criminal conviction. Such "penalties," it went on, were the means by which the government "protects a certain order of social relations against future infractions by the criminal himself or by others."[79]

This idea of crime as a "socially dangerous action" directed against the Soviet state was a key element in the 1922 and 1926 criminal codes. Lenin and other Bolshevik jurists still viewed law as a bourgeois phenomenon that, according to Stuchka, would ultimately "die out altogether."[80] The 1922 code, the model for all future Soviet criminal codes,[81] used the principles of retroactivity and analogy to deal with alleged criminal actions, meaning that courts could consider crimes prior to the enactment of the code itself, and consider certain actions criminal even if not specified in the criminal code. This, coupled with a strong spirit of "class favoritism," gave judges a great deal of "judicial discretion" to deal with cases based on their "socialist legal consciousness."[82] Though some members of the code's drafting committee argued strongly for the inclusion of the traditional legal concept of *nullem crimen* [*nulla poena*] *sine lege* (no law, no crime), Kursky and others said that as a new state there was no way to anticipate the crimes judges might have to consider in the future, and they needed broad authority to adjudicate such crimes. The 1926 code further strengthened analogy as a "key principle of Soviet criminal law,"[83] and it remained so until 1958.[84]

The actual practice of criminal law in Russia during the NEP was extremely unsophisticated and reflected, to some degree, Soviet concern about moving away from some of the more harsh punishments meted out during the tsarist period. According to a 1927 study by Rabkrin (*Raboche-krest'yanskaya Inspektsiya*, Commissariat of Workers and Peasants' Inspection), a vast majority of the cases investigated by the police in 1926 were dropped by justice officials. Moreover, when defendants were found guilty, they were often given "lenient, usually noncustodial" sanctions, a reflection of the corruption in the legal system.[85]

Soviet officials were sensitive to these problems and tried to initiate reforms in 1927 and 1928 that centered on the idea that the legal organs of state had to be run and staffed by "our people" who were deeply committed to Soviet ideals. In the end, one's legal credentials were considered far less important than a person's "redness." Equally important was "efficiency," which encouraged Soviet legal specialists to find ways to rid the system of the large number of cases that dealt with minor offenses. This, coupled with overcrowded prisons, led Rabkrin and Sovnarkom (*Sovet Narodnyikh komissarov*, Council of People's Commissars) to decree that judges use "compulsory work" instead of prison sentences to handle minor cases. When some judges resisted, central authorities threatened them with prosecution, which resulted in the return of the "noncustodial sanction of compulsory work" as a central feature of the "penal arsenal of Soviet courts." Unfortunately, Soviet law was not changed to underscore this new shift, creating a precedent used by political and legal authorities to dictate legal policy "without adjusting the law."[86]

All of this took place in the midst of two dramatic changes in the young Soviet state—the leadership struggle between Joseph Stalin and Leon Trotsky to succeed Lenin, who died in 1924, and the end of the NEP. Part of the power struggle centered on criticism of the NEP by Trotsky and other leftists.[87] Stalin, who had increasing doubts about the viability of the NEP vis-á-vis the prospect of developing socialism in Russia, told the Seventh Enlarged Plenum of the Executive Committee of the Communist International in 1926 that it was possible to build socialism in the Soviet Union by "welding agriculture and socialist industry into one integral economy." Failure of the party to follow this path would negate the party's claim to power and justify working class efforts to hang, draw, and quarter its leaders.[88]

In early 1928, concerned over inadequate grain supplies to the cities, Stalin and a select group of party leaders visited Siberia, where they demanded a dramatic increase in grain deliveries from local agricultural leaders. He backed this up with "searches and arrests" that subjected Siberian villages "everywhere to violence and lawlessness."[89] Stalin soon coupled this with a plan to dramatically increase industrial production that would transform the country into a "military power which could defend itself" from Britain, France, and Japan. For the most part, party leaders, already dissatisfied with the NEP and its capitalistic "excesses," supported the shift to a socialist economy.[90] The result was the first of a number of Five Year Plans that sought dramatically to increase agricultural production, whose surpluses would fund an equally ambitious increase in industrial production. To achieve this, Stalin adopted a campaign that Robert Service calls "terror economics" that used ideas about "class warfare" and "revolutionary spirit" to rally the country to embrace a plan that would transform the political, economic, and social face of Soviet Russia.[91] His campaigns also resulted in the deaths of millions of peasants, particularly in Ukraine, where almost 4 million died in what some now considered to be a genocidal crime—the *Holodomor*.[92]

Stalin responded to these upheavals with a series of "show" trials during the early phases of his collectivization-industrialization campaigns to send a message about the price anyone would pay if they resisted his programs. The background to the first of these trials centered around the Shakhty Affair which was based on a local party report in the Donbas, one of the principal mining areas in the Ukraine, in March 1928. It noted widespread drunkenness and violence among miners who refused to work full time, which affected production totals. After investigating the matter, Stalin ordered a public trial of fifty Russians and three German engineers who were charged with deliberate acts of "wrecking" or sabotage in the region.[93] According to a March 10, 1928, article in *Pravda*, the Soviets and the Germans had been paid "to wage systematic sabotage" in the mines so that they "would be paralyzed during the coming [Western] war of intervention."[94]

Stalin chose Andrei Vyshinsky, the rector of Moscow State University, to serve as chief judge in the trial and Krylenko as its top prosecutor.[95] It was held in Moscow's House of Soviets to accommodate the large contingent of reporters from Russia and abroad, and about 2,000 Russians in the gallery. The trial was also filmed and shown throughout the country after it ended. Prominent foreign correspondents like Eugene Lyons, Louis Fischer, and Walter Duranty covered the entire trial for *The Times*, the *Evening Post*, and *The New York Times*.[96]

In preparation for the trial, the renamed OGPU used harsh interrogation methods to exact confessions from the Russian defendants. Stalin also ordered Krylenko and Vyshinsky to maintain tight control over the proceedings to ensure the outcome he wanted. Consequently, prosecutors made certain that evidence presented during the proceedings included stories that proved that there had been "'a powerful counterrevolutionary organization operating for many years' in the Donestsk Coal Trust to 'the collusion of German and Polish nationals.'"[97]

The highly publicized trial was a legal fiasco since the charges, drawn principally from Article 58 of the 1926 criminal code, dealt with "counterrevolutionary" activity "directed toward the overthrow, subversion, or weakening" of the Soviet Union.[98] Eugene Lyons called the trial a "Roman circus," a "court-martial in the midst of a strenuous social war, where ordinary notions of fairness must be suspended." In the end, he concluded, "the innocence or guilt of these individuals [the defendants] was of no importance."[99]

Vyshinsky's role in all of this was to do what he could to prod the defendants to admit their guilt or at least to implicate other defendants. In the end, the judges found forty-nine of the defendants guilty of various acts of sabotage, and Krylenko demanded that twenty-two of them be sentenced to death. However, Stalin, who was sensitive to concerns about the impact of the trial on the country's small pool of engineers and relations with Berlin, ordered that only eleven receive the death penalty. Six of these sentences were commuted to life in prison, while the rest were sentenced to prison terms of one to ten years. Two of the Germans were found not guilty while the third received a suspended sentence. Before the trial, the Soviet foreign office assured the German ambassador, Count Ulrich von Brockdorff-Rantzau, who attended the trial, that "Vyshinskii could surely be expected to show sufficient wisdom and moderation not to jeopardize German-Soviet relations."[100]

The Shakhty trial proved to be an important launching pad for the legal careers of Krylenko and Vyshinsky. The former, a well-educated lawyer, was a devout Bolshevik who briefly served, at Lenin's behest, as head of what remained of Russian military forces after the Bolshevik Revolution. During the civil war he helped Lenin develop the Soviet legal system "as a weapon against" anti-Bolshevik forces. He quickly emerged as a key prosecutor in various revolutionary tribunals set up to deal with those who opposed the Bolsheviks and, later, served as the Kremlin's chief prosecutor in its early "show" "trials."[101]

Vyshinsky, who was born in Odessa in 1883, was an active Menshevik who was arrested a number of times and kicked out of law school at Kiev University for his revolutionary activities, particularly during the 1905 revolution in Baku. One of the people he met while in jail was Joseph Dzhugashvili—later Joseph Stalin. After his release, Vyshinsky finished law school and worked in Moscow as a legal assistant in a prominent law firm. After the February Revolution, he became active again in Menshevik politics, and headed a small district council.[102]

He continued his involvement in Menshevik politics after Lenin took power in 1917 and worked for the People's Commissariat for Food Supplies (*Narodnyi Kommissariat Prodovolstviya*). Vyshinsky did not join the Bolshevik Party until the early 1920s, which later led to charges of "careerism" and a temporary loss of his party membership.[103] He served briefly as a member of the workers' faculty at Moscow State University (MSU) and in 1923 joined the prosecutorial staff of the RSFSR's Supreme Court (*RSFSR Verkhovnyi Sud*). He was purged again, which led him to beg Aron Solts, a member of the Supreme Court, the legal department of Rabkrin and the party's extremely important Central Control Commission (*Komitet Partiinogo Kontrolya*), for his reinstatement. Solts, considered by some to be the "conscience of the Party," decided to restore Vyshinsky's party membership, arguing:

> What do you expect of him? The fellow tries as hard as he can. He works hard; one must give him a chance. People are not born Bolsheviks, they become them. If he does not turn out right, we'll expel him again.[104]

In 1924–1925, Vyshinsky published a two-volume work on the history of communism—*Essays on the History of Communism* (*Ocherki po istorii kommunizma*)—that was criticized for numerous ideological and historical errors. But this did not affect his career, and he was appointed to the law faculty at MSU and later, its rector, presumably with Stalin's input.[105] He further impressed his mentor as rector by purging professors and students he deemed "hostile to the proletariat."[106]

Stalin was also impressed by some of his writings on Soviet law. In one article, Vyshinsky argued that "the defense in a Soviet court, as well as the prosecutor and the court itself," is to serve "the interests of truth and the state."[107] In another article, he wrote that "the law 'was merely an expression of economic relations'". He also thought that "only recently has the proletariat succeeded in advancing *its own law* against bourgeois law" (Italics in original).[108]

In 1925, Vyshinsky published a series of entries in the three-volume *Encyclopedia of State and Law* (*Entsiklopediya gosudarstva i prava*) that was edited by Stuchka. In one, Vyshinsky said that he did not anticipate the development of a "class theory of evidence," and concluded that lawyers should rely on "social legal consciousness" when dealing with evidentiary questions.[109] Though not highly regarded at the time, his essay became the basis for his seminal work—*Theory of Court Evidence in Soviet Law* (*Teoriya sudebnykh dokazatel'stv v Sovetskom prave*, 1946)—which was awarded the Stalin Prize in 1947.[110]

Some of his ideas differed considerably from some of Russia's more radical, influential jurists, particularly Pashukanis, whose exchange theory argued that law was a reflection of the key economic features of bourgeois society. As such, civil and criminal law was based on "evident relations of subordination." With the withering away of capitalism, Pashukanis argued, and in this instance, the NEP, "there will be no more Law [*otmiranie prave*—the 'withering away of law'], but mere technical regulation."¹¹¹ Pashukanis's theories gained center stage in the growing debate over the whole question of law in post-NEP Russia,¹¹² while Vyshinsky's ideas about the existence of a criminal system based on "compulsory legal norms" with "definite economic, social, and class relations" were not taken seriously by many who supported the idea of *otmiranie prave*.¹¹³

Stalin, who kept close tabs on the works and opinions of the country's most important public figures, wanted to create a new, politically reliable intellectual class that would be part of his larger plan to channel "artistic ideas towards raising the level of the masses."¹¹⁴ In Vyshinsky, he seemed to have found someone who could help develop this new group of leaders. He was impressed by Vyshinsky's book on the Shakhty trial, *Aspects and Lessons of the Shakhty Trial (Itogi i uroki shaktinskogo dela)*, as well as his articles on economic counterrevolutionary crimes.¹¹⁵ Stalin was a strong advocate of the "use of criminal sanction in the economy," and thought it should be used widely in the actual "management of the Soviet economy."¹¹⁶

Stalin was also concerned about the education of young technical specialists and thought that such education was "too bookish and removed from production and practical needs." He was also worried about "capitalist encirclement" and "bourgeois" opponents of his plans to "transform Soviet agriculture and industry."¹¹⁷

He blamed the Commissariat of Education for its failure "to cope with this task [of educating a new technical intelligentsia]," and asked Vyshinsky to oversee the creation of a new technological elite that would play a key role in the industrial transformation of Soviet society.¹¹⁸ Vyshinsky quickly grasped the importance that Stalin put on creating this new group of Soviet leaders, and lost no time using "'military measures' . . . to achieve 'maximum results in the shortest time.'"¹¹⁹ This included the purge of "bourgeoisie" professors from the new Institute of State and Law (*Institut gosudarstva i prava*), the most important legal institution in the Soviet Union. Stalin was so impressed by Vyshinsky's actions that he asked him to oversee plans for several new "show" trials in the early 1930s.¹²⁰

The first, the Industrial Party (*Prompartiya*; *Promshlennaya partiya*) trial,¹²¹ charged eight highly respected engineers of being part of a massive conspiracy that involved thousands of engineers from Russia and abroad of plotting to disrupt the economy and prepare the way for a French invasion of the Soviet Union. The charges were based on reasonable complaints about efficiency and practicality that prosecutors claimed were really personal attacks against Stalin and efforts to "wreck" his economic policies. The trial also provided a glimpse into Stalin's growing paranoia about domestic and international plots against the Soviet state and his hold on power.

The highly orchestrated, widely publicized trial in Moscow was a legal fiction that was preceded by tens of thousands of workers marching through the streets carrying banners that proclaimed

"Death to the agents of imperialism!," "Kill the wreckers!," [and] "No mercy to these class enemies!"

When the trial opened on November 25, 1930, in the House of Unions, Krylenko, the chief prosecutor, was unable to present any "hard evidence" to back up the charges against the defendants because he claimed the defendants had destroyed it. Regardless, on cue, each of the defendants readily admitted their guilt and provided vivid details about their crimes.[122] According to Eugene Lyons, who covered it for UPI, Stalin pulled out all of "the gadgets of ballyhoo . . . to bring the fears and angers of a nation to a boil" throughout the trial.[123]

Stalin, as he did with all of the "show" trials, including Nuremberg, played an extremely active role in every facet of the Industrial Party trial. On October 2, he wrote to Viacheslav Menzhinsky, the head of the OGPU who gathered the "evidence" for the trial, including the defendants' testimony, that he was most interested in the testimony of Leonid. K. Ramzin, the most important defendant. "What I specifically want to know," he wrote to Menzhinsky, were details about

> the intervention [i.e., invasion] generally and its timing. It looks as though they proposed to invade in 1930, but put it off until 1931 or even 1932.

Stalin added that it was important for Menzhinsky to be certain that the testimony of the other defendants accurately reflected Ramzin's confession.[124]

> Vyshinsky, the presiding judge, had become

> the punitive sword of Soviet justice. He self-assuredly assumed the role of the prosecutor who would soon be declaiming at the Great Moscow Trials. In point of fact, he became a second prosecutor actively [during the Industrial trial] helping Krylenko to "unmask" the accused. Whenever he considered that Krylenko was being insufficiently astute, pushing or deft, he would butt into the examination, "helping" his colleague along and giving him—and everyone present as well—a graphic object-lesson in the tactics of conducting a political trial.[125]

At the end of the trial, Vyshinsky sentenced five of the eight defendants to death and the rest to ten years imprisonment. The death sentences were soon commuted to ten years and the others to eight years.[126]

The trial was widely criticized internationally, particularly by French president Raymond Poincaré, who was mentioned as a key figure in the alleged French plot to invade the Soviet Union. He denied any involvement in the fictitious plot and said that

> if by chance there are still judges in Moscow, they would do well to unmask the accusers and the accused, who are acting against their own interests in this strange affair and are participating in the dissemination of falsehood.[127]

Such criticism, however, did little to dissuade Stalin from staging a new trial in the spring of 1931 that accused alleged Menshevik plotters in and out of Russia of efforts to wreck the economy.[128] A series of articles in the Soviet press in early 1931 prepared the public for the new trial that began on March 1, 1931. Vyshinsky was not involved in it because of his Menshevik past, which gave Krylenko a chance to shine in his role as chief prosecutor. Unfortunately, Krylenko and the chief judge, Nikolai Shvernik, were not able to prevent some of the defendants from straying from their prepared testimony and admissions of guilt, despite the fact that they had been promised that they would "be secretly released and rewarded" if they did so.[129]

Many of the thirteen former Mensheviks on trial were prominent economists who had abandoned politics after the Tenth Party Conference outlawed all socialist parties in 1921. Karl Radek, a high-ranking Comintern (Communist International) official, explained at the time that "if the Mensheviks are left at liberty now that we have adopted their policies [the NEP], they will claim power."[130] The indictment focused on various charges of "wrecking" and ties to former opponents of the Bolsheviks, particularly Leon Trotsky, who had been Lenin's choice to succeed him. He lost out in a bitter power struggle with Stalin, and, in exile, waged an ongoing campaign that highlighted Lenin's concern about Stalin's "moral coarseness and unscrupulousness."[131] Consequently, Stalin saw Trotsky, who still had followers in Russia, as one of the key threats to his hold on power.[132] Fortunately for the defendants, Stalin's fear of an alleged Trotskyite plot against him had not reached the fever pitch that it would later in the 1930s, and they only received five- to ten-year prison sentences.[133]

The last of these early "show" trials—the Metro-Vickers trial—took place from April 12 to 19, 1933. Though Stalin ended the First Five Year Plan in early 1933, twelve months earlier than planned, he remained paranoid about what he called the "remnants of the dying classes" who had

> all wormed their way into our factories, our institutions and trading bodies, our railway and river transport enterprises and for the most part into our collective and state farms. . . . They set fire to warehouses and break machinery. They organized sabotage. They organized wrecking in the collective and state farms . . . some of them . . . go so far in their wrecking activities as to inject the livestock in collective and state farms with plague and anthrax, and encourage the spread of meningitis among horses and so on.[134]

In the summer of 1932, the government had issued an edict, *On Revolutionary Legality*, which was written principally by Vyshinsky. It detailed the excesses of officials during the collectivization-industrialization campaigns and called for the prosecution of those responsible for them. It added that the "observance of laws would take on new significance in the future." It was followed in August by a new law that promised severe punishments for anyone stealing grain. Vyshinsky wrote that this new, post-NEP spirit of "revolutionary legality," which was based on these new decrees and laws, should become a "pillar of Soviet criminal policy."[135]

He added in a publication that fall, *Revolutionary Legality in the Contemporary Era* (*Revoliutionnaia zakonnost' na Sovremennon etape*), that the "observance of law . . . was a method of the dictatorship of the proletariat or 'socialist legal consciousness.'" Many of his contemporaries disagreed with him and seemed unaware that a subtle change was taking place in the Soviet Union that placed new emphasis on the importance of law as a means furthering strict adherence to Stalin's multifaceted economic and political programs.[136]

The Metro-Vickers trial, which took place in Moscow a few months before the publication of *On Revolutionary Legality*, centered on charges that six British engineers, who worked for the Metropolitan-Vickers Electrical Company, along with twelve Russian counterparts, had committed acts of "wrecking," and espionage in factories all over Russia.[137] The British government was outraged when it learned of the charges, withdrew its ambassador and threatened a trade embargo against the Soviet Union. And though Stalin was concerned about this threat, he also thought that the trial was a way to shift blame for some of the failings of the First Five Year Plan and give him time to deal with some of the domestic and political issues he was facing because of these failures.[138]

While the Russian defendants fully admitted their guilt, all but one of the British defendants refused to cooperate with Vyshinsky, the chief prosecutor.[139] This meant that he had to build an airtight case by introducing a body of evidence that was so complicated that it would be hard for the "public to follow."[140] Eugene Lyons, who attended every session of the trial, concluded that what took place was "little more than a shadow play on a screen." The Russian defendants, he added, "watched for the flick of Prosecutor Vyshinsky's whip and obeyed with the frightened alacrity of trained animals."[141] In the end, all but one of the Russians were found guilty and sentenced to terms of eighteen months to ten years in prison. One of the British defendants was acquitted while two others were given sentences of two to three years that were soon commuted, resulting in their release. The other three were ordered to be immediately expelled from the country.[142]

According to Robert Conquest, Vyshinsky's role in some of these early "terror" or "show" trials paved the way for his involvement in the next wave of domestic trials because Stalin found him to be

> a man found capable of mastering such a complexity, and imposing it upon the witnesses; he had also proved himself able to break up, and if necessary to interpret in a manner suitable to the plot, various unforeseen divagations, and he had been able to "refute" a perfectly sound complaint by concentrating heavily and impressively on a discrepancy of detail.[143]

Consequently, despite the widespread criticism of the Metro-Vickers trial internationally, Vyshinsky was soon appointed Deputy Procurator General of the USSR.[144] Afterward, *Pravda* and *Izvestia* published a speech by Vyshinsky under the headline "Soviet Law Is Strong and Hard, a Law That Is Unquestionable." He argued that "Soviet law was indestructible" and that "ignoring the demands of socialist legality is impermissible." According to Peter Solomon, the language Vyshinsky used in the speech seemed as though he "had just returned from a meeting with Stalin,"[145] which was probably true.

Vyshinsky was now Stalin's legal mouthpiece and worked hand in hand with the Soviet dictator to promote greater adherence to "the practice of justice." Vyshinsky set the tone for this new era in Soviet law in a speech in 1934 before a conference of procuracy officials. The era of ad hoc procedures was at an end, he told them, and officials who dealt with legal matters had to "know and apply legal rules."[146] They were to "combine revolutionary legality expressed in rules with socialist legal consciousness," which would mean completely new approaches for everyone who worked for the procuracy nationwide. He also criticized investigators, prosecutors, and judges for their failure to adhere to the new norms in Soviet law. Vyshinsky used the procuracy's new journal *For Socialist Legality* (*Za sotsialisticheskuyu zakonnosti*) to promote the "strengthening of socialist legality and the protection of social property." He was extremely critical of those who did not recognize "the 'absolute and fundamental' distinction" between "Soviet and bourgeois legality" and the important role of "the Soviet statute as a powerful cultural force and a key factor for the state of the proletarian dictatorship."[147]

Vyshinsky, with Stalin's support, also challenged some of the legal theories and powers of Krylenko and Pashukanis, which led to a fierce debate in the Soviet legal community about the new direction Vyshinsky was taking Soviet law. Krylenko, who would become the People's Commissar of Justice in 1936, felt threatened by this, and initially rejected many of Vyshinsky's ideas. His criticism rang increasingly hollow in what was becoming a power struggle between both men and their agencies. In the spring of 1935, Vyacheslav Skyryabin Molotov, one of Stalin's closest associates and his wartime foreign minister, created a special commission to investigate the operations of the national court system. The result was a "scathing" report on the Commissariat of Justice's failure to address and reform the "sins of judges" nationwide. Consequently, Stalin decided it was time to create a special body to discuss revisions of the Soviet constitution, with Vyshinsky as head of the sub-commission on judicial questions.[148]

Stalin intended to use these reforms "to enhance the reputation of the Soviet state, even providing camouflage for illegalities perpetrated out of the limelight."[149] After the Eight Congress of Soviets adopted the new "Stalin Constitution" on December 5, 1936, he proclaimed:

> Today, when the turbid wave of racism is bespattering the Socialist movement of the working class and besmirching the democratic strivings of the best people in the civilized world, the new Constitution of the U.S.S.R. will be an indictment against fascism, declaring that Socialism and democracy are invincible. The new Constitution of the U.S.S.R. will give moral assistance and real support to all those who are today fighting fascist barbarism.[150]

It also enhanced Vyshinsky's powers as the new Procurator General of the USSR. (*General'nyi prokuror SSSR*). According to Article 113, his office wielded

> Supreme supervisory power over the strict execution of the laws by all People's Commissariats and institutions subordinated to them as well as by official persons and by citizens of the U.S.S.R.[151]

Three years later, Vyshinsky published one of his principal works, *The Law of the Soviet State* (*Zakon Sovetskogo Gosudarstva*), and explained that the role of justice in the Soviet Union was "to assure the precise and unswerving fulfillment of Soviet laws by all institutions, organizations, officials, and citizens of the USSR." Working hand in hand with the Supreme Court, he saw his office as the "guardian of legality, an instrument to defend the true interests of the people." The "Soviet prosecuting officer [himself]," he argued, was "the watchman of socialist legality, the leader of the policy of the Communist Party and of Soviet authority, the champion of socialism."[152] Written toward the end of the major Moscow "purge" trials of 1936–1938, he reminded his readers of Stalin's warnings about "capitalistic encirclement" and explained that the purpose of the trials was to root out domestic "anti-Soviet elements" who worked with "bourgeois countries" to "encircle the Soviet Union, awaiting an opportunity to fall upon it and to shatter it—or at least to undermine its power and weaken it."[153]

At the time, the idea of "capitalist encirclement" was more than just an ideological threat. Adolf Hitler saw the Soviet Union as the seedbed of "Jewish Bolshevism" and Marxism a "Jewish doctrine."[154] He added in his *Second Book* (*Zweites Buch*, 1928) that the vast lands of Eastern Europe and the Soviet Union would provide the *Lebensraum* needed to ensure that Germany and its people would, in future, be a "decisive power on land."[155] Japan was also viewed in the Kremlin as a threat because of its commitment "to neutralize the influence of the Soviet Union" in northeast Asia, and its decision to join the German-Italian Anti-Comintern Pact in 1936.[156]

But such threats were not the reason that Stalin decided to initiate a new wave of "show" trials and purges against alleged domestic and political enemies after the murder of Sergei Kirov, one of the most prominent leaders in the Soviet political firmament, at the end of 1934. While there were suspicions that Stalin played a role in his murder, recent studies have suggested the opposite.[157] But what has not changed was the fact that Stalin used Kirov's murder as an excuse gradually to begin a purge of old political enemies. His initial targets were Grigory E. Zinoviev and Lev Kamenev, Old Bolsheviks who had once aligned themselves with Trotsky and embraced his leftist critiques of the NEP. They were expelled from the ruling Politburo in 1926 and a year later the party.[158] Though readmitted after confessing their "anti-Leninist" errors, they were kicked out in 1932 because of their alleged ties to the Riutin Platform, a document that was extremely critical of Stalin's policies. Though readmitted after pledges of loyalty to Stalin, they again became targets of the Soviet leader's deadly ire after Kirov's murder.[159]

Immediately after he learned of the assassination, Stalin issued a five point decree that dealt with acts of terror "against the functionaries of Soviet power." It ordered that investigations of such crimes be concluded within ten days, while those charged would only receive a copy of the indictment twenty-four hours before trial, which they could not attend. A court's decision was to be final and the "supreme punishment" was to be carried out immediately, meaning "summary execution" without recourse to a review or "petitions of clemency."[160]

Initially, it was thought that Kirov's assassin, Leonid Nikolayev, had acted alone. However, it was soon alleged that he was a member of a "Leningrad Center" with ties to Zinoviev, Kamenev, and other prominent party leaders. On December 28–29, Nikolayev and thirteen others were secretly tried and charged with being part of a plot not only to murder Kirov but also Stalin, Molotov, and Lazar Kaganovich, secretary of the Central Committee. Their goal was to "replace the leadership with Zinoviev and Kamenev." All fourteen refused to cooperate with the prosecution and were found guilty and executed on December 19.[161]

Three days later, Stalin ordered the arrest of Zinoviev, Kamenev, and five others who were implicated in the plot. However, the NKVD (*Narodnyy Komissariat Vnutrennikh*

Del; People's Commissariat for Internal Affairs), which replaced the OGPU in the summer of 1934, concluded that there was insufficient evidence to try them. Instead, Stalin decided to bring all of the accused before a "Special Board" with the idea of "sending them into administrative exile."[162] In the meantime, the NKVD continued to interrogate the accused, particularly Zinoviev and Kamenev, who refused to admit that they were part of a plot against Stalin.[163] On the other hand, they agreed to "'confess' . . . in a general way" to the fact that their "former anti-party group could bear 'political responsibility'" for Kirov's murder.[164] This seemed to satisfy Stalin and Vyshinsky, and on January 15–16, 1935, Zinoviev, Kamenev, and seventeen others were tried and convicted of their alleged crimes and given sentences of five to ten years. Hundreds of their supporters were also arrested and exiled to Siberia.[165]

Two days after this "Leningrad/Moscow Centre" trial ended, the Central Committee sent out a secret letter to party organizations that discussed Stalin's interpretation of the facts in the case—Kirov's murder was orchestrated by "Zinoviev followers" whose ultimate goal was to gain "high party and government posts." From his perspective, the Zinovievites were "a White Guard organization in disguise." The letter ended by reminding party leaders of the importance of studying the tactics of various anti-party groups throughout Bolshevik history as a necessary tool for "fully securing the revolutionary vigilance of party members."[166]

Stalin's fears were driven by concerns about the invasion of the Soviet Union by a coalition of European powers or Japan. He was now convinced that a fifth column was trying to "weaken Soviet defences and exacerbate disaffection with the regime."[167] New diplomatic agreements with France and Germany did little to ease his fears and this, coupled with news of various problems meeting quality and production goals in the new Five Year Plan, and Hitler's announcement of total German rearmament in the spring of 1935, convinced Stalin that the threat of war was far greater than at any time since he had taken power.[168]

In early June, over 100 Kremlin bureaucrats were convicted of "terrorist acts," which a Central Committee report attributed, along with Kirov's murder, directly to Zinoviev and Kamenev.[169] On June 17, the Central Committee issued a decree that stated that the arrests of prominent Soviet officials had first to be approved by the "appropriate procurator [Vyshinsky]," and arrests of members of the Central Executive Committee by its chairman, Mikhail Kalinin.[170]

The NKVD noted in some of its investigative reports about those accused of such crimes that they were often doing nothing more than expressing disillusionment with Stalin and his efforts to rebuild the Soviet economy and society.[171] Stalin read the same reports, and concluded that

> they reveal in fine detail the true criminal face of the killers and provocateurs Trotsky, Zinoviev, Kamenev, and Smirnov [i.e., leftist party critic of Stalin]. It's now absolutely clear that the mercenary whore Trotsky was the gang leader. It's about time to declare him "beyond the law" and shoot the other bastards we have here.[172]

The die was now cast for the beginning of a series of major "show trials" that took place over the next three years—the "Trotskyite-Zinovievite Terrorist Centre" (August

1936), the "Anti-Soviet Trotskyite Center" (January 1937), and the "Anti-Soviet Bloc of Rights and Trotskyites" (March 1938).

In his secret speech before the 20th Party Congress in 1956, Nikita Khrushchev was extremely critical of Stalin for deeming anyone who disagreed with him as an "enemy of the people." The "sins" of Zinoviev, Kamenev, Bukharin, and others were ideological, he argued, while the prosecution of those deemed a threat to Stalin "actually eliminated the possibility of any kind of ideological fight or the making of one's views known on this or that issue, even those of a practical character." And

> the only proof of guilt used, against all norms of current legal science, was the "confession" of the accused himself; and, as subsequently proved, "confessions" were acquired through physical pressures against the accused. This led to glaring violations of revolutionary legality and to the fact that many entirely innocent persons, who in the past had defended the party line, became victims.[173]

The trials themselves were overseen by Stalin, who worked closely with Vyshinsky to select those to be tried, write the indictments, and decide on the sentences.[174] With the exception of the secret one-day trial of the Trotkyist Anti-Soviet Military Organization in the summer of 1937, the other major "show" trials lasted from one to two weeks. But unlike the earlier "show" trials, they were orchestrated to limit the impact of possible outbursts from some of the defendants and criticism by foreign journalists in attendance. In addition, the NKVD carefully selected the 150 or so Soviet citizens and 30 foreign journalists allowed to attend the proceedings, and trained the former to respond on signal "if any untoward outbreak from one of the prisoners took place."[175]

The trials were conducted by the Military Collegium of the Supreme Soviet of the USSR (MCSS; *Voennaya Kollegiya Verkhovnogo suda* CCCP), which was headed by Vasili Ulrikh. Created in 1924 to try senior personnel in the Red Army, it began handling political cases in 1934 under Article 58 of the criminal code. The fourteen-point article, which first appeared in the 1926 penal code, carefully defined different counterrevolutionary acts including treason, espionage, armed uprising, adherence to a foreign state, terrorist acts, propaganda, damaging or hindering economic production, and any other activities deemed detrimental to the interests of the state and people.[176]

The powers of the MCSS were vast, and, according to a 1989 article in *Red Star* (*Krasnaya Zvezda*), the Soviet Ministry of Defense's official newspaper, it tried over 36,000 cases during this period, and sentenced almost 85 percent of the defendants to death. A far greater number of cases were handled by the NKVD—800,000 in 1937—that relied on a Special Board in Moscow and three (*troiki*) and two (*dvoiki*) person tribunals in other parts of the country. The Special Board was made up of representatives of various branches of the NKVD, the police, and Vyshinsky's procuracy. As caseloads increased, Vyshinsky ordered his prosecutors in late 1937 to begin to rely on the *troiki* instead of local and regional courts in cases where "the evidence of guilt will not allow its use at trial," meaning when such evidence "featured denunciations or false testimony from provocateurs."[177]

During the purges, the MCSS gained increasingly broad powers to interpret Article 58 in ways that would ensure that anyone viewed suspiciously by the NKVD would be brought to trial. Its powers had been further enhanced by the introduction of the death penalty in 1932 for "a wide range of offenses against State property."[178] Vyshinsky increased the MCSS's powers by ordering investigators to look at the political elements in any alleged crime dealing with the destruction of state or public property. Moreover, he reminded them that the primary concern of any investigation into such crimes should be the question of "counter revolutionary intent." And once a case came to trial, Vyshinsky added, the "probability of guilt was perfectly adequate," while the evaluation of evidence had to be handled with "so-called 'political flair.'"[179]

Though Vyshinsky worked closely with the NKVD, he began to complain to Stalin after he became Procurator General about the excessive powers of the secret police, particularly when it came to "prosecutions for anti-Soviet agitation and propaganda." He was particularly concerned about the fact that up to a third of the NKVD cases involved "commonplace critical remarks, often by ordinary persons ('toilers'), about an official, institution, or policy." He argued that it was excessive and "groundless" to prosecute such individuals.[180] Consequently, he urged Stalin to look into this matter and allow local courts rather than the NKVD's Special Council (*Osoboe Soveshchanie pri NKVD CCCP*), which had the power to punish alleged criminals without trial, to handle such cases.[181]

Such criticism did nothing to affect Vyshinsky's relationship with Stalin, who worked closely with him on all of the major cases before the MCSS. At Stalin's instigation, for example, Vyshinsky changed the draft of the indictment for the "Trotskyite-Zinovievite" trial to ensure that Zinoviev was named the principal conspirator in the case. Vyshinsky met frequently with Stalin and took copious notes about suggestions for the conduct of the trials. These included "instructions" about how to obtain confessions from each of the defendants, and how to conduct the trial. Stalin also rewrote Vyshinsky's opening remarks, and in joint meetings with Ulrikh, decided on the fate of each defendant.[182]

The Moscow "purge" trials were pure legal shams, and Stalin depended on Vyshinsky and Ulrikh to keep things moving, prevent disruptions, and maintain the façade of legitimacy. The Soviet press played an important role in helping mold public opinion about the "crimes" of the defendants, which would play a role in helping Stalin decide whether to move forward with other trials against his real and imagined enemies. The same was true for the foreign reporters in attendance, since "unanimously hostile criticism might have prevented further performances."[183] This would not be the case after the Kamenev-Zinoviev trial since the international reactions to it were, at best, mixed. While some international observers thought the trial was disturbing, other foreign commentators found it hard to believe that it was a pure sham, since all of the defendants had confessed to their crimes.[184] The other unspoken element in all of this was that, given the growing international tensions in Europe and Asia, some foreign observers saw what they wanted to see—a new Soviet state trying to transform itself into a modern industrial power in the midst of threats from Nazi Germany and Japan. Perhaps, some argued, all Stalin was trying to do was to deal legally with some of the same disruptive political, social, and economic problems that were sweeping the world.

Consequently, the staging and orchestration of the Kamenev-Zinoviev trial was extremely important. Each day, all three judges walked sternly into the bright courtroom wearing full military dress with breeches. Ulrikh headed the three judge panel, which included I. O. Matulevich, vice chair of the MCSS, and Iona. I. Nikitchenko, an unknown regional military jurist who would later serve as chief Soviet judge at the Nuremberg IMT trial.[185]

One of the principal concerns of Stalin, Ulrikh, and Vyshinsky during the trial was the recantation of carefully prepared, forced confessions by the defendants. To protect against this, Stalin assured Zinoviev and Kamenev that their lives, as well the others on trial, would be spared if they confessed their crimes. And just before the trial opened, Genrikh Yagoda, the head of the NKVD and Nikolai Yezhov, who would soon replace him, met with the principal defendants and reassured them of Stalin's promise. They added that if there was "a single attempt at 'treachery'" this would be "regarded as implicating the whole group."[186] Though most of the defendants did admit to being part of a Trotsky-directed plot to assassinate a number of major party figures including Stalin, a few denied being actively involved in these plans.[187]

The most dramatic moment in the trial was Kamenev's implication of other suspected opposition leaders such as Bukharin, Tomsky, Rykov, and Radek.[188] A few days later, Vyshinsky announced that he was initiating an investigation of the new suspects for their possible involvement in "criminal counter-revolutionary activities for which the accused in the present case are being tried."[189] In his closing argument on August 22, Vyshinsky called the defendants "mad dogs of capitalism" who had "killed one of the men of the revolution who was most dear to us"—Kirov.[190] He ended by demanding "that dogs gone mad should be shot—every one of them!"[191] After pleas by the accused, the judges found all of the defendants guilty of all charges and ordered them to be shot. In addition, a number of the defendants' family members as well as about 160 of their associates were eventually arrested and executed for their role in the alleged conspiracy.[192]

Soon after the trial ended, Vyshinsky launched an investigation into those implicated in the trial, while the following month Bukharin and Alexei Rykov, once head of the powerful Council of People's Commissars, met with Yezhov and Vyshinsky, and denied any involvement in the Trotsky-Zinoviev conspiracy. Afterward, Vyshinsky announced that there was not enough evidence against the two to indict them. This did not deter Yezhov, whose interrogations of other "former rightists" convinced him that both men were involved in a plot against Stalin.[193] He presented his evidence before a Central Committee plenum in early December 1936, where Bukharin and Rykov denied charges that they were part of a large, nationwide "back-up" conspiracy that planned to assassinate major Soviet leaders. Stalin countered that they had a platform that advocated the

> restoration of capital[ism] . . . the restoration of private enterprise in agriculture . . . the curtailment of the kolkhozy . . . the restoration of the kulaks . . . [and] moving the Comintern out of the USSR.

Furthermore, he added, they wanted to "open the gates" to English capital and to foreign capital in general and had ties with France and the United States.[194]

When Bukharin questioned the charges, Mikhail Kaganovich explained that he was responding to "juridical matters" and not addressing "political matters."[195] In other words, the charges against Bukharin had less to do with legal questions and more with his failure to support "the party line."[196] Vyshinsky added that Bukharin's attempt to defend himself was evidence that he put himself above the party. In doing so, he argued, Bukharin was, among other things, "denying the nomenklatura's [prominent bureaucrats] right to establish the dominant narrative."[197]

But Stalin was not ready to try Bukharin, one of the most storied figures in the history of the party. Instead, he moved ahead with plans to conduct a trial of those accused of involvement in the "Anti-Soviet Trotsky Center" who were charged with colluding with Germany and Japan to undermine the Soviet economy. They were also accused of plans to assassinate major communist leaders and transfer resources and territory to the fascist powers, who would allow the Trotskyites to take power in Moscow.[198] As plans for the trial moved forward, Stalin met frequently with Vyshinsky and Yezhov. He also told Vyshinsky to move the trial along.

Don't allow them to talk much about the disasters. Shut them up. They caused so many disasters, don't let them blab too much.[199]

Stalin, who edited Vyshinsky's closing statement, suggested the death penalty for the principal defendants and lesser sentences for the others.[200]

The executions of the accused in the Kamenev-Zinoviev trial had a chilling effect on the defendants in the January 1937 trial, who were subjected to intense, tortuous NKVD questioning before they confessed to their fictitious crimes. Stalin carefully studied the interrogation transcripts and made suggestions about what each defendant was to say in their testimony during the trial. Karl Radek, a former Comintern leader and journalist, balked at admitting guilt until he met with Stalin, who convinced him to confess.[201]

The principal defendants in the trial other than Radek were Georgii Pyatakov, a former supporter of Trotsky's leftist ideals who had presided over the 1922 SR trial and later held important positions in Soviet finance and industry. Lenin called him one of the "most outstanding" young figures in the party.[202] Another defendant, Gregorii Solkolnikov, was a former ambassador to the UK who had ties to the Kamenev-Zinoviev opposition group. The other defendants were principal functionaries in the railway, coal, and chemical industries.[203]

The trial itself was similar to the other "show" trials and centered on the forced confessions of the accused and "witnesses" who had been told what to say in court. Before the trial opened, Stalin told Vyshinsky that the defendants should provide details about not only Trotsky's central role in wrecking schemes but also their ties to Germany and Japan. He also wanted the defendants to identify new conspirators for future trials. Ulrikh opened the trial on January 23 by asking each of the defendants if they had read the indictment and if they wanted "defense counsel." Most refused because they knew that the best a defense attorney could do was offer modest mitigating evidence for their clients. The defense lawyers, of course, knew that their principal role in the trial was to assist Vyshinsky's case.[204]

That evening, Vyshinsky began his "examination" of the seventeen defendants, which lasted for four days. As the trial drew to a close, the three defense attorneys were given a chance to address the court, preceded by Vyshinsky's closing statement on January 28.[205] He closely followed the script that he and Stalin had agreed to beforehand, and called the trial and the charges against the defendants a summary of the "criminal activities of the Trotskyite conspirators" who, going back to the time of Lenin, had "waged a continual campaign against the Soviet state and the Party." The trial, he added, provided "a searchlight" into the "disgusting hidden crimes of the Trotskyite underground."[206] The trial of the earlier "Trotskyite-Zenovievite terror centre," he continued, underscored the "abyss of [their] degradation!," while the current trial forced the Soviet people to once again hear of "monstrous crimes, monstrous treachery, [and] monstrous treason."[207]

He then summarized the crimes of each of the defendants and called a number of them "direct agents of the German and Japanese intelligence services"[208] who took their orders directly from Trotsky. Each of the accused, Vyshinsky went on, were charged with crimes under Article 58 while their overarching crime was "treason against the country." The victims of these crimes were those who stood beside him in the courtroom and demanded in the name of "the whole of our people" that the court punish each of the accused with "death by shooting."[209] The defense attorneys made brief comments though they noted that "there is no dispute about the facts." In the end, all they could say in mitigation was that their clients had told the truth or that they were naively drawn into working with Trotsky's organization.[210]

Ulrikh allowed the defendants to make final statements or pleas to the court, which most of them did. Pyatakov admitted that he was guilty and refused to ask for clemency or mercy. Radek questioned the idea

> that those who sit here in this dock are criminals who have lost all human shape. I am fighting not for my honour, which I have lost; I am fighting for the recognition of the truth of the testimony I have given, then truth in the eyes of this court, not of the Public Prosecutor [Vyshinsky] and the judges, who know us stripped to the soul, but of the far wider circle of people who have known me for twenty years and cannot understand how I have sunk so low.[211]

On January 30, the judges, noting their crimes under Article 58, found each of the defendants guilty of various counterrevolutionary crimes and sentenced thirteen, including Pyatakov, to be shot. Radek and Sokolnikov were sentenced to ten years in prison, while the other defendants received prison terms of eight to ten years.[212]

International observers had mixed reactions to the trial. Joseph E. Davies, the new US ambassador to the Soviet Union, attended the entire trial and wrote to Washington that while it shocked "our mentality," this had more to do with the charges than its fairness. Davies, an attorney, added that though he had doubts about the facts presented in the trial, he concluded, like other diplomats, that Vyshinsky "established clearly the existence of a political plot and conspiracy to overthrow the government."[213] Walter Duranty, the controversial *New York Times* correspondent in Moscow, went further, and wrote in *The New Republic* that the confessions in the trial were "true."[214]

Others were not so sanguine. The Dewey Commission, which was set up to investigate the charges against Trotsky, conducted a series of hearings in Mexico, where Trotsky lived. Headed by John Dewey, a renowned philosopher and educational reformer, it concluded that the three principal charges against Trotsky and his son, Leon Sedov—terrorism, sabotage, and "agreements with foreign powers," were "incredible," and "preposterous."[215]

The commission was particularly critical of the confessions of many of the defendants and noted that they were obtained using physical and mental torture, common practices, it noted, of the "Soviet police." These methods completely contradicted what was laid out on such procedures in a book edited by Vyshinsky, *Criminal Trials: A Textbook for Law Schools and Judicial Courses* (*Ugolovnykh del Uchebnik dlya Yuridicheskikh Vysshikh Uchebnykh Zavedeniy I Subednykh Kursov*, 1936). It stated, for example, that

> the accused has the right to give evidence but he is not obligated to do so. For refusing to give evidence, just as for giving false evidence, in contrast to the witness, he does not bear criminal responsibility. It is prohibited to force the accused to give evidence and those cases where, during examination, illegal methods for forcing the accused to give evidence are applied (violence, threats, terrorization, tricks, etc.), the person in charge of the investigation is criminally liable according to Section 2, article 115, UK [*Ugolovonyi Kodeks*; Criminal Code].[216]

The commission concluded that the 1936 and 1937 "purge" trials were driven by "the current internal difficulties, economic and political, and by the current foreign relations, of the Soviet regime." In the end, the trials were completely political in nature and, as such were "frame-ups."[217]

By the time the Dewey Commission completed its report, Stalin had also conducted a highly secretive, one-day purge trial of the military before the Military Collegium. Interestingly, Davies told the State Department soon after he arrived of rumors about Stalin's disaffection with some of his military leaders. One of them claimed that the minister of defense, Klement Voroshilov, was "marching on Moscow."[218]

Such rumors had become commonplace within the higher echelons of the party, government, and military. Fear and suspicion were widespread, and the mention of someone's name in one of the trials cast a shadow over that person. This was certainly the case with Marshal Mikhail N. Tukhachevsky, a hero of the Russian civil war and an internationally known military theorist.[219] He was mentioned twice by Radek during the "Anti-Soviet Trotskyite Center" trial in January 1937, though not in a way that directly implicated him in any crimes.[220] Given how carefully Stalin and Vyshinsky planned the trial, particularly when it came to the testimony of each defendant and witness, the mention of Tukhachevsky was ominous, since Stalin was becoming increasingly concerned about a military plot to overthrow him.

Stalin was particularly concerned about Trotsky's ties to the military. The latter had served as Lenin's foreign minister and later commissar of war during the early years of the regime. He also headed the Revolutionary-Military Council during the civil war, which brought him into direct conflict with Stalin. At the time, Stalin, Trotsky's subordinate, was responsible for procuring food in the Tsaristsyn (today, Volgograd) region. Trotsky ran a tight ship, and resented the fact that Stalin constantly challenged his authority in the region. Stalin complained to Lenin about this and suggested that Trotsky was out of control. In the end, Lenin sided with Trotsky, and Stalin never forgave Trotsky for this.[221] Over time, the fact that many of the Soviet Union's top generals had served under Trotsky during the civil war made them vulnerable to charges of collaboration with the Trotskyites in the various fictitious plots against Stalin.

The question of a serious military plot against Stalin first arose in the summer of 1936, when the NKVD arrested several mid-level officers for involvement in a plot to assassinate Marshal Kliment Voroshilov, the People's Commissar of Defense and others. Vyshinsky alluded to this plot during the "Trotskyite-Zinoviev Terrorist Centre" trial and said that the cases of those involved, along with others accused of similar crimes, were "set aside for separate trial" pending the completion of the investigations against them.[222] All of this came to a head during the February–March 1937 Central Committee Plenum when Stalin and Molotov declared that there were spies and others in the military who could undermine efforts in the "struggle against 'enemies of the people.'"[223]

Afterward, Stalin, armed with forged German documents and other fabricated evidence that implicated Tukhachevsky and seven other high-ranking army officers in a plot against him, ordered the NKVD to put together a case against them. Tukhachevsky, whom Kaganovich called a "refined nobleman, handsome, clever, and able," was Stalin's principal target. One of Soviet Russia's most storied and talented military leaders, Tukhachevsky was a self-assured, devout Bolshevik who had no trouble standing up to Stalin or other senior military leaders. Stalin called him "Napoleonchik," while Kaganovich said that he "hid Napoleon's baton in his rucksack."[224]

In May 1937, the suspected officers were arrested and brutally interrogated.[225] On June 2, Stalin met with his new Military Council of the Commissariat of Defense, which was made up of the military elite, and told them that the eight officers were part of a plot led by Trotsky, Rykov, Bukharin, and others who worked closely with the German military. Tukhachevky, the alleged head of the military wing of this conspiracy, was accused of providing the Germans with "our operation plan—our holy of holies." There was also evidence, he went on, that some of the accused also worked with "Japanese intelligence."[226]

On June 7, Stalin met with Vyshinsky and others about the indictment, and two days later Vyshinsky briefly questioned the eight generals in front of their NKVD interrogators to make certain their testimony was "authentic," meaning it conformed exactly to the interrogation transcripts. He had several meetings with Stalin on June 9–10 about the final draft of the indictment, the official statement about the conspiracy, and the arrests of the eight generals. On June 10, Vyshinsky met with the Plenum of the Supreme Court which decided to try them before a Special Judicial Session of the court chaired by Ulrikh and made up of members of the Military Council chosen specifically by Stalin to ensure "the correctness of its verdict."[227] On June 11, *Pravda* reported on the investigation and the arrest of the generals, and explained that "they were accused of '*breaching their military duty, betrayal of the Motherland, betrayal of the peoples of the USSR, and betrayal of the Workers-Peasants Red Army* (Italics in original).'"[228]

The secretive June 11 trial was a judicial farce that lasted only one day. Ulrikh maintained tight control over the proceedings to ensure no deviation from Stalin's game plan for the outcome. The defendants had only seen the charges against them the day before and were given no opportunity to defend themselves. A stenographic record was kept but this was heavily edited by the NKVD after the trial ended. Late on June 11, Ulrikh met briefly with Stalin, who ordered all of the defendants be found guilty and sentenced to death, which Ulrikh announced at 11:35 p.m. Ulrikh and Vyshinsky signed the execution order, and then, as official witnesses, watched as NKVD officers shot each of the convicted in the back of the head with a pistol.[229]

Nikita Krushchev later condemned Stalin for what he called the "annihilation" of the country's military elite "because of his suspiciousness and thorough slanderous accusations."[230] Molotov, on the other hand, told Felix Chuev in 1982 that Tukhachevsky was "a most dangerous conspirator" who was deeply involved in a coup "with Trotskyites and rightists." If not apprehended, he argued, "the consequences could have been catastrophic."[231] Several weeks after the trial ended, Joseph E. Davies wrote that it was "generally accepted by members of the Diplomatic Corps that the accused must have been guilty of an offense which in the Soviet Union would merit the death penalty." Yet he also saw what foreign observers saw—a party leadership determined to stifle even verbal opposition to what military leaders saw as policies that "handicapped the army."[232]

And even though Davies thought that "Stalin's regime" was "probably stronger than before" because of the elimination of "all potential opposition," the "crux of the situation . . . depends upon the attitude of the army."[233] And it was this very concern, whether real or imagined, that led Stalin to mount a major purge of the military. His intentions fed the growing disillusionment and distrust of the military throughout Soviet society and led to large-scale dismissals of soldiers in the months after the Tukhachevsky trial. The first victims were those with the vaguest of ties to the alleged Tukhachevsky conspirators.[234]

By the fall of 1938, when the military purge began to wane, 33,000–35,000 officers had been discharged from the armed forces (though about a third of them were later reinstated). It is impossible to estimate the number that were executed or imprisoned though we do know that the senior ranks were decimated by the purge. Robert Conquest estimates that Stalin had three of his five Marshals, thirteen of his fifteen army commanders, eight of his nine senior admirals, fifty of fifty-seven corps commanders, all eleven vice commissars of defense, and most members of his divisional political commissars and members of Stavka, the high command of the Soviet military, executed.[235] According to Roy Medvedev,

> never did the officer staff of any army suffer such great losses in any war as the Soviet Army suffered in this time of peace.[236]

In late 1940, Hitler told some of his military leaders in talks about his invasion of the Soviet Union that not only were the Russians "inferior . . . [but] the army lacks leadership."[237]

The military purge stimulated a new wave of political terror aimed at "leading cadres in all fields and at all levels."[238] Members of ethnic minority groups, former Kulaks, anyone associated with outlawed political parties such as the Mensheviks and the Socialist Revolutionaries, and others were caught up in this new reign of terror.[239] It began after Stalin sent a secret letter to Yezhov and regional party leaders on July 3, 1937, that ordered that three-man party tribunals should identify the "most hostile" of the "kulaks and criminals" who had recently been released from prison, and execute or exile them.[240] This was followed by Yezhov's Operational Order No. 00447 of July 30, 1937, that established guidelines and regional figures for a wide range of groups that were to be dealt with punitively. The most active were to be shot while the rest were to be imprisoned for eight to ten years.[241] This "wildcat" purge resulted in the arrest of 936,000 suspects in 1937 and 638,000 in 1938, most of whom were convicted of "counterrevolutionary crimes." Of this number, 43 percent were executed for their alleged crimes.[242]

In the midst of this political carnage, Stalin decided to round out his deadly circle of purges by putting on trial one of the most prominent of the Old Bolsheviks with close ties to Lenin—Nikolai Bukharin. The die had been cast against Bukharin when Kamenev implicated him in the 1936 "Trotyskite-Zinovievite" trial as part of a rightist faction in the government that had been supportive of a Trotsky-inspired "terrorist conspiracy." The group's loss of power, Kamenev testified, "deprived us of this trump card."[243] These charges were further discussed at the February–March 1937 Party Plenum. Bukharin, well aware that his days were numbered, fought hard against these allegations, and told leaders at the Plenum that the evidence presented in earlier trials against him was "slanderous."[244] Stalin ordered the immediate arrest of Bukharin and his co-conspirators and the creation of a commission of party leaders to decide their fate. In his final speech to the Plenum, he said that they, like other Trotskyites, were "wreckers and diversionists."[245]

It would take Vyshinsky almost a year to complete his investigation of Bukharin and his alleged co-conspirators in what would be his most challenging "show" trial. Bukharin, one of the Bolshevik's foremost theoreticians, was a popular, highly regarded party leader. His most prominent co-defendants were Genrikh Yagoda, the unpopular former head of the NKVD, and Alexei Rykov, who not only served as Lenin's assistant for three years after his stroke in 1921 but was also premier from 1924 to 1929.[246]

Though the trial resembled some of the other "show" trials, it was different because of the desperate, fearful siege mentally throughout the country, driven in part by a propaganda campaign that focused on pro-Trotskyite conspirators who were plotting to destroy the Soviet Union. They, in turn, were alleged to have strong ties to Japan, which had invaded China only months earlier, and Adolf Hitler, who was making increasingly aggressive statements about German expansion in Europe. This, coupled with the violent purge sweeping the country, created an atmosphere of fear that played well into Stalin and Vyshinsky's hands. Davies attended the Bukharin trial and concluded that, despite serious questions about the defendants' confessions and a judicial system "which affords practically no protection" for the defendants, the accused were guilty as charged beyond any reasonable doubt under Soviet law. He added that many of the diplomats who attended the trial on a regular basis shared this opinion. In 1941, he added that he was convinced that the conspiracy theories were correct and that there were now "no Fifth Columnists in Russia . . . they had shot them. The purge had cleansed the country and rid it of treason."[247]

The indictment charged Bukharin, Rykov, Yagoda, and the other defendants of working with the intelligence services of several countries hostile to the Soviet Union to help plan an attack on the Motherland. The goal was to overthrow Stalin's government, restore capitalism and the bourgeoisie, and "dismember" the Soviet Union. It named Tukhachevsky as head of the conspiratorial group, while Trotsky was considered one of the "inspirers of the conspiracy." It added that earlier trials had revealed the fact that Trotsky had been working with the Gestapo for years. The defendants were also accused of close ties to Zinoviev and other anti-Soviet Trotskyites. Vyshinsky drew heavily on evidence from the earlier purge trials and added Poland to the list of countries that worked closely with the conspirators. And, as he had done in the 1937 trial, he accused Bukharin and the others of earlier plans to assassinate Lenin, Stalin, and Yakov Sverdlov as well as other prominent "Soviet public men" like Maxim Gorky.[248]

All of the defendants pleaded guilty to all of the charges when the trial opened on March 2, 1938.[249] But over time, some wavered when cross-examined by Vyshinsky and questioned by Ulrikh, the chief judge. On the first day of the trial, for example, Ulrikh asked one of the defendants, Nikolai Krestinsky, a lawyer, a close associate of Lenin, and former member of the Politburo and Central Committee, if he was guilty of all charges. He answered that he was still a member of the Communist Party of the Soviet Union and had "never been a Trotskyite" nor a German spy.[250]

His response was unexpected and Vyshinsky did what he could to force him to recant his statement. He did this by referring to a letter that Krestinsky wrote to Trotsky in 1928 in which he claimed that he had severed ties with the former Soviet leader. According to the testimony of another defendant, Khristian Rakovsky, Trotsky had shown him the letter and concluded that it was nothing more than a "manoeuvre" or a bit of "double-dealing" by Krestinsky to protect himself from accusations that he was a supporter of Trotsky after the 15th Party Congress had expelled Trotsky and Zinoviev from the party. Vyshinsky produced the letter and quoted from it.

> It is my profound conviction that the tactics of the opposition [to Stalin] during the past half-year have been profoundly erroneous and detrimental to the aims of the opposition itself, and one might say tragically so.[251]

He then asked Rakovsky if there was any criticism of Trotskyism in this paragraph. "No," Rakovsky replied, "Krestinsky is arguing like a man who belongs to the Trotskyite organization." Vyshinsky read other portions of the letter aloud, and asked Krestinsky if he agreed with Rakovsky's interpretation of it. Yes, said Krestinsky, "what he said was right." If that was the case, Vyshinsky wanted to know, why did his testimony the day before seem like "a piece of Trotskyite provocation"?

> Yesterday, under the influence of a momentary keen feeling of false shame, evoked by the atmosphere of the dock and the painful impression created by the public reading of the indictment, which was aggravated by my poor health, I could not bring myself to tell the truth, I could not bring myself to say that I was guilty. And instead of saying "Yes, I am guilty," I almost mechanically answered "No, I am not guilty."

"Mechanically?" Vyshinsky asked. Yes, Krestinsky answered.

> In the face of world public opinion, I had not the strength to admit the truth that I had been conducting a Trotskyite struggle all along. I request the Court to register my statement that I fully and completely admit that I am guilty of all the gravest charges brought against me personally, and that I admit my complete responsibility for the treason and treachery I have committed.[252]

According to Robert Conquest, Krestinsky was brutally interrogated after his erroneous testimony on March 2, though the NKVD was careful not to do anything that affected his outward physical appearance. He finally agreed to change his confession as long as his letter was presented into evidence the next day.[253]

Once he finished with Krestinsky, Vyshinsky began his examination of Rykov, who had been "tortured quite brutally" during his interrogation.[254] But first, Ulrikh asked him if he would "confirm the testimony you gave in the preliminary investigation" in hopes of avoiding some of the problems they had with Krestinsky. "Yes," he responded, "I do." But once Vyshinsky began to question Rykov, he strayed from the script and only admitted vague involvement in unsuccessful terrorist organizations. On the other hand, Rykov admitted that, like Bukharin, he was traitor. It was apparent that the principal goal of Vyshinsky's questioning of Rykov was to establish Bukharin's dominant role in the "Bloc of Rights" conspiracy. Midway through his examination of Rykov, Vyshinsky began to question Bukharin about some Rykov's testimony. This proved to be a dangerous strategy because Bukharin proved to be a more troublesome witness than Rykov.[255]

After Bukharin was arrested in the spring of 1937, Stalin allowed him to receive books and other materials to continue his research and writing. After his execution, all of his prison writings were sent to Stalin, who kept them in his private papers. This included four letters that Bukharin sent to Stalin that dealt with his "neurotic state," his "devotion" to the Soviet leader, and pleas for his life. According to Vadim Rogovin, Stalin played an "insidious game with Bukharin" that gave him hope that his life would be spared.[256]

Initially, Bukharin refused to admit his guilt in the charges leveled against him. However, after several months of physical and psychological torture, and threats against his family, he agreed to sign a confession. But when he saw Stalin's handwritten changes in it, he repudiated it. In the end, while he accepted responsibility for being the leader of an alleged conspiracy, he refused to admit that he played any role in the assassination of Lenin and rejected the charge that he had been a spy.[257]

Consequently, when the trial began, there was some uncertainty about what Bukharin would say. When Vyshinsky began his formal examination of him on March 5, Bukharin asked Ukrikh if he could "freely present my case to the court," and present "an analysis of the ideological and political stand of the criminal 'bloc of Rights and Trotskyites,'" since few knew anything about a subject of "certain public interest." He added that since Vyshinsky had already asked him about the ideology and politics of the "bloc," a more detailed explanation might be useful. Vyshinsky immediately objected because he thought this might prevent him from asking Bukharin a further questions about "his explanation."²⁵⁸ Ulrikh then asked Bukharin if he confirmed the confession he had agreed to during the pretrial investigation about his "anti-Soviet activities." He said that he did "fully and entirely." He admitted that he was one of the principal leaders of the "bloc of Rights and Troyskyites" and, as a result, guilty for the "sum total" of its crimes even if he did not known of them or participated in them.²⁵⁹

On the other hand, he denied that he played any role in the alleged assassination attempt against Lenin, Stalin, and Sverdlov in 1918. This complicated the case for Vyshinsky, who had to rely on the testimony of Rykov and others to counter some of Bukharin's comments to confirm his guilt.²⁶⁰ Bukharin was also adamant when it came to charges of espionage. On March 7, Vyshinsky asked him about his connection to "Whiteguard circles and German fascists." Bukharin said he did not understand the question and asked him what he had in mind. When Vyshinsky asked him the same question again, Bukharin said he knew nothing about this. His response was the same when Vyshinsky asked him about his ties to anti-Soviet groups.²⁶¹

Vyshinsky shifted the focus of his questions and asked Bukharin and Rykov about their plans to "dismember" the Soviet Union and turn parts of the country over to Germany and Japan. Bukharin picked apart all of Vyshinsky's questions on the subject and played word games with him. Again, he accepted responsibility for the "centre's" negotiations with the Germans but said he either knew nothing about them or simply could not remember any details about the talks. Vyshinsky turned to Rykov and asked him about his pretrial testimony that he and Bukharin had an "espionage connection" with the Poles. Rykov did not respond, which led Vyshinsky to ask another defendant, Vasily Sharangovich, a Belorussian party leader, if Bukharin and Rykov were spies. Yes, he responded, they were both spies.²⁶²

This did not satisfy the chief prosecutor, and he continued to press both men on their work with Polish intelligence services. Both of them sparred with Vyshinsky over his questions which angered him. He became so frustrated that at one point Bukharin tried to calm him down, telling Vyshinsky that "there is nothing for you to gesticulate about" since he had already admitted his involvement in earlier discussions to overthrow Stalin's government. Ulrikh intervened and told Bukharin not to "forget where you are now." Vyshinsky added that if he continued to respond in this manner,

> I will be compelled to cut the interrogation short because you apparently are following definite tactics and do not want to tell the truth, hiding behind a flood of words, pettifogging, making digressions into the sphere of politics, of philosophy, theory and so forth—which you might well forget about once and for all, because you are charged with espionage and, according to all the material of the investigation, you are obviously a spy of an intelligence service. Therefore stop pettifogging. If this is the way you want to defend yourself I shall cut the interrogation short.

Bukharin calmly responded "I am answering your questions."²⁶³

Later that day, Vyshinsky introduced a new witness, Vladimir Karelin, a former SR leader, who Bukharin had met in Vyshinsky's office during the pretrial investigation. Karelin, who had been arrested in 1937 for his former SR activities, appeared "grey and corpse-like" in court. Karelin testified that in late 1917 Bukharin was in favor of overthrowing the new Bolshevik government and, if necessary, supported "the physical extermination of the leaders of the Soviet government and of the Party."[264] Bukharin completely denied this and questioned Karelin about certain details in his testimony.[265] None of this, of course, had any impact on his case since Stalin had already decided his fate.

Vyshinsky began his lengthy closing remarks on March 11 by countering what he called Bukharin's attempt "to reduce the whole nightmare of his heinous crimes to some sort of 'ideological lines.'"[266] He called Bukharin, a "theoretician" whose works were nothing more than "scientific raving babble."[267] But, Vyshinsky went on, he did not act alone, and "here in the dock is [sic] a number of anti-Soviet groups, the agents of the intelligence services of foreign powers hostile to the U.S.S.R."[268] Vyshinsky, perhaps driven by Stalin's frustration with Bukharin's refusal to plead guilty to espionage, asked why he did so in light of the overwhelming body of evidence against him. The only way to understand this, Bukharin told the court, was to carefully review the details of his many crimes as well as those of the other defendants, particularly Rykov and Yagoda.[269]

After carefully going over the testimony and details of the cases against each of the defendants, Vyshinsky said that not all of them participated on a "equal basis in the crimes which were reviewed at this trial," which raised the issue of complicity.[270] This, Vyshinsky argued, should center on "the logic itself of the circumstances of the case." Articles 58 Ia (treason) and 58 II (armed uprising) dealt with the principle charge—"treasonable conspiracy." But one accused of such a crime must be held accountable

> for the sum total of the crimes as a member of a conspiratorial organization whose criminal objectives and aims, and whose criminal methods or carrying out these aims, were known to, approved of, and accepted by each of the accused. Here we observe only a peculiar "division of labour" in criminal activities, depending on the special qualities and means which each member of the gang possessed. This is entirely natural and logical from the point of view of the conspiracy as a whole.[271]

This, Vyshinsky went on, raised questions about the idea of complicity, a new, important concept in Soviet legal theory that would help shape Allied thinking about the nature of war criminality at Nuremberg. Some would argue, Vyshinsky noted, that to prove complicity "it is necessary to establish common agreement and intent on the part of each of the criminals, of the accomplices, for each of the crimes."[272] He disagreed with such a "narrow . . . scholastic" view. To "establish complicity we must establish that there is a common line uniting the accomplices in a given crime, that there is a common criminal design." Moreover, "it was also necessary to establish the existence of a united will directed towards a single object common to all the participants in the crime."[273]

What we are dealing with, he added, was a

> conspiratorial group, with an agency of foreign intelligence services, united by a will common to all of its members, by a criminal aim which is the same for all of them. The concrete crimes which were committed by the individual criminals

were only particular cases of putting into effect their plan of criminal activities, which was common to all of them.[274]

Such crimes, he added, were covered under Article 58 II. He ended by stating that it was important for the judges "to individualize" the crimes and asked for leniency for some of the defendants, such as Khristian Rakovsky and Sergei Bessonov.[275] But those convicted of the most treacherous crimes "must be shot like dirty dogs!"[276]

Later that evening, the two defense attorneys, following the script approved by Stalin, argued for leniency for Lev Levin, Dmitry Pletnev, and Ignaty Kazakov. This was followed over the next two days by the final pleas of the defendants. Some, such as Bessonov, pleaded guilty to crimes not brought up during the trial, though most admitted their "treachery" in hopes that their lives would be spared.[277] Bukharin did the same but refuted in considerable detail some of the charges brought against him. He denied that he was a spy and was involved in plots to assassinate Lenin, Kirov, Gorky, and others. He considered himself a "repentant enemy" who wished only for the "flourishing progress of the U.S.S.R. and its international importance."[278]

Rykov admitted his important role in the "bloc or Rights and Trotskyites" but denied he played any role in the murder of Kirov, Gorky, and others. He also asked all of his former supporters to "lay down their arms" as a prelude to seeking "salvation" by "helping the Party . . . liquidate the remnants, the dregs of the counter-revolutionary organization."[279] Krestinsky reminded the court of his long "revolutionary career" dating back to 1901 and said that his personal involvement in counterrevolutionary activities did not begin until 1937. And while he was willing to accept responsibility for the limited nature of his involvement in such plots from 1933 to 1935, he was not a leader in the "bloc" until 1937. He also told the court that he played no role in the crimes specified in the second portion of the indictment, which dealt with the murder of Kirov and Gorky as well as the assassination attempt against Lenin in 1918. He revisited his denial of the charges against him on the first day of the trial and stated that he was not involved in any way with "the most acute form of struggle—terrorism, diversion and wrecking." He asked the judges to spare his life so he could find a way "to expiate my grave crimes in any way."[280]

The court adjourned at 9:25 p.m. on March 12, and for the next six and a half hours the judges discussed the cases, presumably with input from Stalin and Vyshinsky. During the early morning hours of March 13, Ulrikh read the verdict. Eighteen of the defendants were found guilty of all charges, while Dmitry Pletnev, Khristian Rakovsky, and Sergei Bessonov were sentenced to prison terms of twenty to twenty-five years.[281] Those sentenced to death were shot immediately, while Pletnev, Rakovsky, and Bessonov languished in prison until the fall of 1941, when they were executed.[282]

Conclusion

While the trial of the anti-Soviet "Bloc of Rights and Trotskyites" represented a certain denouement in Stalin's obsessive, paranoid effort to rid himself of those he deemed a threat to his power, it by no means ended his effort to deal with those Robert Conquest called members of the "inner Party." This new, more secretive purge took place without "show" trials and represented a final blow against alleged centers of opposition in the secret police, the military, the foreign ministry, and the party. The removal of Yezhov as head of the NKVD was followed by new "judicial and prosecutorial supervision," which allowed Vyshinsky, without criticizing the new purge campaign, to at least "make suggestions aimed at controlling, regularizing, and even limiting it."[283]

What tempered all of this was Stalin's realization of the damage the purges had done throughout the country, and growing fears that if it continued at its current pace, it would leave the country ill-prepared for what were the serious, growing threats of Nazi Germany and Japan. Hitler was given parts of Czechoslovakia—the Sudetenland—in the fall of 1938 at Munich, followed by his occupation of the rest of Czechoslovakia the following spring. A few months before the conclusion of the Munich accord, border clashes had broken out with Japan on the Soviet-Korean-Manchukuo border that lasted for over a year. On September 17, 1939, Japan, driven partially by the realization that the conclusion of the German-Soviet nonaggression pact of August 23, 1939, put it in an awkward position with its Axis ally, Nazi Germany, agreed to a ceasefire with Moscow.

The outbreak of war in Europe on September 1, 1939, created a conundrum for Stalin who, well aware of the impact of the purges on the Soviet Union's political and military preparedness for war, decided, as Alexander V. Prusin notes in his chapter "Traitors or War Criminals: Collaboration on Trial in Soviet Courts in the 1940s," to instruct military tribunals to intensify its efforts against "traitors of the Motherland." So while the Soviet Union had been weakened by the terror that had swept the country since the late 1920s, the purges and Vyshinsky's "show" trials created a legal mechanism that was able to deal in a variety of ways with the thousands of real and alleged Soviets suspected of anti-Soviet activity before and after the outbreak of war with Germany on June 22, 1941. As Prusin notes, the use of this sophisticated "tool" of repression, with its deep roots going back to the late imperial period reminded the Soviet population of the government's "long reach and memory."

Notes

1 Julie Cassiday, *The Enemy on Trial: Early Soviet Courts on Stage and Screen* (DeKalb, IL: Northern Illinois University Press, 2000), 3.
2 Samuel Kucherov, "The Jury as Part of the Russian Judicial Reform of 1864," *The American Slavic and East European Review*, 9 (April 1950), 77–90 (78).
3 William E. Butler, *Russia and the Law of Nations in Historical Perspective: Collected Essays* (London: Wildy, Simmonds & Hill, 2009), 30; Irina Reshetnikova, "Judicial Reforms in Russia, 1864-2014," *Russian Law Journal*, III (2015), 109.
4 Cassiday, *Enemy on Trial*, 30.
5 Elizabeth Wood, *Performing Justice: Agitation Trials in Early Soviet Russia* (Ithaca: Cornell University Press, 2005), 23.

6   Tatiana Borisova, "Public Meaning of the Zasulich Trial 1878: Law, Politics and Gender," *Russian History*, 43 (2016), 222; Cassiday, *Enemy on Trial*, 30; the Senate Trial of the 50 took place in St. Petersburg from February 21 to March 14, 1877. The prosecution accused the fifty young Socialist Revolutionaries belonging to an organization dedicated to the overthrow of the government. Some of those in the dock used the trial, which was open and public, to make revolutionary speeches. Forty-seven were sentenced to prison terms ranging from three to ten years or exile to Siberia. Three were acquitted; the Senate Trial of the 193 in St. Petersburg was the largest political trial in imperial Russia (October 18, 1877–January 23, 1878). Given official dissatisfaction with the outcome of the Trial of the 50, the government decided to make it more secretive. The Senate acquitted ninety of the defendants though Alexander II ordered that eighty of the acquitted be sent into administrative exile. Those who were sentenced to terms of hard labor prepared a widely circulated "Testament" at the end of the trial that called for revolution. N. A. Troitskii, "Trial of the 50," in Joseph L. Wieczynski, ed., *The Modern Encyclopedia of Russian and Soviet History*, 39 (Gulf Breeze, FL: Academic International Press, 1985), 201–02; "Trial of the 193," in Joseph L. Wieczynski, ed., *The Modern Encyclopedia of Russian and Soviet History*, 39 (Gulf Breeze, FL: Academic International Press, 1985), 203–09.
7   Cassiday, *Enemy on Trial*, 34.
8   Ibid., 32; Richard Pipes, "The Trial of Vera Z.," *Russian History*, 37 (2010), 54.
9   Cassidy, *Enemy on Trial*, 31.
10 Ibid., 32.
11 Ibid.
12 Borisova, "Public Meaning of the Zasulich Trial," 237–38.
13 Cassidy, *Enemy on Trial*, 33.
14 Ibid., 32.
15 Ibid., 34.
16 Gary Rosenshield, *Western Law, Russian Justice: Dostoevsky, the Jury and the Law* (Madison: University of Wisconsin Press, 2005), 131–32.
17 Ibid., 134.
18 G. K. Gradovskii, "Fel'eton," *Golos* (April 1, 1878), 2.
19 Robert Service, *Lenin: A Biography* (Cambridge, MA: Harvard Belknap Press, 2000), 55, 88–89, 133, 155; Marx-Engels-Lenin Institute, Moscow, *Lenin* (London: Hutchinson, n.d.), 35, 48, 49.
20 George Kennan, "Prison Life of the Russian Revolutionists," *The Century Magazine*, 35 (November 1887–April 1888), 284–85.
21 Walter G. Moss, *Russia in the Age of Alexander II, Tolstoy, and Dostoevsky* (London: Anthem Press, 2002), 167, 230–31, 237–38; Vera Broido, *Apostles into Terrorists: Women and the Revolutionary Movement in the Russia of Alexander II* (New York: Viking, 1977), 188–89.
22 Philip Pomper, *Lenin's Brother: The Origins of the October Revolution* (New York: W.W. Norton, 2010), 164.
23 Robert Riggs, *Sofia Perovskaya. Terrorist Princess: The Plot to Kill Tsar Alexander II and the Woman Who Led It* (Berkeley: Global Harmony Press, 2017–2018), 281; George Kennan, "The Russian Penal Code," *The Century Magazine*, 35 (November 1887–April 1888), 884; Jonathan W. Daly, "Criminal Punishment and Europeanization in Late Imperial Russia," *Jahrbücher für Geschichete Osteuropas*, Neue Folge, 48/3 (2000), 341–62 (351).
24 Moss, *Russia in the Age of Alexander II*, 241, 242.

25 Riggs, *Sofia Perovskaya*, 283.
26 Ibid., 289.
27 Moss, *Russia in the Age of Alexander II*, 243.
28 Ibid., 243; Riggs, *Sofia Perovskaya*, 289–90.
29 Arkadii Kravitz, "Rebenok No. A-824, Nizhe izlozhena istoriya odhoi iz hikh—Gesi Gel'fman." *Lekhim*, Iiuon' 1999, Tamuz 5759 – 6 (86), 6–8 (accessed June 28, 2018). https://lechaim.ru/ARHIV/86/kravets.htm.
30 Moss, *Russia in the Age of Alexander II*, 246.
31 Ibid., 247–48.
32 Ibid., 251–52.
33 Ibid., 252.
34 Rosenshield, *Western Law, Russian Justice*, 137; Fyodor Dostoevsky, *The Karamazov Brothers*, trans. and ed. Ignat Ausey (Oxford: Oxford University Press, 1997), 823–948.
35 Pomper, *Lenin's Brother,* 126, 132, 136, 137,152–56, 158.
36 Vera Figner, *Zapechatlennyi Tryd: Vospominaniya v Dvykh Tomakh*, Tom II (Moskva: "mysl,'" 1964), 25–26.
37 Pomper, *Lenin's Brother*, 165. The trial, which was held behind closed doors, began on April 15, 1887. The tribunal was made up of four senators, two prominent aristocrats, the mayor of Moscow, and a peasant leader. Peter A. Deyer was the presiding judge, and Nicholas Neklyudov the chief prosecutor.
38 Ibid., 167.
39 Ibid., 169.
40 Ibid., 169–70, 177.
41 Ibid., 182–86, 186.
42 Ibid., 188–91.
43 Marx-Engels-Lenin Institute, Moscow, *Lenin*, 6.
44 Service, *Lenin: A Biography*, 60.
45 Wood, *Performing Justice*, 23.
46 Michael T. Florinsky, *Russia: A History and an Interpretation*, II (New York: Macmillan, 1970), 1081.
47 *Lenin on Politics and Revolution: Selected Writings*, ed. James E. Connor (New York: Pegasus, 1968), 248–49, 264–65.
48 "War Communism" was the Bolshevik program to destroy the "institution of private property" during the civil war, while the "red terror" was the Cheka-led campaign to strike out against opponents of the regime. Both used violence to achieve its goals though the "red terror" went beyond mass executions and embraced widespread repressive policies that Steinberg said "dominates the revolutionary earth . . . its bloody pinnacle, its apotheosis." The Cheka (the All-Russian Extraordinary Commission for Combating Counterrevolution and Sabotage; *Vserossiyskaya chrezvychaynaya kommisiya po bor'bye s kontrrevolyutsiyei i sabotazhem*) was under the Sovnarkom. Richard Pipes, *The Russian Revolution* (New York: Vintage Books, 1991), 671–72, 792–93; George Leggett, *The Cheka: Lenin's Political Police* (Oxford: Clarendon Press, 1981), 343–45.
49 Pipes, *The Russian Revolution*, 793.
50 V. I. Lenin, "The Socialist Fatherland Is in Danger!," in V. I. Lenin, *Collected Works* (Moscow: Progress Publishers, 1972), vol. 27, 30–33.
51 Pipes, *Russian Revolution*, 794.
52 Ibid., 795.

53 David M. Crowe, "Stucka, Petr Ivanovich (1865-1932)," in Joseph L. Wieczynski, ed., *The Modern Encyclopedia of Russian and Soviet History*, 53 (Gulf Breeze, FL: Academic International Press, 1990), 196; from Lenin's perspective, the purpose of this new legal concept "was to become an arm of the state in its 'major real task—administration, organization and supervision.'" It was also meant to "educate and discipline." Jane Burbank, "Lenin and the Law in Revolutionary Russia," *Slavic Review*, 54 (Spring 1995), 42.
54 Piotr Stuchka, "'Zakonnost' revoliutsionnaia," *Entsiklopediia gosudarstva i prava*, I (Moscow, 1925), 1150-53.
55 P. I. Stuchka, *Select Writings on Soviet Law and Marxism*, ed. and trans. Robert Sharlet, Peter B. Maggs, and Piers Beirne (Armonk, NY: M.E. Sharpe, 1988), 140-41.
56 Matthew Rendle, "The State versus the People: Revolutionary Justice in Russia's Civil War, 1917-22," *The International Newsletter of Communist Studies*, XVIII, 25 (2012), 56; Aaron B. Retish, "Power, Control, and Criminal Activity: The Peasantry and the Soviet Revolutionary Tribunal in Viatka Province, 1918-1921," 1-3 (accessed May 2, 2016). miamioh.edu/cas/_files/havighurst/social-norms-social-deviance/refish.pdf.
57 Cassiday, *Enemy on Trial*, 37-38.
58 Adele Lindenmeyr, "The First Soviet Political Trial: Countess Sofia Panina before the Petrograd Revolutionary Tribunal," *The Russian Review*, 60 (October 2001), 513-16, 518.
59 Wood, *Performing Justice*, 34-36.
60 Ibid., 41-42, 44.
61 Ibid., 70-71.
62 Mark Jansen, *A Show Trial under Lenin: The Trial of the Socialist Revolutionaries, Moscow 1922*, trans. Jean Sanders (The Hague: Martinus Nijhoff, 1982), 27-28.
63 Ibid., 85-91; Richard Johnson, "Kaplan, Fania Efimova (1890-1918)," in Joseph L. Wieczynski, ed., *The Modern Encyclopedia of Russian and Soviet History*, 15 (Gulf Breeze, FL: Academic International Press, 1980), 235-37.
64 Jansen, *A Show Trial*, 50; Samuel Kucherov, *The Organs of Soviet Administration of Justice: Their History and Operation* (Leiden: E. J. Brill, 1970), 52.
65 Jansen, *A Show Trial*, 142, 143.
66 Ibid., 146.
67 Ibid., 5; *Sobranie uzakonenii I rasporiazhenii raboche-krestian'skogo pravitel'stva*, 1922, No. 15, Art. 153.
68 Jansen, *A Show Trial*, 85-95.
69 Ibid., 104.
70 Maureen Perrie, "Socialist Revolutionary Party," in Joseph L. Wieczynski, ed., *The Modern Encyclopedia of Russian and Soviet History*, 36 (Gulf Breeze, FL: Academic Press, 1984), 100-01.
71 Jansen, *A Show Trial*, 3-25, 26, 27, 50-55, 128-31, 170-74; Elizabeth White, *The Socialist Alternative to Bolshevik Russia: The Socialist Revolutionary Party, 1921-1939* (London: Routledge, 2010), 40.
72 Orlando Figes, *A People's Tragedy: A History of the Russian Revolution* (New York: Viking, 1997), 763-64.
73 Ibid., 767-68.
74 Lenin's speech was published in *Izvestia* on December 30, 1921, and in different Stenographic Reports of the Ninth All-Russian Congress of Soviets. Lenin, *Collected Works*, 31, 2nd edn (Moscow: Progress Publishers, 1965), 178-81.

75 Robert D. Warth, "GPU," in Joseph L. Wieczysnki, ed. *The Modern Encyclopedia of Russian and Soviet History*, Vol. 13 (Gulf Breeze, FL: Academic International Press, 1979), p. 87.
76 Peter H. Juviler, *Revolutionary Law and Order: Politics and Social Change in the USSR* (New York: The Free Press, 1976), 27–28.
77 Rudolf Schlesinger, *Soviet Legal Theory: Its Social Background and Development* (London: Kegan Paul, Trench, Trubner & Co., Ltd. 1945), 106.
78 Ibid., 62–63.
79 Ibid., 74.
80 Juviler, *Revolutionary Law*, 28.
81 *Ugolovnyi Kodeks RSFSR (1922)*, 1 iyuonya 1922 goda, 1–39 (accessed December 29, 2017). http://ru.wikisource.org/wiki/%D0%...
82 Peter H. Solomon, Jr. *Soviet Criminal Justice under Stalin* (Cambridge: Cambridge University Press, 1996), 31–33. Though the idea of class discrimination was included in the 1926 criminal code, it was later removed, only to be revived by Stalin a few years later.
83 Ekaterina Mishina, "The Soviet Legacy: The Impact of Early Bolshevik Law Felt Up to the Present," *Institute of Modern Russia*, November 1, 2013, 1–3 (accessed November 11, 2017). http://imrussia.org/en/analusis/law/595-the-soviet-legacy-theimpact-of...; Ekaterina Mishina, "Russia: Presumption of Innocence as 'Legal Fiction,'" *Institute of Modern Russia*, February 5, 2014, 1–4 (accessed November 12, 2017). http://imrussia.org/en/analysis/law664-russia-presumption-of-innocen....
84 Harold J. Berman, *Soviet Criminal Law and Procedure: The RSFSR Codes* (Cambridge, MA: Harvard University Press, 1972), 28.
85 Solomon, *Soviet Criminal Justice*, 50–52, 56–57.
86 Ibid., 66–69.
87 Robert Service, *Stalin: A Biography* (Cambridge: Belknap Press, 2004), 216–17.
88 J. V. Stalin, *On the Opposition (1921-27)* (Peking: Foreign Languages Press, 1974), 535–36.
89 Oleg V. Khlevniuk, *Stalin: New Biography of a Dictator*, trans. Nora Seligman Favorov (New Haven, CT: Yale University Press, 2015), 100–03.
90 Service, *Stalin*, 256, 259.
91 Ibid., 265–75; Khlevniuk, *Stalin*, 108–09.
92 Service, *Stalin*, 274–75; Robert Conquest, *Harvest of Sorrow: Soviet Collectivization and the Terror-Famine* (New York: Oxford University Press, 1986), 306; for more on the detailed planning and background of the First Five-Year Plan, see E. H. Carr and R. W. Davies, *Foundation of a Planned Economy*, I (Harmondsworth: Penguin, 1974), 893–949; Anne Applebaum, *Red Famine: Stalin's War on Ukraine* (New York: Doubleday, 2017), xxvi, 278–83. Overall, about 5 million Russian peasants died during the first years of the collectivization campaign.
93 Annabelle Autin-Perrault, *Conspiracy and Paranoia at Shakhty: The First Stalinist Show Trial, May-June 1928* (Lexington: CreateSpace Independent Publishing Platform, 2014), 29.
94 Gustav Hilger and Alfred G. Meyer, *The Incompatible Allies: A Memoir-History of German-Soviet relations, 1918-1941* (New York: Macmillan, 1953), 218.
95 Jansen, *A Show Trial*, 119–22.
96 Autin-Perrault, *Conspiracy and Paranoia*, 47–48.
97 Stephen Kotkin, *Stalin*, I: *Paradoxes of Power, 1878-1928* (New York: Penguin Press, 2014), 691.

98 "Article 58, Criminal Code of the RSFSR (1934)," 1 (accessed October 6, 2016). http://www.cyberussr.com/rus/uk58-e.html#58-1a; Article 58 was revised in 1934 though its basic definition of "counterrevolutionary" activity remained essentially the same.
99 Eugene Lyons, *Assignment in Utopia* (New York: Harcourt, Brace, 1937), 120.
100 Hilger and Meyer, *Incompatible Allies*, 220; Kendall Bailes, *Technology and Society under Lenin and Stalin: Origins of the Soviet Technical Intelligentsia, 1917-1941* (Princeton, NJ: Princeton University Press, 1978), 90-92.
101 Donald D. Barry, "Nikolai Vasil'evich Krylenko: A Reevaluation," in Piers Beirne, ed., *Revolution in Law: Contributions to the Development of Soviet Legal Theory, 1917-1938* (Armonk, NY: M.E. Sharpe, 2015), 160; James G. Nutsch, "Krylenko, Nikolai Vasil'evich (1885-1938)," in Joseph L. Wieczynski, ed., *The Modern Encyclopedia of Russian and Soviet History*, 18 (Gulf Breeze, FL: Academic International Press, 1980), 119-20.
102 Arkady Vaksberg, *Stalin's Prosecutor; The Life of Andrei Vyshinsky*, trans. Jan Butler (New York: Grove Weidenfeld, 1990), 15-25.
103 Robert Sharlet and Piers Beirne, "In Search of Vyshinsky: The Paradox of Law and Terror," in Beirne, *Revolution in Law*, 141.
104 Vaksberg, *Stalin's Prosecutor*, 38.
105 Sharlet and Beirne, "In Search of Vyshinskii," 141-43.
106 Ibid., 141-43.
107 Ibid., 143.
108 Ibid., (Italics in original).
109 Ibid., 144.
110 Rudolf Schlesinger, "Soviet Theory of the Law of Evidence," *Soviet Studies*, I (June 1949), 74-78; Vaksberg, *Stalin's Prosecutor*, 190.
111 Schlesinger, *Soviet Legal Theory*, 155, 156, 161; Sharlet and Beirne, "In Search of Vyshinsky," 145.
112 For more on the evolution of Pashukanis' ideas, see Michael Head, "The Rise and Fall of a Soviet Jurist: Evgeny Pashukanis and Stalinism," *Canadian Journal of Law & Jurisprudence*, XVII (July 2004), 269-94 *passim*.
113 Sharlet and Beirne, "In Search of Vyshinsky," 145-46.
114 Dmitri Volkogonov, *Stalin: Triumph & Tragedy*, trans. Harold Shukman (New York: Grove Weidenfeld, 1991), 129-30.
115 Ibid., 147.
116 Solomon, *Soviet Criminal Justice*, 138.
117 Bailes, *Technology and Society under Lenin and Stalin*, 88-89.
118 Ibid., 159-60, 170-71; Sharlet and Beirne, "In Search of Vyshinsky," 147-48.
119 David Joravsky, *Soviet Marxism and Natural Science, 1917-1932* (London: Routledge, 2013), 223.
120 Sharlet and Beirne, "In Search of Vyshinsky," 147-48, 162. It was Krykenko who called them "show trials" (*pokazatel'nye protessy*).
121 The trial took place from November 25 to December 7, 1930.
122 Roy A. Medvedev, *Let History Judge* (New York: Vintage Books, 1971), 114-15; Samuel A. Oppenheim, "Prompartiia Trial," in Joseph L. Wieczynski, ed., *The Modern Encyclopedia of Russian and Soviet History*, 52 (Gulf Breeze, FL: Academic International Press, 1990), 5-7.
123 Lyons, *Assignment in Utopia*, 370, 372.

124   James Harris, *The Great Fear: Stalin's Terror of the 1930s* (Oxford: Oxford University Press, 2016), 94.
125   Vaksberg, *Stalin's Prosecutor*, 53.
126   Robert Conquest, *The Great Terror: Stalin's Purge of the Thirties* (Harmondsworth: Penguin, 1971), 225; Robert Conquest, *The Great Terror: A Reassessment* (New York: Oxford University Press, 1990), 143.
127   Medvedev, *Let History Judge*, 115.
128   Aleksandr I. Solzhenitsyn, *The Gulag Archipelago, 1918-1956: An Experiment in Literary Investigation, I-II*, I, trans. Thomas P. Whitney (New York: Harper & Row, 1974), 406; the most detailed study of the trial is Adrian Timofeev's *Perbyi pokazatel'nyi protsess 1931: Soyuznoe byuro men'shebikov, chast' I* (Lexington: CreateSpace Independent Publishing Platform, 2014), and Natalia Skripalshchikova, *The Mensheviks Trial, 1931*, Part 2 (Lexington: Free Siberia Publisher LLC, 2014); Andre Liebich, *From the Other Shore: Russian Social Democracy after 1921* (Cambridge, MA: Harvard University Press, 1997), 201, 202.
129   Conquest, *Great Terror*, 735; Shvernik, a devout Stalinist, had no background in law. But his loyalty to Stalin served him well throughout the 1930s, and he enjoyed a rapid rise in the party. During the Great Fatherland War, he was chairman of the ChGK, Stalin's commission to investigate war crimes. He was later named chairman of the Presidium of the USSR Supreme Court. Edgar C. Duin, "Shvernik, Nikolai Mikhailovich, 1888-1970)," in Joseph L. Wieczynski, ed., *The Modern Encyclopedia of Russian and Soviet History*, 35 (Gulf Breeze, FL: Academic Press, 1983), 87-91.
130   Helene Carrére D'Encausse, *Lenin: Revolution and Power*, trans. Valence Ionescu (London: Longman, 1982), 137.
131   Leon Trotsky, *My Life* (New York: Pathfinder Press, 1970), 480.
132   Service, *Stalin*, 278, 315-16.
133   Medvedev, *Let History Judge*, 116-17; Conquest, *Great Terror*, 735-36.
134   Volkogonov, *Stalin*, 186.
135   Solomon, *Soviet Criminal Justice*, 158-60.
136   pp. 160-62; Sharlet and Beirne, "In Search of Vyshinsky," 150-51.
137   *The Case of N.P. Vitvitsky et al., Charged with Wrecking Activities at Power Stations in the Soviet Union*. Heard before the Special Session of the Supreme Court of the U.S.S.R., Moscow, April 12-19, 1933, I (Sessions of April 12 and 13, 1933) (Moscow: State Law Publishing House, 1933), 11-86
138   G. L. Owen, "The Metro-Vickers Crisis: Anglo-Soviet Relations between Trade Agreement, 1932-1934," *Slavonic and East European Review*, 49 (January 1971), 92, 96-97, 92-112 (103); Curtis Keeble, *Britain and the Soviet Union, 1917-89* (London: Macmillan, 1990), 113-15; Robert D. Warth, "Metro-Vickers Case," in Joseph L Wieczynski, ed., *The Modern Encyclopedia of Russian and Soviet History*, 22 (Gulf Breeze, FL: Academic International Press, 1981), 19-20.
139   *The Case of N.P. Vitvitsky, V.A. Gusev, A.W. Gregory et al., Charged with Wrecking Activities at Power Stations in the Soviet Union*. Heard before the Supreme Court of the U.S.S.R., Moscow, April 12-19, 1933. Translation of the Official Verbatim Report, Vol. I: Sessions of April 12 and 13, 1933 (Moscow: State Law Publishing House, 1933), 84-86.
140   Conquest, *The Great Terror*, 737.
141   Lyons, *Assignment in Utopia*, 565, 567.
142   *Case of N.P. Vitvitsky et al.*, III. Sessions of April 16-19, 1933, 221-34; Gordon W. Morrell, *Britain Confronts the Stalin Revolution: Anglo-Soviet Relations and the*

      Metro-Vickers Case (Waterloo, CA: Wilfried Laurier University Press, 1994), 168–69; Lyons, *Assignment in Utopia*, Ibid., 571; Conquest, *The Great Terror*, 739.
143 Conquest, *The Great Terror*, 739.
144 Ibid., 34.
145 Solomon, *Soviet Criminal Justice*, 162.
146 Ibid., 162–63.
147 Sharlet and Beirne, "In Search of Vishinsky," 151.
148 Solomon, *Soviet Criminal Justice*, 167, 170, 177, 179.
149 Ibid., 155.
150 J. V. Stalin, *Problems of Leninism* (Moscow: Foreign Languages Publishing House, 1947), 567.
151 *Constitution (Fundamental Law) of the Union of Soviet Socialist Republics: Adopted at the Extraordinary Eighth Congress of Soviets of the U.S.S.R., December 5, 1936* (Karagah: H. Dawson, 1937), 13.
152 Andrei Y. Vyshinsky, *The Law of the Soviet State*, trans. Hugh W. Babb (New York: Macmillan, 1948), 498, 532, 537.
153 Ibid., 45–46.
154 David M. Crowe, *The Holocaust: Roots, History, and Aftermath* (Boulder: Westview, 2008), 97–99; Ian Kershaw, *Hitler: 1889-1936 Hubris* (New York: W.W. Norton, 1999), 61.
155 Adolf Hitler, *Hitler's Second Book: The Unpublished Sequel to Mein Kampf*, ed. Gerhard Weinberg and trans. Krista Smith (New York: Enigma Books, 2003), 158.
156 David M. Crowe, *War Crimes, Genocide, and Justice: A Global History* (New York: Palgrave Macmillan, 2014), 127, 128.
157 J. Arch Getty and Oleg V. Naumov, *The Road to Terror: Stalin and the Self-Destruction of the Bolsheviks, 1932-1939* (New Haven, CT: Yale University Press, 1999), 142–45.
158 Conquest, *Great Terror: A Reassessment*, 10–11; Harris, *The Great Fear*, 72–76.
159 Getty and Naumov, *Road to Terror*, 52–58.
160 Zigurds L. Zile, ed. *Ideas and Forces in Soviet Legal History: A Reader on the Soviet State and Law* (New York: Oxford University Press, 1992), 304; Cathy A. Frierson and S. S. Vilenski, eds., *Children of the Gulag* (New Haven, CT: Yale University Press, 2010), 149. 150.
161 Conquest, *The Great Terror: A Reassessment*, 47–48.
162 Ibid., 47.
163 Service, *Stalin*, 315–16; Getty and Naumov, *Road to Terror*, 146–47.
164 Volkogonov, *Stalin*, 208–09.
165 Service, *Stalin*, 315–16.
166 Getty and Naumov, *Road to Terror*, 147–50.
167 Ibid., 126.
168 Ibid., 127, 129–30, 131–32, 142–43.
169 Ibid., 161–65.
170 Ibid., 187.
171 Ibid., 197–200; Harris, *Great Fear*, 145.
172 Harris, *Great Fear*, 152.
173 Nikita S. Khrushchev, *The Crimes of the Stalin Era: Special Report to the 20th Congress of the Communist Party of the Soviet Union*, annotated by Boris I. Nicolaevsky (New York: The New Leader, 1956), 14.
174 Getty and Naumov, *Road to Terror*, 256.

175 Conquest, *The Great Terror*, 152–53.
176 Article 58, Criminal Code of the RSFSR (1934), pp. 1–5 (accessed June 20, 2018). http://www.cyberussr.co./rus/uk58-e.html/#58-1a.
177 Ibid. 282–84; Solomon, *Soviet Criminal Justice*, 234, 238.
178 Conquest, *The Great Terror*, 283.
179 Ibid., 283–84.
180 Solomon, *Soviet Criminal Justice*, 233.
181 Ibid., 233–34.
182 Vaksberg, *The Prosecutor*, 79–80.
183 Conquest, *The Great Terror: A Reassessment*, 91.
184 Ibid., 105–08.
185 Ibid., 91, 92.
186 Ibid., 92–93.
187 Ibid., 93–94.
188 *Report of Court Proceedings: The Case of the Trotskyite-Zinovievite Terrorist Centre.* Heard before the Military Collegium of the Supreme Court of the U.S.S.R., Moscow, August 19–24, 1936 (New York: Howard Fertig, 1967), 65, 67.
189 Ibid., 115.
190 Ibid., 120.
191 Ibid., 164.
192 Ibid., 174–80; Getty and Naumov, *Road to Terror*, 256–57; Alexander Bittelman, "The Zinoviev-Kamenev Trial," *The Communist*, 15 (September 1936), 813–14.
193 Getty and Naumov, *Road to Terror*, 300–01, 303.
194 Ibid., 306.
195 Ibid., 309.
196 Ibid., 323.
197 Ibid., 323–24.
198 Vadim Z. Rogovin, *1937: Stalin's Year of Terror*, trans. Frederick S. Choate (Oak Park, MI: Mehring Books, 1998), 117–19.
199 Ibid., 116.
200 Vaksberg, *The Prosecutor*, 80.
201 Rogovin, *1937*, 115–16.
202 V. I. Lenin, "'Last Testament': Letters to the Congress" (accessed July 10, 2016). http://www.marxists.org/archive/lenin/works/1922/dec/testament/index.htm, 1–5 (2).
203 James Burnham, *Why Did They 'Confess?': A Study of the Radek-Piatakov Trial* (New York: Pioneer Publishers, 1937), 20–22.
204 Ibid., 124; *Report of Court Proceedings in the Case of the Anti-Soviet Trotskyite Center.* Heard before the Military Collegium of the Supreme Court of the U.S.S.R., Moscow, January 23–30, 1937. Verbatim Report (New York: Howard Fertig, 1967), 1–4.
205 Ibid., 124–25, 300–02, 446–61.
206 Ibid., 462.
207 Ibid., 463.
208 Ibid., 507.
209 Ibid., 516.
210 Ibid. 517–29.
211 Ibid., 543–44.
212 Ibid., 579.
213 Joseph E. Davies, *Mission to Moscow* (Garden City, NY: Garden City Publishing, 1943), 29, 30–31.

214 S. J. Taylor, *Stalin's Apologist: The New York Times Man in Moscow* (New York: Oxford University Press, 1990), 267.
215 Preliminary Commission of Inquiry, *The Case of Leon Trotsky: Report of Hearings on the Charges Made against Him in the Moscow Trials* (New York: Harper & Brothers, 1937), 1–617 passim; *Not Guilty: Report of the Commission of Inquiry into the Charges Made against Leon Trotsky in the Moscow Trials* (New York: Monday Press, 1972), 256, 287, 319, 372.
216 *Not Guilty*, 22, 372.
217 Ibid., 394.
218 Davies, *Mission to Moscow*, 30.
219 Norma C. Noonan, "Tukhachevskii, Mikhail Nikolaevich (1893–1937)," in Joseph L. Wieczynskii, ed., *The Modern Encyclopedia of Russian and Soviet History*, 40 (Gulf Breeze, FL: Academic International Press, 1985), 79–80.
220 *Report of Court Proceedings in the Case of the Anti-Soviet Trotskyite Centre*. Heard before the Military Collegium of the Supreme Court of the U.S.S.R., Moscow, January 23–30, 1937 (New York: Howard Fertig, 1967), 105, 146.
221 Service, *Stalin*, 160, 165, 167, 168–69.
222 *Case of the Trotskyite-Zinvoviev Terrorist Center*, 36.
223 Conquest, *The Great Terror: A Reassessment*, 192.
224 Simon Sebag Montefiore, *Stalin: The Court of the Red Tsar* (New York: Alfred A. Knopf, 2004), 221, 222.
225 Conquest, *The Great Terror: A Reassessment*, 198–99; Getty and Naumov, *Road to Terror*, 445.
226 "Shvernik Report on the Trial against Tukachevsky and Other Members of the RKKA [*Raboche-krest'yanskaya Krasnaya armiya*; Workers' and Peasants' Red Army] II," April 28, 2009, 3 (accessed September 20, 2016). http://skoblin.blogspot.com/2009/04/shvernik-report-on-trial-against_28....; for more on the council, see A. Pechenkin, *Stalin I voenny soviet* (Moskva: VZFEI, 2007).
227 "Shvernik Report," 6–7.
228 Ibid., 7.
229 Ibid., 7–9; Montefiore, *Stalin*, 225.
230 Khrushchev, *Crimes of the Stalin Era*, 39.
231 *Molotov Remembers*, 280.
232 Davies, *Mission to Moscow*, 125–26.
233 Ibid., 126.
234 Peter Whitewood, *The Red Army and the Great Terror* (Lawrence: University Press of Kansas. 2015), 252–54, 255, 257.
235 Conquest, *The Great Terror: A Reassessment*, 450; Getty and Naumov, *Road to Terror*, 450–51; Whitewood, *The Red Army*, 264; Vadim Z. Rogovin, *Stalin's Terror of 1937-1938: Political Genocide in the USSR*, trans. by Frederick S. Choate (Oak Park, MI: Mehring Books, 2009), 197–201, 202–203.
236 Medvedev, *Let History Judge*, 213.
237 Ian Kershaw, *Hitler: 1936-1945 Nemesis* (New York: W.W. Norton, 2000), 335.
238 Getty and Naumov, *Road to Terror*, 451.
239 Harris, *The Great Fear*, 174–75.
240 Getty and Naumov, *Road to Terror*, 470–471.
241 *30.07.1937 No. 00447*, 1–16 (accessed October 27, 2016). https://ru.wikisource.org/wiki/___30.07.1937_No. 00447.
242 Getty and Naumov, *Road to Terror*, 470, 492.

243 *Case of the Trotskyite-Zinovievite Terrorist Centre*, 65. Kamenev later told Vyshinsky that Bukharin, along with others, "sympathized with" the Trotskyite conspirators, 68.
244 Roy A. Medvedev, *Nikolai Bukharin: The Last Years*, trans. by A. D. P. Briggs (New York: W.W. Norton, 1980), 136.
245 Donald Rayfield, *Stalin and His Henchmen* (New York: Random House, 2004), 319; J. V. Stalin, "Defects in Party Work and Measures for Liquidating Trotskyite and Other Double Dealers," Report to the Plenum of the Central Committee of the RKP(b), March 3, 1937 (parts 21-3, 5) (Moscow: Cooperative Publishing Society of Foreign Workers in the USSR, 1937), 8 (accessed August 20, 2018). https://www.marxists.org/reference/archive/stalin/works/1937/03/03.htm.
246 Medvedev, *Nikolai Bukharin*, 10, 122–23, 125; Stephen F. Cohen, "Bukharin, Lenin and the Theoretical Foundations of Bolshevism," *Soviet Studies*, Vol. 21 (April 1970), 436; Getty and Naumov, *Road to Terror*, 277; Samuel A. Oppenheim, "Rykov, Aleksei Ivanovich (1881–1938)," in Joseph L. Wieczynski, ed., *The Modern Encyclopedia of Russian and Soviet History*, 32 (Gulf Breeze, FL: Academic International Press, 1983), 239–42.
247 Davies, *Mission to Moscow*, 163, 168–69.
248 *Report of the Court Proceedings in the Case of the Anti-Soviet 'Bloc of Rights and Trotskyites.'* Heard before the Military Collegium of the Supreme Court of the U.S.S.R., March 2–13, 1938 (Moscow: People's Commissariat of Justice of the U.S.S.R., 1938), 5–6, 35. The indictment stated that twenty-one defendants would be tried, while the eleven others mentioned in it would be tried at a later date; a rumor spread after Gorky's death in 1936 that he had been poisoned by the NKVD. Service, *Stalin*, p. 302. In reality, he died of natural causes in his dacha outside of Moscow. Stephen Kotkin, *Stalin: Waiting for Hitler, 1929-1941* (New York: Penguin, 2017), 295.
249 *Case of the Anti-Soviet 'Bloc of Rights and Trotskyites,'* 1–3.
250 Ibid., 36.
251 Ibid., 156.
252 Ibid., 157–58.
253 Conquest, *The Great Terror*, 510.
254 *Case of the Anti-Soviet 'Bloc of Rights and Trotskyites,'* 348.
255 Ibid., 158, 160, 163–64, 179, 180, 182–83, 189, 192.
256 Rogovin, *Stalin's Terror of 1937-1938*, 34–37.
257 Conquest, *The Great Terror: A Reassessment*, 364–65.
258 Ibid., 369–70.
259 *Case of the Anti-Soviet 'Bloc of Rights and Trotskyites,'* 369–70, 372–73.
260 Ibid., 377, 413, 415–17.
261 Ibid., 396, 397–401.
262 Ibid., 403–04, 409–10, 413, 414.
263 Ibid., 423.
264 Ibid., 499; Karelin was executed on September 22, 1938. *Protsess Bukharina 1938 g.*, sostavileli: Zh. V. Artamonova and N. V. Petrov (Moskva: Mezhdunarodnyi Fond 'Demokratiya', 2013), 910.
265 *Case of the Anti-Soviet 'Bloc of Rights and Trotskyites,'* 504–06.
266 Ibid., 627.
267 Ibid., 627–28.
268 Ibid., 629.
269 Ibid., 632, 693.
270 Ibid., 693.

271 Ibid., 694.
272 Ibid., 693, 694.
273 Ibid., 695.
274 Ibid.
275 Ibid., 695–96.
276 Ibid., 697.
277 Ibid., 698–705, 715–16, 721, 725, 730, 737, 743, 748, 753, 758, 764, 766, 781, 783–84, 786–88, 790, 791.
278 Ibid., 767–68, 770, 778, 779.
279 Ibid., 737, 740, 741.
280 Ibid., 720–29, 730–33, 734, 735–36.
281 Ibid., 799–800.
282 Rogovin, *Stalin's Terror of 1937-1938*, 102; Conquest, *The Great Terror: A Reassessment*, 395.
283 Conquest, *The Great Terror*, 419.

2

Traitors or War Criminals: Collaboration on Trial in Soviet Courts in the 1940s

Alexander V. Prusin

Throughout the existence of the Soviet Union, the Soviet leadership stressed that the struggle against the enemies of the state must be "decisive, energetic, and merciless without any reservations."[1] A key role in this struggle belonged to the justice system, which treated political offenses as most dangerous to the existence of the Soviet state. Prosecution of alleged political opposition reached its zenith during the Stalinist purges in the 1930s and continued through the Second World War, when the Soviet courts convicted 2.5 million people, including 471,988 people for "counterrevolutionary crimes." The latter term also included what the Western courts termed war crimes, and until the late 1980s the Soviet government tenaciously pursued policies of retribution, seeking to punish their own countrymen whose behavior was severely compromised during the war.[2]

As long as Soviet archival documents were inaccessible for researchers, the prosecution of war crimes and collaboration in the Soviet Union remained largely unexplored. The situation changed in the 1990s, when the opening of archives generated the appearance of several stimulating studies, which shed light on the Soviet methods of investigation, the presentation of trials in official propaganda, and their place in the context of the Soviet internal and international politics.[3]

This chapter seeks to contextualize the prosecution of high treason and collaboration (*sotrudnichestvo*)—with the latter term referring to assistance to the enemy in different capacities—within the larger framework of Soviet retributive justice. Like most European countries, the Soviet legal system was partially based on Roman law (as opposed to Anglo-Saxon Common Law) and, as such, considered treason to be a serious crime. Consequently, the charge of treason played a central role in Soviet "courtrooms" during the war. The Soviet criminal code defined high treason as the most grievous political crime against national sovereignty and it encompassed a whole range of offenses, from anti-Soviet propaganda to flight abroad, all punishable by the death penalty.

In the aftermath of the Second World War, the Soviet trials of alleged war criminals and collaborators played an important part in a comprehensive campaign to reintegrate the territories that had remained outside of state control for several years. The Soviet leadership was particularly concerned about the volatile situation in the provinces, which were annexed by the Soviet Union in 1939–1940, and in some areas of with significant ethnic minorities, where substantial segments of population collaborated with the occupiers. The prosecution of war crimes and collaboration were predominantly the domain of the extrajudicial courts—military tribunals, which used the charges of treason and collaboration interchangeably or simultaneously, often differentiating the two only by vague criteria, such as the motives one had for interaction with the enemy.

High treason and collaboration in Soviet legislation

In November 1917 the Bolshevik government abolished the imperial justice system, discarding the terms "state crime" and "high treason" as belonging to the legal phraseology of the empire.[4] Nonetheless, the Soviet state eventually inherited and expanded the concept of political justice, which in its traditional Russian form was not a part of the court system but a government tool for suppressing the opposition. Since the Bolsheviks aimed at the total transformation of Soviet society, they conceived repression as both a key element of this transformation and a preventive police measure.[5]

Consequently, the earliest decrees of the Bolshevik legislation termed any acts inimical to the Soviet state as "counterrevolutionary" or "state" crimes. Thus, on the day of the Bolshevik revolution, November 7, 1917, a decree by the 2nd Council of Soviets announced the arrest of the ministers of the Provisional Government and stated that any assistance to it was to be treated as a "grievous state crime," punishable retroactively.[6] Adjudication of "counterrevolutionary" and "state" crimes was delegated to the jurisdiction of revolutionary tribunals, subordinated to the Commissariat of Justice. As the Russian civil war gained momentum, the Soviet government accorded tribunals more power. On April 12, 1919, a special statute authorized tribunals to act in accordance with "revolutionary conscience" rather than traditional legal procedures. On June 20 the All-Russian Central Executive Committee reintroduced the imperial clause of high treason; in September the Commissariat of Justice defined high treason as one of the most dangerous "counterrevolutionary" crimes but did not provide any specifics about its judicial meaning. The tribunals, therefore, had a free hand in interpreting the "counterrevolutionary" and "state" crimes and could use both terms interchangeably as any act directed against the Soviet system, imposing verdicts of forced labor or the death penalty.[7]

Since Soviet lawmakers were more concerned about the alleged social threat of a criminal offense than in its specific characteristics, legalistic flexibility became a critical feature of the Soviet criminal legislation. According to the *Basic Principles of Criminal Legislation* of the USSR issued in 1924, repressive measures could be applied against individuals guilty of commission of crimes as well as against those who were considered "socially dangerous" due to their criminal background or political affiliations.[8] Such formulation, on one hand, accorded the courts substantial leeway in determining the level of "social threat," and on the other hand, underscored the courts' total dependence on the party and the state apparatus. Critically, both guided the justice system through numerous decrees, instructions, and directives, which had precedence over the existing laws.

The evolution of the Soviet criminal legislation vividly demonstrated its tractability and its key function as an arm of the government. In 1922 the first Soviet criminal code (specifically, Article 57) described "counterrevolutionary" crimes as "any act to depose the toiler-peasant government or to help the elements of the international bourgeoisie, which aspired to depose the communist system through intervention, blockade, espionage, financing [counterrevolutionary] press, and similar actions." Critically, the code defined high treason as "collaboration with a foreign state in pursuance of counterrevolutionary aims," thus conflating the two terms.[9] Lenin, who took part in the preparation of the code, emphasized that "elements of the international bourgeoisie" meant both foreign and domestic enemies. In July 1923 the term "counterrevolutionary crimes" was reworded as "any act directed to overthrow or undermine the Soviet government."[10]

International tensions and the activities of the White émigré groups in the 1920s were reflected in the introduction of additional "counterrevolutionary" crimes in the criminal legislation. In 1926 the new criminal code enumerated fourteen forms of such acts, which included high treason and its main features were espionage and defection to the enemy. On February 25, 1927, the Central Executive Committee of the USSR issued the Statute of State Crimes, which specifically included "counterrevolutionary crimes and particularly dangerous crimes against the state order."[11]

Integrated into the 1926 Criminal Code as Article 58, the Statute contained thirteen clauses (one more was added in June 1937) that stipulated death penalty and long prison terms for a range of political offenses. Article 58-1 defined "counterrevolutionary" crimes as acts "against the sovereignty and political system of the USSR and . . . national gains of the proletariat revolution." Article 58-1a imposed the death penalty and lengthy prison terms for high treason (committed by civilians); the same crime committed by the military personnel was punishable exclusively by death (Article 58-1b). Article 58-3 defined collaboration with the enemy as "maintaining contacts with a foreign state or its representatives, guided by counterrevolutionary aims" and "assisting a foreign state in war against the USSR." Similarly, Article 58-4 described collaboration as "assisting the international bourgeoisie," without specifying what sort of assistance was involved (Articles 58-3 and 58-4 carried prison terms and the death penalty). Articles 58-6, 58-8, and 58-9 covered espionage, political terror, and subversive activities respectively. Of particular significance was Article 58-11, which equated "any organizational activity towards the preparation or implementation of criminal acts [enumerated in the Statute] to commission of such acts, punishable under the relevant articles of the Criminal Code." In practice it meant that the Soviet courts could qualify any political, civic, or religious groups as "counterrevolutionary" and indict their members under any of the charges, stipulated by the Statute. Finally, Article 58-13 made retroactively punishable all anti-Soviet acts committed under the imperial regime and during the civil war.[12]

The provenance of the Statute of State Crimes clearly indicated that the rights of the individual were subordinated to the interests of the state, and the latter could modify or overrule the criminal legislation at will. In November 1929 the Presidium of the Central Executive Committee empowered the courts to charge with high treason state employees who refused to return from abroad.[13]

On June 8, 1934, the Central Executive Committee issued the "Statute of Criminal Responsibility for High Treason," which became the guiding tool for the Stalinist purges. The statute provided the most specific definition of high treason (*izmena Rodinie*) to date and was integrated into the criminal code as "acts, committed by the citizens of the USSR to the detriment of its military might, independence, and state sovereignty through espionage, betrayal of military or state secrets, defection to the enemy, and escape or flight across the border."[14]

The wording of the Statute had immense significance, for it effectively highlighted the three key elements of the Soviet criminal legislation—object of crime (state interests), objective side ("social threat" or effect of crime), and subjective side (criminal intent). Critically, from the official standpoint, since the object of high treason was state interests, high treason could be committed *only* with criminal intent (*prestupnyi umysel*), which alone constituted corpus delicti. The courts, therefore, were not obligated to distinguish between intent and motive. It meant that all defectors or escapees from the Soviet Union were liable to punishment for high treason, regardless whether they left the country looking for better economic opportunities or were driven by ideological reasons. Similarly, the courts could qualify as high treason the refusal to serve in the armed forces out of religious convictions. The Statute also made the family members of those who had escaped from the Soviet Union liable to the deprivation of civil rights and exile, if they did not inform proper authorities (effectively replicating the Russian imperial decree of 1649).[15]

Furthermore, on July 10, 1934, the Central Executive Committee and the Council of People's Commissars subordinated all cases of high treason, espionage, terrorism, and subversive activities to the jurisdiction of military tribunals (through the Military Collegium of the Supreme Court), which were empowered to apply Article 58 retroactively and to adjudicate any act as a political crime ipso facto, based on alleged intent.[16] Adjudication of "counterrevolutionary" crimes was drastically simplified—an indictment was handed over to the defendant twenty-four hours before the trial, defense counsel was not mandatory, and the death penalty was carried out immediately after passing the verdict. The objective proof in form of documentary evidence or witness testimony was sidelined in favor of confession, which was termed the "queen of evidence" by the notorious prosecutor Andrei Vyshinsky.[17] In November 1934 the People's Commissariat of Internal Affairs (NKVD) received its own extrajudicial organ—the so-called Special Commission (*Osoboye Soveshchaniye*). It had power to convict without trial solely on the results of investigation and could overrule the decisions of the Military Collegium.[18]

The Soviet government's suspicions over potential disloyalty of its subjects increased with the outbreak of the Second World War, reflected in further instructions to the courts. In August and December 1940 the Political Bureau of the Central Committee called for the "intensification of struggle against traitors of the Motherland" and instructed military tribunals to expedite trials against the escapees from the Soviet Union. In such cases, tribunals had to hand down sentences in the course of forty-eight hours. In April 1941 a special ordinance sanctioned the courts to charge with high treason individuals who had escaped from prisons.[19]

Wartime trials

On the day of the German invasion of the Soviet Union, June 22, 1941, the Soviet government decreed that martial law took precedence over civil laws in many areas of the country. In these areas, the military tribunals were empowered to try the military personnel and civilians who committed high treason, collaboration, and espionage; the tribunals also were authorized to try the cases concerning the "theft of socialist property," brigandage, first-degree murder, speculation, spreading false rumors, shirking of labor in military industries, and any offense considered dangerous by the local military command.[20] In peacetime, military tribunals functioned only at the level of army corps and military districts, but the June decree authorized the creation of military tribunals in divisions, corps, armies, and army groups (fronts). The NKVD, the Border Troops, and the railroad and river-traffic departments formed their own military tribunals. All tribunals were subordinated to the Military Collegium of the Supreme Court of the USSR (in 1942 they were temporarily subordinated to the Main Department of Military Tribunals of the Commissariat of Justice).[21]

The tribunals were made up of three judges—the so-called troika (trio)—who had to be the party members and could adjudicate cases without the defense counsel. The tribunal's key figure was the military prosecutor (*voennyi prokuror*), who was answerable to the Chief Military Prosecutor (the latter functioned under the auspices of the Chief Prosecutor of the USSR) and acted in two overlapping capacities— supervising investigation and the trial and representing the state as chief prosecutor, having exclusive control over pressing the charges.[22] In the areas under the martial law, tribunals' verdicts were not subject to appeal. If death sentence was rendered, the tribunal's chairman informed the Military Collegium and the Chief Military Prosecutor. If these two offices did not change the sentence in the course of seventy-two hours, it was carried out. The commanders of the military districts, armies, fleets, and fronts had the right to commute the death penalty, but their decisions could be overruled by the Military Collegium.[23]

Heightened during the Great Purges, the struggle against "internal enemies" reached its zenith, especially in the initial stages of the war, when the Red Army suffered crushing defeats. From the official standpoint, in such situation all "counterrevolutionary crimes" automatically acquired the character of high treason since they played into the hands of the enemy. On July 17, 1941, the State Committee of Defense (headed by Stalin) issued a special directive 187 that called for the "merciless suppression of spies, subversives, deserters, cowards, and panic-mongers in the army and the navy."[24] Moreover, on August 16, 1941, the Soviet Supreme Headquarters (Stavka) issued a decree "On the responsibility of servicemen for surrender and abandonment of arms to the enemy," which effectively equalized falling into captivity to high treason. Accordingly, Soviet courts would try those who had surrendered to the enemy and those who were captured as the "traitors to the Motherland."[25] In

Ukraine alone, between June 22 and September 25 the security services arrested 7,694 people for political offenses. Between June 22 and October 10 the Special Sections (the NKVD branches in the armed forces) arrested 25,878 soldiers and officers of the Red Army; 10,201 of the arrested were shot; the NKVD and the Red Army units often executed alleged collaborators on the spot. Such practices became official, when in November 1941 Moscow was declared under siege and the State Committee of Defense decreed that "spies, provocateurs, and other enemy agents," who tried to cause panic and disorder would be executed without trial.[26]

On December 12 the NKVD chief Lavrentii Beria ordered "special measures" against individuals who "assisted [the enemy] in anti-Soviet activities" in the territories liberated from German occupation. On December 16, the NKVD of Ukraine issued a directive to the same effect, ordering its branches to find and "remove" (*izyat'*) all individuals, who worked in the German administration and helped the Germans and "their accomplices in atrocities and other activities." On December 27 Stalin signed another directive that authorized repressions against the family members of "traitors" and "accomplices."[27]

By 1943 about 70 million Soviet residents had found themselves under the Axis occupation. While many joined the resistance, up to 1 million people collaborated with the occupiers in different capacities.[28] Accordingly, since the outbreak of the war, the Soviet security services meticulously collected information about individuals who were employed in the Axis military, administrative, and police organs. In January 1942 the 4th department of NKVD was specifically directed to this task; the Special Sections carried out the same functions in the rear of the Red Army. In February 1942 the NKVD issued a circular letter, which enumerated categories of offenders to be apprehended. These included the members of the Axis security and intelligence services, functionaries of the civil administration, owners and the service personnel of the buildings, where German offices were located, terrorists and the members of anti-Soviet, "counterrevolutionary," and nationalist organizations. People who kept radio-transmitters and munitions left by the occupiers and the party members who had registered by the Germans (and survived occupation) were considered as dangerous as women married to the German personnel, managers of brothels, and employees and laborers of industrial sites. Among potential offenders were also individuals (and their relatives) who had retreated with the Germans. The circular letter also named "traitors," "turncoats," and the "German hirelings," without defining these terms.[29]

Such extensive "black lists" meant that most people in the occupied territories fit at least one of the aforementioned categories since living under foreign rule entailed performing some sort of work, which accorded a minimum economic security, but simultaneously translated into fulfilling the German orders. For the Soviet leadership, living with the enemy effectively meant "laboring for the enemy" and entailed appropriate repressive measures.

To prosecute the growing numbers of potential culprits, military tribunals were expanded from 298 in 1941 to 823 in March 1942. Simultaneously, tribunals' proceedings were simplified. Judges often pronounced verdicts upon superficially collected information or solely on the arguments of the prosecution. As a result, thousands of people, who deserted from the Red Army, shirked labor service, or carried out their professional duties under German occupation were charged with high treason and sentenced to death or long prison terms. To compensate for the shortage of trained jurists in the tribunals, in July 1942 the Presidium of the Supreme Soviet decreed that upon recommendation of the army command or its political department any member of the Red Army could sit in judgment, regardless whether they had any legal experience.[30]

Still, the Soviet government insisted that these measures were not enough and sent out numerous directives and instructions to this effect. On May 15, 1942, the Chief Prosecutor of the USSR Viktor Bochkov issued a directive which stated that the tribunals often charged deserters who had actively participated in the enemy's punitive organs under Article 58-3 as "accomplices." Since the charge of "complicity" more often resulted in milder prison terms and did not carry the same ideological weight, Bochkov stressed that such cases were to be governed by Article 58-1a instead of Articles 58-3 and 58-4 (which covered what came closest to the Western definition of collaboration). On October 11, 1942, the State Committee of Defense ordered that deserters engaged in banditry and robbery be tried for high treason under Article 58-1b. The directive applied the principle of collective responsibility to the families of collaborators and deserters, leaving the security services and tribunals to decide appropriate repressive measures.[31] On November 2, 1942, the Presidium of the Supreme Soviet decreed the creation of the "Extraordinary State Commission for Ascertaining and Investigating Crimes Perpetrated by the German-Fascist Invaders and their Accomplices" (ChGK), which was authorized to investigate war crimes committed on Soviet soil. Later in the war, materials collected by the ChGK would constitute the evidence for prosecution in many trials.

The retribution drive gained momentum in the spring of 1943, when the Red Army began reconquering the occupied territories. Beria's deputy Vsevolod Merkulov reported to Stalin and the Politburo that by March 10 in the liberated regions the security organs arrested 30,750 individuals, including spies and "German hirelings."[32] Experiences with trials in 1941–1942 compelled the Soviet government to create a sort of legalistic umbrella, which provided a common mechanism for the prosecution of the Axis personnel and native collaborators. Upon Stalin's authorization, four Soviet officials—the secretary of the Central Committee of the Communist Party Georgii Malenkov, the chairman of the Soviet Supreme Court Ivan Goliakov, the secretary of the Presidium of the Supreme Soviet Alexander Gorkin, and Bochkov—drafted a special decree. After Stalin approved the text, on April 19, 1943, the Presidium of Supreme Soviet signed it as Decree 39, "Of the Punishment Measures against the German-Fascist Villains, Spies, the Traitors of the Motherland, and Their Accomplices Guilty of Murder and Mistreatment of the Soviet Civilian Population and POWs."[33] The decree stressed that the Axis forces and their native helpers committed countless crimes, but

> the punishment meted out to all these criminals clearly do not merit the gravity of their crimes. Since massacres and violence against defenseless Soviet citizens and POWS are the most shameful, horrible, and heinous atrocities, the Presidium of the Supreme Soviet of the USSR decided that

1. The German, Italian, Romanian, Hungarian, and Finnish military and civilian personnel and spies and traitors of the Motherland guilty of atrocities will be executed by hanging.
2. Accomplices from the local population guilty of assisting in the same crimes will be sentenced to forced labor for between fifteen and twenty years.[34]

In accordance with the decree, the extreme nature of crimes committed by the Axis powers necessitated the most extreme form of punishment to be carried out by the field courts-martial (*voenno-polevye sudy*) of the frontline divisions. The field courts-martial included the chairman of division's military tribunal, the chief of the Special Section, and a political officer. In contrast to regular military tribunals, the field courts-martial were to prosecute culprits who were caught on the spot, immediately after the liberation of a Soviet territory, when cases required no further investigation. The expected outcome of such trial was most likely the death sentence and if confirmed by a division's commander, it was carried out immediately. Furthermore, "to satisfy the popular sense of justice in regards to the German-fascist criminals and their hirelings" public executions by hanging were to underscore the shameful nature of crime and the utter disgrace of the culprits. To the same effect, corpses of traitors were to be left on the gallows for several days, so that "everyone was aware of retribution for violence against the civilian population and for betrayal of the Motherland." Such wording vividly underscored the April decree's main objectives—to stress that by waging the war of extermination, Germany and its allies placed themselves outside the conventional laws of warfare, and to warn the population of inevitable and harsh retribution for collaboration with the enemy.[35]

However, although the April decree specified the forms of punishment, its legal terminology remained ambivalent, for it neither defined a highly emotional term "atrocities" (*zlodeianiia*) nor explained the degree of responsibility in "assisting in atrocities." In practice it meant that the courts tried only two categories of offenders—either the defendant was a perpetrator (*zlodei*), spy, or traitor, who deserved death or a hireling (*posobnik*) to be sentenced to hard labor.

Such vague interpretation of war crimes was further confounded by numerous directives, guidelines, and instructions, which attempted to clarify its application. On April 26, 1943, a special instruction emphasized that the April decree alone sufficed for the qualification of "atrocities," without the application of the Criminal Code, enabling the courts to speed up investigation process and complete each trial in five days.[36] On May 18 the Main Department of Military Tribunals ruled that for culprits who were charged under Part I of the April decree there would be no statute of limitation; they also could be charged retroactively. On June 26 Bochkov enumerated crimes that fell under the decree's jurisdiction: murder, mistreatment, torture of civilians and POWs, and impressment into hard labor. Still, his directive was vague in regard to the qualification of the decree's key terms—atrocities, traitors, and accomplices.[37] As unclear remained the difference between traitors (*izmenniki*) and the more equivocal term "turncoats" (*predateli*). The latter was neither mentioned in the April decree nor in the Soviet criminal code, but it carried heavy emotional resonance in popular mentality since the medieval origins of the Russian state.

Consequently, the field courts-martial and tribunals used both terms interchangeably, particularly in public trials.

The first trials under the April decree were conducted in the liberated provinces of southern Russia. In May 1943 the court-martial of the 32nd Guard Division sentenced to death a former policeman F. Dembovskii, who was publicly hanged in the Cossack village Krymskaia. In accordance with the decree, his corpse remained on the gallows for two days. Between June 11 and 25 at least four trials ended in the public hanging of native collaborators.[38] The trial of Petr Sosnovskii, the former chief of auxiliary police in Armavir, received a lot of attention in the press. Sosnovskii was captured in January 1943, when the Soviet army liberated the city and the tribunal of the city garrison sentenced him to death by shooting for participation in the murder of Jews, the Soviet POWs, and the partisans. However, after the passing of the April decree, the military tribunal of the North-Caucasian Front (to which the garrison tribunal was subordinated) revoked the sentence as "too soft." Since the decree had a retroactive power, the case was reviewed and Sosnovskii was sentenced to hang. Appropriate public announcements made sure that the execution became a public spectacle and on June 24 about 12,000 people gathered in the city central square. Once Sosnovskii dangled in the noose, the crowd pushed aside the cordon, tearing off the cloth and mutilating his body; the corpse remained on the gallows for three days.[39] Such reaction emanated from genuine euphoria over liberation, but also may have reflected the psychological atmosphere of the day, whereby the population's own culpability for large-scale accommodation with the enemy was projected upon a single "traitor."

After a series of local trials, the Soviet government decided to stage a large public hearing that would have national and international resonance. It aimed at several objectives at once—deterring potential collaborators, demonstrating the Soviet government's determination to punish war criminals in accordance with its public announcements, and indicting the German political and military leadership as a whole. In preparation for the trial, which was to take place in the regional capital Krasnodar, the regional party committee sent a special directive to local party branches, initiating a series of propaganda measures. The party activists and agitators were dispatched to explain to the population that there was "no more grievous crime than the betrayal of the socialist Motherland and that Soviet justice punishes by death all those who violate the Stalinist Constitution and the military oath."[40]

On July 14, 1943, in a movie theater, packed with spectators and journalists, the military tribunal of the North-Caucasian Front charged eleven men with participation in atrocities, committed by a German killing unit (*Sonderkommando* 10a) in the Krasnodar region. The trial became a blueprint for similar proceedings, for each participant fulfilled a carefully orchestrated function. In vogue with the "classic" show trials of the 1930s, the defendants described in detail their crimes and admitted their guilt (most likely, under constant pressure during the investigation stage, they either resigned to their fate or were promised leniency in exchange for confession). One defendant hailed from the "kulak" (rich peasant in the Soviet political phraseology) background and three others had previous criminal records, which accorded the prosecution the ground to highlight their alleged anti-Soviet inclinations.[41] Since the remaining defendants were of peasant background, the state prosecutor Major-General

Leonid Yachenin portrayed them as cowards, bereft of will and morals. According to the Soviet court traditions, the judges acted in an "inquisitorial" fashion, highlighting the most horrific episodes of German occupation. The prosecution paraded two dozen witnesses, who testified to the atrocities committed by the German occupiers but offered little on the actual activities of the defendants. Instead, Yachenin used his podium for a vitriolic propaganda campaign, referring to the defendants as "traitors, fascist hirelings," and "boot-lickers." In his final peroration he warned the German leadership and native collaborators of inevitable retribution:

> Today the avenging hand of Soviet justice falls upon the heads of traitors, fascist hirelings and lackeys. Tomorrow the court of history, the court of freedom-loving people will pronounce its inexorable verdict over bloodthirsty rulers of Nazi Germany and all its collaborators—enemies of mankind, who plunged the world into the bloody abyss of the present war. None of them will escape the merciless punishment. Blood for blood, death for death![42]

At the end of the trial, the judges sentenced eight of the defendants to death by hanging, and three to terms of twenty years of forced labor. The trial and the public hanging were filmed (the execution was attended by 30,000 spectators) and highlighted in the Soviet press. Numerous pamphlets about the trial were published in Russian, English, and German.[43]

The Krasnodar and subsequent trials (e.g., in Krasnodon in August 1943) clearly underscored the ideological and retributive character of the Soviet legal system and the state's unrelenting will to punish political offenders. Public trials also effectively fused official ideological objectives and popular desires to place the blame on selected individuals, partially exonerating the population from its compliant conduct under foreign occupation. Still, too much publicity ran a risk of revealing that collaboration with the enemy was a massive phenomenon, thus running afoul to the official interpretation of the "Great Patriotic War." Accordingly, after the trial of four defendants in Kharkov in December 1943, where three Germans and one Russian were sentenced to hang, the Soviet government decided that similar trials should be conducted with much less fanfare.

The hunt for native collaborators gained momentum as more Soviet territories were liberated. A secretary of a military tribunal recalled that in the Kuban' area alone there were thousands of suspects. By the end of 1943 the NKVD arrested 80,926 individuals, including 4,822 German agents, 14,626 "traitors," 5,663 policemen and *karateli* (individuals who participated in punitive actions), and 21,022 accomplices.[44] To demonstrate their zeal, the police functionaries often fabricated cases or forced innocent individuals to accuse themselves of war crimes and collaboration. To expedite proceedings, on September 8, 1943, the Presidium of the Supreme Council decreed that regular military tribunals were also empowered to adjudicate under the April decree. Accordingly, if in 1941 tribunals tried 15,743 individuals for high treason, espionage, and collaboration, 65,957 people were tried in 1942, and in 1943 these numbers grew to 158,477. In a blanket fashion, courts-martial and tribunals indicted thousands of defendants under the Part 2 of the April decree, solely on the basis of membership in the military, civil, or police organs of the occupiers or for desertion.[45]

However, although in 1943 the numbers of convictions grew, the death penalty was applied more selectively. Indeed, the end of the year marked a gradual (though not immediately visible) departure from the lynch-format trials to a more pragmatic approach of dispensing wartime justice. Indeed, if the courts were to apply the April degree systematically, such practices would have evolved into the mass executions, mirroring the Great Terror of the 1930s rather than the "liberation of the Motherland," glorified by Soviet propaganda. Critically, shooting tens of thousands of people deprived the Soviet state of a massive pool of costless labor force, including many specialists—engineers, doctors, teachers, and managers—necessary for the economic reconstruction and re-integration of the liberated territories into the Soviet state.[46]

Accordingly, on November 25, 1943, the Supreme Court sent out an instruction that clarified the distinction between "traitors" and "accomplices." The former term referred to activities that exceeded a mere compliance with German orders and encompassed a whole range of culprits—the Gestapo employees, city mayors, chiefs of native police, and those who directly participated in mass murder, violence, and destruction of property, but also individuals who divulged state secrets or took part in the persecution of the Soviet military personnel, resistance members, and their family members; the members of the military personnel who defected to the enemy were also classified as "traitors." All these categories were to be tried under Part 1 of the April decree, or Articles 58-1a, 58-1b, and the corresponding articles of the criminal codes of the Union Republics. In contrast, individuals who collected food supplies and contingents for the German Army, or labored in industries, transport, and agriculture were to be tried as "accomplices" under Article 58-3 or Part 2 of the April decree.[47]

Despite these clarifications, the field courts-martial and tribunals continued adjudicating collaboration and high treason as the same offense. Therefore, on March 7, 1944, the Presidium of the Supreme Soviet sent out a directive, which was to clarify the difference once and for all. Judges were instructed to treat crimes committed out of ideological grounds (termed "hostile intentions towards Soviet power") as aggravating factors, charged under Article 58-1a or under Part I of the April decree. Desertion was also to be qualified as high treason. If "hostile intentions" were lacking, offenders should be charged with collaboration under Article 58-3. On March 23 the Supreme Court of the USSR issued a similar instruction, accentuating that anti-Soviet ideological inclinations exacerbated guilt and should be punished accordingly.[48] These guidelines effectively replicated the terminology of the revolutionary era, highlighting the key element of the Soviet justice system—its ideological foundation. A prominent Soviet jurist argued that in wartime the courts were obligated to qualify any offenses—political or criminal—as particularly dangerous to the state and charge them under Article 58 or the April decree.[49]

Since the Bolshevik revolution, the Soviet state was involved in a ferocious struggle against "bourgeois nationalism"—the official propaganda label of national independence movements—which played a key role in the court charges against native collaborators in the Crimea, the Caucasus, the Baltic region, and in the eastern Polish provinces annexed by the Soviet Union in 1939–1940. Thus, in the interwar period the Soviet government subjected the Crimea to radical transformation, which dramatically affected its religious, cultural, and sociocultural traditions. In particular, an assault on the Islamic religious practices generated resentment among the substantial segments of the Tatar population, which perceived the German invasion as liberation from Bolshevism. Conversely, the Soviet leadership's anxieties over potential disloyalties of the Tatars crystalized upon the German conquest of the region, when thousands of the natives served the occupiers in different capacities, including the propaganda and terror apparatus. Such a situation provided the Soviet government with a pretext to remove the entire Tatar population, and in May 1944 about 194,000 Crimean Tatars were deported to different parts of the Soviet Union.

Simultaneously, the security organs unremittingly tracked down the members of the Tatar police forces and the so-called national committees. In such trial-cases, when the defendants were judged to have been acting out of ideological considerations, the death penalty or high prison terms were a norm. For example, in June 1944 the NKVD military tribunal of the Crimea charged Miknil Ramazanov with high treason under Article 58-1b. In November 1941 Ramazanov, deserted from the Red Army, joined a Tatar police unit, which operated under the supervision of the German security service (SD) and participated in the roundups of Soviet activists and guerrillas. For zeal and bravery in combat, he was promoted to the rank of platoon commander and received a bronze medal from the German command. Under investigation, Ramazanov admitted that he had personally shot at least one partisan and functioned as an SD informer. In the latter capacity, he tracked down and betrayed several Soviet activists, who were subsequently shot; in November 1943 the SD inserted him into a partisan unit for obtaining intelligence on its strength and location.[50]

The NKVD functionaries, who interrogated Ramazanov, were not well-versed in the structure of the German police and referred to the auxiliary unit in which he served as "an SS company." Such detail, in combination with Ramazanov's service record, determined his fate. The indictment emphasized that he was an ideological enemy, "hostile to Soviet power, [who] betrayed the Motherland and remained loyal to the German-fascist state to the end."[51] On June 12, 1944, the tribunal pronounced its verdict, which emphasized that Ramazanov "voluntarily joined an SS company . . . was then transferred to a punitive battalion," participating in anti-partisan operations. At the end of the war, to conceal his wartime activities Ramazanov joined the partisans and the tribunal ruled that this attempt to "avoid responsibility for betrayal of the Motherland" exacerbated his guilt. The tribunal, therefore, sentenced Ramazanov to death.[52]

In June 1944 the military tribunal of the 8th Airforce Army in Simferopol charged seven members of the so-called Muslim Committee with "counter-revolutionary activities." Under German occupation, the committee regulated the inner life of the Tatar community, carried out propaganda activities among the Tatars for the recruitment into the auxiliary police, and published a newspaper "Azat Krym" (Liberated Crimea), which hailed the German invasion as long-awaited deliverance from oppressive Soviet rule. Operating under the supervision of the SD, the committee also compiled the lists of Soviet activists, who were then arrested and imprisoned or executed.[53]

Although the tribunal did not elaborate the concept of criminal association, it determined that the defendants were driven by ideological convictions and common criminal intent (*prestupnyi umysel*). The indictment, therefore, emphasized the committee's "nationalist, pro-fascist, slanderous, and counter-revolutionary" activities, exacerbated by the fact that it was organized by the members of *Milli Firka*, the Tatar "bourgeois-nationalist" party organized in the Crimea in 1917. Defendant Izet Nuriev was the chief-editor of *Azat Krym* and the investigators obtained several issues of the newspaper, replete with vehement anti-Soviet and anti-Semitic articles.[54]

During the investigation stage, Nuriev and the other defendants denounced each other and fully admitted that they promoted "counterrevolutionary" ideology and collaborated with the SD. In line with the Soviet courtroom procedure, they repeated their testimonies during the trial.[55] Although the committee's activities clearly fell under the jurisdiction of Article 58-10—"dissemination of anti-Soviet agitation," punishable by prison terms (no less than six months)—and certainly appeared less grievous than the activities of Ramazanov, the tribunal found that the defendants' criminal intent—rooted in the anti-Soviet ideology—was particularly dangerous and sentenced Nuriev and two other defendants to death under Articles 58-1a and 58-11; four other defendants were sentenced to long prison terms.[56]

Criminal intent was also a key charge in the trial of four defendants by the NKVD Special Commission in the Crimea in April 1945. Defendant Abdulla Ablayev deserted the Red Army and voluntarily joined the auxiliary police in Simferopol', partaking in the arrests of Soviet citizens. Later he served in the SD and in the Romanian intelligence. Ilmi Kermenchekli was also a deserter, who joined the Tatar police unit subordinated to the Simferopol' SD. In this capacity, Kermenchekli guarded and escorted prisoners to labor and execution sites (although the investigation could not prove his participation in executions). Appointed to head the political department of the Simferopol' Muslim Committee, Kermenchekli became an SD informant, responsible for detecting anti-German sentiments among the population.[57]

Trying to save their lives, the defendants revealed facts about each other, previously unknown to the investigation. Thus, Kermenchekli denounced his former colleague Ashim Mustafa as the warden of the so-called Peasant House, an organization that collected funds for propaganda activities among the Tatar population. In turn, Mustafa revealed that Kermenchekli was an SD agent, forcing the latter to confess that he had betrayed a Soviet partisan who was subsequently executed.[58]

Charged under Articles 58-1a, 58-1b, and 58-3, the defendants certainly faced the death penalty. However, Ashim Mustafa turned out to be an NKGB[59] informant, and the investigators and the military procurator of the Black Sea Navy handed the case over to the NKVD Special Commission, which recommended long prison terms instead of the death penalty. On April 28, 1945, the Commission sentenced Ablayev and Kermenchekli to fifteen years in prison, while Mustafa and the fourth defendant received ten years in prison.[60]

Postwar retribution policies

After the war, the prosecution of wartime offenders became a key element of a comprehensive campaign for reestablishing the state's control, which was loosened by the war. To this effect, since 1941 the Soviet security services had methodically collected all available information on real and alleged collaborators. For example, in June 1942 and in May 1943 the Chief Prosecutor of the USSR Viktor Bochkov ordered that all appropriate information about crimes committed by the occupiers and their native helpers be compiled and preserved.[61] In December 1943 Stalin ordered the collection of all documentary materials, regarding the organs of self-rule created by the occupiers. Accordingly, upon entering a liberated territory, the security service operatives seized all available German documents, archives, and newspapers. They copied writings left by inmates in German prison cells on walls and questioned local residents to record the names of those who had served the enemy in various capacities.[62]

The NKVD and NKGB also created special registries, which contained information on all individuals suspected in anti-state activities—spies, terrorists, "wreckers," and members of anti-Soviet groups, in addition to those who "due to their dubious political past" were to be placed under surveillance. The collected data was constantly expanded upon receiving reports from secret agents and informants. On May 29, 1945, the NKGB issued a special instruction 00252 "regarding the registration and apprehension of the members of the intelligence, counterintelligence, punitive, and police organs of the countries that fought against the USSR [and] traitors, accomplices, and hirelings of the German-fascist occupiers."[63]

In 1945–1947, several public trials highlighted German atrocities and accentuated the determination of the Soviet government to adhere to the wartime agreements between the Allies in regard to the punishment of war crimes, especially in light of the Nuremberg Trial of major Nazi criminals. Thus, about two hundred members of the German military and civil personnel were put on trial for war crimes in Leningrad, Minsk, Kiev, Smolensk, and other cities. In August 1946 the Soviet press reported on the trial and executions of the leadership of the Russian Liberation Army.[64] The same month, a former commander of the anti-Bolshevik forces in the Far East during the Russian civil war Grigorii Semenov and several other individuals, accused for collaboration with the Japanese, were sentenced to death and executed. In January 1947 the Military Collegium of the Supreme Court sentenced to death the commanders of the anti-Soviet Cossack formations, which fought on the side of the Germans. Most of the defendants in these trials were charged under Part 1 of the April decree as "spies," "terrorists," and "traitors" (the latter category referred to those who were Soviet citizens).[65]

By 1947, however, the Soviet press reports on the trials of native collaborators had dwindled in numbers, for highlighting such cases distorted the official interpretation of the Great Patriotic War as the second (after the October revolution) foundational myth of the Soviet Union. According to it, all Soviet people fought side by side against the invaders, while those who sided with the enemy were but a "handful" of asocial, anti-Soviet, or criminal elements. Moreover, from the official standpoint, the "traitors to the Motherland" had to possess some particular sociological traits such as a "bourgeois" background, membership in the non-Bolshevik parties, or criminal records. However, often such negative qualities were lacking—many defendants were members of the "working class"— toilers or peasants; many held membership in Komsomol or in the Communist Party.[66]

The trials, therefore, continued but behind closed doors. Investigation of such cases began after the security service received information about an alleged criminal, often in the form of denunciation or when a suspect's name was mentioned in a different case. Then a whole arsenal of methods—surveillance of the suspect's family, passport control, perusal of correspondence, and questioning of survivors, eyewitnesses, or the suspect's former colleagues—was brought to bear. The security operatives searched for a culprit in localities where he or she had functioned under occupation; if not found, search would be conducted nationwide, sometimes for years on end. Sometimes suspects were arrested after they were accidentally recognized by their victims or neighbors.[67]

Upon arrest, the suspect was placed in custody and subjected to long hours of questioning, pressed to reveal his activities during the war and to divulge the names of former confederates. In accordance with the long-tested interrogation tactics, investigators questioned the suspect about his background, presumably to reveal particular traits that may have contributed to his ideological inclinations. To this end, the suspect was forced to formulate his answers in conformity to official terminology, often implicating himself. Under duress or hoping for a more lenient treatment, most suspects compiled lists of their colleagues, including the personal data, physical description, detailed characterization, specific criminal activities, and possible residence. A single defendant often revealed a dozen or more names; surveillance and search network would then spread further, encompassing up to a hundred individuals. By 1947 the MGB[68] had compiled tens of thousands of names of alleged German agents and traitors on its wanted lists. Upon the completion of investigation, the investigators set the tone for the courts by formulating indictment under specific articles of the criminal code or the April decree and handed the case over to the military or state security tribunals.[69]

As a rule, the military prosecutor's office approved the indictment. In turn, the tribunal's proceedings were based entirely on investigation records and indictment. In accordance with the Soviet criminal-procedural code, judges questioned the defendants and witnesses and determined punishment (such practices were customary for many European courts).

Although during the battle of the Caucasus in the summer-fall 1942 the two Georgian, three Azerbaijani, and two Armenian divisions fought alongside other Soviet troops against the advancing German Army, the Soviet government was concerned that the ethnic minorities lacked the requisite loyalty to the state. Such suspicions were heightened when a number of soldiers and officers of these divisions deserted to join the enemy or were captured. Since the fall of 1941, the Germans began forming units, made up of deserters and the POWs of the North-Caucasian, Georgian, Armenian, Azerbaijani, and Central Asian nationalities.[70]

The court case of Mikhail Dondua mirrored the fate of thousands of Soviet soldiers, who fell into German hands. In May 1942 the Soviet army in the Crimea suffered a crushing defeat (popularly known as the "Crimean catastrophe") and entire Soviet units surrendered or were captured. Alongside other captives, Dondua was sent to a POW camp in Feodosiya and then in Dzhankoy, where inmates starved and labored in extremely poor sanitary conditions. When a representative of the Georgian national committee (which functioned under German auspices) appealed to the prisoners of Georgian nationality to join the so-called Georgian Legion, the prospect of delivery from suffering and hunger made the proposition irresistible. According to Dondua, all Georgian captives accepted it.[71]

Transferred to a special camp near Poltava, the legionaries were trained in combat tactics and received ideological indoctrination by the representatives of the Georgian committee. Dondua revealed to the investigators that in November 1942, he and several other legionaries who had high school or college education were sent to Berlin to see firsthand the advantages of "supreme" German culture. After the trip, the group was dispatched to carry out anti-Soviet propaganda in the Legion.[72]

In July 1946 the military tribunal of the Transcaucasia Military district sentenced Dondua as an "accomplice" to ten years of forced labor under Article 58-1b. The verdict enumerated the defendant's criminal activities such as "a voluntary enlistment in the nationalist Georgian Legion, created by the Germans to fight against the Red Army and talks of fascist content with a White émigré." Furthermore, the tribunal stressed the defendant's anti-Soviet inclinations, reflected by his conduct as a propagandist in the Legion. Still, a relatively mild sentence indicated that Dondua was surely lucky—the judges may have taken into account that he sided with the enemy exclusively out of desperate situation in POW camps.[73]

Collaboration with the enemy on the basis of nationalism was a key charge in many trials in Western Ukraine, where the Organization of Ukrainian Nationalists (OUN) and its armed hand, the Ukrainian Insurgent Army (UPA) resisted the Soviets during and long after the Second World War. Armed with the ideology of integral nationalism, the OUN-UPA partook in the destruction of the Polish and Jewish communities in Volhynia and East Galicia and impeded the Sovietization of Western Ukraine. Accordingly, the Soviet government prioritized the suppression of the "Ukrainian bourgeois nationalists" by any methods. On August 7, 1944, the Supreme Court issued a special resolution, authorizing the courts to qualify the activities of the OUN members under Articles 54-1a, 54-1b, and 54-11 of the Criminal Code of the Ukrainian SSR as high treason. Accordingly, from 1946 to 1957 Soviet courts tried 52,610 alleged guerrillas and their sympathizers for guerrilla activities, in contrast to 41,585 individuals sentenced for treason, collaboration, and defection to the enemy,[74] and the Soviet propaganda consistently portrayed the guerrillas as collaborators and "German lackeys." In many cases, however, such propaganda method was not too far-fetched as thousands of defendants had indeed served in the German administration and police forces and directly participated in roundups, executions, and brutal "pacifications."[75]

In May 1945 the NKVD tribunal of the Volhynia oblast charged ten OUN members with being "active enemies" of the Soviet state. The key defendant Mikhail Yarmoliuk joined the Ukrainian auxiliary police in the Volhynia region in August 1941 and took part in arrests and mistreatment of local residents suspected in anti-German activities. He also participated in the anti-partisan operations and guarded the Jewish ghetto in Kovel. In June 1943 Yarmoliuk deserted from the police and joined the UPA (alongside many other Ukrainian policemen); as an experienced policeman, he graduated from the OUN security service school and became a district security chief. In this capacity, he fought the Soviet partisans, the NKVD, and the Red Army units, and organized the murder of residents suspected in pro-Soviet sympathies. Yarmoliuk's brother Mina and the other defendants had similar records, participating in combat against the Red Army and carrying out executions of alleged Soviet sympathizers.[76]

According to Article 54-11 (participation in anti-Soviet organizations), membership in OUN alone sufficed for harsh sentences. The defendants' guerrilla activities, murder of civilians (although the prosecution possessed no evidence except the defendants' confessions), arson, and fight against the Red Army were absorbed into the charge of high treason.[77] As the most active members of the group, Yarmoliuk and his brother were sentenced to death under Article 54-1a and Article 54-1b (the equivalents of Article 58-1a and Article 58-1b in the Ukrainian criminal code) respectively; the remaining defendants were sentenced to forced labor as accomplices under Article 54-1a and Part 2 of the April decree.[78]

Similar to Western Ukraine, the crush of Sovietization campaign in 1940–1941 in the Baltic lands generated strong anti-Soviet sentiments, which erupted during the German invasion and thousands of people initially accorded the German troops enthusiastic reception. Although such attitudes were soon dampened by the Nazi contempt for the national aspirations of the Estonians, Latvians, and Lithuanians, they were allowed some veneer of national self-rule. Thousands volunteered for or were drafted in the native police and security forces, which played a crucial role in the German terror system and in the genocide of Jews.[79]

In January 1947 the security service arrested Adolf Skaistkalns, a member of the notorious Arajs commando—a special killing unit that murdered thousands of people (mostly Jews) throughout Latvia.[80] During the investigation, Skaistkalns admitted that he served in the political police of the "bourgeois" Latvia and that the police "combated the revolutionary movement in Latvia." Moreover, he admitted that in September 1941 he voluntarily joined the "punitive Arajs commando ... which fought for the establishment of the fascist power" and described in detail the commando's participation in the murder of 10,000 Jews in the Rumbula forest in December 1941. Skaistkalns described to the investigators how he had escorted Jews to the murder site but denied that he took direct part in the executions. In 1942–1943 alongside other members of the commando, Skaistkalns fought against the Red Army and the Soviet partisans.[81] Similarly, in another investigation case, Vasilii Purvinsh, Janis Labans, and Karl Roshkalis were also volunteers to the Arajs commando, participating in anti-partisan operations and in the executions of the "Soviet citizens of Jewish nationality."[82] Admissions of guilt and the voluntary enlistment in the commando made it clear for the investigation and the courts that Skaistkalns, Purvinsh, Labans, and Roshkalis acted out of ideological convictions and deserved the ultimate penalty. They were lucky, however, for in May 1947 the death penalty in the Soviet Union was temporarily abolished (it was reinstated in January 1950) and they were sentenced to prison or hard labor terms for "anti-Soviet activities" under Article 58-1a.[83]

The cases of Skaistkalns, Purvinsh, Labans, and Roshkalis underscored several key features of the postwar Soviet investigation methods and court proceedings. Most trials were conducted behind closed doors, without defense counsel, and often without a prosecutor, whose role was carried out by the judges. As a rule, all defendants attempted to conceal their wartime activities, often admitting guilt only under pressure during the nightly, or long hours of, questionings. To catch suspects lying, interrogators repeatedly asked the same questions and searched the execution sites, collecting evidence, which was then attached to criminal cases. More often than not documentary evidence was lacking, but in rare cases the investigation obtained defendants' reports of their wartime activities.[84] The investigation also found witnesses who offered chilling testimonies on the participation of the accused in the genocide. For example, seven former members of the Arajs commando testified in the case of Skaistkalns.[85]

Critically, in many court cases, the Holocaust played the critical role as the basis of the indictment. Traditionally, in the official Soviet presentation of the war the Holocaust was subsumed into the broad category of "murder of peaceful citizens." Thus, the April decree referred to "tens of thousands of innocent women, children, and the elderly were bestially tortured to death, hanged, shot, or burned alive." After the war the genocide of Jews almost completely disappeared from public discourse, but at the same time it often constituted the sole provable charge in the courtroom. For example, the investigation and trial records of Skaistkalns, Labans, Purvinsh, and Rozhkalns (as well as thousands of others) unequivocally referred to the "punitive Arajs commando created by the German Security Service (SD) for the mass murder of the Jewish population," in which the defendants actively took part. Similarly, a member of the Arajs commando Arnold Laukers was charged with participation in the murder of "17,000–18,000 Jews and Latvian communists."[86]

According to the Soviet criminal-procedural code, judges did not elaborate how the verdicts measured defendants' crimes against the existing legal norms. Although the indictments against Skaistkalns, Labans, Purvinsh, and Rozhkalns enumerated concrete instances of participation in mass murder and in roundups and arrests of Soviet citizens, all these deeds were inclusively classified as high treason.

Conclusion

By definition, the concept of high treason entails an attempt on a country's sovereignty and security. In the context of the Soviet political system, external security was inextricably linked to its domestic situation and Soviet law did not separate high treason from a much broader concept of "counterrevolutionary crimes." Accordingly, the Soviet war crime trials displayed an extreme degree of ideological prejudice, particularly as the postwar retributive justice played a crucial role in the state's agenda of consolidating its control over the territories that for some time remained under the enemy occupation. Suspicious of its own people and convinced that "traitors of the Motherland" revealed their true identities in time of crisis, the Soviet government continuously urged the security services and courts to be ruthless in expurgating society from such elements. Between 1941 and 1954 about 400,000 individuals were tried for collaboration with the enemy under Articles 58-1a and 58-1b and the April decree.[87] The trials were thus integrated into a continuous purification drive that aimed at eliminating dangerous, unreliable or counterproductive elements from Soviet society.[88]

At the first sight, these trials resembled the notorious "purges" of the 1930s. The military tribunals often applied "counterrevolutionary" articles of the Criminal Code and the government decrees as instruments of retribution, often disregarding the nuances of individual cases. Importantly, the Stalinist purges had decimated the Soviet security services and the judiciary, directly affecting the quality of the tribunals' members. Subjected to psychological pressure or physical abuse, many individuals admitted guilt and became innocent victims.[89]

However tempting it is to discard Soviet trials as a façade of ideologically contaminated justice, they should not be perceived merely as the blunt and blind instrument of Stalin's justice. During and after the war, the security services and the tribunals collected a massive amount of materials pertaining to crimes committed by the Axis powers and their native helpers. Many NKVD and NKGB operatives possessed considerable professional experience and meticulously investigated alleged criminal acts.

Critically, many defendants who were tried for nationalist or "anti-Soviet" activities had indeed collaborated with the Germans in different capacities, and were essential to the implementation of the Nazi terror system and the genocide of Jews. As a result, although by the late 1940s the Holocaust had virtually disappeared from the official discourse, Soviet courts consistently prosecuted those involved in the persecution and murder of Jews. In other words, many charges against individual perpetrators were real and many cases were prosecuted on their own merits. Also, while public opinion mattered much less in the Soviet Union than in Western Europe, by and large the Soviet population understood the trials as a fair punishment for the Nazi crimes.

The relentless pursuit and punishment of "traitors" and "collaborators" was a part of complex ideological, social, and administrative measures and although the charge of high treason was applied as a blanket repressive tool, it covered various criminal acts, largely conforming to contemporary international concepts of war crimes. The war crimes trials, therefore, served several functions at once: they rendered state justice, exposed political culture that profoundly affected the Soviet justice system, and reminded the alienated population of the regime's long memory and reach.[90]

Notes

1 V. M. Chebrikov, G. F. Grigorenko, N. A. Dushin, and F. D. Bobkov, *Istoriia sovetskikh organov gosbezopasnosti* [History of the Soviet Security Services] (Moscow: Vysshaia Krasnoznamennaia shkola KGB pri Sovetie Ministrov SSSR imeni F. E. Dzerzhinskogo, 1977), 21.
2 Viacheslav Zviagintsev, *Voina na vesakh Femidy: voina 1941-1945 gg. v materialakh sudebno-sledstvennykh del* [War on the Scale of Lady Justice: The War of 1941-1945 in the Judicial-Investigative Cases] (Moscow: Terra, 2006), 15–16; Tanja Penter, "Local Collaborators on Trial: Soviet War Crimes Trials under Stalin (1943-1953)," *Cahiers du monde russe et soviétique* 49/2–3 (2008), 342.
3 For example, Tanja Penter, "Collaboration on Trial: New Source Material on Soviet Postwar Trials against Collaborators," *Slavic Review* 64/4 (2005), 782–90; Ilya Bourtman, "'Blood for Blood, Death for Death': The Soviet Military Tribunal in Krasnodar, 1943," *Holocaust and Genocide Studies* 22/2 (2008), 246–65; Vanessa Voisin, "*Au nom des vivants*, de Léon Mazroukho: rencontre entre denunciation officielle et hommage personnel," in Valérie Pozner and Natacha Laurent, eds., *Kinojudaica. Les représentations des Juifs dans le cinéma russe et soviétique des années 1910 aux années 1980* (Paris: Nouveau Monde éditions, 2012), 365–407.

4 V. N. Riabchuk, *Gosudarstvennaia izmena i shpionazh: ugolovno-pravovoe i kriminologicheskoe issledovanie* [High Treason and Espionage: Criminal-Legal and Criminological Research] (Sankt-Peterburg: Izdatel'stvo R. Aslanova "Iuridicheskii tsentr Press," 2007), 54.

5 V. N. Kudriavtsev and A. I. Trusov, *Politicheskaia iustitsiia v SSSR* [Political Justice in the USSR] (St. Petersburg: Iuridicheskii tsentr Press, 2002), 19–22; Amir Weiner, *Making Sense of War: The Second World War and the Fate of the Bolshevik Revolution* (Princeton-Oxford: Princeton University Press, 2001), 21–22.

6 S. M. Rakhmetov, S. A. Krementsov, and M. O. Kolkobaev, *Prestupleniia protiv osnov konstitutsionnogo stroia i bezopasnosti gosudarstva* [Crimes against the Fundamentals of the Constitutional Order and State Security] (Almaty: TOO "Baspa," 1998), 3.

7 Riabchuk, *Gosudarstvennaia izmena*, 53–54; V. I. Kurlianskii and M. P. Mikhailov, eds., *Osobo opasnye gosudarstvennye prestupleniia* [Particularly dangerous state crimes] (Moscow: Gosudarstvennoe izdatel'stvo iuridicheskoi literatury, 1963), 49–52; Rakhmetov, Krementsov, and Kolkobaev, *Prestupleniia protiv osnov*, 4.

8 A. A. Gertsenzon, Sh. S. Gringauz, N. D. Durmanov, M. M. Isaev, and B. S. Utievskii, *Istoriia sovetskogo ugolovnogo prava* [History of Soviet Criminal Law] (Moscow: Iuridicheskoe izdatel'stvo Ministerstva Iustitsii SSSR, 1948), 321.

9 Riabchuk, *Gosudarstvennaia izmena*, 55.

10 V. D. Men'shagin and I. S. Romashkin, eds., *Nauchno-prakticheskii kommentarii k zakonu ob ugolovnoi otvetstvennosti za gosudarstvennye prestupleniia* [Scientific-Practical Commentary to the Law on Criminal Responsibility for State Crimes] (Moscow: Gosudarstvennoe izdatel'stvo iuridicheskoi literatury, 1960), 4–5; M. V. Turetskii, *Osobo opasnye gosudarstvennye prestupleniia* [Particularly Dangerous State Crimes] (Moscow: Izdatel'stvo Moskovskogo universiteta, 1965), 13–14.

11 "Polozhenie o presupleniiakh gosudarstvennykh (kontrrevolutsionnykh i osobo dla Soiuza SSR opasnykh prestupleniiakh protiv poriadka upravleniia)," [Regulation on State Crimes (Counter-Revolutionary and Particularly Dangerous Crimes against the USSR and the State Order)], *Svod zakonov SSSR*,[Code of Laws of the USSR] March 11, 1927, n. 12, article 123, pp. 283–88; Turetskii, *Osobo opasnye prestupleniia*, 14; M. I. Iakubovich and V. A. Vladimirov, eds., *Gosudarstvennye prestupleniia: uchebnoe posobie po sovetskomu ugolovnomu pravu* [State Crimes: The Manual for the Soviet criminal law] (Moscow: Gosudarstvennoe izdatel'stvo "Vysshaia shkola," 1961), 17–18.

12 S. S. Askarkhanov, *Ugolovnyi kodeks RSFSR redaktsii 1926 goda s postateino-sistematizirovannymi materialami* [Criminal Code of the RSFSR of the 1926 Edition with Article-Systematized Materials] (Moscow: Iuridicheskoe Izdatel'stvo NKIu RSFSR, 1927), 122, 126.

13 Rakhmetov, Krementsov, and Kolkobaev, *Prestupleniia protiv osnov*, 5.

14 Postanovlenie TsIK SSSR ot 8 iunia 1934 g. "O dopolnenii Polozheniia o prestupleniakh gosudarstvennykh (kontrrevolutsionnykh i osobo dlia Soiuza SSR opasnykh prestupleniiakh protive poriadka upravleniia) stat'yami ob izmenie Rodinie," [Decree of the CIK USSR of June 8, 1934, "On the Appendage of the Clauses of High Treason to the Regulation on State Crimes (Counter-Revolutionary and Particularly Dangerous Crimes against the USSR and the State Order by)"] in I. N. Kuznetsov, ed., *Istoriia gosudarstva i prava Rossii v dokumentakh i materialakh 1930-1990-e gg.* [History of State and Law of Russia in Documents and Materials] (Minsk: Amalfeia, 2003), 73–74. In 1958 the "Statute of Criminal Responsibility for High Treason" was replaced by the "Law of Criminal Responsibility for State Crimes."

15 Riabchuk, *Gosudarstvennaia izmena*, 58–59; Kurlianskii and Mikhailov, *Osobo opasnye gosudarstvennye prestupleniia*, 74–75.
16 I. T. Goliakov, *Sovetskoe pravo v period Velikoi Otechestvennoi voiny* [Soviet Law During the Great Patriotic War] (Moscow: Iuridicheskoe izdatel'stvo Ministerstva Iustitsii SSSR, 1948), 2: 203; Oleg V. Khlevniuk, *Master of the House: Stalin and His Inner Circle* (New Haven: Yale University Press, 2008), 196.
17 Solomon, *Soviet Criminal Justice*, 236–37.
18 Khlevniuk, *Master of the House* 204; Gábor T. Rittersporn, "Extra-Judicial Repression and the Courts: Their Relationship in the 1930s," in *Reforming Justice in Russia*, 208; Peter H. Solomon, Jr., *Soviet Criminal Justice under Stalin* (Cambridge: Cambridge University Press, 1996), 28–29; Chebrikov, *Istoriia organov*, 274.
19 Directives of the Politburo, August 17, 1940, December 7, 1940, in V. N. Khaustov, V. P. Naumov, and N. S. Plotnikova, eds., *Lubianka: Stalin i NKVD-NKGB-GUKR "Smersh" 1939-March 1946* [Lubianka: Stalin and NKVD-NKGB-GUKR "Smersh" 1939-March 1946] (Moscow: Mezhdunarodnyi fond "Demokratiia," 2006), 184, 201–04; Zviagintsev, *Voina na vesakh Femidy*, 549.
20 A. E. Epifanov, *Otvetstvennost' za voennye prestupleniia, sovershennye na territorii SSSR v gody Velikoi Otechestvennoi voiny* [Responsibility for War Crimes Committed on the Territory of the USSR during the Great Patriotic War] (Volgograd: Volgogradskaia akademiia MVD Rossii, 2005), 38–39; P. Zorin, *Soviet Military Tribunals* [Soviet Military Tribunals] (New York: Research Program on the U.S.S.R., 1954), 1–4.
21 Yakov Aisenshtat, *Zapiski sekretaria voennogo tribunala* [Notes of a Military Tribunal's Secretary] (London: Overseas Publications Interchange, Ltd., 1991), 5–6.
22 "Voennye tribunaly v usloviiakh Velikoi Otechestvennoi voiny," [The Military Tribunals in the Conditions of the Great Patriotic War] *Sotsialisticheskaia zakonnost'*, 7 (1942), 1–3; M. Grodzinskii, "Osobennosti ugolovnogo sudoproizvodstva v usloviiakh voennogo vremeni," [The Peculiarities of Criminal Proceedings in Wartime Conditions] *Sotsialisticheskaia zakonnost'*, 13–14 (1942), 10–11.
23 Goliakov, *Sovetskoe pravo*, 2: 173–74; Kurlianskii and Mikhailov, *Osobo opasnye prestupleniia*, 63; Zviagintsev, *Voina na vesakh Femidy*, 28–29; Aisenshtat, *Zapiski sekretaria*, 88.
24 Directives of the NKVD, December 16, 1941, February 18, 1942, in V. M. Lytvyn et al., *Kyiv u dni natsyts'koi navaly: za dokumentamy radians'kykh spetssluzhb* [Kiev during the Days of the Nazi Invasion: According to the Documents of the Soviet Special Services] (Kiev: Natsional'na Akademiia Nauk Ukrainy-Instytut Istorii Ukrainy, 2003), 372–85; Chebrikov, *Istoriia organov*, 361.
25 O.Iu. Makarov, "Kollaboratsionism i sotrudnichestvo v Velikoi Otechestvennoi Voine" [Collaborationism and Collusion in the Great Patriotic War], *Vestnik Nizhegorodskogo universiteta im. N.I. Lobachevskogo* 3/1 (2011), 187.
26 V. M. Nikol'skyi, *Represyvna diyal'nist' orhaniv derzhavnoi bezpeky SRSR v Ukraini (kinets' 1920-x-1950-ti rr.): istoryko-statystychne doslidzhennia* [Repressive Activities of the Soviet Security Services in Ukraine (late 1920s-1950s): A Historical-Statistical Research] (Donets'k: Vydavnytstvo Donets'koho natsional'noho universytetu, 2003), 205; report to Beriia, October 1941, in Khaustov, *Lubianka*, 317–318; Penter, "Local Collaborators on Trial," 343.
27 V. P. Iampol'skii, *Organy gosudarstvennoi bezopasnosti SSSR v Velikoi Otechestvennoi voinie: sbornik dokumentov* [The Soviet Security Services in the Great Patriotic War: Collection of Documents] (Moscow: Izdatel'stvo "Rus," 2008), 2/2: 423–14;

T. Vrons'ka, "Phenomen 'posobnytstva': do problem kvalifikatsii spivpratsi tsyvil'noho naselennia z okupantamy u pershyi period Velykoi Vitchyznianoi viiny," [Phenomenon of Collaboration: To the Problem of Qualification of Collaboration of Civil Population with the Occupiers at the Initial Period of the Great Patriotic War] p. 90, in http://www.history.org.ua/index.php?article=war_2008_11_88 (accessed on December 20, 2013). I am grateful to Tetjana Pastushenko for referring me to this site.

28 For example, see Tanja Penter, "Die locale Gesellschaft im Donbass under deutscher Okkupation 1941-1943," in Christoph Dieckmann et al., eds., *Kooperation und Verbrechen: Formen der "Kollaboration" im östlichen Europa, 1939-1945* (Göttingen, 2003), 183–223 in series *Beiträge zur Geschichte des Nationalsozialismus*, vol. 19; Martin C. Dean, *Collaboration in the Holocaust: Crimes of the Local Police in Belorussia and Ukraine, 1941-1944* (New York, 2000).

29 Vrons'ka, "Phenomen 'posobnytstva,'" pp. 90–91.

30 Epifanov, *Otvetstvennost'*, 39.

31 V. S. Khristoforov, *Organy bezopasnosti SSSR v 1941-1945 gg.* [The Soviet Security Services in 1941-1945] (Moscow: Izdatel'stvo Glavnogo arkhivnogo upravleniia Moskvy, 2011), 174–75; Epifanov, *Otvetstvennost'*, 39.

32 A memo of V. N. Merkulov to Stalin and the Politburo, March 19, 1943, in Khaustov, *Lubianka*, 361–71.

33 Sergey Kudriashov and Vanessa Voisin, "The Early Stages of 'Legal Purges' in Soviet Russia (1941-1945)," *Cahiers du monde russe* 49, 2/3 (2008), 290.

34 The text of the decree in *Velikaia Otechestvennaia* (The Great Patriotic War) (Moscow: "Terra-Terra," 1993–1999), 2/3: 130–31.

35 *Velikaia Otechestvennaia*, 2/3: 130–31; Kudriashov and Voisin, "The Early Stages of 'Legal Purges,'" 291. The decree was no longer used after February 1953, when the Supreme Court of the USSR ruled that war crime trials were to be adjudicated in accordance with the Criminal Code of the USSR. Officially, the decree was terminated on January 11, 1983, by the Presidium of the Supreme Council of the USSR. Epifanov, *Otvetstvennost'*, 25.

36 Zviagintsev, *Voina na vesakh Femidy*, 624; Goliakov, *Sovetskoe pravo*, 2: 51. Epifanov, *Otvetstvennost'*, 22–23, 40.

37 Epifanov, *Otvetstvennost'*, 25, 29, 69.

38 A. M. Beliãev et al., *Kuban' v gody Velikoĭ Otechestvennoĭ Voĭny, 1941-1945: khronika sobytiĭ* [Kuban' during the Great Patriotic War 1941-1945: The Chronicle of Events] (Krasnodar: Sov. Kuban': 2000–2003), 2: 354–55.

39 Epifanov, *Otvetstvennost'*, 180; Aisenshtat, *Zapiski sekretaria*, 87–90; *Kuban' v gody Voĭny*, 2: 356–57.

40 *Kuban' v gody Voĭny*, 2: 418.

41 Vanessa Voisin, *L'URSS contre ses traîtres L'Épuration soviétique (1941-1955)* (Paris: Publications de la Sorbonne, 2015), 259.

42 Ilya Bourtman, "Blood for Blood, Death for Death," 250–56; "Rech' gosudarstvennogo obvinitielia general-mayora iustitsii tov. L.I. Yachenina," [Summation of the State Prosecutor Major-General L. I. Yachenin] http://wolfschanze.narod.ru/krasnodar/prok.htm (accessed February 7, 2014).

43 Bourtman, "Blood for Blood," 256.

44 Aisenshtat, *Zapiski sekretaria*, 75; Beria's memo to Stalin, January 8, 1944, in Khaustov, *Lubianka: Stalin i NKVD*, 407; a memo of the military procurator of the 56th Army, November 17, 1943, Iampol'skii, *Organy gosudarstvennoi bezopasnosti*, 4/2: 205–14.

45 Riabchuk, *Gosudarstvennaia izmena*, 920–21; Aisenshtat, *Zapiski sekretaria*, 21–23; Iampolskii, *Organy gosudarstvennoi bezopasnosti*, 4/2: 337; Epifanov, *Otvetstvennost'*, 39; Oleg Borisovich Mozokhin, "Statistika repressivnoi deiatel'nosti organov bezopasnosti SSSR," [Statistics of the Repressive Activities of the Soviet Security Services] http://istmat.info/node/255 (accessed on August 25, 2012).
46 Franziska Exeler, "The Ambivalent State: Determining Guilt in the Post-World War II Soviet Union," *Slavic Review* 75/3 (2016), 618–19; Voisin, *L'URSS contre ses traîtres*, 236–37.
47 Decree of the Plenum of the Supreme Court, November 25, 1943, in Iampol'skii, *Organy gosudarstvennoi bezopasnosti SSSR*, 4/2, 572–73; Epifanov, *Otvetstvennost'*, 19.
48 Epifanov, *Otvetstvennost'*, 19, 49.
49 Gertsenzon, Gringauz, Durmanov, Isaev, and Utievskii, *Istoriia sovetskogo ugolovnogo prava*, 454.
50 *United States Holocaust Memorial Museum* (USHMM), RG-31.018M, "Post-war crimes trials related to the Holocaust, 1937-1943 from the Archives of the Security Service of Ukraine," reel 56, case 19376, frame 000001203-1204. Due to problematic pagination, archival documents will be quoted according to contents or frame number.
51 Ibid., frame 000001203-1204.
52 Ibid., frame 000001204-1206.
53 USHMM, reel 57, case 13135, frame 00000923-925, 00000927.
54 Ibid., frames 0000936-939, 0000957, 0000983, 0001013-1014.
55 Ibid., frames 00001266, 00001274.
56 Ibid., frames 00001302-1305.
57 USHMM, reel 77, case 20347, frame 00001371-1373.
58 Ibid., frame 00001460-1461.
59 In April 1943 NKVD was divided into two branches—NKVD (internal affairs) and NKGB (state security). The Special Sections were fused into the Main Department of Counter-Intelligence (known by its abbreviation "SMERSh"), which was directly subordinated to the State Committee of Defense.
60 USHMM, reel 77, case 20347, frame 00001489-1492.
61 Chebrikov, *Istoriia organov*, 344–45; Epifanov, *Otvetstvennost'*, 69.
62 Khristoforov, *Organy bezopasnosti*, 260–61, 265–66; Epifanov, *Otvetstvennost'*, 75; a report of the 7th NKVD Infantry Division, November 4, 1943, in Iampolskii, *Organy gosudarstvennoi bezopasnosti*, 4/2: 506–09.
63 Chebrikov, *Istoriia organov*, 356, 477; Olaf Mertelsmann and Aigi Rahi-Tamm, "Cleansing and Compromise: The Estonian SSR in 1944-1945," *Cahiers du monde russe* 49/2 (2008), 327–28.
64 Headed by General Andrei Vlasov, who surrendered to the Germans in 1942, the Russian Liberation Army (*Russkaya osvoboditel'naya armiya*, ROA) was made up of Soviet POWs and defectors, fighting on the German side. In popular Soviet parlance they were referred to as "vlasovtsy."
65 E. Samoilov, "Ot beloi gvardii k fashizmu," [From the White Guard to Fascism], 122–46, and N. Chistiakov, "Razgrom semenovshchiny," [Destruction of Semenovshchina] pp. 147–66, in S. S. Maksimov and M. E. Karyshev, eds., *Neotvratimoe vozmezdie: po materialam sudebnykh protsessov nad izmennikami rodiny, fashistskimi palachami i agentami imperialisticheskikh razvedok* [Inevitable Retribution: On the Records of the Trials of the Traitors of the Motherland, Fascist Henchmen and Agents of the Imperialist Intelligence Services] (Moscow: Voennoe izdatel'stvo, 1987).

66 For example, Alexander V. Prusin, "Ukrainskaia politsiia i Kholokost v General'nom okruge Kiev, 1941-1943: deistviia i motivatsii," [The Ukrainian Police and the Holocaust in the General-Bezirk Kiev, 1941-1943: Actions and Motives] *Kholokost i suchasnis't'* 1 (2007): 30–59.

67 Chebrikov, *Istoriia organov*, 478; Igor Panchishin, "V rozyske oborotni," [In search of turncoats] in V. K. Kirilov and V. P. Krasnopevtsev, eds., *Kontrrazvedka* [Counter-intelligence] (Pskov: Izdatel'stvo organizatsionno-metodicheskogo tsentra, 1995), 254–76.

68 In 1946 the Soviet security organs were re-structured—NKVD and NKGB were turned into the ministries of internal affairs (MVD) and state security (MGB) respectively.

69 Chebrikov, *Istoriia organov*, 455.

70 Iu. N. Semin and O. Iu. Starkov, "Kavkaz 1942-1943 gody: geroism i predatel'stvo," [The Caucasus 1942-1943: Heroism and Betrayal] *Voenno-istoricheskii zhurnal*, 6 (1991), 38.

71 USHMM, RG-38.001, "Post-War War Crimes Trials from the Archives of the Ministry of Interior of Georgia SSR (ex-KGB archives)," reel 23, case 46198, frame 000020-000024.

72 Ibid., frame 000024-000032.

73 Ibid., frame 000032-000036.

74 Nikol'skyi, *Represyvna diial'nis't'*, 111–12, 210.

75 USHMM, RG-31.018M, reel 2, case 43111, interrogation minutes; reel 3, case 46872, interrogation minutes.

76 Ibid., reel 73, case 1058, frame 00000498-502.

77 Ibid., frame 00000502-00000505.

78 Ibid., frame 00000535-00000536.

79 For example, the natives made up the overwhelming majority of the SD apparatus in Estonia. See, Mertelsmann and Rahi-Tamm, "Cleansing and Compromise," 323–24.

80 Subordinated to the SD, the "Sonderkommando Arajs" was named after its commander Viktors Arājs.

81 USHMM, RG-06.027, "Latvian State Archives of the Former Latvian KGB (State Security Committee) records from Fond 1986 relating to war crimes investigations and trials in Latvia, 1941-1995 (bulk 1944-1966)," microfiche 1, case 702, interrogation minutes and indictment.

82 Ibid., microfiche 1, case 909, arrest warrants and interrogation minutes. Names are spelled in accordance with investigation and trial records.

83 Ibid., microfiche 1, case 702, verdict; microfiche 3, case 909, verdict.

84 USHMM, RG-26.004M, "War crimes investigation and trial records from the former Lithuanian KGB Archives, 1944-1992," reel 1, case 9559, activity report of defendant Kasis Makauskas, June 28, 1941.

85 USHMM, RG-06.027, reel 1, case 24618, minutes of confrontation between defendants.

86 Ibid., microfiche 1, case 909, arrest warrant and indictment; microfiche 3, case 182, indictment.

87 The April decree was a wartime extraordinary measure and after the war, its application rapidly decreased—2,159 in 1947, 165 in 1950, 89 in 1951, 11 in 1952, and 6 in 1953. Mozokhin, "Statistika repressivnoi deiatel'nosti organov bezopasnosti SSSR." http://istmat.info/node/255 (accessed February 3, 2018).

88 See, for example, Juliette Denis, "Identifier les 'éléments ennemis' en Lettonie: Une priorité dans le processus de resoviétisation (1942-1945)," *Cahiers du monde russe*, 49, 2/3 (2008), 297–318.
89 Penter, "Local Collaborators," 346. For example, USHMM, RG-31.018M.0077, reel 7, case 19288, vol. 4, frame 0004704, defendant's appeal.
90 In the 1960s, the Soviet government resumed a widely publicized campaign of judicial persecution of wartime collaborators. See, Alexander Prusin, "The 'Second Wave' of Soviet Justice: The 1960s War Crimes Trials," in Norman J. W. Goda, ed., *Rethinking Holocaust Justice: Essays across Disciplines* (New York: Berghahn Press, 2018), 129–57.

3

Nikto ne zabyt: The Politicization of Soviet War Dead

Thomas Earl Porter

Emblazoned onto virtually every one of the war memorials in the former Soviet Union is the slogan "nikto ne zabyt, nichto ne zabyto" (no one will be forgotten, and nothing will be forgotten). The Soviet Union played a major role in the establishment of the International Military Tribunal (IMT) by resolutely promoting the idea of an international trial of Nazi Germany's leaders for the criminal actions perpetrated by its forces upon both civilians and prisoners of war during its invasion and occupation of the Soviet Union during the Second World War. At the very outset of the conflict the Soviet Union established "flying" military committees which collected evidentiary materials for later use in a future international judicial forum. Later, they would go to great lengths to document virtually every cow or pig that had been requisitioned or slaughtered by the invaders. Subsequently, a veritable cult of the Great Patriotic War would serve to buttress the regime's legitimacy and even today the anniversary of the end of the war is arguably the most important of Russian holidays. But the enormous death toll was composed of millions upon millions of non-Russians as well, and their story has been subsumed into the legitimizing narrative started with Stalin's famous "toast to the Russian people" upon the conclusion of hostilities.[1]

To be sure, the conduct of German forces after the invasion of the Soviet Union was recognized as criminal almost from the very start. On October 27, 1941, both US president Franklin Roosevelt and British prime minister Winston Churchill condemned their atrocities, with the latter opining that "the punishment of these crimes must now be included among the major aims of the war."[2] The Nazis' callous indifference to the peoples of the Soviet Union pointed to the difference between Hitler's war in the West and the brutal *Rassenkampf* (racial struggle) in the East. The racist nature of this conflict can be seen in the plans for the war of annihilation outlined in the "General Plan for the East" drawn up by Heinrich Himmler. It called for the "removal" of 80 million people from Russia to allow for its colonization by Germans. This document, which was to have been presented to Hitler upon the occasion of the final defeat of the Soviet Union, was to be the blueprint by which all of Russia would be turned into a colony to furnish raw materials and slave labor for Germany while also obtaining the *Lebensraum* (living space) Hitler had been dreaming of since he dictated *Mein Kampf*

(My Struggle) to Rudolf Hess in Landsberg Prison in 1924. Stalin, in an address to his generals underground in Moscow on November 6, 1941, asserted this link between the plans of the Nazi leadership and the actions of German forces in the field when he stated that "the German invaders want a war of extermination with the peoples of the USSR," and "if the Germans want a war of extermination they will get it."[3] Throughout the war the Soviet Union continually pointed out not only the glaring violations by the Nazis of international treaties regarding the conduct of war and treatment of both civilians and prisoners of war but also this direct link to and criminal responsibility of the civilian and military leadership of Nazi Germany for any actions committed by their subordinates in the field.

Only a handful of Western scholars have noted that the Soviets were not only early proponents of the use of the legal principle of conspiracy (which had been used in the infamous show trials domestically but had no place in continental European jurisprudence) but also played an instrumental role in establishing the principle that aggressive war in and of itself could be legally construed as a criminal act.[4] Of course, neither of these concepts were entirely novel. The Preamble of the Covenant of the League of Nations adumbrated the aim of the international movement to outlaw aggressive war by asking its members "to promote international cooperation and to achieve international peace and security by the acceptance of obligations not to resort to war."[5] Article 10 of the Covenant still more specifically inveighed against "aggression." Of even more significance was the General Treaty for the Renunciation of War (also known as the Kellogg-Briand Pact) which was signed by fifteen nations (including Weimar Germany) on August 27, 1928, and registered as part of the League of Nations Treaty Series a week later, which explicitly called for the renunciation of war between the contracting parties as a solution to any kind of conflict. Article II of the treaty stated that "the settlement or solution of all disputes or conflicts of whatever nature or of whatever origin they may be . . . shall never be sought except by pacific means."[6]

Eventually, another forty nations (including the Soviet Union just two days later, on August 29) indicated their intention to subscribe to the treaty's provisions. The Soviet Union also concluded supplemental treaties with Latvia, Estonia, Poland, and Romania (the so-called Litvinov Protocols) on February 9, 1929, which reiterated the Pact's provisions and were signed separately since that treaty had not yet been ratified by enough states to come into legal force. The Soviet Union never formally signed the Pact but its entrance into the League of Nations in 1934 legally required it to assent to any treaties that had been adopted by that body. The Soviet Union also signed a series of nonaggression pacts with its neighbors in the 1930s (including, of course, the notorious Molotov-Ribbentrop Pact) which made the Soviet Union a leading advocate for the diplomatic principle of collective security. To that end, as Francine Hirsch has observed, the brilliant Soviet jurist Aron Trainin had in 1937 published his *The Defence of Peace and Criminal Law* in which he castigated the League of Nations for failing to make aggressive war a criminal offense and for not providing for any sort of international court to punish aggressors. Notable in this regard was the fact that Andrei Vyshinsky, Stalin's procurator general, wrote an introduction to the book in which he asserted that "criminal law must be utilized for defending peace, and must be mobilized against war and against the instigators of war."[7] Kirsten Sellars notes, however, that

Trainin was not the first to put forward this precept and that it had not developed as the result of "any single national monologue, but as an intermittent *international* dialogue involving jurists in the Soviet Union, Britain, and the United States."[8]

But Trainin had indeed forcefully "advanced the idea of individual responsibility for international crimes . . . the realization of which was established during the course of the Nuremberg deliberations." Trainin's second major work, *On the Criminal Responsibility of the Hitlerites* (*Ob ugolovnoi otsvetsvennosti gitlerovtsev*) was published in 1944 and had also been almost immediately translated into English, had reiterated the argument that "peace is the greatest social value" and that war itself should be a punishable criminal act. Ginsburgs called it "a pioneering attempt to gain recognition for the phenomenon of crimes against peace."[9] Even though the legal principle of conspiracy to commit a criminal offense had no place in continental European law the Soviets had earlier found it a useful tool with which to prosecute the accused in their Show Trials and they now seized upon the concept as a vehicle to try the Nazi leadership. Francine Hirsch notes that "the Soviets were keen proponents of this charge from early on, recognizing its great utility."[10] Trainin would vigorously advocate for the charge of "conspiracy" to commit aggressive war as well by devoting a chapter to the concept of complicity, defining it as "a complex phenomenon" that "embraces various understandings among criminals" and can include "the dangerous form of participation in an organization." Members of such organizations may not know each other "but should answer for all their criminal activities."[11] Many Western accounts do indeed wholly attribute the use of the conspiracy charge as well as the concept of "aggressive" war to American ingenuity but there is at least some evidence that the Soviets also contributed to the jurisprudence at Nuremberg.[12]

The Soviet leadership would in fact consistently call for individual political, military, and business leaders to be tried for their complicity in the launching of a war of aggression after the invasion of the Soviet Union. In the first of his four wartime notes on November 25, 1941, People's Commissar for Foreign Affairs Molotov had described the reprehensible treatment of Soviet prisoners of war and laid "all responsibility for these inhuman actions of the German military and civil authorities on the criminal Hitlerite government."[13] For their part the Germans asserted that they were not bound to adhere to such strictures since the Soviet Union had not been a signatory to international agreements such as The Hague Conventions of 1899 and 1907, and especially the Geneva Convention in 1929. This was immaterial since, unlike the Kellogg-Briand Pact that only called for no force to be used between signatories in a dispute, the Geneva Convention's stipulations concerning the treatment of POW's were binding upon any state that acceded to the agreement so long as the opposing side accepted and applied the provisions. The Soviets insisted they had de facto agreed to adhere to the rules governing the conduct of military forces vis-à-vis prisoners of war. In Molotov's note of April 27, 1942, by which time the scope and enormity of Nazi crimes against Soviet prisoners was all too apparent, with over 2 million of them dead, he wrote:

> Being true to the principles of humanity and respect for its international obligations, the Soviet government even in present circumstances does not intend to resort to reprisals against German war prisoners, and continues to abide by

the undertakings as regards the regime of war prisoners, which the Soviet Union assumed under The Hague Conventions of 1907, which was signed, but is now treacherously violated in all its provisions, by Germany.[14]

Of course, the Soviet government had also completely disregarded these international laws concerning the treatment of POW's during its campaigns against Finland and Poland in 1939 and 1940. And it has been irrefutably established and acknowledged by the Russian government that the Soviets executed over 25,000 Polish officers in the spring of 1940.[15] But the Soviet government's public pronouncements consistently demanded that the entire Nazi leadership be held accountable for war crimes committed by its forces. The Kremlin insisted that "severe punishment must overtake all who are guilty of these most atrocious crimes against culture and humanity, all the Hitlerite criminals without exception—from the lance-corporal in the army to the lance-corporal on the throne."[16] The atrocities perpetrated by German forces upon the prisoners of war and the civilian population were part of a criminal conspiracy to pursue a deliberate war of annihilation. In his note of January 6, 1942, Molotov delineated the "wholesale robbery, despoliation of population and monstrous atrocities" committed by the Germans in the Soviet Union and noted that "the inhuman regime which has been established by the German-Fascist authorities for prisoners of war has become the lot of the civilian population."[17] Molotov once again took pains to emphasize the criminal conspiracy that was at the heart of Nazi policies in the Soviet Union:

> Irrefutable facts prove that the regime of plunder and bloody terror against the non-combatant population of occupied towns and villages constitutes not merely the excesses of individual German officers and soldiers, but a definite system previously planned and encouraged by the German Government and the German High Command.[18]

Molotov continued to put forward the Soviet demand for a war crimes trial using the conspiracy principle. He argued that "in reporting all these atrocities committed by the German invaders to all governments with which the USSR has diplomatic agreements the Soviet government lays all the responsibility for these inhuman and rapacious acts committed by the German troops on the criminal Hitlerite government of Germany."[19] Just one week later representatives of nine occupied states met in London and issued a declaration that demanded that the Allies

> place among their principal war aims the punishment, through the channels of organized justice, of those guilty or responsible for these crimes, whether they have ordered them, perpetrated them, or in any way participated in them.[20]

The signatories to this document also established a Commission for the Punishment of War Crimes. The principle that the entire political and military chain of command was just as guilty as the actual perpetrators in the field for any violations of the norms of war was already on its way to being established; the claim of "obedience to orders" would not be admissible as a defense.

On April 27, 1942, ten months after Hitler's invasion of the Soviet Union, Molotov sent a long, single-spaced note to "all embassies and ambassadors with which the USSR has diplomatic relations." The missive, "Concerning the Monstrous Crimes, Atrocities, and Acts of Violence of the German State in the Occupied Soviet Regions and the Responsibility of the German State for these Crimes," was a virtual indictment of the Nazi regime's conduct in the Soviet Union. In this extremely detailed explication of the atrocities committed by German forces Molotov noted that these transgressions were not random but instead were calculated and "not manifested as the episodic excesses of undisciplined military units."[21] The Soviet government collected countless battle reports, orders, and other documents that clearly proved that the Nazis' "bloody crimes and atrocities had been undertaken in accordance with the carefully compiled and elaborate plans of the German government and German High Command." This diplomatic note broke down the Nazis' heinous transgressions in Russia into a half dozen categories, including the methodical plunder of the country's population, the complete destruction of cities and villages, the enslavement of her people and deportation of several million more to Germany for forced labor, the veritable extermination of the Soviet population and prisoners of war, and the liquidation of Russian national culture and the cultures of other peoples of the Soviet Union.

Molotov took pains to point out that the evidence presented "not only supports the assertions of the Soviet government of the planned nature of these evildoings as outlined in the notes of 25 November 1941 and 6 January 1942," but also "shows that the Hitlerite government and its accomplices have reached the limits of cruelty and moral depravity in its bloody criminal attack on the freedom, welfare, culture and very life of the Soviet peoples."[22] The document went into explicit details of the myriad atrocities and crimes of German forces in Russia and connected the perpetration of those crimes with the military orders that had been captured, including several from Hitler and Göring. The grisly specifics of some of the many massacres of men, women, and children were presented, as well as detailed retellings of the numerous summary executions of citizens and the horrific treatment of Soviet prisoners. The wanton burning and looting of villages and destruction of equipment, buildings, and entire cities was chronicled and the looting of property was also carefully catalogued. The idea that these acts were not only criminal but committed as part of a plan determined by the highest civil and military authorities would become a key part of the Nuremberg Trial. Molotov promised in conclusion that "Hitler's government and its accomplices will not escape severe responsibility and deserved punishment for all their unparalleled crimes perpetrated against the peoples of the USSR and against all freedom loving peoples."[23]

The idea that the Nazi war effort was essentially a criminal undertaking and Germany's leading political and military figures ought to be brought before the bar of justice was being advanced forcefully by the Soviets by early 1942. Representatives of the European governments in exile had also met on January 13, 1942, in London at St. James's Palace and issued what became known as the Declaration of St. James. It demanded that the allies try war criminals for their crimes.[24]

In September of that year, in a speech in the House of Commons, Winston Churchill seemingly supported the Soviet position when he pledged the support of Great Britain in ensuring that "those who are guilty of the Nazi crimes will have to stand up before tribunals in every land where their atrocities have been committed in order that an indelible warning may be given to future ages" and Franklin Roosevelt declared that it would be US policy "that the successful close of the war shall include provision for the surrender to the United Nations of war criminals."[25] In October 1942 Roosevelt and Sir John Simon (the British Lord Chancellor) both proposed that a "United Nations Commission for the Investigation of War Crimes" be established to collect evidence and identify suspects. Two months later a joint declaration by the US, Britain, and the European governments in exile publicly accused the Nazis of "a bestial policy of extermination of the Jewish people in Europe," but the United Nations War Crimes Commission (UNWCC) did not meet until over a year had passed and the Soviet Union never even became a member of the commission.

The Soviets did seize upon the declaration by the United Nations to call yet again for the establishment of a war crimes tribunal for both civil and military leaders as well as the actual perpetrators. A diplomatic communiqué was sent that noted:

> The Soviet government approves and shares the just desire expressed in the collective note received, that those guilty of the crimes indicated shall be handed over to judicial courts and prosecuted, and that the sentences passed on them shall be put into execution.
>
> The Soviet government is ready to support all practical measures to this end on the part of the Allied and friendly governments, and counts upon all interested states giving each other mutual assistance in seeking out, handing over, bringing to court and passing sentence on the Hitlerites and their accomplices guilty of the organization, promotion, or perpetration of crimes on unoccupied territory.[26]

It was the Soviet government, however, that insisted upon an *international tribunal*, considering it

> essential to hand over without delay for trial before a special international tribunal, and to punish severely to the fullest extent of criminal law, any of the leaders of Fascist Germany who during the war have fallen into the hands of states fighting against Hitlerite Germany.[27]

Given Churchill's speech in Parliament and Roosevelt's repeated expressions of moral outrage one might think that the Allies were on the same page insofar as the idea of convening a postwar international war crimes trial was concerned. But that was manifestly *not* the case. Though the United States and Britain promised "retribution" through "organized justice," an undertaking that was echoed by the declaration of the governments in exile that "punishment, through organized justice of those guilty and responsible for those crimes, whether they have ordered them, or in any way participated in them" neither ally had any real interest in creating such a tribunal.[28] Both thought that the UNWCC should merely collect and catalogue evidence of war crimes while the Soviet Union pressed for its conversion into an international court that would be empowered to try war criminals such as Rudolph Hess. But the British and Americans were concerned lest retaliation be taken against their own men in German hands, and they much preferred simply pursuing justice through "executive action" after the war. In any case, the British pushed for the inclusion of representatives of their dominions in the UNWCC and the Soviets countered by demanding that representatives from Byelorussia, Ukraine, Moldavia, and the Baltic states then also be admitted. This was correctly understood to be but a cynical ploy for recognition of the incorporation of the Baltic states into the Soviet Union, and despite Roosevelt's assurance to Stalin at Tehran that he did not object to the annexation of these territories, the Soviets never joined the commission but instead would form their own.[29]

As Howard Ball has noted, as late as 1945 the Western Allies were largely agreed on a plan to summarily execute Nazi war criminals and tried to convince the Soviet Union to go along.[30] Most scholars are aware of US Secretary of the Treasury Henry Morgenthau's proposal drawn up in late 1944 to turn Germany into a veritable potato farm after the war.[31] Less well known, however, was the provision to distribute a list of 2,500 Nazi war criminals (including political and military leaders, police officials, industrialists, among others) to the advancing Allied troops so that they could be summarily executed upon capture.

Roosevelt and Churchill had met in Quebec in September 1944 and agreed with a proposal put forward by Lord Simon that called for the execution of Nazi war criminals. They further agreed "to put to Marshal Stalin Lord Simon's proposal for dealing with the major war criminals, and to concert with him a list of names."[32] Winston Churchill, writing just a week before Hitler's suicide and two weeks before Germany's formal unconditional surrender, had agreed with this idea, writing to Roosevelt of his unease with the Americans' conversion to the Soviet idea of an international war crimes trial:

> [His Majesty's Government is] deeply impressed with the dangers and difficulties of this course [judicial proceedings], *and they think that execution without trial is the preferable course* [italics mine]. [A trial] would be exceedingly long and elaborate, [many of the Nazis deeds] are not war crimes in the ordinary sense, nor is it at all clear that they can properly be described as crimes under international law.[33]

Churchill would later claim that Stalin's remark at the Tehran conference that fifty thousand of Hitler's henchmen ought simply to be "rounded up and shot at the end of the war" was in fact indicative of Stalin's "serious intent." Since the historical record clearly shows otherwise it is probable that Stalin was merely poking fun at the prime minister for his reluctance to endorse the idea of an international war crimes trial. Even ruthless dictators can have a sense of humor. Stalin's true intentions can be seen in the agreements ultimately agreed upon at the Moscow Conference in 1943. It was reported that

> the Russians . . . insisted on a declaration concerning the punishment of those individuals responsible for German atrocities . . . [and] contended that the category of such war criminals embraced everyone from the Nazi higher-ups . . . down to the meanest *Wehrmacht* private . . . in the gruesome fulfilment of . . . directives.[34]

The joint resolution issued by the Big Three at the behest of the Soviet Government had only agreed that major political and military figures whose crimes had "no particular localization" would be "punished by the joint decision of the Governments of the Allies." Of course, this vague formulation was merely a sop to the Soviets who were still insisting on an international war crimes trial. It was, however, agreed that "petty associates" would be "brought back to the scene of their crimes and judged on the spot by the peoples they have outraged" and further pledged to "pursue them to the uttermost ends of the earth and . . . deliver them to their accusers in order that justice be done."[35] The Soviets, however, continued to demonstrate their commitment to justice; just a week after the Moscow Conference Stalin said:

> Together with our Allies, we must adopt measures to ensure that all the Fascist criminals responsible for the present war and the sufferings of the people, should bear stern punishment and retribution for all the crimes perpetrated by them no matter in what country they may hide.[36]

Stalin had already called for the implementation of such a framework for justice a year earlier in his speech of November 6, 1942: "We know who the men are that are guilty of these outrages . . . their names are known to tens of thousands of tormented people. Let these butchers know that they will not escape responsibility for their crimes or elude the avenging hands of the tormented Nations." US Secretary of War Henry Stimson had disagreed with Morgenthau's plan and had also believed all along that an international judicial proceeding was required.[37] It was his department that devised the outlines of the criminal indictment that ultimately would be utilized at Nuremberg. The plan charged the Nazi regime with a criminal conspiracy to wage aggressive war and commit crimes against humanity:

> The whole movement had been a deliberate, concerted effort to arm for war, forcibly seize the lands of other nations, steal their wealth, enslave and exploit their populations, and exterminate the . . . Jews of Europe.[38]

This idea, of course, had already been put forward by Trainin and espoused by the Soviets. Francine Hirsch has made the argument that it was in fact Trainin's book, translated immediately into English, French, and German, that proved instrumental in preparing the groundwork for the legal justification for the charges leveled at Nazi leaders at the IMT. Using archival materials she showed how the book was discussed in October 1944 at a meeting of the United Nations War Crimes Commission and ultimately was reviewed by officials in both the State and War Departments of the United States. One of those officials was a War Department lawyer named Murray Bernays. It would be he who ultimately drew up the American plan to charge the German leadership with criminal conspiracy. Bernays even cited Trainin's definition of a "crime against peace" in his memo to the White House. Eventually, Bernays's use of the legal charge of "conspiracy" (as opposed to Trainin's use of the term "complicity") would enshrine the former as the progenitor of the charge leveled at Nuremberg. But Robert Jackson, who would act as the US chief prosecutor at Nuremberg, had also agreed with Trainin's argument.[39] Trainin's definition would essentially form the basis for the charges of "war crimes" and "crimes against humanity" lodged against the Nazi leadership at Nuremberg. And his definition of "complicity" was subsumed by the charge in the Nuremberg Charter that agreed that "leaders, organizers, instigators, and accomplices participating in the formulation or execution of a common plan or conspiracy to commit" war crimes "are responsible for all acts performed by any persons in execution of such plan."[40]

So, even though most histories credit the United States with the major legal innovations of the Nuremberg Trials, Hirsch concludes that the Soviets played at least an equal role in formulating the legal rationales for crimes against peace and complicity. Moreover, as we have seen, they had insistently called for an international trial to bring the Nazi criminals to justice; unlike Roosevelt and Churchill who had met in Quebec in September 1944 and agreed with a proposal put forward by Lord Simon that called for the summary execution of Nazi war criminals. It was here that they agreed to compile the list of names of those to be prosecuted for war crimes.[41] Roosevelt had himself evidently not seriously entertained the idea of a postwar trial, and extrajudicial executions in keeping with Lord Simon's and Morgenthau's plans remained the official policy until early 1945 when, after the massacre of captured US Army soldiers at Malmedy in Belgium on December 17, 1944, an enraged American public demanded justice. The massacre of these eighty-four American soldiers had finally galvanized public and official opinion as to the criminality of the Nazis. Although undoubtedly sympathetic to the reports of the millions upon millions of murdered Jews, Soviet prisoners of war, and civilians that had taken place so far away, it was this event that led to the demand for the punishment of those responsible for such atrocities.

Even US attorney general Francis Biddle, who had opined that there should not be any prosecution of prewar acts or acts against German nationals and that the War Department's idea of charging Nazi political and military leaders with conspiracy should be dropped, now wrote that Malmedy was just part of a "purposeful and systematic conspiracy to achieve domination of other peoples by deliberate violations of the rules of war as they have been accepted and adhered to by the nations of the world."[42] The fact that the massacre was perpetrated by the *Waffen SS* (Armed SS) also led Biddle to agree with the plan (as finally drawn up by Murray Bernays) to charge the German leadership with criminal conspiracy. He later wrote that it "was the shooting of American officers and soldiers after their surrender at Malmedy by an SS regiment, *acting under orders*" (italics mine) that convinced him. Stimson and Secretary of State Cordell Hull seized on this opportunity to argue:

> While [executive action . . . arrest and execution] has the advantage of a sure and swift disposition, it would be violative of the most fundamental principles of justice, common to all the United Nations. This would encourage the Germans to turn these criminals into martyrs and in any event, only a few individuals could be reached in this way. Consequently, [although there are serious legal difficulties involved in a judicial proceeding], we think that the just and effective solution lies in the use of the judicial method . . . [which] will, in addition, make available for all mankind to study in future years an authentic record of Nazi crimes and criminality.[43]

Roosevelt finally agreed and brought up the idea of an international war crimes trial with Churchill and Stalin at the Yalta Conference in February 1945. For Stalin, who had been calling for precisely such a trial for several years now, it must have indicated that the criminal nature of the Nazi occupation in the East was finally being recognized by his allies. But Churchill instead continued to insist on the summary execution of top Nazis through to the beginning of April 1945. It was only after the liberation of the Nazi concentration camps and extermination centers that the British grudgingly assented to the idea. Even then, as late as the summer of 1945 (this after Churchill's departure from office and the London Conference had already convened in June to determine the procedures for the IMT) the British again asserted it would be far easier and save everybody time by simply shooting the defendants.

But the Soviet Union had been preparing for several years for just such a trial. In July 1942 a draft proposal by G. Aleksandrov, head of the Propaganda and Agitation section of the Central Committee of the Communist Party, was circulated that called for the establishment of an "Extraordinary State Commission for the investigation of atrocities, violence and other crimes committed by the German army on the regions of Soviet territory temporarily occupied and an account of the damage inflicted by the German-Fascist forces on the population of the USSR and to the Soviet state."[44] Aleksandrov asserted that the "violence, mass murders, destruction of priceless material and cultural treasures of the Soviet people, and establishment of the forced labour regime" were the result of "a systematic plan which had earlier been devised and authorized by the German government and the German High Command."[45] Therefore, the "Soviet people demand retribution for the crimes of the German Fascist forces" and to that end it "was necessary to conduct an exact inventory of all the evil crimes of the Hitlerite army on the territory of the USSR, the violation of the norms of international law, of the rules and customs of the conduct of war."[46]

Aleksandrov, however, also noted the ad hoc nature of efforts to compile evidence for future use in war crimes trials. He wrote that "a series of organizations had taken it upon themselves to undertake such an inventory as well as the collection of materials concerning the crimes of the German army." Such activities were "undertaken without a unified plan" and "organized poorly," therefore it was "necessary to provide for the formation of an Extraordinary State Commission which would be engaged in the investigation and inventory of crimes, atrocities, violence, and thievery of the German Fascist army and an accounting of this army's material damage to the Soviet state and to Soviet citizens." The commission would need to be invested with "special authority for the collection of all necessary materials" and would be responsible to the Sovnarkom (Council of People's Commissars, the Soviet government's cabinet).[47] On October 28 Aleksandrov forwarded to Molotov a draft decree from the Presidium of the Supreme Soviet concerning the establishment of an "Extraordinary State Committee [sic] for the inventory of the German-Fascist invaders' evildoings."[48] Molotov made extensive corrections on the proposal (including the name of the commission) and added that the principal purpose of the commission would be to oversee "the unification and conformity of the inventory already being conducted by Soviet state organs of the crimes and damage inflicted by the invaders."[49]

In addition to a full accounting of the damages inflicted upon the Soviet Union, the commission would also be charged with "establishing, in all cases where circumstances permitted, the identity of the German-Fascist criminals, the guilty in organizations which have committed evildoings on occupied Soviet territory, with the goal of bringing these criminals to justice and to their most severe punishment."⁵⁰ Thus, on the basis of the October 1942 declaration the Soviets in November set up an "Extraordinary State Commission for ascertaining and investigating crimes perpetrated by the German-Fascist invaders and their accomplices, and the damage inflicted by them on citizens, collective farms, social organizations, State enterprises and institutions of the USSR." Announced in *Pravda* as a decree of the Presidium of the Supreme Soviet and as a resolution from the Council of People's Commissars, this body was charged with compiling the evidentiary materials for a future war crimes trial. A policy paper submitted to the commission by a Soviet jurist in February 1943 entitled "Organization of criminal prosecution for crimes connected with the war" called for the trial of Hitler and his minions on conspiracy charges before an international court in order to lay bare the evils of Nazism; the commission's charter was formally approved in March 1943.⁵¹

The Soviets had in fact already begun to lay the foundation for such a tribunal with the trial of three German prisoners of war in the city of Kharkov in December 1943. In his August 1943 article "The Responsibility for Nazi Crimes," which was then broadcast (in English) two months prior to the meeting of the allies' foreign ministers in Moscow (and then reprinted in *Soviet Monitor*, again in English, and distributed to government agencies abroad by Soviet embassies), Trainin had reiterated his arguments on conspiracy and the criminal responsibility of the German political and business leadership. The Kharkov trial featured three accused war criminals who confessed to atrocious crimes but more important was the statement made by one of them that the principal war criminals were Hitler, Himmler, and Rosenberg.⁵² In addition, Trainin would later point to these proceedings and draw two more important conclusions. Although the Soviets were insisting that prisoners of war be treated in accordance with The Hague Conventions of 1907, Trainin was concerned lest war criminals use their status as prisoners to avoid their just punishment by being classified as both "bandit and as military personnel." But in perhaps his most important observation he said that these criminals might well try to find "legal" methods to evade responsibility by claiming they were acting under orders. One defendant in the Kharkov trial had made just such an argument by saying he had simply been following the orders of his superiors. Trainin noted the defendants "were tried for the misdeeds they themselves committed, with their own hands, for the crimes they committed personally. And for these crimes a command is not a defence."⁵³ The "orders are orders" defense eventually used at Nuremberg would, of course, be inadmissible.

In delivering the verdict, the judge said that these proceedings were "only a prototype of the coming of the not far distant court of peoples, which will mete out punishment to the band of leaders of fascism for all their loathsome crimes."⁵⁴ The Western Allies, of course, were not nearly as far along since as we have seen they had not yet definitively agreed to the idea of a postwar international war crimes tribunal but had merely agreed that the Germans' conduct of the war had in fact been criminal and that individuals could be tried at the scene of their crimes by the responsible authorities. But the Soviets had forged ahead in planning for the future war crimes tribunal. On April 3, 1943, a staff of 116 people with a budget of 2,669,000 roubles was approved.⁵⁵ Nikolai Shvernik was appointed as head of the commission. Other notables included Andrei Zhdanov (both he and Shvernik were also members of the Politburo), Andrei Vyshinsky, Trofim Lysenko, the writer Aleksei Tolstoi, and Semyen Budennyi. A secretariat was established to coordinate the gathering and collation of the evidentiary materials to be used in future war crimes trials; P. I. Bogoiavlenskii was appointed as its executive secretary. The secretariat included departments charged with recording the evidence of atrocities against Soviet citizens, damage to state and collective farms, damage to industry, transportation, and communications, damage to cooperatives, trade unions, and other civic organizations, damage to cultural, scientific, and medical institutions, churches, and so forth, and finally a department to collect the evidence of damage to Soviet citizens. Much like the party and state apparatus, sub-commissions were established at the republic and regional levels. Members always included the first secretary of the Central Committee of the Communist Party at each level (Nikita Khrushchev was head of the Ukrainian SSR's commission) as well as the chair or deputy chair of the Council of People's commissars and representatives from the local political police.[56]

Care was taken to ensure the participation in the commission's work of a representative cross section of Soviet officials and citizens, and in fact more than 7 million people supposedly took part in the process.[57] Instructions were adopted by the Commission on May 31, 1943, which required the staff of the commission to travel around the recently liberated areas of the Soviet Union and empower local committees to investigate Nazi crimes and atrocities. The statute required that these investigations be completed within one month of the area's liberation. Dossiers were meticulously compiled listing the details of Nazi crimes, the units and persons that had committed them, accomplices, and so forth, along with forensic reports, statements by local citizens and captured German documents. The commission ultimately collected more than a quarter million statements and estimated the damage to the regions surveyed at almost 700 billion roubles. Members of the commission reopened graves, exhumed bodies, and interrogated German prisoners of war. These prisoners

> went through a screening which divided officers from men, separated party and army SS troops, and Gestapo members from non-party men, and singled out individuals held accountable for specific atrocities, on the basis of evidence compiled by the ubiquitous War Crimes Commission, which had branches in every army division and every local soviet.[58]

In those areas that had seen enormous devastation, and where the local organs of government had not yet been reconstituted, special Red Army military intelligence units composed of officers and medical doctors investigated the crimes and drew up the protocols (*akty*), or findings of fact, which were then forwarded to the Main Political Administration of the Workers and Peasants Red Army (GLAVPURKKA) and from there sent on to the Extraordinary Commission.[59] These particular documents have not yet been studied and offer interesting contrasts with the records filed by the civilian local and regional commissions. Research into these documents indicates that the military committees faithfully recorded the eyewitness testimony of the locals and were extremely diligent in revealing the human cost of the war (as compared with the protocols of the Extraordinary Commission which seemingly were more attentive to material damage, perhaps with an eye toward future reparations). Of special interest is the fact that many of these Red Army officers were Jewish, especially the medical staff.

Both the civil and military commissions took down the testimonies of the eyewitnesses at the scene of the crimes and atrocities. In those reports where the victims were Jews, the term was at first written down as these eyewitnesses clearly indicated that Jews had been the principal victims. Yitzhak Arad has shown that these testimonies were often then altered and the word "Jews" replaced with "Soviet citizens." At the next level in many of the civilian *akty* the word "Jew" was found less frequently, and finally in the reports from the republic committee's the word was almost never to be found. The fact that some reports were indeed edited can be seen through a simple comparison of the initial reports by Red Army committees with those ultimately forwarded to Moscow by the union republic committees. For example, one of the earliest protocols documenting Nazi atrocities was submitted by a "flying" military committee to GLAVPURKKA in January 1942 by senior political instructor (*politruk*, or *politicheskii rukovoditel'*) Kriuchkin, political instructor Fadeikin, and medical officer Gurvich, which recorded the eyewitness testimony of several persons from the village of Alfer'evo, Volokolamsk district, Moscow region. In it the villagers recounted how "upon arrival in November 1941, the German soldiers and officers rounded up without exception all the Jews . . . they held them for hours in the cold after having taken from them all their warm clothing. Most of these people were women, old men and children. They shot these unfortunates and out of 100 persons 80 were killed and 20 were wounded. The Germans forbade the rendering of any kind of medical assistance to the wounded and the other 20 froze to death."[60] Other atrocities were also recounted in detail including the rape and "cruel treatment of our women and girls." The corresponding report forwarded by the regional committee to Moscow in 1944 repeated this information verbatim but read simply that "100 peaceful Soviet citizens" had been murdered.[61]

In other words, a deliberate decision was made as to which victims would be commemorated. Arad has asserted that this concealment of the fate of Soviet Union's Jewish citizens was a policy set by Stalin from the very beginning of the war. To be sure, in public pronouncements the massacred Jews would, with very rare exceptions, usually be referred to only as "Soviet citizens" as Stalin used nationalism to rally support for the war effort.[62] Of course, one could argue that "Soviet" was not necessarily the same as "Russian" but the "fifth row" (*piataia grafa*) of the Soviet internal passport contained one's "national" identification and there is no doubt that most Russians saw themselves as the leading people of the Soviet Union; Stalin's famous wartime toast "to the Russian people" at the conclusion of hostilities well illustrates this conflation of identities. Molotov mentioned the Nazi effort to annihilate the Jews in just one of his four wartime diplomatic notes, and even then, while discussing the massacres at Babi Yar in September 1941 in his January 6, 1942, note, he included "Ukrainians, Russians, and Jews" among the tens of thousands murdered, despite the fact that virtually *all* of the victims were Jewish and were identified as such in their internal passports (and *not* as Ukrainians or Russians) and that two months after the massacre *Izvestiia* had noted that "information has been obtained from the reliable sources that in Kyiv, the Germans executed 52 thousand Jews—men, women, children."[63] While the evidence for Arad's assertion might seem prima facie to be compelling, this may have not been policy and may well have simply been the practice of Soviet *chinovniki* anticipating Stalin's wishes in a somewhat similar fashion to Nazi officials "working toward the Fuhrer."

In Molotov's working papers one can indeed often find specific, explicit discussion of the Nazi efforts at extermination of the Jews. To be sure these references were usually deleted or toned down prior to publication but it is doubtful that Molotov (whose own wife was, as is well known, Jewish) would have discussed this so forthrightly and openly in documents that were marked for distribution to Stalin if in fact it might have served to displease his master (and, as is also well known, he eventually divorced his wife at Stalin's behest and stood by silently when she was arrested and sent to Siberia after the war). For example, in the first draft of the October 1942 "Declaration of the Soviet Government Concerning the Implementation of the Plan of the Hitlerite Criminals for the General Extermination of Jews on Europe's Occupied Territory and the Responsibility of the German Government and all its Accomplices for this Bloody Evildoing," he specifically noted that the victims at Babi Yar, "more than 30,000 people," were Jews.[64]

And *Pravda* did publish the text of the December 18, 1942, joint declaration of twelve nations "On the Hitlerite Regime's Extermination of Europe's Jewish Population." As mentioned earlier this document noted that German forces have "brought to life Hitler's oft-expressed desire to eliminate the Jewish people in Europe." The declaration had concluded with the statement that the signatories "again emphasize their firm resolve to guarantee jointly with all of the United Nations, that the individuals responsible for these crimes will not escape their deserved retribution and they (the signatories) will accelerate their implementation of the necessary practical measures for the achievement of this stated goal." Two days later, in their own declaration the Soviets again highlighted the sufferings of the Russians, Ukrainians, and Byelorussians and opined that the Slavic peoples had also been marked for extermination.[65] The ministry of foreign affairs draft indignantly cast aspersions on the foreign perception that "allegedly, the requisitions, robbery and executions were directed 'only' against Jews." This sentence was crossed out by Molotov himself and not included in the final version.

And yet in still another draft version of the declaration (again with marginalia in Molotov's own hand) he waxed grandiloquent about the tolerance and lack of racism in the Soviet Union and the complete absence of such thoughts in Marxism-Leninism and asserted that "the younger generation of Jews [in the Soviet Union] had had absolutely no experience with anti-Semitism and racial chauvinism was unknown." He quoted Lenin as saying that "the use of the vile prejudices of the most uncivilized strata of the population against Jews to encourage . . . the monstrous slaughters of peaceful Jews, their wives and children . . . evokes such disgust from the entire civilized world." Molotov's exegesis also included, undoubtedly deliberately so, not just one but *two* quotes from Stalin. In the first instance Molotov noted that as the result of Hitler's racial theories Stalin had correctly pointed out that "the German people were the first, and would also be the final, victims of Hitlerism and that their anti-Semitism was the highest form of racial chauvinism, which will turn out to be the most dangerous form of cannibalism for them." In conclusion Molotov then quoted from one of Stalin's frequent notes to the Red Army that reminded its soldiers that they were "fighting in its great liberation struggle free from feelings of racial hatred . . . and free from such degrading sentiments because it [the Red Army] has been raised in the spirit of racial equality and respect for the rights of all people."[66]

In the final analysis then, the Soviets were of course very much aware of the Nazis' ongoing effort to exterminate the Jews. Molotov's working papers contain numerous documents detailing the extent and scope of the Holocaust in both the Soviet Union and the West. The highly specific information in these reports undoubtedly made it clear to the Soviet regime that the Jews were marked for total annihilation, despite the occasional snide aside about how "it was not only the Jews . . . but the entire [Soviet] population" that was targeted for such a fate. Molotov's papers included the observation that it was Hitler's "plan to concentrate 4 million Jews in Eastern Europe by the end of 1942 with the aim of their physical annihilation" and that "ultimately the plan contemplates the complete destruction of the multi-million Jewish population."[67] But the regime's official declarations made statements such as the following:

> The crimes and atrocities committed by the Hitlerite robbers, rapists, and hangmen against peace-loving Soviet citizens have already been revealed to the entire world. The large majority of the victims of these bloody riots are farmers, laborers, clerks and members of the Russian, Ukrainian, and Belorussian intelligentsia. Many are the victims among the Lithuanians, the Latvians, and the Estonians, among the Moldavians and people of the Karelo-Finnish Republic. *The Jewish minority in the Soviet population, which is not very large in number,* has suffered particularly at the hands of the blood-thirsty Hitlerite animals.[68] (Italics mine)

And *Pravda* continued to print articles that talked of Hitler's "plans to annihilate the Slavs . . . to expel and exterminate Russians, Poles, Czechs, Slovaks, Yugoslavs, Ukrainians, Belorussians."[69] In addition, at the end of the war, when the noted Soviet (and Jewish) writers Il'ia Ehrenburg and Vasilii Grossman tried unsuccessfully to publish *The Black Book*, their accounting of the magnitude of Jewish suffering at the hands of the Nazis, Georgii Aleksandrov, the head of the agitprop department and the individual who had been entrusted with setting up the Extraordinary Commission, wrote of the effort that they

> allege that the destruction of the Jews was a particularistic provocative policy and that the Germans established some kind of hierarchy in their destruction of the peoples of the Soviet Union. . . . The documents of the Extraordinary State Committee convincingly demonstrate that the Hitlerites destroyed, at one and the same time Russians, Jews, Byelorussians, Ukrainians, Latvians, Lithuanians, and other people of the Soviet Union.[70]

After hostilities were concluded the Americans were often able to dictate the specific protocols of the postwar judicial proceedings, such as the trial being held in Nuremberg instead of Berlin as the Soviets wished; in part this was because they had the major Nazi war criminals in their custody.[71] But it should be kept in mind that it was the Red Army that liberated the extermination camps of Auschwitz, Treblinka, Sobibor,

Belzec, Chelmno, and Majdanek. The photographs and films of the concentration camps in Germany itself were as close as most Americans or Britons came to the industrial murder carried out by the Nazis and, of course, they had not witnessed the wholesale industrial slaughter of millions of human beings in the East. Much of the documentation and evidence needed to convict the Nazi criminals would necessarily have to come from the Soviet investigations. The GPU "flying" military intelligence committees continued their work as the Red Army crossed into Poland. The first *Vernichtungslager* (extermination camp) liberated by the Soviets was Majdanek on July 23, 1944. One might think that after suffering through three years of German occupation and documenting the myriad atrocities and inhumane acts of the "fascist invaders" the members of the committee investigating the "death camp" outside of Lublin would have been inured to Nazi barbarism. But this was manifestly not the case as the reports of the second committee of the 1st Belorussian Front, which were immediately sent on to Aleksandrov via the Central Committee of the All-Russian Communist Party (Bolshevik), did not quite manage to conceal the shock the members felt at finally coming face to face with the depths of Nazi depravity.

One of the 1st Belorussian Front military committees present at the liberation of Majdanek submitted a preliminary report the very same day that stated that this camp "was not an ordinary camp . . . rather, it was a camp designed for the extermination of people."[72] The report detailed the discovery "of gas chambers, and two ovens for the cremation of corpses." The victims "included Russian [*sic*] prisoners of war, Poles that had been captured in 1939, political prisoners from various countries, and a significant number of Jews."[73] The members requested that "representatives of the Extraordinary Commission be sent immediately for the investigation of the Nazis' atrocities in this camp." The committee further requested that "moviemakers and photographers be sent as well in order adequately to document the unprecedented barbarism of the German Fascists as mere words simply cannot convey the horrors that have taken place here."[74]

Ultimately, the Soviets would get their international war crimes trial for the major planners and organizers of the myriad atrocities committed by the Nazi regime in the East and the actual perpetrators would indeed be tried at the scene of their crimes. Even before Hitler's suicide the United Nations Conference on International Organization met in San Francisco on April 25, 1945, to establish a successor to the discredited League of Nations. Representatives of the Soviet Union, United States, Great Britain, and France discussed a draft of a proposal by the United States that an IMT be convened to try Nazi war criminals. The following basic principles were agreed upon:

> First, trial of major war criminals rather than political disposition; second, return of criminals whose crimes had fixed geographical localization to the countries where their crimes were committed; third, an international military tribunal to hear the cases of the major war criminals.

The Four Powers then met in London in June 1945 to hammer out the framework for this process. The representatives agreed that the Nazi political and military leadership were to be charged with not only war crimes, crimes against humanity, and the violation of the rules of warfare but also launching a war of aggression.

Interestingly, both the Soviets and Americans argued that the treaties and conventions that had existed prior to the Second World War clearly showed that the world's peoples had recognized aggressive war as being an international crime and that, unlike the new concept of genocide, the sanctions that might be levied against individuals for their participation in this crime would not be "ex post facto." But while the Americans wanted to move forward and define "aggression," the Soviets insisted that this was a task for the United Nations, and Great Britain and France agreed with this position. Many general histories credit the United States with being in the forefront of the campaign to bring Nazi war criminals before the bar of justice, and as Francine Hirsch noted "Conventional wisdom about the trials give little attention to the substantive role that the Soviets had in all aspects of the IMT."[75] But it was the Soviet Union that immediately recognized the uniquely criminal aspects of the German war of annihilation and insistently called for such a tribunal. Many of the voluminous eyewitness protocols that were compiled by the Extraordinary Commission would be admitted as evidence *without further corroboration* both at the IMT and at other war crimes trials. The countless official military documents, reports, and orders, as well as the interrogation records of captured German POWs and the official court records of war crimes trials held in the Soviet Union prior to the Nuremberg Trials were also accepted as evidence. [76]

The nature of Nazi warfare on the Eastern front had, of course, been criminal from the outset. The Soviets had been subjected to inhuman and barbaric acts which the regime went to great lengths to chronicle. The murder of millions of prisoners of war in violation of international law, the wholesale slaughter of Jews and the deaths of millions of other civilians from famine and deprivation during the occupation, the plundering of Soviet resources as well as the still untold story of the suffering of millions more Soviet citizens abducted for forced labor in Germany were all monstrous crimes. These were all meticulously documented by the Soviets in an enormous effort which was in marked contrast to the efforts undertaken by the United Nations War Crimes Commission. According to Telford Taylor, the Chief US prosecutor at Nuremberg, the commission "had no investigatory staff or, for that matter, adequate staff for any substantial undertaking."[77]

Looking through the voluminous files and reports of the Extraordinary Commission one is at first appalled by the sheer scale of the destruction but ultimately it becomes clear that Stalin hoped to recoup these losses through war reparations and an exact accounting would be necessary to press for future reparations.

To be historically accurate it must be acknowledged that it was the Soviet leadership that had consistently called for a postwar international criminal trial with the Nazi ringleaders in the dock for criminal conspiracy to commit aggressive war. National histories generally tend to highlight the positive contributions of their subjects and it should come as no surprise that American narratives emphasize the leading role played by the United States in bringing the Nazis to account for their heinous crimes. But as Hirsch again correctly asserts "There is compelling evidence that the Soviet Union made significant contributions to the legal framework of the IMT."[78] Not surprisingly, Russian scholars and school children alike are keenly aware of the strenuous efforts made by the Soviet Union to see that justice was done for the victims of Nazi aggression. The Soviet contributions to international justice for the victims of the Nazi tyranny rightly deserve to be acknowledged.

The cult of the Great Patriotic War would be used to give Stalin's regime legitimacy. But there is also no doubt that the evidentiary material compiled by the Extraordinary Committee and the military committees proved of enormous importance both for the Soviets' domestic war crimes trials and for the prosecution of the Nazi war criminals at Nuremberg. And the Soviets' insistence on such an international trial and their contributions to jurisprudence, regardless of the political cynicism sometimes displayed, should also be applauded. But the deliberate downplaying of the Jewish identities of many of the Hitler's victims both during and since the war is unconscionable. The cynicism with which Stalin tried to gain political recognition for the Soviet Union's annexation of the Baltic states by refusing to enter the UNWCW and the obvious cataloguing of material damages for a future monetary reckoning (of course, while there were no reparations paid per se there was a wholesale movement of equipment and entire factories, etc., to Russia during the occupation) aside, it was this political manipulation of the identity of the dead that was, and still is, bone-chilling. That the Soviet Union suffered grievously is beyond doubt, but Putin's annual calls for the remembrance of the 27 million "Russian" war dead of course include many millions that were *not* ethnic Russians and some were only "Soviet" as a result of the Molotov-Ribbentrop Pact. The postwar monument erected to the massacre victims at Babi Yar had noted only that "peaceful Soviet citizens" had been slaughtered there. Decades later, during Gorbachev's era of glasnost (publicity), another, supposedly more truthful plaque was installed, this time in Hebrew. But even this plaque also read simply "peaceful Soviet citizens." It was only after the collapse of the Soviet Union that three separate plaques with inscriptions in Russian, Hebrew, and now Ukrainian as well were installed that finally read "Jews." While of course the sheer enormity of the numbers matter, more importantly all these victims had specific identities, culture, and beliefs and deserved to be converted back into the individual human beings they once were. Indeed, no one should be forgotten.

Notes

1 Nina Tumarkin, *The Living and the Dead: The Rise and Fall of the Cult of World War II in Russia* (New York: Basic Books, 1995).
2 Quoted in George Ginsburgs, *Moscow's Road to Nuremberg: The Soviet Background to the Trial* (The Hague: Martinus Nijhoff, 1996), 25.
3 Ibid., 31.
4 Notable exceptions include Francine Hirsch's excellent article "The Soviets at Nuremberg: International Law, Propaganda, and the Making of the Postwar Order," *American Historical Review* 113/3 (2008): 701–30 and George Ginsburgs's *Moscow's Road to Nuremberg: The Soviet Background to the Trial.*
5 Quoted in Kirsten Sellars, *Crimes against Peace and International Law* (Cambridge: Cambridge University Press, 2013), 12.
6 Michael R. Marrus, *The Nuremberg War Crimes Trial, 1945-46: A Documentary History* (Boston/New York: St. Martin's Press, 1997), 15.

7 Quoted in ibid., 706.
8 Sellars, *Crimes against Peace,* 50.
9 Sellars, *Crimes Against Peace,* 49; Ginsburgs, *Moscow's Road,* 78-79.
10 Hirsch, "Soviets at Nuremberg," 707.
11 Quoted in Hirsch, "Soviets at Nuremberg," 707.
12 Marrus, *The Nuremberg War Crimes Trial 1945-46,* 28, "Officials in the Pentagon worked to refine a scheme that emerged from the desk of the chief of the War Department's Special Projects Office, Lieutenant Colonel Murray Bernays. An attorney who worked in civilian life with the Securities and Exchange Commission (SEC), Bernays developed a plan that used the law of conspiracy (commonly referred to in SEC cases but hitherto unknown in international law) to organize a grand strategy for the prosecution of major Nazi war criminals." To the same effect, Telford Taylor, *The Anatomy of the Nuremberg Trials* (New York: Alfred A. Knopf, 1992), 35, "Bernays resorted to the Anglo-American law of criminal conspiracy."
13 *Soviet Government Statements on Nazi Atrocities* (London, 1946), 7-10.
14 Ibid., 50 and *Nota Narodnogo Komissara Inostrannykh Del Tov. V. M. Molotova o Chudovishchnykh Zlodeianiiakh Zverstvakh i Nasiliiakh Germanskikh Vlastei v Okkypirovannykh Sovetskikh Raionakh i ob Otvetstvennosti Germanskikh Vlastei Za Eti Prestupleniia* (People's Commissar of Foreign Affairs Comrade V. M. Molotov's Note Concerning the Monstrous Deeds, Atrocities and Acts of Violence of the German State in the Occupied Soviet Regions and About the Responsibility of the German State For These Crimes), RG-22.009.01.06 United States Holocaust Memorial Museum (hereafter USHMM),13. Records Group (RG) 22.009 contains Soviet Ministry of Foreign Affairs archival records from the Molotov Secretariat which document early Soviet knowledge of the Holocaust and interaction with the Allies about a joint policy declaration, materials relating to the creation of the Extraordinary State Commission to Investigate German-Fascist Crimes Committed on Soviet Territory and miscellaneous reports of the SovInformBuro including articles prepared for the Soviet press. It also holds archival materials from the Central State Archive of the Ministry of Defense (TsGAMO) located in Podolsk which document atrocities perpetrated by the Nazis as does RG.04.050.
15 R. G. Pikhoia and V. P. Kozlov, eds., *Katyn"* (Moscow: ROSSPEN, 1997).
16 A. N. Trainin, *Ugolovnaia otvetsvennost" gitlerovtsev,* ed. A. Ia. Vyshinsky (Moscow: Iurid. Izdatel'stvo NKIU Soiuza SSR, 1944), 87.
17 *Statements,* 16.
18 Quoted in Ginsburgs, *Moscow's Road,* 33.
19 Quoted in Ginsburgs, *Moscow's Road,* 33-34.
20 Quoted in ibid., 34.
21 *Nota,* 1.
22 Ibid., 2.
23 Ibid., 13.
24 Quoted in Taylor, *The Anatomy of the Nuremberg War Trials,* 25.
25 Quoted in *Nuremberg War Crimes,* 19. The term "United Nations" was often used by the Allies and refers to the Declaration of the United Nations of January 1, 1942, signed by twenty-six nations calling for a united war effort against Germany and Japan.
26 *Vneshnaia politika Sovetskogo Soiua v perio otechestvennoi voiny* (Moscow, 1946), vol. 1, 52-53.
27 Ibid., 54.

28 Arieh Kochavi, *Prelude to Nuremberg: Allied War Crimes Policy and the Question of Punishment* (Chapel Hill: University of North Carolina Press, 1998), 20.
29 Ibid., 61.
30 Howard Ball, "The Path to Nuremberg: 1941-1945," in *The Genocide Studies Reader*, Samuel Totten, ed. (New York and London: Routledge, 2009), 427.
31 Bradley Smith, *The American Road to Nuremberg: The Documentary Record, 1944-1945* (Stanford: Stanford University Press, 1982), 28–29.
32 Quoted in Taylor, *Nuremberg Trials*, 31.
33 Quoted in ibid.
34 Quoted in Ginsburgs, *Moscow's Road*, 48.
35 Quoted in Ibid., 49.
36 J. Stalin, *War Speeches, Orders of the Day and Answers to Foreign Press Correspondents During the Great Patriotic War* (London, n.d.), 82.
37 *Foreign Relations of the United States: The Conference at Quebec, 1944* (Washington, 1972), 123–25.
38 Quoted in Joseph Persico, *Nuremberg: Infamy on Trial* (New York: Viking, 1994), 17.
39 Ibid., 708.
40 Ibid., 709
41 Quoted in Taylor, *Nuremberg Trials*, 31.
42 Quoted in Bradley Smith, *The Road to Nuremberg* (New York, 1981), 117.
43 Quoted in Richard Minear, *Victor's Justice: The Tokyo War Crimes Trial* (Princeton: Princeton University Press, 1971), 9–10.
44 USHMM, RG 22.009.01.07, 12 (Memorandum of G. Aleksandrov to V. M. Molotov dated July 14, 1942).
45 Ibid.
46 Ibid.
47 Ibid., 14.
48 Ibid., 17.
49 Ibid., 19.
50 Ibid.
51 N. S. Lebedeva, *Podgotokva Niurnbergskogo protsessa* (Moscow: Izdatel'stvo Nauka, 1975), 26–30.
52 *The Spectator*, December 23, 1943, 1.
53 Quoted in Arieh J. Kochavi, *Prelude to Nuremberg: Allied War Crimes and the Question of Punishment* (Chapel Hill: University of North Carolina Press, 2005), 69.
54 Quoted in ibid., 65.
55 Ginsburgs, *Moscow's Road*, 38.
56 Ibid., 38–39, USHMM, RG 22.009.01.07, 25–31 (Memorandum of G Aleksandrov to V. M. Molotov dated April 3, 1943).
57 Ginsburgs, 38.
58 E. Snow, *The Pattern of Soviet Power* (New York: Random House, 1945), note 18, 97.
59 There were three to five of these committees assigned to each Red Army "front." There were several dozen of these "fronts" and although they were usually identified with a geographic region (1st Baltic Front, 2nd Ukrainian front, Caucasus Front, etc.) they were in fact military formations unique to the Russian and Soviet military; composed of three to five armies and they should not be confused with the Western usage of the term which denotes a broad geographic area of military operations.
60 USHMM, RG 22.008M, 72–73 (*Akt* of V. F. Kriuchkin to GLAVPURRKA dated January 17, 1942).

61 *Soobshchenia Chrezvychainoi Gosudarstvennoi Kommissii po Ustanovleniiu i Rasledovaniiu Zlodeianii Nemetsko-Fashistikh Okkupantov i ikh posobnikov na Vremenno Okkupirovannoi Territorii SSSR*, Moscow, 1944, tom 27, 864.
62 Yitzhak Arad, *The Holocaust in the Soviet Union* (Lincoln and Jerusalem: University of Nebraska Press and Yad Vashem, 2009), 539–40.
63 Quoted in Aleksandr Burakovskiy, "Holocaust Remembrance in Ukraine: Memorialization of the Jewish Tragedy at Babi Yar," *Nationalities Papers*, 39/3 (May 2011), 373.
64 USHMM, RG 22.009.01.04, 33. Draft Memorandum by V. M. Molotov of Soviet "Declaration of the Soviet Government Concerning the Implementation of the Plan of the Hitlerite Criminals for the General Extermination of Jews on Europe's Occupied Territory and the Responsibility of the German Government and all its Accomplices for this Bloody Evildoing" dated September 8, 1942.
65 USHMM, RG 22.009.01.04, 24–25.
66 USHMM, RG 22.009.01.04, 39–40. Molotov's Second Draft Memorandum dated September 27, 1942.
67 Ibid.
68 Ibid., 32.
69 *Pravda*, July 26, 1943, 1.
70 Quoted in Amir Weiner, *Making Sense of War: The Second World War and the Fate of the Bolshevik Revolution* (Princeton: Princeton University Press, 2001), 216.
71 Though the opening session of the IMT was in fact first convened at Soviet insistence in Berlin before being moved to Nuremberg.
72 USHMM, RG 22.008.01.05, 459. *Akt* of D. B. Nikolaev to GLAVPURKKA July 30, 1944.
73 Ibid.
74 Ibid., 460.
75 Hirsch, "Soviets at Nuremberg," 702.
76 For a complete discussion of the Soviet's impressive effort at the compilation of evidence see Marina Sorokina "People and Procedures: Toward a History of the Investigation of Nazi Crimes in the USSR," *Kritika: Explorations in Russian and Eurasian History*, 6/4 (2005), 797–831.
77 Taylor, *Nuremberg Trials*, 27.
78 Hirsch, "Soviets at Nuremberg," 703.

4

The Human Face of Soviet Justice? Aron Trainin and the Origins of the Soviet Doctrine of International Criminal Law

Valentyna Polunina

On July 16, 1938, six hundred legal scholars, academics, and legal practitioners from different regions of the Soviet Union gathered in Moscow for the "First conference on the doctrine of the Soviet state and law." The meeting was organized by Andrey Vyshinsky, the head of the Institute of State and Law in the Soviet Academy of Sciences and state prosecutor in notorious Stalin's Moscow trials, with the ambitious goal of adopting a unified Marxist-Leninist-Stalinist vision of Soviet legal doctrine. The new theory of Soviet law was to replace the approaches and concepts of earlier Soviet jurists, which had been branded as "hostile" and "anti-Marxist."[1] For instance, Vyshinsky condemned the idea of Evgeny Pashukanis that once the state of communism was achieved, law and the state would wither away. Instead, morality was supposed to be a replacement.[2]

In his speech, Vyshinsky introduced a new official definition of law, while other approaches to law were declared to be "wrecking." Vyshinsky defined law as "a set of rules of behavior . . . that express the will of the ruling class as well as . . . the customs and rules of coexistence, authorized by the state, the application of which is guaranteed by state power in order to protect, consolidate, and develop the public relations and orders beneficial and acceptable for the ruling class."[3] This definition shows that Vyshinsky understood law as a coercive instrument in the hands of state that was to be used for the regulation of human behavior. At the same time, Vyshinsky, like many of the earlier legal scholars he had criticized, forgot to mention that Marx and Lenin had themselves rejected the idea of a new proletarian or socialist law which would wholly replace capitalist law in a socialist society.

Vyshinsky introduced a concept new to Soviet legal thought—"a branch of law." Among the branches of law that received official sanction, like administrative or criminal law, a special role was given to the Soviet doctrine of international law due to the complicated geopolitical constellation of the Soviet state "in capitalist encirclement."[4] One of the most important topics for analysis was the notion of aggression that, claimed Vyshinsky, "had first been defined by Soviet diplomats."[5]

Vyshinsky also called for more attention to aspects of criminal law such as issues of guilt, complicity, and the legal instrument of analogy. They would later prove to be useful, not only during the Soviet but also during the Allied and international war crimes tribunals.

Vyshinsky's vision of how Soviet legal doctrine should evolve was distributed throughout the Soviet Union. Just a week after the conference, parts of his speech were reprinted in *Pravda* under the title "About the tasks of the Soviet socialist law science." From then on, the Soviet government would elaborate a practical approach to international law and criminal justice; international trials were seen as a good opportunity to present the benefits of a communist state to the world. The era of more open theoretical debate was over, and legal theory became nothing but a tool for the exigencies of official policy.[6]

In his research, Andrey Vyshinsky developed a close and somewhat unlikely cooperation with legal scholar Aron Trainin—a brilliant lawyer, already known as one of the founders of Soviet criminal law science.[7] Educated before the October Revolution and proficient in several foreign languages, Trainin was known not only in the Soviet Union but also abroad due to his participation in international meetings and bodies as well as through translations of his most important writings. Trainin himself was not isolated from his foreign colleagues and, as his works show, even extensively drew upon the ideas of Western legal scholars.

Trainin published around 300 works,[8] many of them with Vyshinsky's support. Specifically, his formulation of "crimes against peace" would be incorporated into the Charter of the Nuremberg Trial (IMT), "becom(ing) a part of the recognized body of contemporary international law."[9] In this regard, "the Soviets played an important, if not a dominant, role in the formulation of the principle of the criminality of aggressive war."[10] Trainin also influenced the adoption by the Allies of the legal concept of "conspiracy" against peace, traditionally thought to be an invention of the Western powers.[11] Besides his work on international aggression and conspiracy, Trainin published studies on international crime, international terrorism, crimes against humanity, and genocide.[12]

Trainin and Vyshinsky closely cooperated in their intellectual efforts, but it was Vyshinsky who defined and led this cooperation. Vyshinsky had deep interest in Trainin's scholarship; he edited his books, wrote introductions, and suggested possible themes. He even praised Trainin's book *Criminal Intervention* (*Ugolovnaya interventsiya*) in his foreword as nothing less than "a matter of huge political importance."[13] Such involvement of Vyshinsky, who was the Procurator General of the USSR by the late 1930s, in Trainin's legal scholarship indicates that the latter not only expressed his personal opinion but also the official position of the Soviet state. Vyshinsky and Stalin trusted Trainin so much that they relied on him to represent Soviet interests at the highest level: first at the London Conference in the summer of 1945 he signed along with Iona Nikitchenko, the future Soviet judge at the IMT, the London agreement. Later, he served as adviser to the Soviet prosecution team at the IMT.

This chapter seeks to briefly address the evolution of the Soviet doctrine of international criminal law during the interwar period and then proceed to a more detailed analysis of the wartime and postwar period with an emphasis on Aron Trainin's legal innovations and the influence of his legal thinking on Trainin's colleagues abroad. An unconventional biographical approach to Trainin allows a better understanding of the impact of his background—his "Western" education, progressive views, and his paradoxical cooperation with Andrey Vyshinsky—on the evolution of the Soviet approach to international criminal law.

The development of the Soviet doctrine of international law: From rejection to use

Before we proceed to the development of the Soviet doctrine of international criminal law during and immediately after the Second World War, it is important to give a short overview of the origins of the Soviet international law doctrine. First of all, the Soviet Union's interest in international criminal justice began relatively late. Before the 1930s, the Soviet state had suffered from international isolation and concentrated its foreign policy mainly on the goal of achieving "world proletarian revolution." After the revolution of 1917, the Bolsheviks rejected bourgeois law, including bourgeois international law. They believed that international law was biased in favor of the West, because it presupposed the superiority of "civilized" European nations over the rest of the world.[14] In its place, the Soviets advanced a vision of Moscow as the home of a new "socialist" version of international law.

This drastic turn can to a certain degree be described as the "first wave of decolonization."[15] After belonging for two centuries to the European club, and still not being "civilized" enough (at least from the European perspective), the Soviets chose to turn their back on Western legal tradition, despite the fact that socialism itself was a Western import.

The Bolsheviks began to actively implement their idea of a just international order from the first days of existence of Soviet Russia. With the Decree on Peace of October 25, 1917, they declared the principle of "just and democratic peace ... without annexations and contributions."[16] The Soviet government opposed "any incorporation into a large and powerful State of a small or weak nationality without a precise, clear, and voluntary expression of consent" by that nationality, "regardless of whether the nationality lives in Europe or in distant overseas countries."[17] They emphasized the right of peoples to self-determination and political orientation in the Declaration of the Rights of the Peoples of Russia (November 15, 1917). They denounced both unequal treaties and secret diplomacy between imperialist powers. The Bolsheviks even published more than 100 such treaties they had found in Tsarist archives, causing scandal. Moreover, they refuted the previous regime of capitulations—extraterritorial rights colonial powers enjoyed in non-Western countries (Tsarist government enjoyed these rights in China, Persia, Turkey, and Afghanistan).

In the early 1920s, the most prominent Soviet lawyers of that time rejected any possibility of cooperation between the capitalist and communist states, arguing that these states were *a priori* destined to compete with each other. The isolationist approach to international law ended after the recognition of the Soviet Union on the international stage. The "First conference on the doctrine of the Soviet state and law" in 1938 officially put an end to this approach. The idea of the "world revolution" faded into the background and the prospect of cooperation with the capitalist countries looked more promising than isolation. In this situation the Soviet leadership turned to such lawyers as Aron Trainin who happened to catch the spirit of the time early enough with his 1935 book *Criminal Intervention*,[18] his first book dedicated to some aspects of international criminal law such as international terrorism or a nature of an international crime.

Aron Trainin: "An agreeable man to do business with"

Aron Naumovich Trainin was born in 1889 in Vitebsk, now Belarus, to a Jewish family. He attended a gymnasium in Kaluga and after graduating with honors in 1903, Trainin entered the Moscow University's law faculty. Even though he enjoyed education in "Western European legal traditions,"[19] he embraced revolutionary ideas quite early. Trainin was even arrested twice for participation in student demonstrations. Upon the graduation from the university in 1908, the promising lawyer was offered a position at the Department of Criminal Law in his alma mater. In 1912, Trainin, together with many leading professors, left the Moscow University in protest against the "reactionary policies"[20] of the Minister of Education and started working at the People's University of Shanyavsky as an assistant professor. After publishing his dissertation "Insolvency and bankruptcy" in 1920 and several other papers on criminal law, criminology, and criminal procedure, Trainin returned to the Moscow University and became one of the first Soviet professors.

In 1935 Trainin published *Criminal Intervention*, his first study in the field of international law that marked the beginning of Trainin's work on the concept of international crime and modes of liability for committing an international offense. Moreover, for the first time Trainin turned his attention to terrorism as an international crime. Trainin accused his colleagues in the International Bureau for the Unification of Criminal Law of "slanderous attempts to identify terrorism and communism."[21] The author came to the conclusion that the primary goal of the bureau was not "to fight individual political terror but the struggle against mass revolutionary actions."[22]

More importantly, Trainin addressed the issue of aggression in international law, which would become one of his main areas of interest. In 1935, Trainin had analyzed the writings of colleagues like Professor Nikolaos Politis of Greece and Professor Vespasien Pella from Romania. Trainin had recognized that "military aggression is a huge, immeasurable consequence for the evil which threatens death and devastation to millions of workers."[23] Furthermore, he was inspired by the idea of Polish Professor Emil Rappoport that the incitement of aggression should be punishable under criminal law, an idea that Trainin would share till the end of his academic career.

In 1937, two years after *Criminal Intervention*, Trainin published his new work *The Defense of Peace and Criminal Law* (*Zashchita mira i ugolovnyy zakon*), dedicated to aspects of defense of peace by means of criminal justice. In his study he defined the "urgent duty of Soviet criminologists" as the revelation of "theoretically incorrect and politically harmful trends (in legal science) and at the same time (the transformation) of criminal law into a real weapon against a common enemy—war and fascism."[24]

In 1938, Aron Trainin joined the Academy of Sciences of the USSR where he worked until his death on February 7, 1957. He worked as the head of the department of criminal law of the Moscow University from 1942 to 1954. In the early 1950s, Trainin became a target of ideological attacks alongside other Jewish intellectuals as part of the campaign against "cosmopolitans"[25] and was forced to resign from the head of the department. He continued to work at the university as a professor of criminal law until 1957.

Trainin, together with Iona Nikitchenko, one of the drafters of the Nuremberg Charter, represented the Soviet Union at the London conference in 1945 and worked with delegations from the United States, Britain, and France on the document. Later, he participated in the trial as an advisor of the Soviet prosecution team (from November 20, 1945, to October 1, 1946). Despite his close cooperation with the infamous Soviet prosecutor Andrey Vyshinsky, Trainin was remembered by his Western colleagues as a "distinguished legal academician"[26] and as "an agreeable man to do business with"[27] unlike some other Soviet lawyers. Aron Trainin was one of the founders and vice president of the International Association of Democratic Lawyers (1947–1948) and a member of the editorial board of one of the most prominent Soviet legal journals "Soviet State and Law" (1950–1951). From 1935 until the late 1950s, Trainin focused his research on different aspects of international criminal law.

Trainin's doctrine of complicity

In 1941, the first monograph on the Soviet doctrine of complicity "Uchenie o souchastii" was published at Vyshinsky's urging in his 1938 speech.[28] The concept of complicity was not new for the Soviet criminal law; it was introduced by Vyshinsky and successfully used at Moscow purge trials (1936–1938). To prove the guilt of a defendant and his complicity in the commission of a crime, it was mostly enough to prove his membership in an anti-Soviet Trotsky-led conspiracy.[29]

Trainin defined complicity as "a joint participation of several persons in committing the same crime, provided each of the perpetrators has a relation to the criminal result of complicity and can be held legally accountable for this result."[30]

Trainin did not support the theory that merely intentional participation of several persons in the commitment of a crime was enough to be defined as complicity.[31] He believed that the joint effort of multiple people in crime meant that conspiracy was a greater threat to public order than the crimes of individuals.[32] In Trainin's interpretation, there were four types of conspirators—instigator, organizer, agent, and perpetrator. The most dangerous of whom was the organizer: "The role of the organizer is to *establish* a criminal group, recruit its members, then to *develop a plan* of criminal actions and, finally, to *control* the committing of the offence" (author's italics).[33] The organizer "bear[s] the greatest responsibility for committed crimes."[34]

There were also three levels of complicity, the most important of which, in terms of its later influence on international law, was "special complicity *sui generis*," referring to participation in a criminal association.³⁵ According to Trainin, this was "the highest level of a joint criminal activity," in which members might not know one another but were united in "serving the same goal."³⁶

"International legal principles" for trying Nazi war criminals

In 1944, several months after the first public Soviet trial of Nazi war criminals,³⁷ Trainin published his work *On the Criminal Responsibility of the Hitlerites*,³⁸ the first monograph on the subject of war crimes in the Soviet Union.³⁹ In his book, Trainin proposed a set of "international legal principles" for trying the Nazis and other Axis powers and dedicated a whole chapter to complicity,⁴⁰ defining it as "a complex phenomenon" that "embraces various understandings among criminals" that can include "the dangerous form of participation in an organization, bands, blocs, gangs, conspiracies," and so on. In such cases, he explained, a member of an organization "may not know all the other members" of the organization "but should answer for all their criminal activities."⁴¹

The author acknowledged the "complexity and exceptional uniqueness of the responsibility for complicity in international crimes" which are "created by the extremely complex relationship between the individual accomplices in international offenses."⁴²

Trainin argued that the leadership of Nazi Germany bore the biggest responsibility for the crimes committed:

> From the standpoint of criminal law the members of the fascist organization of international criminals playing the following roles: Hitler and his ministers, leaders of the fascist party, the command of the German army . . . and other members of Hitler's clique are the organizers and *perpetrators*; their supporting heads of financial and industrial concerns—organizers and *agents* of the gravest assault on the foundations of international relations and human morality.⁴³ (Trainin's italics)

Trainin's proposal to try German industrialists along with government officials attracted attention.

Trainin's idea of making aggressive war a criminal offense itself was a "pioneering attempt" with no less than a "revolutionary" implication for the international law doctrine.⁴⁴ Some historians believe that the main innovation of Trainin's *Criminal Responsibility* was that war criminals should be tried not just for war crimes committed during the course of war but also, and more importantly, for launching a war of aggression—and thus committing a fundamental crime against peace.⁴⁵ For Trainin, nothing could be more serious than a crime against peace, which was "the greatest social value" and the basis of all "international association."⁴⁶

According to Trainin, "crimes against peace" included "acts of aggression," "propaganda of aggression," "the conclusion of agreements with aggressive aims," "the violation of treaties which serve the cause of peace," "provocation designed to disrupt peaceful relations between countries," "terrorism," and "support of armed bands (fifth columns)."⁴⁷

In his book, Trainin distinguished between different kinds of liability: merely political, moral, and material liability could be attributed to the state, whereas only physical persons were to bear legal responsibility. He claimed that "none of the fundamental principles of criminal justice is adapted to . . . bring before a criminal court anything so complicated and unique as a modern state."[48]

The author did go back again to complicity, this time in international crimes. According to him, international crimes are committed with *different degrees of complicity*.

> There is still another peculiarity in the interpretation of complicity in international violations—in the sphere of international criminal law there arises a peculiar form of "ideal associations": here by means of the same acts certain crimes are perpetrated with various forms of complicity. Concretely this may be expressed as follows: Hitler and his clique, who created with the help of a number of measures a system of militarized banditry, are in the first place planners and instigators of ordinary criminal bandit crimes (murders, rape, robbery, and other kinds perpetrated by soldiers of the German army) and in the second place they are perpetrators of international crimes (violation of conventions, and of the laws and usages of warfare etc.).[49]

Criminal Responsibility was translated into several languages and circulated among the Allies during the preparations to the Nuremberg Tribunal. Representatives of the four powers at the London Conference[50] Sir David Maxwell Fyfe and Lord Jowitt from Great Britain, Robert Falco from France, General Nikitchenko and Aron Trainin from the Soviet Union, and Robert Jackson as a representative of the United States actively discussed Trainin's book. It was especially useful for finding the common ground among the delegates from "different schools of thought as to whether that is an existing offense against international law" and whether they were "breaking new ground."[51]

Unlike the French delegate Gros,[52] the American representative Robert Jackson was more influenced by Soviet legal concepts than one might have expected. At the conference he made numerous references to Trainin's opinion that "a war of aggression or initiating war in violation of treaties is an international crime."[53] Furthermore, he seemed to acknowledge Trainin's view on the nature of an international offense:

> The American representatives conceive of this case as more than the trial of many particular offenses and offenders. It involves our whole attitude towards the waging of aggressive war, which, we think, as Professor Trainin has pointed out in his book, is an international crime.[54]

Eventually, American position regarding aggression was very close to that of Trainin, perhaps due to the fact that it offered a valid justification for America's entering the war:

> As I have understood Professor Trainin's book, which I have read carefully in the effort to understand the Soviet views, I gather that his view comes very close to the view which we entertain in the United States. Our attitude as a nation, in a

number of transactions, was based on the proposition that this was an illegal war from the moment that it was started, and that therefore, without losing our rights as neutrals or nonbelligerents, it was our right to extend aid to the nations under illegal attack, and the lend-lease program.

Therefore, our view is that this isn't merely a case of showing that these Nazi Hitlerite people failed to be gentlemen in war; it is a matter of their having designed an illegal attack on the international peace, which to our mind is a criminal offense by common-law tests, at least, and the other atrocities were all preparatory to it or done in execution of it.[55]

Trainin, in his turn, was quite a cooperative colleague. During the negotiations he even went as far as pointing to similarities between Soviet and American law. Jackson noticed in his report, not without a certain surprise, Trainin's position on the fair trial for the defendants: "He would like to take this as a basis and redraft it so as to make it even somewhat broader than the American draft."[56]

But there were at least two things Trainin was intransigent about: he insisted that Berlin be the permanent trial venue, archival location, and place of detention. In this case Trainin was without a doubt trying to fulfill Stalin's wishes since the placement of the tribunal in the Soviet occupation zone of Berlin would make it easier to influence. Nevertheless, he did not manage to achieve this goal and in the end Berlin was just a nominal location of the tribunal. Moreover, Trainin tried to ensure that the charter of the future trials would refer only to Nazi war crimes, so as to avoid the possibility of Soviet war crimes becoming a topic in the courtroom.

It should be pointed out that another member of the Soviet delegation in London, General Nikitchenko, also lobbied during the conference for some of Trainin's ideas, like the definition of aggression or the rejection of the criminal responsibility of states. It is further confirmation that Trainin's writings expressed the official position of the Soviet leadership.

At the London Conference, the Allies decided to integrate the complicity charge into the Nuremberg Charter, agreeing that "leaders, organizers, instigators, and accomplices participating in the formulation or execution of a common plan or conspiracy to commit specific crimes are responsible for all acts performed by any persons in execution of such plan."[57]

It should be noted that participants of the London Conference such as the head of the American and British delegations, Robert Jackson[58] and D. Maxwell Fyfe, acknowledged the importance of *Criminal Responsibility* for their task in London.[59] In her latest book on the Soviet participation in the Nuremberg Trial, Natalya Lebedeva mentions a personal letter of D. Maxwell Fyfe in which he praised Trainin's book: "He and his colleagues did not have a vaguest idea what to do—Americans were putting pressure on them but after all the Soviet people who had suffered a hundred times more should have very clear ideas on (complicity)."[60]

Trainin's *Criminal Responsibility* not only influenced his Western colleagues but also inspired Central European exile lawyers, among others Bohuslav Ečer, the Czechoslovak representative to the United Nations War Crimes Commission (UNWCC).[61] Soviet legal ideas seemed to be an attractive alternative for the exile lawyers, disappointed over weak British support for their legal innovations.⁶² Ečer, who had helped to translate Trainin's work, met delegates of the United States and France at the London Conference but was particularly impressed by his meeting with the Soviet delegate Trainin.⁶³ Kerstin von Lingen suggests that Trainin's intellectual endeavors may have even inspired Ečer's further development of concept of crimes against humanity.⁶⁴ Moreover, Ečer maintained a pro-Soviet position in his public speeches and in one of them went so far as to deny any fundamental differences between "Western" and "Eastern" legal conceptions. He supported his claim with a statement that there was no difference between categories of war crimes proposed by Professor Trainin and those suggested by the London International Assembly (LIA).⁶⁵ Aron Trainin, in his turn, supported the work of LIA on crimes against humanity and heavily criticized the restrained attitude of the British government toward the assembly as no less than an attempt "to prevent the struggle against crimes against humanity by insisting that investigations should only be concentrated on war crimes."⁶⁶

Judge Pal turns to Trainin

The charter of the next international war crimes tribunal—the International Military Tribunal for the Far East (IMTFE)⁶⁷ generally followed the model set by the Nuremberg Trials. The Tokyo Charter, unlike the Nuremberg Charter, did not foresee prosecutions of the so-called criminal organizations described by Trainin. Nevertheless, it reflected some of his views on conspiracy and aggression. Thus, Article 5(a) of the Tokyo Charter provided for the Tribunal's jurisdiction over

> *crimes against the peace* . . . the planning, preparation, initiation or waging of a declared or undeclared war of aggression, or a war in violation of international law, treaties, agreements of assurances, or *participation in a common plan or conspiracy* for the accomplishment of any of the foregoing (Italics in original).⁶⁸

Article 5(a) was based on Article 6 of the Nuremberg Charter and thus reaffirmed the policy decided upon at the London Conference that war was a criminal offense, an attack on international peace. This policy was reflected in two charges: conspiracy to commit aggression, and the substantive offense of aggression itself, which includes planning, preparing, initiating, or waging war.⁶⁹

Thus Aron Trainin's intellectual legacy influenced not only the framework of war crimes trials in Europe but also of those with regard to the former Japanese empire. The Tokyo Trial raised more questions and criticism than the Nuremberg Trial. The IMTFE's alleged legal flaws such as the retrospective creation of the charges, the unsatisfactory interpretation of the facts, and the misapplication of the law led to three dissenting votes from Indian judge Radhabinod Pal, Dutch judge Prof. Bert Röling, and French judge Henri Bernard.

It was Radhabinod Pal who expressed keen interest in Trainin's works, especially in his ideas about the criminal nature of aggressive wars and his concept of an international crime. In his voluminous dissenting vote, Pal dedicated more than twenty pages to a detailed, chapter by chapter, analysis of Trainin's *Criminal Responsibility*.

But unlike those legal scholars who agreed with his point of view and drew upon Trainin's ideas, in the case of Judge Pal it was rather the criticism of Trainin's work that helped him to prove his opinion about the ex post facto application of the aforementioned charges, namely conspiracy to commit aggression, and the substantive offense of aggression (planning, preparing, initiating, or waging war).

Pal acknowledged the fact that "Mr. Trainin's is a very valuable contribution to deep juridical thinking"[70] and pointed out that the charges of crimes against peace as a new international criminal concept may be traced directly back to *Criminal Responsibility*.[71] Moreover, he mentioned that Trainin's ideas had some supporters among "distinguished international jurists" like Harvard Law professor Sheldon Glueck or the chairman of UNWCC, Lord Robert Wright, who "placed great reliance on the views of Mr. Trainin."[72]

First of all, Pal found it convincing that the concept of criminal responsibility for wars can arise only after a society reaches a certain stage in its development. He still mentioned an important reservation that this concept can be introduced after one is "in a position to say that life itself is established on some peaceful basis: International crime will be an infringement of that base—a breach or violation of the peace or pax of the international community."[73]

Nevertheless, Pal rejected Trainin's idea about "criminal responsibility in international life."[74] He did not agree with the Soviet scholar about the idea that a new international society had developed since the Moscow Declaration of 1943 which required a new system of international law that would reflect this new order and "dictate to the conscience of nations the problem of criminal responsibility for attempts on the foundations of international relations."[75] For Pal the Moscow Declaration was only a declaration that a new epoch of international life was *going to begin*[76] and Trainin "at most . . . only established a demand of the changing international life."[77] He rejected Trainin's idea that Soviet legal scholars had an "honourable obligation" to "give legal expression to the demand of retribution for the crimes committed by the Hitlerites."[78] In his opinion, a judge should not be guided by such an idea: "I hope this sense of obligation to satisfy any demand of retribution did not weigh too much with (Trainin). A judge and a juridical thinker cannot function properly under the weight of such a feeling."[79]

Cold War: New challenges, new ideas

The most important monograph written by Trainin in the postwar period was published in 1956 under the title *Protection of peace and the fight against crimes against mankind* (*Zashchita mira i bor'ba s prestupleniyami protiv chelovechestva*). The book was a result of twenty years of research in the field of international criminal law. The term *prestupleniya protiv chelovechestva* is nowadays usually understood as "crimes against humanity" in Russian legal scholarship, but Trainin used this concept in his book as an overarching category, a synonym for what we understand as "international crimes" now. For him, the notion of "crimes against mankind" covered "the whole range of criminal acts which threaten the peace and security of nations."[80] He differentiated between *prestupleniya protiv chelovechestva* (crimes against mankind) and *prestupleniya protiv chelovechnosti* (crimes against humanity). This somewhat confusing term will be discussed in a greater detail hereinafter.

Along with the concept of "the crimes against mankind" Trainin analyzes in his work the notion of crimes against the laws and customs of war, the concept of genocide, criminal liability of legal persons and individuals, and comes back to the topic of aggression.

It is important to point out the changed political situation in the Soviet Union and in the world at the moment of the publication that was reflected in Trainin's book. Changes in the country after Stalin's death in 1953 and criticism of the "cult of personality of Stalin" at the 20th Congress of the Communist Party of the Soviet Union had consequences for Soviet legal scholarship too. The official legal thinking introduced by Vyshinsky in 1938 prevailed until the second half of the 1950s when it finally became possible for Soviet lawyers to express different opinions. But, analyzing Trainin's work, it seems that the conditions of the Cold War and the new challenges that superpower competition posed an even greater influence on the development of his ideas.

In his monograph, Trainin reflected on the changing geopolitical constellations and "easing of tensions in international relations."[81] It is evident from the manuscript that Trainin's new comprehensive volume was an attempt to rethink the main aspects of the Soviet doctrine of international criminal law in light of the changed circumstances of "peaceful coexistence of states with different social and political systems . . . proclaimed by the resolution of the 20th Congress."[82] For Trainin international criminal law was more than science; it was a means of domestic and international politics, a tool that could be used against the new "warmongers" and "fascist reactionaries."[83] Unlike several years before, the fascists and warmongers were now understood to mean the new archenemy of the Soviet state—the United States.

In this context, "crimes against mankind" were defined as "encroachments on the foundations of the existence and progressive development of nations."[84] According to Trainin, "crimes against mankind" refer to a "substantial and diverse group of offences, united in a single notion . . . of the crimes against mankind."[85] These included murder, torture, forced labor, robbery, destruction, and so on.

As for the classification of "crimes against mankind," Trainin distinguished between three categories: "Crimes against the foundations of peaceful coexistence of nations. Crimes against the laws and customs of war. Crimes against the foundations of the physical existence of the nations—genocide."[86]

The first category of "crimes against the mankind" closely resembles the concept of aggression Trainin elaborated before and during the Second World War. Later on, he introduced some changes to the concept and suggested differentiating between two forms: direct military aggression and indirect aggression—economic and ideological. For instance, ideological aggression was an especially important political concept for the Soviet state in the period of the nuclear arms race and the attempt by the Soviet Union to lead the peace movement. It included not only the incitement of war but also the propagation of weapons of mass destruction (nuclear, hydrogen, and bacteriological weapons), as well as the promotion of fascist and Nazi views, racial and national exclusiveness, hatred and contempt for other nations.[87]

For the first time, Trainin moved away from a concept of aggression that criminalized all kinds of wars: he distinguished between illegal aggressive wars and just wars of liberation. Stating in the spirit of official Soviet position with regard to colonized nations, the author stated that a war "which aims to protect people from foreign attacks and attempts at enslavement or to liberate colonies . . . from the yoke of the imperialists cannot be regarded as a war of aggression."[88] Moreover, any intervention in a civil war was to be qualified as aggression in its severe form.[89] As to reiterate connection between his opinion and the geopolitical situation in which the Soviet Union and the United Stated were competing for spheres of influence, Trainin gave an example of an illegal war—"American aggression in Korea."[90]

With regard to liability for "crimes against mankind," Trainin reiterated his previously well-known opinion that the "state and other legal entities can and should bear political and financial responsibility for crimes against mankind, but the subjects of criminal liability may only be individuals."[91] Moreover, he used an opportunity to stress once again his opinion that POWs should not be excluded from prosecution. At this point the author criticized Western "humanism inside out"[92] shared by the International Committee of the Red Cross during the wartime.[93]

Trainin was of the opinion that a crime against mankind represented not just an episodic action but a system of actions like preparation of aggression, policy of terror, persecution of civilians, and so on. These specific activities, in turn, required the "extensive and cohesive work of many units and individuals."[94] Therefore, according to Trainin, complicity in its most primitive form—simple complicity, where the relation between the partners has the least intensive character, where there is just a mutual awareness of partners about their criminal acts—is rarely the case in terms of "crimes against mankind." The second form of complicity, complicity by prior agreement, is in Trainin's opinion possible with regard to "crimes against mankind." However, the complexity of the actions necessary for the implementation of criminal activities directed "against the interests of all mankind" led to the conclusion that the most typical form of complicity in the commission of this kind of crime is complicity sui generis that "involves lasting and cohesive activities in the form of participation in a criminal association."[95] According to Trainin, the term "criminal clique," an association of political, military, and financial leaders, best describes a criminal association.[96]

Again, in line with the official Soviet position that the Soviet Union was the only country in the world genuinely interested in establishing world peace, Trainin stressed the necessity of prohibiting weapons of mass destruction, accusing again "new imperialists" on the head with the United States of using chemical and bacteriological warfare in Korea.[97]

The last crime in Trainin's classification of "crimes against mankind" is the crime of genocide. He analyzed this topic for the first time in a 1948 article "The Fight Against Genocide as an International Crime" published in "Soviet state and law." A specific feature of genocide, which distinguished it from all previously known crimes, was that the object of genocide is not a single individual but a group of people. In genocide the killing of a person is not a goal but a means to the destruction of the whole group.[98]

Trainin distinguished three forms of genocide: physical genocide—"direct physical extermination of people belonging to a certain race or nation," biological genocide—"prevention of childbirth, sterilization, prohibition of marriage, complete separation of the sexes, forced abortions," and the third special form—"a national and cultural genocide aimed at destroying the national culture of persecuted peoples, its achievements and heritage."[99]

Just as with aggression, the United States with its racial segregation was given as an example of a country in which genocide was taking place, thus reinforcing the official Soviet narrative.

Conclusion

Despite the specific Soviet understanding of international law ranging from complete rejection due to its "bourgeois nature" to the practical view of it as a tool for securing the Soviet state and achieving its geopolitical and ideological goals, there is reason to believe that Soviet scholars made valuable contributions to the framing of the IMT and IMTFE and thus helped to shape modern international criminal law.

Surprisingly, the "crimes against peace" described in the charters of the IMT and IMTFE had been elaborated by a Soviet jurist. Aron Trainin had significantly influenced the formulation of the idea of complicity in the prosecution of Nazi leaders as a conspiracy against peace, deriving it from domestic Soviet precedents that had been used in show trials in Stalinist Russia in the late 1930s.

It is important to stress that Aron Trainin was not the only lawyer of his time who was interested in advancing the concept of crimes against peace, the doctrine of complicity, or the crime of aggression. The aim of this chapter was to demonstrate that despite the common understanding that modern international law was created under the influence of the Anglo-American legal doctrine alone, Soviet legal scholars and Trainin in particular made a valuable contribution too.

Unlike many members of Soviet delegations at the international level, Trainin was perceived by his Western colleagues as an intelligent and reasonable person with whom one could be on an equal footing and not as an unpredictable "Russian bear" or a puppet of Vyshinsky. At the same time it would be a too far-reaching if we branded him as a "Western man" lost in the Soviet reality. Despite the fact that he received a classical "bourgeois" education, was fluent in foreign languages, and produced high-quality scholarship, his passion for revolutionary ideas early on and cooperation with the mastermind behind Stalin's purge trials, Vyshinsky, suggest something different. It is hard to imagine that Trainin was coerced to write about something he did not believe in. The great scientific value of his works itself shows the opposite. Everyone who is familiar with the propaganda tomes of Soviet scholars citing Stalin on every page would notice a difference between these opportunistic works and Trainin's books and articles. In his "Doctrine of complicity," Trainin, for example, referred to Stalin just once. Moreover, talking about victims of Nazi war criminals, he often mentioned Jews and did not opt for the politically loyal term of "peaceful Soviet citizens." It was a happy coincidence for him that he was able to capture the spirit of the time and that the Soviet leadership of the period valued his field of expertise. After the main wave of war crimes trials was over, Trainin lost his importance and even became a target of anti-Semitic attacks at the Moscow University and at the Academy of Sciences.

With the absence of Trainin's personal correspondence or memoirs, it is difficult to know to what extent he realized the scale of wrongdoings committed by his immediate supervisors—Vyshinsky and Stalin. Leaving aside the question of his motives, Trainin deserves credit for promoting ideas of justice for international crimes and peace as the greatest good of the international community.

Notes

1. Vyshinsky's speech quoted from Y. N. Umanskiy, "Pervoye soveshchaniye po voprosam nauki sovetskogo gosudarstva i prava (16–19 iyulya 1938)," *V Akademii Nauk SSSR*, 7 (1938), 53.
2. Evgeny Pashukanis, *Obshchaya teoriya prava i marksizm. Opyt kritiki osnovnykh yuridicheskikh ponyatiy* (Moscow: Izd-vo Sots. akad., 1924).
3. Vyshinsky's speech quoted from Y. N. Umanskiy, "Pervoye soveshchaniye po voprosam nauki sovetskogo gosudarstva i prava (16–19 iyulya 1938)," 50–51.
4. Vyshinsky's speech quoted from Y. N. Umanskiy, "Pervoye soveshchaniye po voprosam nauki sovetskogo gosudarstva i prava (16-19 iyulya 1938)," 49.
5. Ibid., 51–52. See also Kirsten Sellars' "Treasonable Conspiracies at Paris, Moscow and Delhi," in Sellars (ed.) *Trials for International Crimes in Asia* (Cambridge: Cambridge University Press), 25–54; here 35.
6. China Miéville, *Between Equal Rights. A Marxist Theory of International Law* (Leiden: BRILL, 2005), vol. 6, 60.
7. On cooperation between Trainin and Vyshinsky and Trainin's concept of crime against peace, see Kirsten Sellars, *Crimes against Peace* (Cambridge: Cambridge University Press, 2013), 48–58.
8. Here and further information about Trainin's biography is taken from his personal file at the Russian Academy of Sciences. ARAN, f. 411, op. 4A, d. 127.
9. George Ginsburgs, *Moscow's Road to Nuremberg. The Soviet Background to the Trial* (The Hague, Boston, London, 1996), 26.
10. Ibid.
11. On Trainin's participation in the London Conference and the influence of his ideas on the legal framework of the Nuremberg Trial, see Francine Hirsch, "The Soviets at Nuremberg: International Law, Propaganda, and the Making of the Postwar Order," *American Historical Review*, 2 (2008), 701–30; here 707.
12. Aron Trainin (ed. and foreword by Andrey Vyshinsky), *Zashchita mira i ugolovnyy zakon* (Moscow: Yuridicheskoye izdatel'stvo NKU SSSR, 1937); Aron Trainin, *Ucheniye o souchastii* (Moscow: Yuridicheskoye izdatel'stvo NKU SSSR, 1941); Aron Trainin (ed. Andrey Vyshinsky), *Ugolovnaya otvetstvennost' gitlerovtsev* (Moscow: Yuridicheskoye izdatel'stvo NKU SSSR, 1944); Aron Trainin (ed. and foreword by Andrey Vyshinsky), *Ugolovnaya interventsiya. Dvizheniye po unifikatsii ugolovnogo zakonodatel'stva kapitalisticheskikh stran* (Moscow: Sovetskoye zakonodatel'stvo, 1935); Aron Trainin, "Bor'ba s genotsidom kak mezhdunarodnym prestupleniyem,"

in *Sovetskoye gosudarstvo i parvo*, 5 (1948); Aron Trainin, *Zashchita mira i bor'ba s prestupleniyami protiv chelovechestva* (Moscow: Izdatel'stvo AN SSSR, 1956).
13 Aron Trainin (ed. and foreword by Andrey Vyshinsky), *Ugolovnaya interventsiya*, 5.
14 Lauri Mälksoo, "Russia-Europe," in Bardo Fassbender, Anne Peters, and Simone Peter, eds., *The Oxford Handbook of the History of International Law* (Oxford: Oxford Univ. Press, 2012), 764–86; here 781.
15 Bardo Fassbender, Anne Peters, and Simone Peter, eds., *The Oxford Handbook of the History of International Law* (Oxford: Oxford University Press, 2012), 782. The Bolsheviks directed their message primarily to the nations outside Europe, in the world colonized by the Europeans. Nevertheless, the Soviet Union took up the legacy of the Tsarist empire too easily and never properly admitted that Russia too had been a colonial power. The Bolshevik leaders hoped that their anti-colonialist project would territorially affect primarily Western European empires.
16 Decree on Peace of October 25, 1917, http://bit.ly/1HECAFx (accessed October 20, 2016).
17 Ibid.
18 Aron Trainin (ed. and foreword by Andrey Vyshinsky), *Ugolovnaya interventsiya. Dvizheniye po unifikatsii ugolovnogo zakonodatel'stva kapitalisticheskikh stran* (Moscow: Sovetskoye zakonodatel'stvo, 1935).
19 Hirsch, "The Soviets at Nuremberg," 705.
20 ARAN, f. 411, op. 4A, d. 127.
21 Aron Trainin, "Ugolovnaya interventsiya," in N. F. Kuznetsova, ed., *Trainin, Izbrannie proizvedenia* (St. Petersburg: Yuridichesky Center Press, 2004), 433.
22 Ibid., 428.
23 Ibid., 414.
24 Aron Trainin, "Zashchita mira i ugolovnyy zakon," in N. F. Kuznetsova, ed., *Trainin, Izbrannie proizvedenia* (St. Petersburg: Yuridichesky Center Press, 2004), 464.
25 The "struggle against cosmopolitanism" was an anti-Semitic campaign designed to punish Soviet Jews for their suspected disloyalty. Soviet Jews were accused of being "rootless cosmopolits" hostile to the patriotic feelings of Soviet citizens. Those condemned for cosmopolitanism lost their jobs; some were expelled from the Communist Party and arrested.
26 Hirsch, "The Soviets at Nuremberg," 713.
27 Ibid.
28 The author would like to thank Professor Kirsten Sellars (The Chinese University of Hong Kong) for her academic guidance. This part of the chapter is based on research conducted in collaboration with Professor Sellars in 2014. The result of this collaboration can be found in Kirsten Sellars', "Treasonable Conspiracies at Paris, Moscow and Delhi," in Sellars, ed., *Trials for International Crimes in Asia* (Cambridge: Cambridge University Press), 25–54, especially 33–35, 39–43. In the following, the original quotes of Trainin are cited in the footnotes, where preferable.
29 A. Trainin, "Uchenie o souchastii," in N. F. Kuznetsova, ed., *Trainin, Izbrannie proizvedenia* (St. Petersburg: Yuridichesky Center Press, 2004), 270, see assessment also in Sellars, "Treasonable Conspiracies at Paris, Moscow and Delhi," 45.
30 A. Trainin, "Uchenie o souchastii," 265.
31 Ibid.
32 Ibid., 254.
33 Ibid., 293. See assessment also in Sellars, "Treasonable Conspiracies at Paris, Moscow and Delhi," 37–38.

34 A. Trainin, "Uchenie o souchastii," 293.
35 Ibid., 267. See assessment also in Sellars, "Treasonable Conspiracies at Paris, Moscow and Delhi," 43.
36 A. Trainin, "Uchenie o souchastii," 270, 285–86.
37 The first Soviet trial of Nazi war criminals took place in the Ukrainian city of Kharkiv from December 15 to 18, 1943. The Military Tribunal of the 4th Ukrainian Front, better known as the Kharkiv Trial, was established directly after the liberation of the city and concerned the atrocities committed in the city of Kharkiv and the Kharkiv region.
38 A. Trainin, *Ugolovnaia otvetstvennost' gitlerovtsev*, ed. A. Ia. Vyshinsky (Moscow, 1944), translated into English as *The Criminal Responsibility of the Hitlerites*, ed. A. Y. Vyshinsky (Moscow, 1944). (In this example I am citing the Russian-language version of Trainin's work in the text, which is consistent with the English version.) See also Sellars, *Crimes against Peace*, 51–52; Hirsch, "The Soviets at Nuremberg," 706–08.
39 For the analysis of Trainin's book, see also Irina Schulmeister-André, *Internationale Strafgerichtsbarkeit unter sowjetischem Einfluss. Der Beitrag der UdSSR zum Nürnberger Hauptkriegsverbrecherprozesspp* (Berlin: Duncker & Humboldt, 2017), pp. 63–71.
40 "Souchastie v mezhdunarodnykh prestuplenniiakh: Gitlerovskaia klika" ("Complicity of the Hitlerite Clique in International Crimes" in the English-language version).
41 A. Trainin, *Ugolovnaia otvetstvennost' gitlerovtsev*, 81–82.
42 Ibid., 80.
43 Ibid., 87.
44 Ginsburgs, *Moscow's Road to Nuremberg*, 79. See also Hirsch, "The Soviets at Nuremberg," 710.
45 Hirsch, "The Soviets at Nuremberg," 706–07; John Quigley, ed., *Soviet Legal Innovation and the Law of the Western World* (Cambridge, NY: Cambridge University Press, 2007), 151.
46 A. Trainin, *Ugolovnaia otvetstvennost' gitlerovtsev*, 35–36.
47 Trainin, *Criminal Responsibility of the Hitlerites*, 54. (In this case I am citing the English-language version.)
48 Ibid., 102.
49 Ibid., 112.
50 London Conference (June 26–August 2, 1945) was a conference of legal scholars from four Allied nations (United States, France, United Kingdom, and the Soviet Union) which had a task to elaborate a charter for the trial of major Nazi war criminals.
51 Minutes of Conference Session, June 29, 1945, in *Report of Robert H. Jackson, United States Representative to the International Conference on Military Trials* (Washington, DC: Department of State, 1949), 98.
52 Gros did not consider the launching of a war of aggression as a criminal violation. He pointed out that the existing law did not foresee a criminal sanction for starting aggressive wars. He wanted to avoid "criticism in later years of punishing something that was not actually criminal." As for Trainin's book, Gros claimed that he himself "recognized that international law, as it now stands, does not make it punishable." Minutes of Conference Session, July 19, 1945, in *Report of Robert H. Jackson*, 295–296.
53 Minutes of Conference Session, July 23, 1945, in *Report of Robert H. Jackson*, 126.
54 Revised draft of agreement and memorandum submitted by American delegation, June 30, in *Report of Robert H. Jackson, United States Representative to the International Conference on Military Trials*, 1945, 126.

55 Minutes of Conference Session, July 19, 1945, in *Report of Robert H. Jackson, United States Representative to the International Conference on Military Trials*, 299. On Jackson's position on aggression, see Sellars, *Crimes against Peace*, 88–89.
56 Report of American member of drafting subcommittee, July 11, 1945, in *Report of Robert H. Jackson, United States Representative to the International Conference on Military Trials*, 189–90.
57 Article 6 of the Nuremberg Charter, Nuremberg Trial Proceedings, vol. 1, published online through the Avalon Project at Yale Law School, http://avalon.law.yale.edu/subject_menus/imtproc_v1menu.asp (accessed May 21, 2016).
58 "Smart and dignified position of the Soviet delegation . . . compelled Justice Jackson . . . to abandon pressure techniques and switch to sober, business-like discussions." Ginsburgs, *Moscow's Road to Nuremberg*, 97.
59 Natalya Lebedeva, ed., *SSSR i Nyurnbergskiy protsess. Neizvestnyye i maloizvestnyye stranitsy istorii* (Moscow: MFD, 2012), 23.
60 Ibid., 24.
61 The United Nations War Crimes Commission was a commission of the United Nations that was in charge of investigations of war crimes committed by Nazi Germany and the other Axis powers in the Second World War. The commission started its work already during the war in 1943 before the establishment of the United Nations under a different name.
62 Kerstin von Lingen, "Fulfilling the Martens Clause: debating 'Crimes Against Humanity,' 1899–1945," in Fabian Klose, Mirjam Thulin, eds., *Humanity: A History of European Concepts in Practice From the Sixteenth Century to the Present* (Göttingen: Vandenhoeck & Ruprecht, 2016), 187–208; here 199.
63 Kerstin von Lingen, Transnationale Debatten um die Zivilisierung von Kriegsgewalt, 1864–1945. Eine intellectual history des Konzepts von crimes against humanity, unpublished manuscript of Habilitation, 311.
64 von Lingen, "Fulfilling the Martens Clause," 200.
65 The London International Assembly was created in 1941 under the auspices of the British League of Nations Union (LNU).
66 Aron Trainin, "Zashchita mira i bor'ba s prestupleniyami protiv chelovechestva," in N. F. Kuznetsova, ed., *Trainin, Izbrannie proizvedenia* (St. Petersburg: Yuridichesky Center Press, 2004), 874.
67 International Military Tribunal for the Far East was held from April 29, 1946, to November 12, 1948. It was proclaimed by the Supreme Commander or the Allied Powers (SCAP) General Douglas MacArthur and conceived as a legal response to Japan's military actions in East Asia and the Pacific between 1928 and 1945. The trial consisted of representatives from eleven countries: United States, United Kingdom, France, Australia, Canada, New Zealand, Holland, China, India, Philippines, and Soviet Union.
68 Charter of the International Military Tribunal for the Far East, https://www.uni-marburg.de/icwc/dateien/imtfec.pdf (accessed May 21, 2016).
69 Neil Boister and Robert Creyer (eds.) *Documents on the Tokyo International Military Tribunal. Charter, Indictment and Judgements* (Oxford University Press, 2008), xlvii.
70 "Judgement of the honorable Mr. Justice Pal, member from India" in Boister and Creyer (eds.) *Documents on the Tokyo International Military Tribunal*, 897.
71 Ibid., 885.
72 Ibid., 842, 893.
73 Ibid., 898.

74　Ibid., 843.
75　Ibid., 844.
76　Ibid., 897.
77　Ibid., 898.
78　Ibid., 897.
79　Ibid.
80　Trainin, "Zashchita mira i bor'ba s prestupleniyami protiv chelovechestva," 701.
81　Ibid., 874.
82　Ibid., 689.
83　Ibid., 706.
84　Ibid.
85　Ibid., 708.
86　Ibid., 713.
87　Ibid., 705.
88　Ibid., 765.
89　Ibid.
90　Ibid., 762.
91　Ibid., 730.
92　Ibid., 737.
93　During the war, the International Committee of the Red Cross was concerned over war crimes trials against POWs even though it changed its position after the war. Mark Lewis, *The Birth of the New Justice: The Internationalization of Crime and Punishment, 1919–1950* (Oxford: Oxford University Press, 2014), 235.
94　Trainin, "Zashchita mira i bor'ba s prestupleniyami protiv chelovechestva," 739.
95　Ibid., 740.
96　Ibid.
97　Ibid., 851.
98　Trainin, "Bor'ba s genotsidom kak mezhdunarodnym prestupleniyem," 3.
99　Trainin "Zashchita mira i bor'ba s prestupleniyami protiv chelovechestva," 848.

5

"May Justice Be Done!" The Soviet Union and the London Conference (1945)

Irina Schulmeister-André and David M. Crowe

The London Conference, which ended on August 8, 1945, with the signing of the London Four-Power Agreement[1] with annexed statute, was a crucial step in the planning of the Nuremberg IMT trial of major German war criminals. The joint development of the statute is regarded as an important example historically of the cooperation of the Allied Powers, who, despite their different legal traditions, found ways to reach a consensus acceptable as the legal basis for their common goal: to carry out a trial of the major war criminals. This was particularly remarkable, given that they had to negotiate the substantive, procedural foundations of the future tribunal in just a little over six weeks (June 26 to August 8, 1945).

Given this, it is important to take into account the existing differences and conflicts between each nation's representatives. The minutes of the London Conference published in the *Report of Robert H. Jackson*,[2] the US chief prosecutor in 1945, revealed that each of the four delegations openly viewed the trial from the perspective of their own legal origins, experiences, and agendas, which caused quite a few problems during the negotiations. There were also questions about whether a trial of major German war criminals should even take place. This was further complicated by the fact that no serious political discussions had taken place between the Allies before the end of the war about the nature of the trial. That led to different opinions among the delegates about the binding nature of the decisions made in London. The Soviet delegation, for example, had a very different view of the purpose of the trial and the authority of the tribunal that was to conduct it. These conceptual differences caused the serious conflicts during the London Conference. Jackson noted in his report that the "antagonistic concepts"[3] between the Soviet and Anglo-American representatives about the independence of the judiciary were particularly troublesome. However, it is important to question this allegation critically, particularly given the fact that Jackson's attitude toward the Soviet negotiators was far from impartial.[4]

The appointment of the Soviet representatives

After the Big Four decided at the San Francisco conference in early May 1945[5] to deal with the major German war criminals judicially and not politically, the United States asked the Soviet government three times to appoint a representative to take part in the negotiations in London about a possible war crimes trial. On May 19, 1945,[6] Washington informed the Soviet government that Supreme Court Justice Robert H. Jackson had been appointed the American representative to these talks.[7] The US note also stated that the American government considered it essential to begin such negotiations about the trial as soon as possible, and asked Moscow to appoint a delegate to take part in these important talks. When the note went unanswered, George F. Kennan, a highly regarded Soviet specialist and deputy chief of mission at the US embassy in Moscow, contacted Andrei Vyshinsky, the deputy commissar for External (Foreign) Affairs (NKID), about this matter six days later.[8] It emphasized the urgent need to begin negotiations and reach an agreement on the treatment of major war criminals, and again urged Moscow to appoint its own representatives to the London talks as soon as possible. When the Kremlin failed to answer Keenan's letter, another was sent by William Averell Harriman, the American ambassador in Moscow, to NKID on June 11, 1945.[9] Harriman underscored the importance of the talks and noted that the British government had appointed Attorney General David Maxwell Fyfe as its representative, and that the French were about to follow suit. He also asked the Soviet government to appoint without delay a prosecutor and other key persons so that the Four Powers could begin the negotiations as soon as possible. Furthermore, Harriman informed the Soviet government about the proposal to choose London as the conference location. The next day, Vyacheslav Molotov, the Soviet foreign minister, received a letter from Archibald John Kerr, the British ambassador in Moscow, officially inviting the Soviets to send a representative to the negotiations scheduled for June 25 in London.[10]

When the American and the British representatives gathered in London on June 21 for informal discussions, there was still no official answer from the Soviet government about participating in the conference. Two days later, Vyshinsky informed Archibald Kerr that his government would take part in the talks in London, but asked that the opening be delayed until June 26, which the British government quickly agreed to.[11] Vyshinsky then announced that Iona Timofeevich Nikitchenko, deputy chairman of the Supreme Court of the USSR, would head the Soviet delegation, assisted by Professor Aron Naumovich Trainin.[12] In addition, he stated that Oleg Aleksandrovich Troyanovsky, who would later serve as Moscow's ambassador to the United Nations, would be the Soviet delegation's translator. In reality, Troyanovsky's role was more expansive, since he also became Nikitchenko and Trainin's secretary, travel guide, and administrator.[13] Nikitchenko had been nominated for his position by Ivan Terent'evich Golyakov, the president of the Supreme Court who had worked closely with him in the 1930s.[14] Trainin's appointment was something of a fait accompli, given that Vyshinsky had served as his mentor since the 1930s and, along with Stalin, played a key role in the appointments, fully trusting him to serve Soviet interests at the conference and the trial. Consequently, Trainin was the most appropriate choice to match legal wits with the other renowned jurists in London and later Nuremberg. But it was Nikitchenko, a proven legal and political veteran with experience in one of Stalin's early show trials in the 1930s, who would oversee Soviet efforts in London and Nuremberg.[15]

The size of the Soviet delegation at the London Conference was modest, particularly when compared to that of the British and Americans.[16] The latter included such high-ranking individuals as the famous English criminal barrister Geoffrey D. Roberts and Treasury Solicitor Thomas Barnes, as well as many other representatives of the Lord Chancellor's Office, the Foreign Office, the War Office, and other government agencies.[17]

Given the American and British commitment to the discussions in London, there are questions about what seemed to be the delayed Soviet response to the invitation to participate and appoint representatives to the talks. Some of reasons for this seeming hesitancy center around the substantial practical difficulties of a government, which, though interested in a speedy trial of major war criminals, was not adequately prepared to deal with the international cooperation needed to create and take part in such a trial. This, coupled with the selection and appointment of adequate personnel needed considerable coordination in the higher echelons of the Soviet legal community that, in the end, needed Stalin's personal approval.

Even after the Soviet foreign office received the third American invitation to take part in the talks on June 11, no one in the Kremlin had any idea about whom else to appoint to the Soviet delegation other than Trainin and Nikitchenko.[18]

Directives to the Soviet delegation before leaving for London

The changes proposed by the Soviets to the American draft submitted by the Soviet government in San Francisco, as well as the NKID directives that Vyshinsky gave to Nikitchenko and Trainin shortly before their departure for London provide some insight into the Soviet perspective on the creation of the tribunal.[19] The origin of the directives can largely be reconstructed on the basis of the documents contained in the Vyshinsky fund in the AVP RF (Arkhiv Vneshnei Politiki Rossiiskoi Federatsii; Foreign Policy Archives of the Russian Federation).

Before they left for Nuremberg, Vyshinsky, in consultation with Stalin and Molotov, identified, in eight directives, the topics that he would need to discuss with the Soviet delegation before it left for London.[20] He prepared a preliminary draft for each directive, which he submitted to Molotov for review.[21] Molotov made changes to the draft and proposed that the Soviet delegates provide a detailed assessment and justification for any proposed amendments raised by the other delegations during the conference.[22] After making this change, Vyshinsky sent the new draft to Molotov[23] and Stalin[24] on June 24, 1945, for final approval. Once they gave their consent, Vyshinsky gave Nikitchenko and Trainin their final instructions a day before they left for London.

Directives 7 and 8, which dealt with the mode and intensity of reports sent back to the Kremlin from London, are revealing. They provide information on the limits of their independent decision-making and an essential structural element of how the Soviet delegation operated in London and, later, in Nuremberg. In the case of proposals made by other delegations that had not been considered by the Soviet leadership,

Nikitchenko and Trainin had to submit a report to the Kremlin without delay. This included their assessment about any proposal as well as suggestions about how best to receive instructions from Moscow.[25] Directive 8, for example, prohibited the Soviet delegation from making any arbitrary decisions on issues that were not covered by the directives without the Kremlin's approval.[26] There were no exceptions to this requirement, which gave Nikitchenko and Trainin little room to make independent decisions, which seriously limited their decision-making authority.

The organizational framework of the conference and the course of the negotiations

The first official meeting of the conference was held in London on June 26, 1945. Over the course of the next six weeks, there were fourteen additional plenary negotiating sessions of the Four-Power Drafting Subcommittee (FPDS).[27] From June 26 to July 13, there were a number of Four-Power Committee (FPC) and FPDS meetings that considered a number of draft proposals. On July 11, the FPDS presented the FPC with a British draft for an Agreement and Charter, and two days later the latter began its discussion of the proposal. Sir Maxwell began by suggesting that the committee first discuss the draft agreement, which dealt principally with the Four-Power decision to create an International Military Tribunal to try war criminals, and the basic steps they would take to create it.[28] Jackson, who noted that he and his staff had full authority to conclude any agreement and were ready to "start preparing for trial," wondered if the other delegations were able to do the same, or had to await the authorizations of their governments. Nikitchenko said he only had the authority to enter into discussions about a trial. Robert Falco, the top French delegate, said he could sign an accord but was not certain his government would appoint him as prosecutor. Sir Maxwell Fyfe noted he had the same powers as Jackson and would serve as the British chief prosecutor. Jackson then asked the Soviets if they had the authority to sign an agreement or if it had to be returned to Moscow for signature. Nikitchenko said the latter though he was not sure who would serve as the Soviet prosecutor. Jackson added that he was concerned about the time frame for all of this, given that President Truman had promised him that he would be able to return to his position on the US Supreme Court in October, a date he now thought unlikely. But he did want everything completed, including the trial, by year's end. Fyfe and Nikitchenko expressed similar concerns but reassured the committee that if all went well in the forthcoming discussions, then the trials could start before early October. The latter added that "our task here is to prepare such an instrument as will insure the efficient operation of the prosecution and the Tribunal when it gets down to work."[29]

Jackson followed up with a discussion of the detailed report that he had sent to President Truman on June 6[30] that stated that the United States would move ahead with the trial of the major war criminals it had in custody regardless of whether the other conferees were able to reach an accord for an international trial. He then noted the complexities of setting up such a trial, particularly given the widespread destruction throughout Germany. He added that US military engineers were studying the prospect of such a trial in Nuremberg, which was in the US zone, since the United States could not wait until the "last moment" to prepare for a trial. Fyfe suggested a target date for the submission of the indictment, something Falco and Nikitchenko said might be difficult to set at this time. Jackson then asked how long it would take the Soviets to appoint its prosecutorial staff. Nikitchenko said that the appointments would be made once the committee had reached an agreement on the charter. Both Fyfe and Jackson hoped that the chief Soviet and French representatives would be appointed Chief Prosecutors, since this would greatly enhance plans to conduct the trial.[31]

According to Telford Taylor, Jackson "*was* (italics in original) making 'a show of force'" and underscoring his discomfort in working with the Soviets on the trial. In fact, Jackson told Sidney Alderman, his "first assistant," that "he would not much mind a breakup of the conference." Fortunately, the other delegations were determined to move forward with plans for a trial, with Fyfe serving as a mediator who constantly sought to convince the delegates of the importance of reaching a middle ground on controversial issues.[32]

The modus operandi of the Soviet delegation in London

Directives 7 and 8 required Nikitchenko and Trainin to submit a report to the Kremlin, which included their own assessment,[33] on all new proposals made by other delegations.[34] Consequently, they sent reports continuously to the NKID in Moscow. In most cases, they sent a report one to two days after a meeting in London which included drafts and requests for how to proceed. For example, at the beginning of the talks, Nikitchenko sent the English text of the American draft to Moscow on June 25, 1945, and its Russian translation two days later.[35]

They were immediately reviewed in Moscow, often by G. Osnitskaya, an employee of the NKID and expert on international law. In many instances, she prepared the documents and requests for Vyshinsky's review. She also compared the new drafts with old drafts and identified relevant changes in each of them.[36] Given the urgency of all of this, her reports were often sent to Vyshinsky the day after she received the telegrams from London.[37] This proved to be time-consuming approach, despite the need to respond quickly to the reports from London.[38] This process was further complicated by the fact that almost all of the issues confronted by the Soviet delegation at the London Conference had to be reviewed and approved by Stalin.[39]

On July 25, 1945, Vyshinsky prepared a report on the proceedings in London and immediately sent it to Molotov.[40] It stated that the Soviet representatives were to object to two of the criminal offenses in the draft statute: (a) "invasion or threat of invasion or incitement to war against other countries in breach of treaties, agreements or representations between countries or in any other violation of international law" and (b) "participation in an overall plan or a single act aimed at gaining control over other nations."[41] Furthermore, Vyshinsky added, the delegates had still not decided where the trial would be held. But he was sure that the Soviets would sign the IMT statement and agreement if these issues could be resolved, which Stalin agreed to two days before the signing of the Four-Power Agreement in London.[42]

Between compromise and persistence: The creation of the IMT Charter under the influence of the Soviet delegation

Like the history of most international conferences with historical significance, the story of the London negotiations is one of compromise. On the one hand, there were many points of negotiation that could be solved without significant debates. On the other hand, there were highly controversial issues that took time to discuss before reaching mutual decisions about them. What follows is a discussion of those easily dealt with and those that were more difficult to resolve.

The structure—the agreement and the charter of the IMT

The formal distinction between the London Agreement and the Charter of August 8 goes back to a suggestion by Nikitchenko, in response to the June 14 American draft about a Four-Power accord. He argued that there should be a separate but brief text for the Four-Power Agreement with the Charter as an annex.[43] The Soviets made a similar suggestion in its June 28 draft, which the other delegations accepted.[44]

The constitution of the IMT

The Soviets also made another important contribution during discussions about the first part of the IMT Charter—the constitution of the IMT. Soviet ideas were particularly important when it came to discussions about Article 4, which dealt with questions about the presidency of the trial and the role of the president in a tie vote. The American drafts merely stated that court decisions would be made by a vote of the majority of judges but did not deal with a tie vote.[45] At the first meeting, Nikitchenko suggested that in the case of a tie, the president should have the authority to break the tie.[46] Ultimately, with some modest changes, the delegations adopted the Soviet proposal. Article 4 stated that while decisions would be made by a majority of the judges, in situations where "the votes are evenly divided, the vote of the President shall be decisive: provided always that convictions and sentences shall only be imposed by affirmative votes of at least three members of the Tribunal."[47]

Article 6 lit. (a) IMT Charter: Crimes against peace

Both the influence of the Soviet delegation on the legal foundations of the IMT and the conceptual differences between the Soviets and its Western Allies can be seen in the debates about Article 6 of the charter, especially the idea of crimes against peace (Article 6 lit. [a]). The delegates thoroughly discussed the fundamental question about whether a war of aggression could be a crime punishable under international criminal law and whether a universal definition of aggression should be included into the IMT charter. Equally contentious were questions about the need for an initial statement that the three offenses to be listed in the article—crimes against peace, war crimes, and crimes against humanity—were international crimes. The Americans and the British hoped to avoid a discussion about this issue, particularly since they viewed this question quite differently than the French and the Soviets.

The American concept: Statutory definition of aggression

The United States was a strong advocate of the idea of making aggressive war an international crime. The origins of this controversial new legal concept can be traced back to earlier proposals of the United Nations War Crimes Commission and Col. Murray C. Bernays, one of the early authors of the US proposals about the legal basis for prosecuting German war crimes.[48] Jackson considered the development of new principles of international law a key part of the trial's mission.[49] He declared at the conference on numerous occasions that war was "illegal from its outset," and that this was what had led the United States to take sides in the war.[50] Consequently, it was extremely important that the charter include a statement that aggressive war was an international crime. Without such a definition, he argued, it was possible that a defendant could challenge this concept in an effort to prove that it was not an international crime.[51] This would then leave it up to the tribunal to determine the conditions for the existence of a war of aggression. A pretrial definition would help the judges with their decision and help avoid a political controversy about it during the trial.[52] Consequently, on July 19, the American delegation submitted a draft to the delegates that included a definition of aggression.[53]

The Soviet concept: Exclusion of justiciability in relation to specific aggression allegations

From the Soviet perspective, the main purpose of Article 6 was to set the stage for the concrete punishment of various atrocities committed by the Germans during the war, and aggression was one of the principal crimes committed by the Nazis.[54] Each of the Allied delegations expressed their views on such crimes in various common or unilateral declarations. Nikitchenko argued that

> the policy which has been carried out by the Axis powers has been defined as an aggressive policy in the various documents of the Allied nations and of all the United Nations, and the Tribunal would really not need to go into that.[55]

The Soviets hoped the London Conference would provide the legal basis for trying the Germans for the crimes they committed in the midst of waging aggressive war. This was a decision to be made by the Big Four at London, and should not be left up to the tribunal. On July 19, he told the delegates that

> the Tribunal would not be competent to judge really what kind of war was launched by the defendants; neither would it go into the question of the causes of war. It would really be up to the United Nations or the security organization which

has already been established to go into questions of that sort. . . . The task of the Tribunal is to try war criminals who have committed certain criminal acts.[56]

Against this backdrop, the Soviets wanted the trial limited to a certain type of offender (major Nazi war criminal) and certain offenses (atrocities committed by the Nazis). According to C. A. Pompe, the Soviets wanted the trial to be purely ad hoc in nature.[57] This meant that the basic question about whether such crimes can be punished under international criminal law was of secondary importance.

The genesis of a compromise formula

Although the Soviet delegates argued for the criminalization of aggressive war,[58] this, along with other issues, led to some fundamental conflicts with Jackson. Nikitchenko, for example, rejected the American proposal for the formulation of Article 6 lit. (a) (crimes against peace) because of its overly general wording. On July 23, the Soviet delegation submitted its own draft for Article 6,[59] which the British revised the same day. It limited acts of aggression to the Axis powers and stated that such actions be considered as crimes.[60]

The Soviets followed this up with a new draft a few days later that generally embraced the British draft.[61] It retained the key elements of the British proposal but slightly shortened the introduction. Subsequent US drafts accepted these changes and suggested that there be no limits placed on the list of crimes in the article.[62]

At the final meeting on August 2, the delegations reached a compromise, and allowed the crimes to be formulated in general terms. They also agreed that the court's jurisdiction was limited to the prosecution of members of the European Axis powers, while retaining the general headings in Article 6—(a) crimes against peace, (b) war crimes, and (c) crimes against humanity. Nikitchenko had initially opposed the use of such headings in the charter but thought that the use of the term "crimes against peace" was justified in Article 6. Others had also[63] suggested that "crime of war" might also be applicable though the delegates finally settled on "crimes against peace," a term that Trainin had used in his book, *On the Criminal Responsibility of the Hitlerites*.[64]

The trial of criminal organizations: Articles 9–11 in the charter

Articles 9–11, which deal with the trial of criminal groups and organizations, generated the most controversy at the conference. The concept of "organization crime" and conspiracy were some of the principal, fundamental elements of the initial American draft for the tribunal.[65] By introducing these concepts, the US delegation hoped to create a clear precedent for a judicial verdict based on the criminal nature of an organization and its individual members so that the latter could be prosecuted in national proceedings for their membership in criminal organizations.[66] In future trials of members of such organizations, the voluntary nature of their membership and knowledge of its criminal objectives would place the burden of proof on the individual defendant to prove otherwise.[67] This was carefully laid out in Control Council Law No. 10, Article II. 1 lit. (d)—"Membership in categories of a criminal group or organization [is] declared criminal by the international Military Tribunal."[68]

Initial Soviet opposition to the prosecution of Nazi organizations

Most publications about the Nuremberg IMT trial often emphasize the negative attitude of the Soviet delegation to the idea of the prosecution of organizations.[69] This, however, applied only to the Soviet position on the eve of the London Conference. At the initial meeting on June 26, Nikitchenko noted that the Soviet *Aide-Mémoire* dated June 14 stated that the articles on the trial of criminal organizations should be eliminated because, according to the Yalta Conference's Crimea Declaration, the Allied Control Council would have the power over the "dissolution and prohibition" of "fascist organizations."[70] Furthermore, the instructions that Trainin and Nikitchenko received from Vyshinsky on June 24 prior to their departure for London stated that they were to insist on certain changes to the American draft first proposed at the San Francisco conference.[71] Consequently, Nikitchenko insisted that the delegates adhere to the Crimea Declaration that "Nazi organizations [be] declared . . . illegal and criminal and therefore . . . utterly destroyed." He also argued that any accord reached in London should follow "the decision of the Thee Powers in the Crimean agreement,"[72] a point he reiterated four days later.[73]

Misinterpretations, efforts for mutual understanding, and the coordination of the Soviet and the American positions

Part of Soviet unease with the idea of declaring and prosecuting Nazi organizations was Trainin and Nikitchenko's difficulty fully comprehending American ideas on this question.[74] The first American drafts—the San Francisco Memorandum and its June 14 revision—did not sufficiently explain exactly how criminal organizations would be brought to trial. The ambiguity of the wording used in the American drafts, such as "organizations . . . may be charged . . . with criminal acts,"[75] "conviction of an organization,"[76] or "bring to trial . . . the major criminals, including organizations,"[77] confused the Soviet representatives and led to the assumption that the organizations themselves would be indicted and punished. On July 2, Nikitchenko told the delegates that

> when we examined the first draft of the American proposal, we actually made our notes on that draft, and what we were protesting against really was the wording of 21 and 22 [June 14 draft, article 21, 22]. We understood from this, perhaps incorrectly, that it was the question of the trial of organizations without individuals and that the organization would simply be tried as a body. We considered that to be wrong. We considered that the trial of the organization should be through the individuals, and therefore we suggested the exclusion of that portion of the memorandum.[78]

He added that though Soviet criminal law did recognize the "trials of gangs or organizations and the responsibility of the members of such organizations in addition to any criminal responsibility they may carry for individual acts," it did not recognize the criminal responsibility of non-physical bodies.[79]

Consequently, the initial Soviet demand for the elimination of all relevant provisions regarding the trial of organizations caused the American delegation to conclude that the Soviets opposed the trial of Nazi organizations.[80] In a lengthy discussion about this matter on July 2, Jackson admitted that the US perspective on the criminal nature of organizations was not much different from that of the Soviet delegation. The key, he explained, was to "reach the organization through proof of what individuals did," as Nikitchenko had suggested. By the end of the session, the delegates had a more clear idea about the nuanced differences on this issue.[81] On July 12, a day after the delegates had received the British Draft Agreement and Charter (which now became the principal draft under discussion), the NKID told the Soviet delegation to no longer oppose the idea of the trial of criminal organizations.[82] The following day, Trainin expressed full Soviet support for the statement in Article 10 about the trial of organizations, and praised it as an example of how the collective work of the delegates had resulted in the creation a "model of what an article should be."[83] In the end, this willingness on the part the delegates, particularly the Soviets, to seek a middle ground on complex, and at times, contentious legal matters, underscores the determination and flexibility of those at the conference to reach an accord acceptable to each of the nations in attendance.

The rules of procedure—Articles 13 and 14

Discussions about Articles 13 and 14 of the Charter[84] dealt with rules of procedure. Article 13 gave the tribunal the authority to create "rules for its procedure," while Article 14 laid out the responsibilities and powers of each nation's Chief Prosecutor.[85] Article 15 lit. (e) stated that the Chiefs of Counsel (chief prosecutors) would "draw up and recommend to the Tribunal draft rules of procedure" which the tribunal could accept, amend, or reject.[86]

Jackson thought that the rules of procedure should not be codified in detail, and instead be developed by the tribunal during the trial. From his perspective, the idea of a "liberal rule-making power left in the court,"[87] which was common in American jurisprudence, allowed the court the opportunity to react flexibly to "all unforeseen situations."[88] Nikitchenko agreed with him in principle,[89] but stated that, in league with the British delegation, the basic rules of procedure should be laid out in the charter. If not, then it could delay the work of the prosecutors and might later "lead to duplication and delay."[90] Trainin added on June 29 that there was a difference between the "basic rules on which the Tribunal will operate" and "the question of actual procedure."[91] He argued during a discussion of new Soviet and American drafts on July 11 that basic rules should be determined by the tribunal and not the chief prosecutors. To do otherwise would "demean the court."[92]

The issue of defining the rules of procedure and Trainin's ideas caused long debates in the Drafting Subcommittee.[93] Article 4 of the Soviet draft of July 2 served as a basis for discussion in the report of subcommittee on July 11, which included a substantial redraft of the charter.[94] While the idea to incorporate basic rules of procedure in the charter was quickly agreed upon, the question about the right of the prosecution to propose these rules remained controversial. The French and Soviet representatives argued that the participation of the members of the prosecution in a process that is reserved only for the tribunal would affect the court's powers.[95] In contrast, the British and American delegates saw no problem with such rights for the prosecution since the final determination of the procedural rules would be left to the court itself. It was finally agreed in Article 13 to allow the tribunal to "draw up rules for its procedure," while Article 14. (e) stipulated that the Chief Prosecutors' Committee could present draft rules of procedure that the tribunal could accept, change, or reject.[96]

Committee for the investigation and prosecution of major war criminals (Articles 14 and 15)

On July 16, the committee began to discuss Articles 14 and 15, which were particularly important because they specified the roles of the four Chief Prosecutors and their staffs. Article 14 of the charter[97] stated that each signatory power would appoint a Chief Prosecutor who would work with his three peers as a committee to develop a plan for "the individual work" of his staff, decide which "major war criminals" to indict, approve the indictment and its accompanying documents, and present such evidence to the tribunal. It would, as mentioned earlier, also develop "draft rules of procedure," which the tribunal could accept, alter, or deny. Finally, the Chief Prosecutors, acting as the Committee for the Investigation and Prosecution of Major War Criminals, would appoint a chairman based on the "principle of rotation." In the case of a tie vote on the selection of a defendant or on the charges against him, the committee would adopt those made by the party that proposed his selection and the charges against him.[98] Nikitchenko and Trainin both questioned the necessity of this latter point in section 14. (e). After Fyfe explained it was necessary to ensure that questions on the selection of defendants and the charges against them not slow down the trial, Trainin argued that to allow the prosecutor from one country to "carry a case through himself" would completely destroy "the international character of the whole case." Instead, he suggested that the delegates consider something similar to Article 4. (c), which would allow the committee's chairman to have the decisive vote in a tie. In the end, it was decided to leave this section as it was because several of the prosecutors had not yet completed their cases.[99]

Jackson's goal in all of this was to give each Chief Prosecutor as much independence as possible, something he brought up on July 3 when he noted that his delegation did not "think of the prosecution as a commission but rather as four separate representatives."[100] To underscore his point, Jackson brought up the case against Hjalmar Schacht, who had served as the head of the *Reichsbank* and Hitler's economics minister before the war. Jackson was determined to have him indicted for war crimes, while others were skeptical about the charges that he had directly abetted Hitler's "aggressive intentions."[101] Nikitchenko, who had no problem indicting Schacht, strongly disagreed with Jackson's point on this matter.

> To provide for the right of one, or in case of equal division, of two prosecutors to act on their own initiative, is to adopt a principle which is contrary to the whole charter of the International Tribunal.... The whole agreement and the charter are based on combined action, on cooperation between the Four Powers. Now, if we introduce at one point in one paragraph a principle which departs from this and allows the action of only one power independently, then we are going completely contrary to the whole idea on which the charter is based, and the introduction of

that one exception would mean that a whole series of regulations would have to be provided as to what would be done when that happens. It is quite contrary to the whole spirit of the charter.[102]

Nikitchenko also raised questions about Article 15, which spelled out the roles of the Chief Prosecutors individually. He suggested, for example, that it be divided into two articles (15 and 16) because it was "too lengthy and clumsy."[103] Article 15 also stipulated that the Chief Prosecutors, both individually and collaboratively, would investigate, collect, and produce "all necessary evidence before and during the Trial." They would also prepare the indictment for the committee as stipulated in Article 14. (c), do the preliminary examination of "all necessary witnesses and of all Defendants," act as the trial's prosecutor, "appoint representatives" to fulfill whatever duties were assigned to them, and undertake any other tasks deemed necessary in "preparation for and conduct of the trial." Finally, it stated that "no witness or Defendant detailed by the Signatory shall be taken out of the possession of that Signatory without its assent,"[104] something that Nikitchenko questioned.

Sir Thomas Barnes, one of the British delegates, explained that since portions of Article 15 provided for the individual preparation of cases initially, this clause would prevent one of the signatory states from requesting the "attendance or testimony of defendants" in their custody by another country "without the consent of the detaining country."[105] This was an extremely important issue, particularly to the Soviets, since eighteen of the twenty-four defendants that would later be tried were in American or British custody in their zones of occupation.[106] But Fyfe assured Nikitchenko that if the Soviets wanted to ask a prisoner in British custody "some questions" during a preliminary investigation, then that would be arranged "at a convenient spot."[107]

Fair trial for the defendants (Article 16)

There were also differences of opinion over Article 16, which dealt with a fair trial for the defendants. This was particularly the case when it came to 16. (b), which stated that during "any preliminary examination or trial of a Defendant he will have the right to give any explanation relevant to the charges made against him."[108] Both Nikitchenko and Jackson agreed that it was better to say that he "had the right to give *testimony*" than "an explanation." Nikitchenko wanted further clarity on this section of Article 16, which Fyfe explained meant that the defendant had the right to offer any statement and evidence he wished to make during the preliminary examination, as stipulated in Article 16. (e)—"A defendant shall have the right through himself or through his Counsel to present evidence at the Trial in support of his defense, and to cross-examine any witness called by the Prosecution."[109]

Powers of the tribunal and conduct of the trial (Articles 17 and 24 IMT Charter)

This was followed by a discussion of Article 17, which dealt with the powers of the tribunal and the conduct of the trial. It gave the judges the right to summon witnesses and required them to be in attendance when they gave such testimony, to interrogate the defendants, administer oaths to witnesses, and to appoint officers to carry out any tasks required of the court including taking evidence "on commission."[110] The principal question raised by several of the delegates was whether the court could force a defendant to testify, something Jackson argued could result in "compulsory self-recrimination." He added that the United States was willing to accept the continental system which would require defendants to testify, though he did not think "it would accomplish a great deal." Trainin added that he thought it important to allow the prosecution and tribunal to question a defendant though it should not "compel him to answer," noting that the powers of the prosecutor under the charter were much greater than what you had in the continental system, and that prosecutors should have the right to question the defendants, something not included in Article 24, which dealt with the trial's proceedings.[111]

On July 17, the delegates returned to this question in the context of Article 24, and the right of the defendant not to answer questions before the court, something Nikitchenko called "the order of interrogation." He preferred that the tribunal be the first to question a defendant followed by the prosecution and his defense attorney. Fyfe explained that sections Article 24. (d) and (e) would allow the prosecution and the defense to do so if they had any evidence they wanted to present to the court, while witnesses for either side could be examined and cross-examined by the prosecution and the defense. After both sides were finished with their questioning, then the tribunal would have the right to ask questions.[112] Trainin stated that while the Soviet delegation agreed with this perspective, he thought that the "line of authority" should be followed when it came to questioning. Furthermore, since the tribunal was the "highest authority," it "should be the first to interrogate," which Falco said was "also my thought."[113]

Nikitchenko added that it was a bad idea to give the defendant the right not to answer, since this might encourage him to do so. On the other hand, such a refusal would not be held against a defendant. Both Jackson and Fyfe concurred, noting that it was accepted under German law, something that SHAEF (Supreme Headquarters Allied Expeditionary Force) accepted with a slight modification when it was setting up its military court system.[114]

The Soviets also raised questions about the tribunal's right to "appoint special officers" to obtain evidence from a distance and "report to the Tribunal." Trainin argued that this was a matter of procedure that should not be in the charter. Jackson responded that a trial could not function properly if the court did not have the power to seek evidence in such a way. "Such a situation is entirely conceivable under *our type of trial; it could not arise undoubtedly under the Soviet type of trial, where the case is largely made before the trial starts.*" Fyfe noted that Trainin was not objecting to the power of the court to do so, since its right "would be inherent under the rules of procedure." Jackson disagreed, arguing that the tribunal had no "inherent power; all must be conferred upon it. It cannot acquire power by its own rules."[115]

Trainin then offered a compromise—to allow the tribunal, in certain cases, "for technical reasons" to send a "special officer out to investigate and interrogates, et cetera."[116] Fyfe and Falco saw merit in this compromise, while Jackson argued that

Trainin's suggestion "points up a fundamental difference between your system of procedure and ours." In the US system, he noted, to be evidence, it had to be "produced before the Tribunal itself or some master representing the Tribunal." The mere fact that prosecutors obtained and looked at the evidence would not be "sufficient to bring it to the attention of the court." And if such evidence was not given to a "master representing the court, it might not be admissible." In a trial as serious as this one, he went on, it would be important for the court to have the right to send out a master to gather evidence about incidents in different parts of Europe that would be important to making a point in the case. In the US court system, he explained, masters were used in different ways. Moreover, their usage was based on a simple tenet—"our trial requires the production of all documents and oral testimony before the court." If such evidence is not presented in open court, then you "can't have a trial."[117]

What was really at play here were the realities of the significant differences between the US and the Soviet visions of the trial. The American system was based on centuries-old Anglo-American legal practices and precedents, while the Soviet model was developed in the 1920s and 1930s, and meant to ensure, at least in its major "show" trials, that the court and the prosecutor, working hand-in-glove, wielded absolute control over the entire trial and the ultimate decision of the judges. Jackson was well aware of this, and finally, after weeks of frustration with the Soviets, chose obliquely to discuss the significant differences between the two systems.

The final pathway to an accord: Potsdam and London

What followed during discussions on July 17 were questions about the physical preparations for the trial and its location, a topic raised by Jackson four days earlier. He pointed out that the German courtroom in Nuremberg in the US zone, though not large, had adjacent prison facilities connected to the courtroom by a tunnel. Nikitchenko wondered if Nuremberg was to be the site of the first trial or the administrative seat of the tribunal. He thought that Berlin would be more appropriate for the latter since it was the headquarters of the Allied Control Council.[118] This question ultimately would not be resolved until August 2.

Over the next week there were four more meetings of the Four-Power Committee where the delegates expressed increasing frustration about significant arguments over the interpretation of some of the charter's basic points, particularly aggression, conspiracy or the common plan, and crime itself.[119] As frustrations intensified, Jackson noted on July 20 "that our greatest problem is how to reconcile two very different systems of procedure." And he admitted that "in some ways the Continental and Soviet systems are even better than ours," essentially admitting that the United States was probably the principal stumbling block to reaching an accord on the charter.[120]

As the discussions moved forward, there was a flurry of drafts from the French (one), the United States (nine), the Soviets (three), and the British (six) about different parts of the charter that, in some instances, confused matters more than helping resolve differences. On July 23, Jackson told the other delegates that he was "really getting very discouraged about the possibility of conducting an international trial with the very different viewpoints." He did not really blame anyone for this, instead noting again the delegations' "very different viewpoints." He wondered aloud if it might be best for the United States to withdraw from the talks and either turn the prisoners over to the "European powers to try" or hold "separate trials."[121] Fyfe countered that he was an optimist and that his government would be quite disappointed if the talks failed, while Nikitchenko added that the delegates had already resolved their differences on twenty-seven of the thirty articles. Jackson responded that if the committee wanted to move forward with the talks, then a decision needed to be made about the site of the trial. Nikitchenko said that he had already suggested Nuremberg to his government, and that all that was needed to decide on this matter was the role of Berlin and Nuremberg as the seats of the tribunal and the site of the first trial.[122]

The following day, the delegations began to discuss a new British draft of the agreement and charter.[123] During a discussion about Article 6, which dealt with "jurisdiction and general principles," Jackson, noting his "characteristic stubbornness," said that 6. (d), which was about entering into "a common plan or enterprise aimed at domination over other nations,"[124] was far too broad and would entrap millions of people, which the superior American draft of this article "wasn't intended to reach."[125] The delegates left this question unresolved, and began to discuss other articles. A few days later, Nikitchenko and Jackson agreed that the talks had taken "one or two steps back," which prompted André Gros, one of the French delegates, to remind the other delegates of the importance of moving forward with the talks, since "each day lost is a day lost for the prosecuting officers."[126]

On July 26, Jackson flew to Berlin to talk with American officials in Potsdam to discuss how to proceed with the London talks. In a wire to Assistant Secretary of War, John McCloy, Jackson told him that there was serious disagreement about the "definition of war crimes. All European powers would qualify criminality of aggressive war and not go along on view in my report to President." Secretary of State James Byrnes told him that "as a matter of American policy," Jackson should not "make any sacrifices of or deviations from principle," or make any agreement "which he felt in any way derogated from fundamental axioms of justice."[127] On the other hand, Byrnes said he should "make all reasonable attempts to reach an agreement for complete Russian participation on a sound basis,"[128] though, in the end, it was left up to Jackson to determine what would be an acceptable agreement to US policy makers.

Behind the scenes in London, the British Foreign Office was struggling to find ways to keep the talks going. One Foreign Office memo sent to the British delegation in Potsdam indicated that the real problem with the talks was not the inability to reach common ground on an accord, but Jackson's "explicit distrust of the Soviet[s]."[129] Sidney Alderman, Jackson's top assistant, while admitting that it was, at times, difficult to deal with the Soviets, who would agree to something one day and repudiate it the next, attributed this to the fact that the Soviet delegation had to report back to Vyshinsky and Stalin with regularity during the talks, which undermined their autonomy to make decisions.[130] But Jackson's distrust of Soviet intentions was also a reflection of similar feelings among some American officials about Stalin's postwar intentions, which they hoped would be resolved at Potsdam.[131]

The discussions now branched off in several directions—one in London and another in Potsdam. On July 30, the Soviet and British submitted proposals at Potsdam on the question of trying Nazi Germany's "principal war criminals." The two Soviet drafts emphasized the importance of the Moscow Declaration of November 1, 1943, as the basis of the proposal, something they had argued continually about during the London talks. The drafts also listed twelve (ten in the first draft) members of the "Hitler clique" that should be tried—Göring, Hess, Ribbentrop, Papen, Ley, Keitel, Kaltenbrunner, Frick, Hans Frank, Streicher, Krupp, and Schacht. The British proposal stated that, given "the great public interest throughout the world" in a "just and speedy punishment in the major war criminals," the Big Three in Potsdam, aware of the discussions going on in London about such criminals "whose crimes under the Moscow Declaration of October 1943 have no particular geographical localization," hope they will "result in speedy agreement being reached for this purpose."[132]

On the same day, Byrnes told Molotov and Ernest Bevan, Britain's new foreign minister, that he had spoken to Jackson about the talks in London, who told him that the only stumbling block was the question about the "definition of war crimes." The following day, Truman raised the question of war crimes with Clement Atlee, the UK's new prime minister, and Stalin. Molotov agreed to accept the British draft as long as it included the list of those to be tried, especially Göring, something the British and the Americans opposed. Truman responded that Byrnes needed to talk to Jackson before they could move forward with the discussion about war crimes, and Stalin agreed to wait another day to discuss it.[133]

Jackson called Byrnes on August 1 and found him unavailable. Instead, he talked with Judge Samuel Rosenman, President Roosevelt's former legal counsel who was coordinating US efforts on the war crimes issue. Jackson told Rosenman that he opposed naming any potential defendants, and thought it was a bad idea to hold a "joint trial" because "of the difficulty of working with the Russians in a trial." On the other hand, if Moscow accepted the "various propositions" made by the United States, then he would support such a tribunal. If this did not work out, Jackson suggested individual national trials or even a Franco-British-US trial, something Rosenman said might lead to Soviet "recriminations."[134]

The day before, Sir William Jowitt, Britain's new Lord Chancellor, wrote to Atlee, after discussing the issue with Fyfe, that the United States was making too much of the outstanding differences in the London talks, which "could easily be solved by good will." He added that he thought the United States was using such issues to find a way to abandon the idea of a joint trial so that they could conduct individual trials in their zone of occupation. He said he would meet with the four delegations in London to see if he could move the talks forward.[135]

On August 1, Atlee wired Jowitt that he had talked to Truman, and the president had told him that "it was most important that these trials should be conducted on a quadripartite basis and should be started soon."[136] On the same day, Jowitt met with Jackson and told him that he had been asked by his government to take over the talks. He also mentioned that he had recently spoken to the British delegation, who had outlined for him the "points of disagreement," and wanted Jackson's views on these issues. He expressed "general agreement" with many of Jackson's concerns, but disagreed with him on the "right to terminate the agreement if any of the signatories failed promptly to name prosecutors," something he thought might "imply a distrust in some signatory." He also told Jackson that the new Labour Attorney General, Sir Hartley Shawcross, would be named Britain's Chief Prosecutor, assisted by Sir David Maxwell Fyfe.[137]

The next day, Jowitt met with all four London Conference delegations and told them that they had to reach an agreement now or "adopt some other procedure."[138] He then began to go through each article in the agreement and charter. It was quickly agreed to approve the former, though discussions about the latter were more complex. Yet by the end of the day, Jowitt was able to find middle ground on the various issues that had been stumbling blocks in the past. By mid-afternoon, when he left to go to the rehearsal for the opening of Parliament, almost everything had been resolved. Fyfe took his place, and after a brief discussion about the final text, the talks concluded by selecting Berlin as the administrative center of the tribunal and Nuremberg the site of the first trial. A final decision about Article 6 was left up in the air until Nikitchenko got final approval from the Kremlin. The final, translated agreement, which included the charter, was signed by the head of each delegation on August 8, though, in the Soviet case, by Nikitchenko and Trainin. On October 6, a separate protocol that dealt with some translation discrepancies in Article 6 was signed by the trial's four chief prosecutors.[139]

Conclusion

The role of the Soviet delegation, particularly future IMT judge Iona Nikitchenko and the highly respected international criminal law specialist Aron Trainin, whose *Criminal Responsibility of the Hitlerites* was discussed throughout the talks, should not be seen in a negative light. While there is no question that they were hampered by the need to have their most important decisions approved by Stalin and Vyshinsky, their concerns about various aspects of the agreement and charter not only reflected their own interpretation and perspectives on Soviet criminal law but also those voiced by the French delegation. This, and their nation's wartime experiences, played a key role in their view of aggression and related discussions. On certain issues, such as the definition of the crimes of aggression or the site of the trial and headquarters for the tribunal, the Soviet representatives could be stubborn. Yet, overall, the Soviet negotiators proved to be self-confident and consensus-oriented. And, according to Sidney Alderman, "The Russians were second to none in politeness and tact."[140] They were also very detail-oriented and their numerous comments and queries reflected this. Moreover, their influence can be seen in almost every aspect of the agreement and charter. Even the formal structure—a separate agreement as a prelude to the charter—was initially proposed by the Soviet delegation. Other important contributions to these documents include, among others, the Charter's Article 4 (b) and (c) (the tribunal's presidency and voting majorities), Article 13 (creation of the tribunal's procedural rules), Article 14 (Committee of Chief Prosecutors), Article 22 (the tribunal's permanent seat in Berlin), and Article 24 (f) (right of the judges to question witnesses or defendants at any time).

On the other hand, the practical impact of some of these Soviet contributions was rather insignificant. The principle of the rotation of the tribunal's presidency after the first trial (Article 4 [b]) did not go into force since there were no subsequent Four-Power trials. The same was true about Berlin being the tribunal's administrative center, though the IMT trial's opening session took place there on October 18, 1945. The full trial, which took place in Nuremberg, as did the subsequent US war crimes trials. And it was here, not Berlin, that the tribunal announced its opinion and judgment on October 1, 1946.

Articles 14 and 15 were also ineffective, since the Committee of Chief Prosecutors and its various duties such as the investigation, collection, and production of all necessary evidence (15 [a]), the preparation of the indictment (15 [b]), the preliminary examination of witnesses and defendants (15 [c]), acting as prosecutor at the trial (15 [d]) and other sections proved impractical and unworkable.

Yet, in the end, as the minutes of the London Conference indicate, the role of the Soviet delegation was significant, and set the stage for an equally important role in the Nuremberg IMT trial that begin several months later. This role certainly reflects the equally significant role that the Soviet Union played in the outcome of the Second World War in Europe.

Notes

1 Agreement for the Prosecution and Punishment of the Major War Criminals of the European Axis, AJIL 39 (1945), Suppl. 257, 257–58; Internationaler Militärgerichtshof Nürnberg (ed.) ([2001] 1947), Frechen: Komet, Vol. I, 8–9. For the Russian text version see 'Soglašenie o sudebnom presledovanii i nakazanii glavnych voenych prestupnikov evropejskich stran osi', *Socialističeskaja Zakonnost'*, 1945 № 9: 8–9; Ministerstvo Inostannych Del SSSR (ed.), *Sbornik dejstvujushich dogovorov, soglašenij i konvencij, zakljuchennych SSSR s nostrannymi gosudarstvami: Dejstvujushie dogovory, soglashenija i konvencii, vstupivšie v silu meždu 22 iyunja 1941 goda i 2 sentjabrja 1945 goda*. Vyp. 11 (Moscow, 1955), Doc. № 472, 163–65; A. M. Rekunkov, N. S. Lebedeva, N. Alekseev, M. Ju. Raginsky, K. S. Pavlishev (eds.), *Njurnbergsky process*, sbornik materialov v 8-mi tomach, Vol. 1 (Moscow, 1987), 144–46; Lebedeva, N. S. (ed.), *SSSR i Njurnbergskij process*. Neizvestnye i maloizvestnye stranici istorii: Sbornik dokumentov (Moscow: Mezdunarodny fond Demokratiya, 2012), Doc. № 69, 216–18. For the official German text: *Londoner Viermächte*-Abkommen, 8. August 1945, IMT, Vol. I, 7–9; Pursuant to Article 2 of the London Agreement the Charter of the International Military Tribunal formed an integral part of the Agreement, IMT, Vol. I, 7 (8); Charter of the International Military Tribunal, AJIL 39 (1945), Suppl. 257, 258–63; IMT, Vol. I, 10–16. For the Russian text version see 'Ustav Meždunarodnogo Voennogo Tribunala', *Socialisticheskaya Zakonnost'*, 1945 № 9, 9–14, MID SSSR (ed.), *Sbornik dejstvujushich dogovorov*, Vyp. 11, Doc. № 472, 166–83; Rekunkov et al. (ed.), *Njurnbergskij process*, Vol. 1, 146–53; Lebedeva (ed.), *SSSR*, Doc. № 70, 218–24. For the German text version of the *Statut für den Internationalen Militärgerichtshof* see International Military Tribunal (ed.) ([2001] 1947), *Der Prozess gegen die Hauptkriegsverbrecher vor dem Internationalen Militärgerichtshof*, Frechen: Komet, Vol. I, 10–18.
2 *Report of Robert H. Jackson, United States Representative to the International Conference on Military Trials* (Washington, DC: Department of State, 1945).
3 *Jackson Report*, Preface, VI.

4   See Annette Weinke, *Die Nürnberger Prozesse* (Munich: Beck, 2006), 19; Telford Taylor, *Die Nürnberger Prozesse, Hintergründe, Analysen und Erkenntnisse aus heutiger Sicht* (Munich: Heine, 1996), 82, 91, 95, 102; Bradley F. Smith, *Der Jahrhundert-Prozeß. Die Motive der Richter von Nürnberg—Anatomie einer Urteilsfindung* (Frankfurt am Main: S. Fischer, 1977), 68. See the note of Samuel Rosenman to the Secretary of State Byrnes, August 1, 1945, FRUS, The Conference of Berlin (the Potsdam Conference) 1945, Vol. II, 987–88.

5   For the protocol of the meeting, see the Memorandum of Conversation held in San Francisco, May 3, 1945, FRUS 1945, Vol. III, 1161-64; see also Golunskij's protocol, Soveščanie po voprosu o nakazanii voennych prestupnikov, 3 maja 1945, AVP RF, f. 06, op. 7, p. 20, d. 209, Bl. 1–5, printed in Diplomaticheskyi vestnik 1995 № 4, 79–80; Lebedeva (ed.), *SSSR*, Dok. № 40, 160-63. The Soviet side was represented by the People's Commissar of Foreign Affairs Vjačeslav Michailovič Molotov, the Soviet ambassador in the United States, Andrej Andreevich Gromyko, a representative of the law department of the des NKID, Sergej Aleksandrovich Golunskij, a representative of a central department of the NKID, Boris Fëdorovich Podcerob, and the Chief translator of the NKID, Vladimir Nikolaevich Pavlov.

6   Note dated May 19, 1945, AVP RF, f. 06, op. 7, p. 45, d. 711, l. 1= AVP RF, f. 07, op. 13, p. 41, d. 1, l. 1 = AVP RF, f. 07, op. 13, p. 41, d. 3, l. 46, printed in Lebedeva (ed.), *SSSR*, Dok. № 43, 170.

7   Executive Order by President Truman, May 2, 1945, *Jackson Report*, Doc. III, 21.

8   Note from Kennan to Vyshinsky May 25, 1945, AVP RF, f. 06, op. 7, 45, d. 711, l. 2, printed in Lebedeva (ed.), *SSSR*, Dok. № 44, 171. The Ministry of External (Foreign) Affairs was also known as the People's Commissariat for Foreign Affairs (*Narodnyi Kommissariat po Inostrannym delam*) or the *Narkomindel* (*NKID*).

9   Note from Harriman to Dekanozov June 11, 1945, AVP RF, f. 06, op. 7, p. 45, d. 711, l. 3, printed in Lebedeva (ed.), *SSSR*, Dok. № 49, 177–78.

10 Kerr to Molotov June 12, 1945, AVP RF, f. 07, op. 13, p. 41, d. 3, l. 49 = AVP RF, f. 06, op. 07, p. 24, d. 278, ll. 1–2 (Russian translation on l. 1, English text on l. 2); Russian text version is printed in Lebedeva (ed.), *SSSR*, Dok. № 50, 178–79; see also J. P. Laufer and G. P. Kynin (eds.), *Die UdSSR und die deutsche Frage 1941-1949, Dokumente aus dem Archiv für Außenpolitik der Russischen Föderation*, Vol. 2: 9. Mai 1945 bis 3. Oktober 1946 (Berlin: Duncker und Humblot, 2004), LXXXVI.

11 Kerr to Vyshinsky, June 24, 1945, AVP RF, f. 06, op. 7, p. 24, d. 278, l. 4.

12 Vyshinsky to Kerr, June 23, 1945, AVP RF, f. 06, op. 7, 24, d. 278, l. 3, printed in Lebedeva (ed.), *SSSR*, Dok. № 53, 185.

13 Oleg Troyanovsky, *Cherez gody i rasstoyaniyaj. Istoriya odnoy sem'i* (Moscow: Vagrius, 1997), 106.

14 Report from Erofeev and Bazarov to Vyshinsky, June 14, 1945, AVP RF, f. 07, op. 13, p. 41, d. 3, ll. 51–52.

15 Nikitchenko was one the judges in the Moscow show trial against Kamenev and Zinoviev in 1936, K. A. Zalessky, *Kto est' kto v istorii SSSR, 1924-1953 gg.* (Moscow: Vece, 2009), 424f.

16 Taylor, *Nürnberger Prozesse*, 77. The Roster of Representatives and Assistants contained in the *Jackson Report* names Jackson as the official representative for the American side as well as ten assistants, *Jackson Report*, 441; Roster of Representatives and Assistants, *Jackson Report*, 441.

17 Taylor, *Nürnberger Prozesse*, 79.

18 Report from Erofeev and Bazarov to Vyshinsky, June 14, 1945, supra note 14.

19 Directives of the NKID, handed over on June 24, 1945. AVP RF, f. 07, op. 10, p. 8, d. 83, ll. 40–43 = AVP RF, f. 07, op. 13, p. 41, d. 3, ll. 72–75, Diplomatičeskij vestnik 1995, № 12, S. 74–75; Lebedeva (ed.), SSSR, Dok. № 55, S. 187–88; see also Laufer/ Kynin (eds.), Dokumente, Vol. 2, LXXXVI.
20 AVP RF, f. 07, op. 13, p. 41, d. 3, Bl. 70–71; Lebedeva (ed.), SSSR, Dok. № 54, 186.
21 Draft of the directives June 22, 1945, AVP RF, f. 07, op. 13, p. 41, d. 2, ll. 12–15.
22 Draft of the directives June 22, 1945, AVP RF, f. 07, op. 13, p. 41, d. 2, ll. 12, 15.
23 Draft of the directives from Vyshinsky to Molotov, June 24, 1945, AVP RF, f. 07, op. 13, p. 41, d. 2, ll. 19–22.
24 VyshinskyAVP RF, f. 07, op. 10, p. 8, d. 83, ll. 40–43, Lebedeva (ed.), SSSR, Dok. № 54, 186–89.
25 Diplomatichesky vestnik 1995, № 12, 74, 75.
26 Diplomatichesky vestnik 1995, № 12, 74, 75.
27 The meetings in the Four-Power Drafting Subcommittee took place daily between July 5 until July 11, 1945, with the exception of Saturdays and Sundays. See Report of American Member of Drafting Subcommittee, July 11, 1945, *Jackson Report*, Doc. XXIV, 185–93. An additional meeting was held July 19, 1945, Report of American Member of Drafting Subcommittee, July 19, 1945, *Jackson Report*, Doc. XXXIV, 291–92.
28 Office of United States Chief of Counsel for Prosecution of Axis Criminality, *Nazi Conspiracy and Aggression*, Vol. I (Washington, DC: United States Government Printing Office, 1946), 1–4.
29 Minutes of Conference Session, July 13, 1945, *Jackson report*, Doc. XXVII, 211–13.
30 Minutes of Conference Session, June 3, 1945, *Jackson Report*, Doc. VIII, 42–54.
31 Ibid., July 13, 1945, Doc. XXVII, 211–15,
32 Telford Taylor, *The Anatomy of the Nuremberg Trials: A Personal Memoirs* (Boston: Little Brown, 1992), 62–63.
33 Para. 7 of the directives, Diplomaticheskyi vestnik 1995, № 12, 74, 75.
34 Para. 8 of the directives, Diplomaticheskyi vestnik 1995, № 12, 74, 75.
35 AVP RF, f. 07, op. 13, p. 41, d. 3, ll. 1–4, here l. 4; Lebedeva (ed.), SSSR, Dok. № 60, 203, 204; AVP RF, f. 07, op. 13, p. 41, d. 3, ll. 54–62 and ll. 63–66. See Nikitchenko's note from June 27, 1945, AVP RF, f. 07, op. 13, p. 41, d. 2, l. 23, Lebedeva (ed.), Dok. № 56, 189–94, here S. 189, and the american draft AVP RF, f. 07, op. 13, p. 41, d. 2, ll. 24–31, Lebedeva (ed.), SSSR, Dok. № 56, 189–94.
36 "Ispolnitel'noe Soglashenyi o sudebnom presledovanii voennych prestupnikov evropejskich stran. Charakteristika 3-go amerikanskogo proekta, sravnitel'no so 2-m amerikanskim proektom i s učetom naših popravok" July 5, 1945, AVP RF, f. 07, op. 13, p. 41, d. 9, ll. 65–75.
37 The draft of the subcommittee dated July 11, 1945 (*Jackson Report*, Doc. XXV, 194–201) was sent by Nikitchenko und Trainin to Moscow on July 16, 1945. On July 17, 1945, Osnitskaya presented her report (Zakljuchenie po podgotovlennomu podkomissiej chetyrech delegacyj Ustavu mezhdunarodnogo voennogo tribunala, soobshchennomu nam tt. Nikitchenko i Trajninym iz Londona 16 ijulja s.g.), AVP RF, f. 07, op. 13, p. 41, d. 2, ll. 51–56, Lebedeva (ed.), SSSR, Dok. № 62, 207–09.
38 Report dated July 17, 1945 (Fn. 36). See also Osniitskaya report about the meetings on July 16 and 17, 1945: K telegrammam iz Londona ot 18 ijulja o stat'jach proekta Ustava, obsuzhdavshimsja v Komissii 16 i 17 ijulja), AVP RF, f. 07, op. 13, p. 41, d. 3, ll. 110–11.
39 See Laufer/Kynin (eds.), *Dokumente*, Bd. 1, XXVIII.

40 Report from Vyshinsky July 25, 1945, AVP RF, f. 07, op. 13, p. 41, d. 3, ll. 119–20 = AVP RF, f. 07, op. 10, 8, d. 83, ll. 44–45, printed in Laufer/Kynin (eds.), *Dokumenty*, T. II, Dok. 20, 182–83, Lebedeva (ed.), *SSSR*, Dok. № 62, 207–09.
41 Report July 25, 1945, Laufer/Kynin (eds.), *Dokumente*, Bd. 2, Dok. 20, 57.
42 Report July 25, 1945, Laufer/Kynin (eds.), *Dokumente*, Bd. 2, Dok. 20, 57.
43 Minutes of Conference Session, June 26, 1945, *Jackson Report*, Doc. XIII, 71.
44 Comments of the Soviet Delegation on the American Draft, June 28, 1945, *Jackson Report*, Doc. XVI, 92.
45 Pt. 6 of the revised American Draft, *supra* note, *Jackson Report*, Doc. IX, 56. The same wording can be found in the point 12 of the American draft of June 30, *Jackson Report*, Doc. XVIII, 123.
46 Minutes of Conference Session, June 26, 1945, *Jackson Report*, Doc. XIII, 73.
47 Art. 10 (Kvorum i golosovanie/Quorum and Voting), of the Soviet Draft, July 2, 1945, *Jackson Report*, Doc. XXIII, 173; Notes of American Representative on Drafting Subcommittee, July 11, 1945, *Jackson Report*, Doc. XXIV, 188. *Charter of the International Military Tribunal, 8 August, 1945,* 1.
48 David M. Crowe, *War Crimes, Genocide, and Justice: A Global History* (New York: Palgrave Macmillan, 2014), 158–59; See also Smith, *Road to Nuremberg*, 91; Taylor, *Nürnberger Prozesse*, 55; Cornelis A. Pompe, *Aggressive War: An International Crime* (Dordrecht: Springer Netherlands, 1953), 191; Bloxham (2008), 'Milestones and Mythologies, The Impact of Nuremberg' in P. Heberer and J. Matthäus (eds.), *Atrocities on Trial, Historical Perspectives on the Politics of Prosecuting War Crimes*, 263–82 (London: University of Nebraska Press, 2008), 272. For the debates about the criminal liability and war of aggression in 1940s, see Daniel M. Segesser, *Recht statt Rache oder Rache durch Recht? Die Ahndung von Kriegsverbrechen in der internationalen wissenschaftlichen Debatte, 1872-1945* (Paderborn, Munich, Vienna, Zurich: Schöningh, 2010), 313, 329; Brown, R. M. (2006), 'The American Perspective on Nuremberg: A Case of Cascading Ironies', in H. R. Reginbogin and Ch. Safferling (ed.), *Nuremberg Trials, International Criminal Law since 1945*, 21-29 (Berlin/Boston: De Gruyter - De Gruyter Saur, 2006), 25. For the formulation of Article 6 lit. (a) IMT Charter, see Clark, Roger S., Nuremberg and the Crime Against Peace, in: *Washington University Global Studies Law Review* 6 (2007), 527–50.
49 Jackson expressed these ambitions in his report to the American President on June 6, 1945: "Unless we are prepared to abandon every principle of growth for International Law, we cannot deny that our own day has its right to constitute customs and conclude agreements that will themselves become sources of newer and strengthened International Law. . . . We therefore propose to charge that a war of aggression is a crime, and that modern International Law has abolished the defense that those who incite or wage it are engaged in legitimate business. . . . Any legal position on behalf of the United States will have considerable significance in the future evolution of International Law. . . . Such occasions rarely come and quickly pass. We are put under a heavy responsibility to see that our behavior during this unsettled period will direct the world's thought toward a firmer enforcement of the laws of international conduct, so as to make war less attractive to those who have governments and the destinies of peoples in their power." *Jackson Report*, Doc. VIII, 51, 53.
50 Minutes of Conference Session, July 25, 1945, *Jackson Report*, Doc. LI, 383–84.
51 Minutes of Conference Session, July 19, 1945, *Jackson Report*, Doc. XXXVII, 305–06.
52 Minutes of Conference Session, July 19, 1945, *Jackson Report*, Doc. XXXVII, 307–08.

53 Definition of "Aggression," Suggested by American Delegation as Basis of Discussion, July 19, 1945, *Jackson Report*, 294.
54 See Minutes of Conference Session, July 19, 1945, *Jackson Report*, Doc. XXXVII, 298. For similar statements made by Nikitchenko, see pages 303 and 377. A clear position can also be found in Trainin's words during the meeting on July 23: "I welcome the fact that in the French draft personal responsibility is well emphasized and that we should try to incorporate it in our draft, but I still think the question of declaration of law remains. That is, the four countries may, for the purpose of this trial, declare certain acts to be criminal; and for the purposes of this trial the laws declared by the Four Powers should be sufficient." *Jackson Report*, Doc. XLIV, 335.
55 Minutes of Conference Session, July 19, 1945, *Jackson Report*, Doc. XXXVII, 303.
56 Minutes of Conference Session, July 19, 1945, *Jackson Report*, Doc. XXXVII, 303.
57 Pompe, *Aggressive War*, 192.
58 Minutes of Conference Session, July 23, 1945, *Jackson Report*, Doc. XLIV, 335; Minutes of Conference Session, July 25, 1945, *Jackson Report*, Doc. LI, 386.
59 Redraft of Definition of "Crimes," Submitted by Soviet Delegation, July 23, 1945, *Jackson Report*, Doc. XLIII, 327: "The Tribunal shall have power to try any person who has in any capacity whatever directed or participated in the preparation or conduct of any or all the following acts, designs or attempts namely: a) Aggression against or domination over other nations carried out by the European Axis in violation of the principles of international law and treaties."
60 Redraft of Soviet Definition of "Crimes" (Article 6), Submitted by British Delegation, July 23, 1945, *Jackson Report*, Doc. XLVI, 359: "The following acts or designs or attempts at any of them shall be deemed crimes on conviction of which punishment may be imposed by the Tribunal upon any person who is proved to have in any capacity whatever directed or participated in the preparation or planning for or carrying out of any or all acts designs or attempts: (a) Aggression against or domination over other nations carried out by the European Axis in violation of treaties, agreements and assurances."
61 Redraft of Definition of "Crimes," Submitted by Soviet Delegation, July 25, 1945, *Jackson Report*, Doc. XLVIII, 373: "The following acts, design or attempts at any of them shall be deemed crimes and shall come within the jurisdiction of the Tribunal: a) Aggression against or domination over other nations carried out by the European Axis in violation of treaties, agreements and assurances."
62 Redraft of Definition of "Crimes," Submitted by American Delegation, July 25, 1945, *Jackson Report*, Doc. XLIX, 374: "The following acts shall be deemed criminal violations of International Law, and the Tribunal shall have the power and jurisdiction to convict any person who committed any of them on the part of the European Axis powers"; Revised Definition of "Crimes," Submitted by American Delegation, July 30, 1945, *Jackson Report*, Doc. LIV, 393: "The Tribunal established by the Agreements referred to in Article 1 hereof shall have the power and jurisdiction to hear, try and determine charges of crime against only those who acted in aid for the European Axis Powers. The following acts, designs and attempts at any of them, shall be deemed to be crimes coming within its jurisdiction: (a) Initiation of a war of aggression"; Revision of Definition of "Crimes," Submitted by American Delegation, July 31, 1945, *Jackson Report*, Doc. LVI, 395: "The Tribunal established by the Agreements referred to in Article 1 hereof shall have the power and jurisdiction to try and determine charges of crime against individuals who and organizations which acted in aid for the European Axis Powers and to impose punishment on those found guilty. The

following acts, or any of them, are crimes coming within its jurisdiction for which there shall be individual responsibility: (a) The Crime of War."

63 Redraft of Soviet Definition of "Crimes" (Article 6), Submitted by British Delegation, July 23, 1945, *Jackson Report*, Doc. XLVI, 359: "The following acts or designs or attempts at any of them shall be deemed crimes on conviction of which punishment may be imposed by the Tribunal upon any person who is proved to have in any capacity whatever directed or participated in the preparation or planning for or carrying out of any or all acts designs or attempts: (a) Aggression against or domination over other nations carried out by the European Axis in violation of treaties, agreements and assurances."

64 A. N. Trainin, *Criminal Responsibility of the Hitlerites*, Part I, ed. A. Y. Vyshinsky (Moscow: Legal Publishing House, NKU, 1944), 55–60.

65 Jackson described the connection between the idea of conspiracy and the trial against criminal organizations as "the heart of our proposal," Minutes of Conference Session, June 29, 1945, *Jackson Report*, Doc. XVII, 129. For further details about the development of the American concept, see Smith, *Road to Nuremberg*, 48; Ann Tusa and John Tusa ([2003] 1983), *Nuremberg Trial*, New York: Cooper Square Press, 54, Stanisław Pomorski (1990), 'Conspiracy and Criminal Organizations', in: G. Ginsburgs and V. N. Kudriavtsev (ed.), *The Nuremberg Trial and International Law*, 213–48 (Dordrecht, Boston, MA, and London: Martinus Nijhoff Publishers, 1990), 215. For the analysis of the origins of the conspiracy concept and the crime of conspiracy in the Charter of the IMT, see Safferling, Christoph M., 'Die Strafbarkeit wegen "Conspiracy" in Nürnberg und ihre Bedeutung für die Gegenwart', *Kritische Vierteljahresschrift für Gesetzgebung und Rechtswissenschaft* 2010, 65–82.

66 See also the American Memorandum Presented in San Francisco, April 30, 1945, *Jackson Report*, Doc. V, 32–33: "The findings of the tribunal in the trial provided for in paragraph a above should be taken to constitute a general adjudication of the criminal character of the groups and organizations referred to, binding upon all the members thereof in their subsequent trials in occupation tribunals or in other tribunals established under this instrument. In these subsequent trials the only necessary proof of guilt if any particular defendant, as regards the charge of complicity, should be his membership in one of those organizations. Proof should also be taken of the nature and the extent of the individual's participation." See also G. Rauschenbach, *Der Nürnberger Prozeß gegen die Organisationen. Grundlagen, Probleme, Auswirkungen auf die Mitglieder und strafrechtliche Ergebnisse* (Bonn: Röhrscheid, 1954), 12; Pomorski, Stanisław (1990), Conspiracy and Criminal Organizations, in: G. Ginsburgs and V. N. Kudriavtsev (eds.), *The Nuremberg Trial and International Law* (Den Haag: Springer Netherlands), 213, 220.

67 Pt. 21, Revision of American Draft of Proposed Agreement, June 14,1945, *Jackson Report*, Doc. IX, 59: "Upon proof of membership in such an organization, the burden shall be upon the defendant to establish any circumstances relating to his membership or participation therein which are relevant either in defense or in mitigation." See also pt. 23 Revised Draft of Agreement and Memorandum Submitted by American Delegation, June 30, 1945, *Jackson Report*, Doc. XVIII, 112; *Jackson Report*, Doc. XXIII, 181–82: "Upon proof of membership in such an group or organization, such person shall be deemed to have participated in and be guilty of its criminal activities unless he proves the absence of voluntary participation."

68 Law No 10, Punishment of Persons guilty of War Crimes, Crimes against Peace and against Humanity, December 20, 1945, entered into force on December 24, 1945 (Official Gazette of the Control Council for Germany, No. 3 [31 January 1946]), 50–55.
69 For example, see Taylor, *Nürnberger Prozesse*, 81; Bradley F. Smith, *Der Jahrhundert-Prozeß. Die Motive der Richter von Nürnberg—Anatomie einer Urteilsfindung* (Frankfurt a. M.: Fischer, 1977), 64.
70 Pt. 8 of the Aide-Mémoire from the Soviet Government, June 14, 1945, *Jackson Report*, Doc. X, 62.
71 Pt. 2 of the directives, June 24, 1945, Diplomaticheskyi vesnik 1995 № 12, 75.
72 Minutes of Conference Session, June 26, 1945, *Jackson Report*, Doc. XIII, 72.
73 Pt. 12 of the Comments of the Soviet Delegation on the American Draft, June 28, 1945, *Jackson Report*, Doc. XVI, 94.
74 Smith, *Jahrhundert-Prozeß*, 64.
75 Article 12 lit. (c) of the American Draft of Definitive Proposal, Presented to Foreign Ministers at San Francisco, April 1945, *Jackson Report*, Doc. IV, 25.
76 Article 12 lit. (d) of the Draft submitted at San Francisco, *supra* note 7576, *Jackson Report*, Doc. IV, 25.
77 Article 10 of the revised American Draft of Proposed Agreement, June 14, 1945, *supra* note, *Jackson Report*, Doc. IX, 57.
78 Minutes of Conference Session, July 2, 1945, *Jackson Report*, Doc. XX, 137; Minutes of Conference Session, July 2, 1945, *Jackson Report*, Doc. XX, 141.
79 See Nikitchenko's statements in the conference meeting, July 2, 1945, *Jackson Report*, Doc. XX, 134.
80 See Jackson's statement in the conference meeting in July 2, 1945, *Jackson Report*, Doc. XX, 129: "I understand the Soviet memorandum to reject the possibility of trying organizations."
81 Minutes of Conference Session, July 2, 1945, *Jackson Report*, Doc. XX, 137–42.
82 Lebedeva (ed.), *SSSR*, Doc. № 62, 207, 208; Draft Agreement and Charter, Proposed by British Delegation, July 11, 1945, *Jackson Report*, Doc. XXVI, 202–10
83 Minutes of Conference Session, July 13, 1945, *Jackson Report*, Doc. XXVII, 218.
84 Articles 8 and 9 in the 14 June draft.
85 Draft Agreement and Charter, proposed by British Delegation, July 11, 1945, *Jackson Report*, 206.
86 Ibid., 206–07.
87 Minutes of Conference Session, June 26, 1945, *Jackson Report*, Doc. XIII, 75.
88 Minutes of Conference Session, June 26, 1945, *Jackson Report*, Doc. XIII, 74 f.
89 Nikitchenko on June 26, 1945: "It is, of course, impossible to foresee all the details that could be included in a statute of this kind, and I agree that the court which is to be set up must have the power to elaborate detailed instructions that will be necessary," Minutes of Conference Session, June 26, 1945, *Jackson Report*, Doc. XIII. 75.
90 Ibid., XIII, 75.
91 Minutes of Conference Session June 29, 1945, *Jackson Report*, Doc. XVII, 98.
92 Minutes of Conference Session, July 5, 1945, *Jackson Report*, Doc. XXIV, 188; Minutes of Conference Session, July 9, *Jackson Report*, Doc. XXIV, 190–91; Minutes of Conference Session, July 10, 1945, Doc. XXIV, 192–93.
93 Notes of American Representative on Drafting Subcommittee, July 11, 1945, *Jackson Report*, Doc. XXIV, 188, 190 f.

94 Ibid., 194–210. Article 4 (Instrukciya/Instructions) of the Soviet Draft, July 2, 1945, *Jackson Report*, Doc. XXIII, 171: "For a more detailed definition of the procedure the Tribunal shall draw up instructions. These instructions shall not be inconsistent with the Statute." For the Russian text version, see *Proekt polozhenija (Statuta) o Mezhdunarodnom Voennom Tribunale*, AVP RF, f. 07, op. 13, p. 41, d. 3, l. 80, printed in Lebedeva (ed.), *SSSR*, Doc. № 59, 198; Notes of American Representative on Drafting Subcommittee, July 11, 1945, *Jackson Report*, Doc. XXIV, 188: "The Tribunal shall draw up rules of procedure which shall not be inconsistent with this Charter."
95 Notes of American Representative on Drafting Subcommittee, July 11, 1945, *Jackson Report*, Doc. XXIV, 190.
96 Rules of Procedure, IMT, Vol. I, 19–23.
97 Article 15 in the July 11 draft.
98 IMT Charter, 3.
99 Minutes of Conference Session, July 16, 1945, *Jackson Report*, Doc. XXX, 249–51, 252.
100 Minutes of Conference Session, July 3, 1945, *Jackson Report*, Doc. XXI, 151.
101 Taylor, *The Anatomy of the Nuremberg Trials*, 264–65. The tribunal later found him innocent of all charges and acquitted him. Office of United States Chief of Counsel for Prosecution of Axis Criminality, *Nazi Conspiracy and Aggression: Opinion and Judgment* (Washington: United States Government Printing Office, 1947), pp. 134–37.
102 Minutes of Conference Session, July 16, 1945, *Jackson Report*, Doc. XXX, 254.
103 Minutes of Conference Session, July 16, 1945, *Jackson Report*, Doc. XXX, 255. The final Charter did not contain Nikitchenko's suggestion to divide it.
104 IMT Charter, 4.
105 Minutes of Conference Session, July 16, 1945, *Jackson Report*, Doc. XXX, 255.
106 Crowe, *War Crimes*, p. 162; The United States had ten potential IMT defendants in custody in their zone, including Hermann Göring, the British five, including Hess and Ribbentrop, the Russians two, and the French one defendant. Taylor, *The Anatomy of the Nuremberg Trials*, 62,
107 Minutes of Conference Session, July 16, 1945, *Jackson Report*, Doc. XXX, 255.
108 IMT Charter, 4.
109 Minutes of the Conference, July 16, 1945, *Jackson Report*, Doc. XXX, 256.
110 IMT Charter, 4–5.
111 Minutes of the Conference, July 16, 1945, *Jackson Report*, Doc. XXX, 257–58; IMT Charter, 6.
112 Minutes of the Conference, July 17, 1945, *Jackson Report*, Doc. XXXII, 262; IMT Charter, 6.
113 Ibid., 262–63.
114 Ibid., 264.
115 Ibid., 264–65.
116 Ibid., 265.
117 Ibid., 265–66.
118 Ibid., 276–79.
119 Minutes of Conference Session, July 25, 1945, *Jackson Report*, Doc. LI, 383.
120 Minutes of Conference Session, July 20, 1945, *Jackson Report*, Doc. XLII, 319.
121 Minutes of the Conference Session, July 23, 1945, *Jackson Report*, Doc. XLIV, 343.
122 Ibid., 343–46.

123 Ibid., 348–58.
124 Ibid., 352.
125 Minutes of the Conference Session, July 24, 1945, *Jackson Report*, Doc., LXVII, 362.
126 Minutes of the Conference Session, July 25, 1947, *Jackson Report*, Doc., LI, 377.
127 Taylor, *The Anatomy of the Nuremberg Trials*, 68.
128 Ibid., 68–69.
129 Ibid., 70.
130 Sidney Alderman, "Negotiating the Nuremberg Trial Agreements, 1945," in Raymond Dennett and Joseph E. Johnson, eds. *Negotiating with the Russians* (Boston: World Peace Foundation), 53.
131 Michael Neiberg, *Potsdam: The End of World War II and the Remaking of Europe* (New York: Basic Books, 2015), 39–44.
132 Proposals by the Soviet and British Delegations, Nos. 1016–18, July 30, 1945, *Foreign Relations of the United States: Diplomatic Papers, The Conference of Berlin (The Potsdam Conference)*, 1945, Volume II, 482, 497, 498, 499.
133 Jackson, *The Anatomy of the Nuremberg Trials*, 71.
134 Ibid., 72; John W. Wheeler-Bennett and Anthony Nicholls, *The Semblance of Peace: The Political Settlement after the Second World War* (New York: Norton, 1974), 397–402.
135 Jackson, *The Anatomy of the Nuremberg Trials*, 72.
136 Ibid., 73. According to Taylor, he found no evidence that Truman spoke directly to Jackson about this though he presumes that Byrnes or Rosenman did, since, according to one Foreign Office official (Jowitt?), "it gave Jackson 'more patience.'"
137 Summary Record of Conference Between the Lord Chancellor and Mr. Justice Jackson, August 1, *Jackson Report*, Doc. LVIII, 398.
138 Minutes of the Conference Session, August 2, 1945, *Jackson Report*, Doc. LIX, 399.
139 Ibid., 400–19; Agreement and Charter, August 8, 1945, *Jackson Report*, Doc. LX, 420–28; Protocol to Agreement and Charter, October 6, 1945, *Jackson Report*, Doc. LXI, 429–31.
140 Alderman, "Negotiating on War Crimes Prosecutions, 1945," 53.

6

The Soviet Union at the Palace of Justice: Law, Intrigue, and International Rivalry in the Nuremberg Trials

Francine Hirsch

In popular histories and on the screen, the Nuremberg Trials of 1945–6 continue to be celebrated as a triumph of the rule of law—in which the victors of the Second World War put the desire for vengeance aside in order to give the Nazis a fair trial, ushering in a new era of international law and human rights. This is an uplifting story, but one that largely leaves out one of the four countries of the prosecution: Stalin's Soviet Union.[1] The English-language scholarly literature on Nuremberg and transitional justice goes deeper and grapples with some of the legal ambiguities of the trials. But even here there is scant attention paid to the critical role of the Soviet Union in shaping and conducting the trials.[2]

There are practical reasons why the Soviet role in the Nuremberg Trials (IMT) has not been fully appreciated or understood. During the Cold War, documents about Soviet participation in the IMT were buried in the former Soviet archives, to which even Russian researchers had limited access.[3] But there were political reasons as well. Western judges and prosecutors, who produced the most enduring early accounts of the Nuremberg Trials, saw Soviet participation as a threat to the legitimacy of the IMT and to the legacy of postwar justice—and for good reason. Germany and the Soviet Union had jointly invaded Poland in 1939; Red Army troops had committed atrocities during their march to Berlin; and the Soviets were carrying out deportations in Eastern Europe even as the IMT was hearing evidence against the Nazis.[4] To some at Nuremburg the Soviets were little better than the Nazi defendants.

And yet to tell the story of the IMT without a real accounting of the role of the Soviet Union is to miss much of the event's essential drama. It is also to skirt over an important contradiction that was at the heart of the Nuremberg moment.[5] The Soviets, with their faith in political trials and their innovative ideas about international law, were key to Nuremberg's success.[6] At the same time, the IMT was largely a failure for Stalin's Soviet Union. The Soviets, who had suffered devastating losses at the hands of the German occupiers and who took the defendants' guilt as a given, saw Nuremberg as an opportunity for a public accounting of Nazi crimes and a validation of their own political system. In response to clamorous allegations of victors' justice from the defense once the IMT was in session, the other countries of the prosecution (the United States, Great Britain, and France) redoubled their efforts to make sure that the accused were seen as receiving a fair trial—going so far as allowing the defendants to introduce eyewitnesses and evidence that incriminated the Soviets in atrocities and crimes against peace. The Soviets had gone to Nuremberg to mark their role as victors and liberators of Europe and to take their place among the postwar powers. By the conclusion of the trials, they were cast in the international public eye as probable co-conspirators of the Nazi regime.[7]

This chapter uses an array of Russian archival sources to present a retelling of the Nuremberg story, restoring the Soviet Union to its proper place at the table and also looking at how postwar politics shaped the narrative that emerged during the trials about the Second World War.[8] Part One argues that the Soviet Union provided much of the inspiration for the Nuremberg Trials and shaped the IMT in fundamental ways. It also shows how the Soviet prosecutors and judges experienced significant difficulties at Nuremberg because of the particularities of the Stalinist system. Part Two turns to the politics of history, focusing on the crafting of the Indictment Act. It illustrates how the Soviets used these deliberations to try to pin one of their own atrocities, the Katyn massacre, on the Nazis. Part Three looks at the forging of a "gentlemen's agreement" among the chief prosecutors on the eve of the trials to keep the crimes of the victors out of the courtroom. It assesses the Soviet delegation's efforts to introduce Moscow's interpretation of events and to suppress information that could embarrass the Soviet Union. Part Four focuses on the unraveling of the alliance between the Soviet Union and the other countries of the prosecution at Nuremberg and in general. The chapter as a whole illuminates how the Nuremberg Trials were grounded in the particular politics of the postwar moment—and how they must be understood both as an artifact of the wartime alliance and as a front of the early Cold War.

Part One: The Soviet contribution and Stalinist dysfunction

Wartime

Soviet ideas about bringing Nazi leaders to justice took shape in the heat of the war, which German forces conducted with particular brutality on the Eastern front. From early on in the conflict Joseph Stalin and his Commissar of Foreign Affairs Vyacheslav Molotov publicly denounced the systematic nature of Nazi crimes and actively called for the punishment of German war criminals by means of a "special international tribunal."[9] The Soviets were far ahead of their wartime allies in this and in their sophisticated arguments about the criminal responsibility of Nazi leaders. Soviet international law experts working as consultants for the Commissariat of Foreign Affairs made the case that not just "war crimes" committed during the course of war but also "the waging of an aggressive war" itself could be considered a punishable criminal act. While the idea of treating aggressive war as illegal had been raised before at international conferences, it was the Soviet law professor Aron Trainin who coined the term "crimes against peace" during the war and gave it its definitive formulation in a series of articles and in his major work *On the Criminal Responsibility of the Hitlerites*. This work was translated into several languages and circulated in high political circles in the West. According to Trainin, "crimes against peace" included "acts of aggression," "propaganda of aggression," "the conclusion of agreements with aggressive aims," "the violation of treaties which serve the cause of peace," "provocation designed to disrupt peaceful relations between countries," "terrorism," and "support of armed bands (fifth columns)."[10]

Soviet legal experts also made a major contribution to an ongoing discussion among the Allied powers during the war about using the legal concept of "complicity" to try the Nazis. Trainin contended that Hitler and his ministers, the leaders of the Nazi Party, the German High Command, and other "higher-ups" should all be tried as the "central group of international criminals" and charged with "creating a system of organized governmental banditry" and executing "a criminal conspiracy" against other nations.[11] The Western powers and the United Nations War Crimes Commission (of which the Soviet Union was not a member) were initially uncomfortable with Soviet ideas about postwar justice, which they criticized as retroactive or ex post facto law.[12] Some British leaders and many American politicians favored summary execution as a more straightforward approach, arguing that a trial would only complicate things. But the Soviet view prevailed. Indeed, the Nuremberg Trials would not have taken shape as they did—and perhaps would not have happened at all—without the Soviets and their legal theories about aggressive war, complicity, individual criminal responsibility, and collective guilt. Crimes against peace would be one of the main charges set out in Article 6 of the Nuremberg Charter, along with war crimes and crimes against humanity.[13] The same Soviet regime that had murdered millions of its own citizens during the Stalinist Great Terror of the late 1930s and other political campaigns became one of the main forces behind the invention of new international law theories and practices.

The Soviets took the lead during the war in arguing for a special international tribunal at least in part because they had tremendous faith in the efficacy of political trials. From the late 1920s Stalin had used the courtroom to publicly take down purported "enemies of the people." Moreover, in the Moscow Trials of the late 1930s, the notorious Andrei Vyshinsky—a brilliant legal manipulator—had prosecuted Lev Kamenev, Grigory Zinoviev, and other "old Bolsheviks" on false charges as supposed Nazi collaborators who had been conniving with Hitler "to establish a fascist dictatorship in Russia."[14] For the Soviets, a trial of the top Nazi leaders was a logical next step. The Soviets wanted to use an international tribunal to establish an official narrative about German guilt for the Second World War. The archival record also makes clear that Soviet leaders saw such a tribunal as their best hope for establishing a legal claim for reparations, especially labor reparations, which they believed would be essential for rebuilding after the war. It was with these ends in mind that Soviet leaders created their own war crimes commission, the Extraordinary State Commission for the Establishment and Investigation of the Crimes of the Fascist German Invaders and Their Accomplices, and directed it to collect evidentiary materials documenting the unprecedented nature of Nazi atrocities in the occupied territories of the Soviet Union.[15]

Political trials and Stalinist shortcomings

The Soviets drew on their extensive experience with domestic show trials in their initial planning for an international military tribunal. Soon after the Allies agreed on the basics of holding a tribunal, Stalin appointed Vyshinsky, who was now Deputy Commissar of Foreign Affairs, to head a secret, Moscow-based Commission for Directing the Work of the Soviet Representatives in the International Tribunal (the Nuremberg Commission for short). This commission would make a vigorous effort to oversee and manage the Soviet delegation from afar and to influence the course of the trials. Included in its ranks were the Procurator General of the USSR, the head of the Commissariat of Justice, and the head of the Counterespionage Division of the People's Commissariat of Defense (SMERSH), as well as major figures from the Commissariat of Internal Affairs (NKVD), the Commissariat of Foreign Affairs, and the Extraordinary State Commission.[16] Stalin also created a shadow commission—the Politburo Commission for the Nuremberg Trials—which also included Vyshinsky as well as other high-ranking figures from the world of Soviet state security and law.[17]

When selecting the prosecutors and judges, Stalin similarly looked to people who had proven their political mettle in Soviet domestic show trials. The Soviet judge Iona Nikitchenko had made his career as a judge in the Moscow Trials of 1936-1938. The Soviet chief prosecutor Roman Rudenko had served as the prosecutor for show trials in Ukraine in the 1930s; in June 1945 he served as the chief prosecutor of a Moscow-based show trial of the sixteen leaders of "the Polish Underground State."[18] Most of the Soviet assistant prosecutors had similar credentials.[19]

Stalin and Molotov initially had believed that the Nuremberg verdicts would be a fait accompli ratifying the results of the war. They soon came to realize their mistake. As preparations for the tribunal began in earnest in the early fall of 1945, Soviet leaders in Moscow began to express apprehension about the whole endeavor. In deliberations that summer, the Soviets had agreed reluctantly to hold the tribunal in American-occupied Nuremberg, after calculating the expense of hosting the trials in Soviet-occupied Berlin. In Nuremberg, the Americans would shoulder the cost of playing host. Moscow learned only in October (a month before the start of the trials) that US authorities in the American zone were intent on maintaining sole control over the defendants in the Nuremberg prison. The tribunal's ruling (over Nikitchenko's objections) that the defendants could retain Nazi attorneys and summon former German generals and diplomats as witnesses made clear to Moscow just how much the IMT would be outside of its control. Soviet leaders were used to trials in which the defendants spoke only to confess their crimes. The Western judges seemed intent on allowing the accused to launch a genuine defense.

While Soviet prosecutors and judges were skilled at staging domestic trials, they lacked critical expertise and experience abroad. From the fall of 1945, when the American, French, British, and Soviet chief prosecutors and their assistants met in London and Berlin to work out the basics of the tribunal, Soviet informants began reporting back to Moscow that Rudenko and his team were at a disadvantage vis-à-vis their Western colleagues because of their inexperience in the practical work of international organizations and relative ignorance about foreign affairs.

A classified report from the Soviet diplomat and consul in London Nikolai Ivanov, dated late September 1945, impressed upon Soviet leaders the gravity of the situation. Ivanov, who had sat in on some of the prosecutors' meetings in London, argued that it was especially important to brief Rudenko about the diplomatic intrigues of the 1930s: to explain to him "the reasons for the war's origins," and to tell him "what position to take and how to respond to questions" relating to the conclusion of the Soviet-German Non-Aggression Pact (Molotov-Ribbentrop Pact) of August 23, 1939. Making matters worse was the Soviet delegation's lack of qualified translators. According to Ivanov, the translator that Rudenko had "at his disposal" in London had a poor command of English and German and could not even begin to translate the huge piles of evidence that the Americans, the British, and the French had turned over to the tribunal for the prosecution. Sounding the alarm, Ivanov warned that the Soviet prosecution would find itself "defenseless" at Nuremberg if "the English or Americans or above all the defendants" attempted to forge or fake "one or another historical fact."[20] Here too, Ivanov was most worried about the Soviet prosecution being taken off guard by the revelation of diplomatic secrets.

There were deep-seated reasons for the Soviet delegation's shortcomings in the world of foreign affairs. Rudenko had served Stalin well in domestic show trials. But he lacked vital experience on the international stage, and Soviet leaders had done remarkably little to prepare him to handle the challenges of an international trial. Rudenko's ignorance about international relations in general, and about the finer points of Soviet-German collaboration, was a direct consequence of the Stalinist policy of sharing information on a strictly need-to-know basis. Soviet leaders, who had been imagining a scripted trial, had not thought initially that it was necessary to share highly classified information with Rudenko. They had not told him about the secret protocols to the Molotov-Ribbentrop Pact, for example, in which the Nazis and the Soviets had plotted out the conquest and division of Eastern Europe. It also did not help the situation that many Soviet officials with foreign-language expertise had been arrested or shot during the Stalinist Terror of the 1930s. Infighting between the NKVD and the Commissariat of Foreign Affairs continued to plague the world of Soviet foreign relations after the war: the NKVD refused to expedite the clearance of translators and other experts for travel abroad.[21]

Complicating matters further, the Soviet regime's centralized command structure discouraged the true delegation of responsibilities. The Moscow-based Nuremberg Commission rewrote the speeches of the Soviet prosecutors, selected evidence, found and groomed witnesses for the Soviet prosecution, and demanded to be consulted on matters large and small. It warned the Soviet prosecutors and the Soviet judges (who, of course, were supposed to be operating independently) to make "no decision" without "the prior approval of the Soviet Government." Such directives made for a complicated and extremely awkward process before and during the trials. In order to seek official approval, Soviet personnel in London and Germany had to smuggle paperwork back to Moscow on tight deadlines. Highly sensitive materials (including lists of evidence and revisions to official documents) were sometimes delayed or lost in transit—resulting in stalling tactics and panic among the members of the Soviet prosecution.[22] This panic was warranted, for Moscow was unyielding about the chain of command. On the eve of the trials, Rudenko and Nikitchenko signed off on some organizational matters without receiving Moscow's approval—and were called back home and severely reprimanded for acting irresponsibly.[23] All of this deprived the Soviet delegation of much needed flexibility, hampering its ability to quickly react when things went wrong during pretrial negotiations and at the Palace of Justice.

Part Two: Indictment act hullabaloo and the politics of history

Contested history

Scholars of the IMT like to point to US assistant prosecutor Robert M. W. Kempner's appealing description of the Nuremburg Trials as "the greatest history seminar ever held."[24] But as Kempner himself knew, the history being told through the IMT was highly contested—not just between the defendants and the prosecution, but also among the victors.[25] Each of the four countries of the prosecution saw the IMT as a forum not just to bring the Nazis to justice but also to pursue their own state interests. They were all concerned about the narrative that would emerge during the trials about the causes and course of the war—and about the allocation of credit and blame. Which countries, and which nationalities or peoples, would be remembered as the main victims of Germany? Which armies would be celebrated as the saviors of Europe? More troublingly, to what extent had the policies of the Soviet Union and the Western powers enabled the rise of the Nazis and Hitler's march across Europe? What would be said about the British and French abandonment of Czechoslovakia to Hitler? What would be said about Soviet actions toward Poland?

These issues came to the fore in September and October 1945, the two months before the IMT convened, during the crafting of the Indictment Act. One of the most important documents for the case, the joint-authored Indictment Act elaborated the main counts against the major war criminals and would also stand as a key component of the historical record. Moscow clearly understood this. Upon reviewing an initial draft, Soviet leaders and the heads of the state security apparatus enumerated a long list of corrections—and simultaneously expressed some grave misgivings.[26] Above all, they complained that the document "belittled" the Soviet Union's role in the war and underestimated Soviet losses. "On the whole, the aggressive war against the USSR is shown palely in the Indictment Act and the USSR is given a significantly smaller place than the various small states," Soviet leaders complained.[27]

In the Soviet wartime narrative, the themes of valor and victimhood went hand in hand. Even as Soviet leaders sought to establish a heroic narrative about the resolve and strength of the Soviet people, they also endeavored to create a detailed account of the terrible damage that the Nazis had inflicted on the lands, industries, institutions, and peoples of the Soviet Union. This was a critical issue for the historical record, and for making the case for reparations. Soviet leaders had expected that the prosecution would make extensive use of Extraordinary State Commission reports, and that the Indictment Act would include a comprehensive list of those places where the Nazis had "committed war crimes and caused material damage in the USSR." After learning that the document would not include this level of detail, Vyshinsky blamed Rudenko for allowing the Western prosecutors to weaken the Soviet case.[28]

In their deliberations in Moscow, Soviet leaders expressed concern that the Indictment Act should make clear that the Nazis had targeted not just the Jews, Poles, and Gypsies but also the Slavic peoples of the Soviet Union. In a report to Vyshinsky, Soviet Commissar of Justice Konstantin Gorshenin advised that the list of "nationalities and racial groups" that the fascists had targeted with their "policies of mass extermination" should include "the Russians." When Vyshinsky read this memo, he crossed out "Russians" and replaced it with "Slavs."[29] Molotov then put forward a different formulation, which stated that the Germans had pursued "the annihilation" of "Russians, Belorussians, and Ukrainians and the systematic extermination of the Jews."[30] In the end, the published version of the Indictment Act described the "deliberate and systematic" extermination of "Jews, Poles, and Gypsies and others" and noted the "annihilation of adults, old people, women, and children, especially Belorussians and Ukrainians." While the final formulation did not specifically list the Russians among the victimized nationalities, the message was clear that the peoples of the Soviet Union had suffered as a whole.[31]

Soviet secrets

Meanwhile, Moscow had decided to use the back-and-forth about the Indictment Act to pin a major Soviet war crime, the Katyn massacre of Polish officers, on German forces. Soviet leaders sent Rudenko and his assistants a rewrite of a part of the Indictment Act that enumerated a long list of German atrocities committed against civilians and prisoners of war on the territory of the Soviet Union. Included on this list was the "German" murder of 925 Polish officers (prisoners of war) in the Katyn Forest near Smolensk.[32] By this point Katyn was already a political hot potato. Back in April 1943 the Nazis had reported the discovery of the bodies of some 10,000 Polish officers buried in pits in the Katyn Forest and had blamed the Soviet security police for the crime. The Soviets had dismissed these allegations as "vile fabrications" and had contended that the "German-Fascist scoundrels" had themselves "murdered the Poles" along with peaceful Soviet citizens in the summer of 1941, after the withdrawal of Soviet troops.[33]

Although it already had been estimated at the time that more than 10,000 Poles had been killed, Soviet leaders had chosen the figure of 925—which corresponded to the number of exhumed bodies reported by a special Soviet investigation commission headed by the President of the Soviet Academy of Medical Sciences Nikolai Burdenko. (Burdenko was also a member of the Extraordinary State Commission.) By late October Soviet leaders in Moscow were proposing additional changes to the Indictment Act, including a revision of the number of Poles killed at Katyn from 925 to 11,000.[34] The final version of this document included the higher figure.

Katyn was just one of the highly controversial issues that came up during the deliberations about the Indictment Act. When it came to thinking about the past, the basic details about international relations of the previous decade proved to be matters of contention. Soviet leaders voiced serious objections to the Indictment Act's characterizations of the Munich Pact of 1938 and the Molotov-Ribbentrop Pact of 1939 and their relationship to the start of the war—noting that the document gave a "disputable" political interpretation of events.[35] In particular, they took great offense that the draft described the Molotov-Ribbentrop Pact as having facilitated the Nazi attack on Poland, while it skirted the issue of French and British appeasement regarding Czechoslovakia. Vyshinsky gave Rudenko firm orders to demand that the document be revised so that the nonaggression pact could "under no circumstances" be interpreted as "the springboard for" Nazi actions. At the same time, he instructed Rudenko to argue for a more accurate account of the Nazi invasion of Czechoslovakia: the Indictment Act's suggestion that Germany had "intimidated" Czechoslovakia into "handing its fate and the fate of its people" over to Hitler in the wake of a "dispute" did not "correspond to the historical facts," he noted, and was insulting to "the Czechoslovak people."[36]

Soviet leaders, not surprisingly, cared most about the revisions relating to the Molotov-Ribbentrop Pact, and ordered Rudenko to push hard for them—even if it meant giving in on other issues.[37] In the short term Rudenko and the other chief prosecutors did reach a successful compromise. The final version of the Indictment Act treaded with care around the issues of appeasement and collaboration. It made a link between the conclusion of the Munich Pact and the Nazi seizure of Czechoslovakia but let the Western powers off the hook by emphasizing that Hitler had acted counter to the pact's provisions.[38] To Moscow's satisfaction, the final document omitted the line that had described the Molotov-Ribbentrop Pact as the catalyst for the Nazi invasion of Poland. It described the nonaggression pact in neutral terms and characterized the Nazi invasion of the Soviet Union in 1941 as a treacherous crime against peace.[39] Unfortunately for the Soviets, this was not the end of the matter. The Molotov-Ribbentrop Pact would continue to vex them at Nuremberg—with the German defense, the Western judges, and at least one member of the US prosecution attempting to force a public discussion about its secret protocols.

Part Three: The Soviet struggle for control

Secrets and lists

The course of the Nuremberg Trials was shaped by the wartime bonds among the Allies—and also by their unraveling. Cooperation among the four countries of the prosecution was at its height in the fall of 1945. Before the trials began, the four chief prosecutors and their assistants agreed that any crimes committed by the victors would not be subject to scrutiny during the trials. The prosecution formed a united front on this issue. On the eve of the trials, at a November meeting in Nuremberg, US chief prosecutor Robert H. Jackson informed the other prosecutors that he had reliable information that the defense was planning to launch "political attacks" on the countries of the prosecution, and was likely to target British, French, and Soviet policies "in connection with the aggressive war charge." Jackson suggested that the US prosecution take the lead to prevent such attacks and asked the other prosecutors to write up and share confidential lists of taboo topics that they wanted to keep out of the courtroom.[40]

Back in Moscow, Vyshinsky expressed skepticism about this latest development in Nuremberg—but set to work on a list, nonetheless. Soviet leaders completed this "blacklist" during the first week of the trials. Predictably, it included a number of items concerning Soviet-German relations: "the relationship of the USSR to the Versailles peace," "the Soviet-German Non-Aggression Pact of 1939 and all questions relating to it," "Molotov's visit to Berlin and Ribbentrop's visit to Moscow," and "the Soviet-German agreement about the exchange of the German population of Lithuania, Latvia, and Estonia with Germany." The list also detailed other potentially controversial topics concerning "the foreign policy of the Soviet Union," including "questions about the [Dardanelle] Straits and about the alleged territorial pretensions of the USSR," "the Balkan question," and "Soviet-Polish relations" (in particular regarding "Western Ukraine and Western Belorussia"). It also declared off limits all questions "connected with the socio-political structure of USSR" and "the Soviet Baltic republics."[41]

Meanwhile, after months of anticipation and planning, the Nuremberg Trials had started on November 20—without key members of the Soviet prosecution. Most notably, Soviet chief prosecutor Rudenko was still in Moscow receiving directions from Soviet leaders. Deputy chief prosecutor Yuri Pokrovsky stood in for Rudenko in the courtroom, accompanied by the Soviet investigator Georgy N. Alexandrov, who had been closely involved in the pretrial interrogation of the defendants. Pokrovsky maintained regular communication with Moscow, sending Vyshinsky frequent progress reports via Berlin. That first evening he sent a reassuring telegram: "The first day of the trial is over. The Indictment Act was read. There were no incidents."[42] In fact, there had been an incident, albeit not in open court. Hermann Göring's attorney, Dr. Otto Stahmer, himself a known Nazi sympathizer, had submitted a four-page petition to the tribunal on behalf of his client and the rest of the defense, complaining that the judges, as representatives of the victors, could not be impartial, and challenging the legal grounds of the case and the creation of ex post facto law.[43] While this petition was ultimately dismissed, it was a sign of things to come.

On November 22, Rudenko set out for Nuremberg with Gorshenin, Trainin, and several other members of Vyshinsky's inner circle, including Mark Raginsky, who had just been added to the Soviet prosecution team.[44] Raginsky, a seasoned investigator, had earned his credentials in the Moscow Trials of the 1930s, where his lack of scruples had helped to seal the fate of Stalin's enemies. While Rudenko and his colleagues were en route to the American zone of Germany, the American prosecution began to present its case on the Nazi conspiracy to wage aggressive war. Jackson and his assistants, who were growing increasingly leery of the Soviets and uneasy about the defense's accusations of victor's justice, described in great detail the careful process that had been used to gather and prepare the evidence against the accused. They wanted to make it clear to all that the defendants were considered innocent until proven guilty: the IMT would not be a show trial.[45]

The Soviet struggle for control

The Soviets had been pressing for an international trial of Nazi leaders from the darkest days of the war. But during the first few weeks of the Nuremberg Trials, the

Soviet delegation found itself dangerously unprepared, and with far less influence over the proceedings than it would have liked. Moscow's answer was to try to assert greater control. On Sunday, November 25, Vyshinsky descended on Nuremberg with a special mission to fulfill: to ensure that Rudenko successfully stood down a proposal for the tribunal to consider highly sensitive evidence about the Molotov-Ribbentrop Pact. Dr. Alfred Seidl, the defense counsel for Rudolf Hess and Hans Frank, had "dug up" some documents about the pact's secret protocols and wanted to introduce them in court. Rumors were circulating that certain members of the US delegation were prepared to support Seidl's request.[46]

For Western observers, Vyshinsky's role in the Nuremberg Trials was never clear—and this was precisely what Soviet leaders had intended. The Moscow-based Nuremberg Commission that Vyshinsky headed was highly secretive. When Vyshinsky appeared at the Palace of Justice, it was as an esteemed visitor (Soviet Deputy Commissar of Foreign Affairs) and guest. While in Nuremberg, Vyshinsky acquainted himself with the day-to-day work of the judges and prosecutors and held several meetings with the Soviet delegation—giving detailed directives about all aspects of the case. Most significantly, Vyshinsky presented Rudenko with Moscow's list of "taboo topics." Vyshinsky did not give Rudenko permission to share a physical copy of this list with his Western colleagues. He directed him instead to work with the other chief prosecutors toward an informal agreement to avoid all "questions that the USSR, USA, England, France, and other United Nations do not want to become subjects of criticism from the side of the accused."[47] Rudenko reported success (after a couple of informal alcohol-infused conversations with the Western prosecutors), and a few days later Vyshinsky headed back to Moscow.[48]

The Soviet Union would be the last of the four countries of the prosecution to present its case against the Nazi leaders. During the first three months of the Nuremberg Trials, the members of the Soviet prosecution spent much of their time watching and waiting. Rudenko and his assistants became increasingly agitated as the American prosecution, and then the British prosecution, expanded their cases far beyond Soviet expectations. Most troubling of all, US chief prosecutor Jackson and his assistants introduced a number of sensational documents about German crimes against humanity in the Soviet Union and the abuse of Soviet soldiers that were supposed to have been reserved for the Soviet prosecution. The Soviets resented Jackson's efforts to steal their thunder. Every week, the world was learning more about Nazi crimes against the Soviet Union. But the Soviets wondered what would be left for them to present when their turn came to appear before the court.

Meanwhile, behind the scenes the defense had launched a campaign to bring dozens of witnesses, many of them Nazis, before the court to testify on behalf of the former German leaders. The Soviets, who had entered into the IMT seeing Nazi guilt as a given, were outraged by this development. They were also worried—and rightly so. The Soviets had the most to hide of all of the countries of the prosecution and were concerned about possible courtroom revelations about their own war crimes and about their collaboration with Nazi Germany before 1941. It was apparent that the accused and their attorneys were planning to launch a vigorous defense; they had already started to do so through the international press. In one interview published by the *Associated*

Press, defendant and former head of the Wehrmacht High Command Wilhelm Keitel had described the German invasion of the Soviet Union as a defensive move, taken because the Soviet Union had been "noticeably preparing for war."[49] Soviet leaders (who had a shaky conception of freedom of the press) interpreted the publication of this interview as definitive proof of the American government's animosity toward the Soviet Union.

Vyshinsky and other Soviet leaders in Moscow were receiving regular updates about the course of the trials and the latest intrigues through back channels, via Soviet agents and informants. By January, Stalin and Molotov had decided that it was imperative to bring in fresh evidence to strengthen chief prosecutor Rudenko's opening speech and the Soviet case in general.[50] The Nuremberg Commission, the NKVD, and SMERSH set to work to secure this evidence, and also to select and screen new witnesses, including former German, Romanian, and Hungarian government and military leaders who were in Soviet custody. One of their primary goals was to expose the falsity of German claims about the "preventive" character of the Nazi invasion.

The Soviet offensive

On Friday February 8, Soviet chief prosecutor Rudenko delivered his long-awaited opening speech before a large and curious crowd at the Palace of Justice. The Nuremberg Commission had rewritten the speech several times during the previous few weeks, while the French prosecution was presenting its case on war crimes and crimes against humanity committed in Western Europe. The French had called as witnesses numerous concentration camp survivors, whose moving testimony had created an international stir. Moscow was determined that the Soviet case should have at least as powerful an effect.

Rudenko spoke forcefully about the Hitlerite attack on Europe and unveiled new details about the Nazi conspiracy. He emphasized that Germany's aggressive actions in Europe from 1938 to 1941 had all been leading up to the attack on the Soviet Union, which Hitler saw as the main source of future living space and food for Germany. Most critically, Rudenko dismissed the defense's argument about the preventive character of the German invasion: he declared that the original documents of the German government and High Command, which the Soviets would present, plainly demonstrated the falsity of such claims. Turning to war crimes and crimes against humanity, Rudenko described how the defendants had turned war into "a system of militarized banditry" in Eastern Europe and the Soviet Union. He spoke of the razing of villages, the torture of prisoners of war, the massacre of men, women, and children, and the horrors of the concentration camps—calling Dachau and Buchenwald "anemic prototypes" of Majdanek and other death camps that the Nazis had set up in the occupied East.[51]

In the days and weeks that followed, Rudenko's team of assistant prosecutors presented evidence on nine different themes (including some that the Americans and the British had already covered)—and shocked the world with their graphic accounts of Nazi barbarism in the East. Soviet eyewitness testimony was especially compelling, as was Soviet documentary film footage. "Terrible things were shown that had been left out of Soviet newsreels during the war," noted the documentary filmmaker Roman Karmen (who was in Nuremberg for most of the trials and had helped put the Soviet film footage together). "Severed heads, severed arms, terrible camps in which we Soviet cameramen appeared with the first detachments . . . naked skeletons, murdered children."[52] The Soviets wanted the world to comprehend the sheer brutality of the Nazi occupation. In this, they succeeded beyond a doubt. The biggest surprise of the Soviet case was the appearance of a special witness for the Soviet prosecution: Field Marshal Friedrich von Paulus, whom the Soviets had captured in Stalingrad during the war (and who had been assumed dead). Less surprising, but of monumental consequence for the Soviet case and for the further course of the trials, was deputy chief prosecutor Pokrovsky's presentation about Katyn.

As Pokrovsky dove into the Katyn affair the Soviet case moved into the realm of fabrication. Pokrovsky characterized "the mass execution of Polish prisoners of war" in the Katyn Forest as one of the most serious criminal acts for which the Nazis were responsible. His key piece of evidence was the January 1944 report of the Soviet investigation commission headed by Nikolai Burdenko. Pokrovsky read the main conclusions of the Burdenko Commission's report, which he said was based on forensic evidence from the mass graves and the depositions of more than 100 witnesses. It accused German military organizations, disguised as a construction battalion (the 537th Engineering Battalion), of carrying out the massacre in the fall of 1941, and named three commanding officers (Colonel Ahrens, Senior Lieutenant Rex, and Lieutenant Hodt) as responsible for the murder.[53]

Did Pokrovsky know that he was presenting fabricated evidence? Possibly. But it is just as likely that Moscow had left him in the dark. The Wehrmacht and the SS had committed numerous mass atrocities in Poland and Pokrovsky had no reason to question the Soviet evidence about this particular crime.

Including Katyn in the Indictment Act must have seemed like a brilliant idea to Stalin back in October—given his expectations of an open and shut case. For the Western powers, however, the Katyn charges raised serious questions about the overall veracity of Soviet evidence. By now, the American and British governments had credible evidence from Polish witnesses, the US Office of Strategic Services (OSS), and other sources that the Soviets were responsible for this massacre. If the Soviets had fabricated forensic evidence and coerced witness testimony for Katyn, how reliable was the rest of their case? The magnitude of Nazi atrocities in the Soviet Union was enormous. But the Katyn charges threatened to undercut the Soviet case—as well as the legitimacy of the entire IMT.

The defense attorneys were keenly aware that the Western judges had serious questions about the Katyn charge and set out to challenge the Soviet evidence. On February 15, Ernst Kaltenbrunner's attorney, Dr. Kurt Kaufmann, complained to the tribunal that reports from the Extraordinary State Commission and other Soviet investigative commissions (like the Burdenko Commission) should be prohibited because they lacked "definite information" about their sources and "their contents cannot be checked." The judges defended the Soviet right to introduce these reports, citing Article 21 of the Nuremberg Charter, which had declared the reports of national war crimes commissions to be "incontrovertible evidence." If the defense wanted to challenge particular reports, the judges added, it could do so later.⁵⁴ The defense would soon do just that.

On March 3, the day before the Soviets wrapped up their part of the case, Göring's attorney, Dr. Stahmer, submitted a petition to the tribunal asking to call witnesses to counter Soviet claims about Katyn. Stahmer asked to summon the three German officers listed in the Burdenko Commission's report. (All were currently in Soviet custody.) He also asked to call two German officers who were not in Soviet hands: General-Major Eugen Oberhauser (who was in American custody) and Senior Lieutenant Count Berg (who was in British custody). Stahmer also submitted an additional petition to call Professor François Naville, a forensic expert at the University of Geneva who had investigated the gravesite in April 1943 at Germany's request, in order to support the German argument that the shooting had taken place in 1940.⁵⁵ The Katyn challenge had begun.

Part Four: On the defensive

Trouble for the Soviets

The Soviets soon found themselves engaged in two propaganda struggles—against the German defense team and, on a larger scale, against the Western powers. On March 5, former British prime minister Winston Churchill delivered his "Iron Curtain" speech in Fulton, Missouri.⁵⁶ The following day newspapers in Nuremberg printed it under a bannered headline reading "Unite to Stop the Russians."⁵⁷ Soviet leaders characterized this speech as "nothing less than an appeal for a new war" and pointed to the fact that Churchill had delivered it in the United States as clear proof of an Anglo-American anti-Soviet alliance.⁵⁸ News of the speech emboldened the defendants in Nuremberg, who began actively looking for fresh opportunities to stir up discord between the Soviets and the other countries of the prosecution.

On March 8, the defense began its turn on the stand. Göring was up first and it soon became clear that one of his main strategies was to launch accusations of tu quoque ("you did it too") against the Soviet Union.⁵⁹ Meanwhile, the Soviet prosecution continued to puzzle over American intentions. That same day, US chief prosecutor Jackson sent Soviet chief prosecutor Rudenko and French chief prosecutor Auguste Champetier de Ribes a memo recalling their mutual pledge to resist "political attacks" from the defense—and again asking them for memoranda listing their taboo topics. (The British had already provided such a memorandum.) Jackson warned that a dangerous situation was brewing: he now had definite "reason to believe" that the defense was planning to attack Soviet, French, and British wartime policies. He cautioned that it would not be possible for him to commit the United States "to the support of undisclosed positions."⁶⁰

The Soviets were caught between the Scylla and Charybdis of German defense tactics and American ambitions. While Soviet leaders mistrusted the Americans, they decided that it was probably in their best interest to take Jackson up on his offer. They gave Rudenko the go-ahead—and on March 11, he shared the Soviet blacklist with

Jackson and the other chief prosecutors. The list was almost identical to the one that the secret commission had discussed (but not submitted) back in November. Rudenko agreed with Jackson that the prosecutors must act "in solidarity" to prevent the defense from using the Nuremberg courtroom to examine "questions without direct relevance to the case." Rudenko also noted the "timeliness" of Jackson's letter. Already, "several of the defendants and their attorneys" were attempting to air issues "not related to the case" and to misrepresent the actions of the Allied governments with "false information whose refutations would entail a loss of time" and delay the trials.[61]

Even as Rudenko was sharing the Soviet blacklist with Jackson, the Katyn affair was exploding behind the scenes. On Monday March 11, Rudenko presented the tribunal with a petition opposing Stahmer's request to call witnesses about Katyn. He invoked Article 21 of the Nuremberg Charter to assert that the Burdenko Commission's report should stand as "sufficient proof of the Soviet charge" of German guilt for the crime. When the tribunal met in closed session the following day, the three Western judges disputed the Soviet interpretation of Article 21. They argued that Article 21 covered only the submission of evidence—and did not prohibit the defense from challenging evidence once it was submitted. "It is not permitted to tell the defendant" that he "may not refute this document," US judge Francis Biddle maintained.[62] That afternoon, a Soviet informant reported to Moscow that the three Western judges had voted to approve of Stahmer's request to call defense witnesses about Katyn; Nikitchenko had "refused to vote" on the grounds that satisfying Stahmer's request "patently contradicts Article 21."[63]

Back in Moscow Vyshinsky assessed the situation and sprang into action. On March 15, he directed Rudenko to present a letter to the judges (which he attached) insisting "on the Soviet interpretation of Article 21" and arguing that the decision to allow for German witnesses about Katyn marked "a direct breach" of the Nuremberg Charter. Rudenko was to seek support from the other chief prosecutors by arguing that it was unconscionable for the tribunal to allow "the direct perpetrators" of the Katyn massacre to take the stand as supposed witnesses to this atrocity and by warning that the tribunal's decision would set a precedent for the rest of the trials. If the judges refused to change their decision, Rudenko was to demand to call Soviet witnesses and forensic experts on Katyn.[64]

Without waiting for the tribunal's response, Vyshinsky set to work shoring up the Soviet charges about Katyn in an effort to avert disaster. The NKVD and SMERSH tracked down and screened Soviet witnesses from Bulgaria, Germany, and Poland as well as Soviet forensic experts, and prepared them to testify. It also put together "certified documents" about the discovered corpses, including the protocols of forensic examinations. These documents had all of the required stamps, signatures, and seals attesting to their authenticity, but this was an elaborate sham: the NKVD had fabricated much of this evidence, certifications and all.[65] Vyshinsky also directed Rudenko to learn more about the requested defense witnesses and their relationship to the 537th Engineering Battalion.[66]

In the Palace of Justice, Göring used his time in the witness box to elaborate his argument about Germany's preventive invasion of the Soviet Union. On March 21, during Rudenko's cross-examination, Göring claimed that Germany had started planning in 1940 for the deployment of the Luftwaffe for Operation Barbarossa "in order to deal with a potential threat from Russia." According to Göring, Hitler had seen "in the attitude of Russia, and in the lining up of troops on our frontier, a mortal threat to Germany."[67] The following morning, Göring attacked the Soviets for their conduct in the war.[68] Jackson supported Rudenko in objecting to Göring's accusations and the court struck a number of the defendant's statements from the trial record. It was a visible moment of cooperation—especially notable during this period of growing US-Soviet tensions.

The defense did what it could over the next couple of weeks to return to the theme of Soviet-German collaboration. Hess's attorney, Dr. Seidl, attempted to present the court with an affidavit from Dr. Friedrich Gaus, the former chief of the Legal Department of the German Foreign Office, about the secret protocols to the Molotov-Ribbentrop Pact. Gaus had accompanied Ribbentrop to Moscow in August 1939 and his affidavit described the contents of these protocols, which he had helped to draft. Seidl's move blindsided Rudenko—who stood speechless until British judge (and tribunal president) Geoffrey Lawrence asked if the prosecution objected "to passages being read from this document." This was "a completely unknown document," Rudenko piped up, and the prosecution needed time "to familiarize itself" with it. Seidl retorted that if Rudenko really claimed to have "no knowledge" of this document then he would have to summon Molotov as a witness. Lawrence told Seidl that he would need to have the affidavit translated into English and Russian before the tribunal would hear him on it.[69]

Seidl circled back around to the secret protocols during Ribbentrop's defense. On April 1, while cross-examining the defendant, Seidl read a short passage aloud and asked him whether a secret part of the Soviet-German nonaggression pact "had approximately that wording." Ribbentrop replied in the affirmative. Seidl then tried again to introduce the Gaus affidavit (which by now had been translated into English and Russian). Rudenko objected that the tribunal had not been convened to discuss the policies of the Allied powers—and that Seidl's questions to Ribbentrop "should be rejected as not relevant" to the case. The judges privately conferred and overruled Rudenko's objection (outvoting Nikitchenko).[70] Seidl then read from Gaus's affidavit, which described negotiations on a "secret document" aimed at demarcating "spheres of interest in the European territories" situated between Germany and Russia. Ribbentrop affirmed that an agreement had been reached in August 1939, after which Soviet and German troops had occupied Poland and the Baltic states. If Germany was guilty of "aggressive war" toward Poland, then surely the Soviets were "guilty of it" too, Ribbentrop maintained.[71]

Missive to Moscow

The Soviets had been intending to use the Nuremberg Trials to elaborate a narrative about Soviet heroism and German guilt—but the story had gotten away from them. On April 4, the Soviet diplomat and informant Mikhail Kharlamov sent party chief Georgy Malenkov a secret report, describing the struggles that the Soviet prosecution were facing at this "new stage of the trial." Earlier, when the prosecution had been presenting its case, the four countries of the prosecution had formed a united front. But this was no longer true, Kharlamov wrote. The situation had shifted most dramatically with the judges' recent decision to dismiss questions relating to the Munich Pact as irrelevant to the case: Rudenko had lost important leverage. In spite of the existing "gentlemen's agreement" among the four chief prosecutors to keep the IMT focused on Nazi crimes, Rudenko could no longer count on "support from the other prosecutors" to keep "the events of 1939" out of the courtroom.[72]

According to Kharlamov, the defense was broadening "the breach" between the Soviet Union and the other countries of the prosecution by focusing on "the Polish problem." He described how the court had allowed Hess's attorney, Seidl, to read out Gaus's testimony "about the alleged conclusion" of "a secret agreement between the USSR and Germany" to divide up Poland and the Baltic states. The tribunal had "allowed Ribbentrop to add" to this "provocative attack": the former German foreign minister had gone so far as to state that the Soviet Union had been "prepared to go to war on the side of Germany in certain circumstances." Making matters worse, Seidl had given a copy of "Gaus' provocative affidavit" to the English newspaper *The Daily Mail*, which had printed it on March 26—even before the judges had ruled on whether or not to allow it to be read in court.[73]

Kharlamov reported that the Gaus affidavit was just the most recent of a series of attacks on the Soviet Union in the Nuremberg courtroom—and that Rudenko and Pokrovsky were not doing enough to protect Soviet interests. The Soviet prosecutors had not managed to stop the defense from "dragging out a story" about preventive war. Nor had they protested the defense's petition to summon "fascist witnesses about the Katyn affair." As a result, "our prosecution lost the opportunity to prevent them from being called." Kharlamov speculated that the most recent Soviet difficulties were a result of "the particularities of this stage of the trial" combined with the tense "international situation." It "sometimes slips from view" that "we, a country of victors, went to Nuremberg to prosecute the German-fascist criminals and not to become the object of their provocative attacks."[74]

The defense offensive

The so-called Polish problem in its dual aspects—Katyn and the secret protocols—continued to haunt the Soviets in Nuremberg in the weeks ahead. On May 7, Seidl submitted a supposed transcript of the secret protocols themselves, with a petition to introduce them as evidence for the defense.[75] That evening, a Soviet informant reported to Vyshinsky that copies of this transcript had also gone to all of the chief prosecutors. The informant further noted that Gaus had signed a second affidavit attesting to the transcript's authenticity. The informant assured Vyshinsky that the Soviet delegation planned to argue that the transcript could not be accepted as evidence, since it had been put together by an unknown person and then read to Gaus, who had certified the accuracy of the text "by memory."[76] The Soviet informant also speculated on whether Seidl really had an original copy of the secret protocols or was bluffing. He reported that Seidl had attempted to initiate a conversation with Rudenko and wondered what kind of fishing expedition he was on.[77]

Acting on Moscow's orders, Nikitchenko did his best to have the supposed transcript of the secret protocols and Gaus's second affidavit thrown out of court. When the tribunal met in closed session on May 11, he insisted that the transcript "did not relate to the case"—and added that its origins were unknown and it had not been properly certified. Nikitchenko admonished his fellow judges that they could not accept such shaky evidence "on such an important question." The Western judges countered that the secret protocols were the addenda to a nonaggression pact that the prosecution itself had introduced as evidence—and thus did have bearing on the case. US judge Biddle further asserted that if the Soviet prosecution disputed "the accuracy" of the defense's copy of the secret protocols then it should present the tribunal with "the original protocols" which "the defense does not have but which is at the disposal of the Soviet government."[78]

Nikitchenko stood firm: Yes, the nonaggression pact related to the case, but only because the accused had violated its provisions; any addenda, he insisted, were irrelevant. Nikitchenko reminded his fellow judges that the tribunal had recently ruled not to allow a discussion of the Munich Pact, determining that its details "were outside of the bounds" of the case. He deemed the issue of the secret protocols to be "analogous." Recognizing that he might not get far with this argument, Nikitchenko then focused in on the juridical shortcomings of the document in question. If the transcript that Seidl had submitted to the tribunal was really "a copy" of the secret protocols, then where was the original? In the end a compromise of sorts was reached. The Western judges stood by their ruling that the secret protocols were germane to the case. But they told Seidl "to obtain and present to the tribunal the original document."[79]

That same day, the Tribunal reviewed a petition from Göring's attorney, Stahmer, to call two more defense witnesses to testify about Katyn (Reinhard von Eichborn and Rudolf Proft). Pokrovsky—who was in hot water with Moscow for failing to block Stahmer's earlier petition to call witnesses for Katyn—made a valiant effort to oppose this latest request. He protested that the Soviet prosecution "from the very beginning" had considered German responsibility for Katyn to be "common knowledge" and had thus limited itself "to reading into the record only a few short excerpts" from the Burdenko Commission's report. If the tribunal approved the requested German witnesses, then the Soviet prosecution "would be forced to present new evidence," read into the record "all of the documents of the Burdenko Commission," and "call about ten more new witnesses" of its own. All of this would "greatly delay the proceedings," he warned.[80] By now, the Western judges had run out of patience with the Soviets: they stood by their decision to allow the defense to summon witnesses about Katyn.[81]

Emboldened by Stahmer's victory, Seidl intensified his efforts to introduce the secret protocols without revealing his source. He saw an opportunity—and took it—on May 21 when former State Secretary of the German Foreign Office Ernst von Weizsaecker took the stand as a witness for the defendant Grand Admiral Erich Raeder. After the conclusion of Weizsaecker's direct examination, when the other defense attorneys were given the chance to question the witness, Seidl stepped forward "waving several typewritten sheets" of paper. Overruling Rudenko's objections (and ignoring Nikitchenko's opposition), the tribunal allowed Seidl to ask Weizsaecker whether "any other agreements" had been concluded between Germany and the Soviet Union on

August 23, 1939, besides the nonaggression pact. Weizsaecker responded yes—and explained that "these agreements were contained in a secret protocol," which he had read in his role as State Secretary. At this point, Seidl attempted to give Weizsaecker his transcript of the secret protocol of August 1939 to confirm its authenticity. Rudenko again protested that the court had no business examining "the foreign policies of other states" and dismissed the document in Seidl's possession as "forged."[82]

The plot thickened when the tribunal pressed Seidl to reveal where the document in question had come from. Seidl replied that he had received it "a few weeks ago from a man on the Allied side" and that he had promised this man not to "divulge its origin." Seidl again insisted that it was "an essential component" of the Molotov-Ribbentrop Pact, which the tribunal had already accepted as evidence. At this point, US assistant prosecutor Thomas Dodd joined Rudenko in objecting to the introduction of this document from an anonymous source. Before Rudenko could catch his breath, Dodd made another suggestion. Why not simply allow Seidl to ask Weizsaecker "about the contents of the agreement"?[83]

While making a show of supporting Rudenko, Dodd had just played to the defense. The judges gave Seidl the go-ahead to question the witness about the secret protocols; when he did, Weizsaecker described "a very far-reaching secret addendum to the nonaggression pact" that "drew a demarcation line" between Soviet and German "spheres of influence." Weizsaecker told the court that the original agreement from August 1939 was amended a month or two later: "The greater part of Lithuania" now "fell into the sphere of interest of the Soviet Union, while in the Polish territory the line of demarcation" was shifted further west. Lawrence then asked Weizsaecker if he would recognize the protocols if they were shown to him. When Weizsaecker replied in the affirmative, the tribunal called a recess. After some deliberation, the judges agreed not to put the transcript to the witness. Their reasons were twofold. First, Seidl still refused to reveal his source. Second, it seemed unnecessary: the contents of the secret protocols had now been discussed several times over in court.[84]

Thwarted from introducing his copy of the secret protocols as evidence for the defense, Seidl took it to the international press—apparently using Dodd as a middleman. On May 22, the *St. Louis Post-Dispatch* published the transcript with an article by Richard L. Stokes, the paper's correspondent in Nuremberg. In his article, Stokes relates that Dodd had "obtained a German copy of the agreements from Dr. Seidl and arranged for their translation into English."[85] Was Dodd's move part of a larger US effort to publicize Soviet crimes? Or had Dodd acted alone? This is unclear, although Dodd's moral outrage at the Soviets was surely in play. (He privately denounced the Soviets in his letters home as "no different from the Nazis.")[86] By now tensions were boiling over between the Soviet Union and the United States: earlier in the month the US government had halted the flow of reparations payments from the American zone in Germany to the Soviet Union.[87]

A dangerous situation

The publication of the secret protocols was a blow for the Soviet prosecution, and Rudenko had every reason to fear Stalin's wrath.[88] Seidl, meanwhile, remained determined to introduce the secret protocols as evidence for the defense. On May 24 he drafted another petition to the tribunal, explaining how he had come to be in possession of these documents. "At the beginning of April 1946 a member of the US Army . . . handed me two documents," he wrote. These were the secret protocols of August and September 1939. Seidl explained that he had questioned his interlocutor about "the origins of these documents" and had been told that they were "copies of photostats" which had "been captured by the armies of the Western Powers." Seidl described how he had shown these documents to Gaus soon after, and how Gaus had said that he had "no doubt whatsoever" that they were "copies of the German wording of the secret pacts." Gaus had then written his second affidavit. Seidl now asked the tribunal to hear Gaus as a witness. "The agreements contained in the secret addenda were a condition sine qua non for fulfillment of the Non-Aggression Pact," Seidl insisted, and were therefore essential evidence "for the defense of Hess."[89]

The Katyn situation too was becoming increasingly dangerous for the Soviets. The Western judges had dismissed the Soviet interpretation of Article 21—fearing (for good reason) that allowing the Soviet prosecution to pin the massacre on the Germans while barring challenges from the defense "would stultify the trial."[90] On May 24 in Moscow, the Politburo Commission for the Nuremberg Trials held an urgent meeting to plan a Soviet strategy for countering German witness testimony about Katyn. The commission focused on the selection and preparation of witnesses for the Soviet prosecution. It also put together a sub-commission—comprised of Soviet law expert Trainin, assistant prosecutor Lev Sheinin, and an NKVD officer—and directed it to review "all of the materials about Katyn" and to select those documents that could be used to expose German guilt. In addition, the commission finalized a written statement for Nikitchenko to circulate to the Western judges in his name, denouncing the tribunal's interpretation of Article 21.[91]

Back in Nuremberg, Rudenko appealed to the Western prosecutors to come to the aid of the Soviet prosecution. At a May 30 meeting of the chief prosecutors, Rudenko called for an "exchange of opinions" about how to respond to the defense's efforts regarding Katyn. The Western prosecutors were non-committal. They agreed with Rudenko that Article 21 gave the prosecution the right to present government documents (such as the Burdenko Commission's report) without additional supporting evidence. But they refused to question the tribunal's ruling that the defense was entitled to dispute the veracity of these documents. They did agree that if the defense were allowed to present new witnesses and documents on Katyn, then the Soviet prosecution should be allowed to do so too.[92]

Rudenko also broached the topic of the secret protocols. "The defense has recently been conducting undermining tactics," Rudenko complained, such as Seidl's petition to introduce "the 'secret' part of the Soviet-German treaty," Describing this as "an intentional attempt" to divide the prosecution, Rudenko invoked Jackson's "March 8th letter" and asked his colleagues to stand together. Here, the Western prosecutors voiced agreement with Rudenko. British deputy chief prosecutor Sir David Maxwell Fyfe concurred that Seidl's petition "did not relate to the case and was ill-intentioned." US assistant prosecutor Dodd agreed that Seidl's claim that a US Army officer had given him the document "was malicious"—and assured everyone that if such a thing had indeed taken place the officer had "undoubtedly exceeded his authority."[93] The prosecutors agreed to appeal collectively to the tribunal to protest Seidl's most recent efforts to introduce a copy of the secret protocols "into the materials of the trial." On June 5, they drafted a joint petition toward this end. They argued that Seidl's recent petitions "should be refused not only because the documents submitted by him are defective" but also because they were part of a general "tactic adopted by the defense counsel" to divert the court's attention away from defendants and toward "the actions of those states" that had "established the tribunal."[94]

This time the judges granted the prosecutors' request and turned down Seidl's petitions.[95] The Western and Soviet prosecutors had stood together and the judges had listened. And yet, this was only a partial victory for the Soviets. The details of the secret protocols had already become an open secret—and would remain so until Soviet leaders officially acknowledged their existence many decades later.[96] Moreover, the failure to control the publication of damning information in the international press would rankle the Soviets long after the verdicts were in. Throughout the course of the trials the defense had achieved real success in using the Western media to their advantage. British and American newspapers and news agencies such as the *Associated Press* had published interviews with the former Nazi leaders, who attempted to cast doubt on Soviet evidence and repeatedly brought up the issue of Soviet responsibility for war crimes and crimes against peace. The Soviets meanwhile experienced great difficulties on the propaganda front. Indeed, the experience of Nuremberg brought home to Soviet leaders the limitations of their "propaganda state" vis-à-vis the Western powers.[97]

Meanwhile, the Katyn fiasco did not end well for the Soviets. The tribunal decided that the German defense and the Soviet prosecution would each be permitted to summon witnesses to testify about the massacre; the Western prosecutors made it quite clear that this time the Soviet prosecution would be on its own. The Katyn affair took center stage at the Palace of Justice over two days in early July. The German defense and the Soviet prosecution each called three witnesses, and the accusations flew both ways. The results were inconclusive—so inconclusive, in fact, that the judgment would include no mention of Nazi responsibility for Katyn.[98] It disappeared from the list of German war crimes, even as the Soviets continued to insist on their own innocence.[99] For decades after Nuremberg, Polish émigrés as well as Western critics of the IMT would censure the Western governments for not taking the Soviets to task for the Katyn massacre. But in allowing German defense witnesses to paint a picture of Soviet guilt in open court, the Western judges had taken the Soviets to task. And the Soviets knew it. With the battle of the Katyn witnesses, the Soviets had visibly lost control over the narrative of the war.

The final reminder to the Soviets that they were not even close to running the show, and the biggest affront to their vision of justice, came with the verdicts in October 1946. Three of the Nazi leaders standing trial (Hans Fritzsche, Franz von Papen, and Hjalmar Schacht) were acquitted on the grounds of "reasonable doubt." In addition, the tribunal did not find the Reich Cabinet, the SA, or the General Staff and the High Command to be "criminal organizations." Moscow was appalled by these verdicts, which it denounced as wholly unfounded. Indeed, Stalin had given Nikitchenko special instructions "to argue and vote for the death penalty" for every single one of the defendants.[100] Nikitchenko gave a dissenting opinion regarding the acquittals, stating that the tribunal's decisions did "not correspond to the facts" and were "based on incorrect conclusions."[101] Soviet leaders responded by blaming Anglo-American reactionary forces for the acquittals—and organized a "mass protest campaign" in the Soviet zone of Germany to show "the support of the German people" for Nikitchenko's dissenting opinion.[102]

Conclusion

Almost two months after the verdicts, the legal expert Trainin gave a speech to his colleagues back at Moscow's Institute of Law, in which he discussed his work in Nuremberg and expressed optimism about the Soviet Union's continuing contribution to "new ideas and norms of international law." He reminded his fellow jurists that the Nuremberg Charter had set out the three most serious types of encroachments—war crimes, crimes against humanity, and crimes against peace—and that the last of these was "the most severe" offense of all.[103] On the very same day, another Soviet international law expert, Evgeny Korovin, delivered a public lecture, also in Moscow, in which he warned of the dangers of international legal institutions. International law "in its progressive forms" could help to "secure international peace," Korovin maintained, agreeing implicitly with Trainin. But the Americans and the British were using international law disingenuously, he warned, posing as "defenders of human rights" in order to expand their reach throughout the world.[104]

Trainin and Korovin captured Soviet ambivalence about the Nuremberg moment. Had it been a success or a failure for the Soviet Union? The Soviets had played a leading role in organizing the IMT. They had sought to use the trials to pursue reparations and justice, to shape the narrative of the Second World War, and to make their presence felt as a world power. But little of this had gone as planned. The IMT had exposed Soviet vulnerabilities; a centralized command structure that discouraged initiative and a closed regime that put a premium on the strict control of information had handicapped the Soviet delegation. The Soviet Union's experience with show trials (and its comfort with fabricating evidence) had ended up working against it: the effort to pin Katyn on the Nazis had backfired and undercut the Soviet case.

The Soviets had come to understand by the end of the trials how even those international institutions that they had helped to organize could be used against them. As one of the countries of the prosecution, the Soviets had not stood trial for their war crimes. But the defendants and their attorneys, with the acquiescence of the Western judges, had used the courtroom to bring Soviet war crimes to light. The defense had also used the Western press to its advantage—trying the Soviets in the court of international public opinion. With Nuremberg, the Soviets got something very different from the cut-and-dried political trial that they had anticipated. As the wartime alliance gave way, international rivalries and intrigue had shaped the IMT in ways that had taken the Soviet delegation as well as Soviet leaders frequently by surprise.

In the postwar world, new international legal institutions were becoming critical sites of power and diplomacy. The question Stalin faced after Nuremberg was how to go forward into this new world. While the Soviet Union had shaped the Nuremberg Trials, the Soviet experience in Nuremberg had also shaped the Soviet Union—creating in Moscow a deep and abiding sense of the perils as well as the possibilities of international law.

Acknowledgments

I am grateful to Kathryn Ciancia, Laura Engelstein, Mark Hessman, Arthur McKee, Jennifer Ratner-Rosenhagen, and Tony Michels for their helpful comments. Support for this research was generously provided by the American Council of Learned Societies (ACLS), the International Research and Exchanges Board (IREX), and the Office of the Vice Chancellor for Research and Graduate Education at the University of Wisconsin-Madison.

Notes

1 The 2000 drama *Nuremberg* is a great example—based on the riveting book by Joseph E. Persico, *Nuremberg: Infamy on Trial* (New York: Penguin Books, 1994). Also notable is the PBS American Experience documentary *The Nuremberg Trials*, which aired in 2006—and which celebrated Nuremberg as the triumph of US chief prosecutor Robert H. Jackson. For a somewhat more balanced popular account based primarily on the British archives and on memoirs, and told from an Anglo-American perspective, see Ann Tusa and John Tusa, *The Nuremberg Trial* (London: Atheneum, 1983).

2 See, for example, Kim Christian Priemel, *The Betrayal: The Nuremberg Trials and German Divergence* (Oxford: Oxford University Press, 2016). Priemel gives an excellent account of Nuremberg's legal ambiguities. In some accounts Soviet participation is held up as Nuremberg's main flaw. See, for example, Gary Jonathan Bass, *Stay the Hand of Vengeance: The Politics of War Crimes Tribunals* (Princeton, NJ: Princeton University Press, 2000). One of the first works to give serious attention to the Soviet contribution to the framing of the trials was George Ginsburgs, *Moscow's Road to Nuremberg: The Soviet Background to the Trial* (The Hague: Martinus Nijhoff Publishers, 1996). I first published on the Soviet role in the trials in 2008, inspired by Ginsburgs' book and by my findings in the Soviet archives. Francine Hirsch, "The Soviets at Nuremberg: International Law, Propaganda, and the Making of the Postwar Order," *American Historical Review*, 113/3 (2008): 701–30. Since then several other scholars have also published on various aspects of Soviet participation in the IMT. See, for example, Kirsten Sellars, *'Crimes Against Peace' and International Law* (Cambridge: Cambridge University Press, 2013). For a new German-language work on the Soviet role in the trials, see Irina Schulmeister-Andre's dissertation, published as *Internationale Strafgerichtsbarkeit unter sowjetischem Einfluss. Der Beitrag der UdSSR zum Nürnberger Hauptkriegsverbrecherprozess* (Berlin: Duncker & Humblot, 2016).

3   The most comprehensive and insightful Soviet-era scholarly work on Nuremberg is Natal'ia Sergeevna Lebedeva's *Podgotovka Niurnbergskogo protsessa* (Moscow: Nauka, 1975). A serious examination of the Nuremberg Trials is currently underway in Russia, led by Lebedeva. See N. S. Lebedeva, ed., *SSSR i Niurnbergskii protsess. Neizvestnye i maloizvestnye stranitsy istorii: Sbornik dokumentov* (Moscow: Mezhdunarodnyi fond Demokratiia, 2012) and N. S. Lebedeva, V. I. Ishchenko, and I. Iu. Korshunov, eds., *Niurnbergskii protsess: uroki istorii: Materialy mezhdunarodnoi nauchnoi konferentsii* (Moscow: Institut vseobshchei istorii RAN, 2007). Also see Aleksandr Zviagintsev, *Glavnyi protsess chelovechestva: Reportazh iz proshlogo obrashchenie k budushchemu* (Moscow: OLMA Media Group, 2011).
4   See, for example, Norman M. Naimark, *The Russians in Germany: A History of the Soviet Zone of Occupation, 1945-1949* (Cambridge, MA: Belnap Press, 1997); Timothy Snyder, *Bloodlands: Europe between Hitler and Stalin* (New York: Basic Books: 2010); Anne Applebaum, *Iron Curtain: The Crushing of Eastern Europe, 1945-1956* (New York: Doubleday, 2012).
5   For a discussion of some of the different ways in which Nuremberg has been invoked as a "human rights moment," see Elizabeth Borgwardt, "Commerce and Complicity: Human Rights and the Legacy of Nuremberg," in Bruce J. Schulman, ed., *Making the American Century: Essays in the Political Culture of Twentieth Century America* (New York: Oxford University Press, 2014), 92–108.
6   Soviet show trials were a form of didactic trial meant to have an instructive purpose. The Soviets viewed Nuremberg through a similar lens—in the sense that they thought that they would be working with their wartime allies to educate the world about Nazi crimes. On Nuremberg as a didactic trial, see Lawrence Douglas, *The Memory of Judgment: Making Law and History in the Trials of the Holocaust* (New Haven, CT, 2001), 2. For a useful discussion of political trials and a good overview of the literature, see Jens Meierhenrich and Devin O. Pendas, "'The Justice of My Cause is Clear, but There's Politics to Fear': Political Trials in Theory and History," in Meierhenrich and Pendas, eds., *Political Trials in Theory and History* (Cambridge: Cambridge University Press: 2016), 1–64.
7   I explore this contradiction in greater depth in *Soviet Judgment at Nuremberg*, forthcoming with Oxford University Press.
8   I draw on materials from the State Archive of the Russian Federation (GARF), the Russian State Archive of Socio-Political History (RGASPI), the Russian State Archive of Literature and Art (RGALI), the Archive of the Foreign Policy of the Russian Federation (AVPRF), and the Archive of the Russian Academy of Sciences (ARAN). Many of these materials were newly available in 2005 and 2006 when I did the bulk of the research for my forthcoming book. Since then, archival access to some of the collections I worked in has again been curtailed.
9   See Molotov's diplomatic note of October 14, 1942, "Zaiavleniia Sovetskogo pravitel'stva ob otvetstvennosti gitlerovskikh zakhvatchikov i ikh soobshchnikov za zlodeianiia, sovershaemye imi v okkupironvannykh stranakh Evropy." AVPRF f. 06, op. 4, p. 137, d. 14, l. 48.
10 Aron Naumovich Trainin, *Ugolovnaia otvetstvennost' gitlerovtsev*, ed. Andrei Y. Vyshinskii (Moscow: Iuridicheskoe izdatel'stvo, 1944), 54; translated into English as *The Criminal Responsibility of the Hitlerites*, ed. Andrei Y. Vyshinsky (Moscow: Legal Publishing House NKU, 1944), 40. On this work and its significance, see Ginsburgs, *Moscow's Road to Nuremberg*, chapter 4. I discuss Trainin's contribution at length in "The Soviets at Nuremberg." Trainin's ideas contributed to a larger international

discussion about the criminality of aggressive war. Sellars looks at this discussion in *'Crimes Against Peace' and International Law*. I follow the archival trail of this discussion in *Soviet Judgment at Nuremberg*.

11 Trainin, *Criminal Responsibility of the Hitlerites*; and Trainin, *Ugolovnaia otvetstvennost' gitlerovtsev*. Here Trainin acknowledged an intellectual debt to Vyshinsky, noting that he was borrowing from the definition of complicity that the latter had elaborated in 1938 during the Moscow Trials. Also see Ginsburgs, *Moscow's Road to Nuremberg*, 79–80.

12 For an account of the UNWCC's deliberations on these issues, see Dr. Bohuslav Ečer's "Contribution to the History of the UNWCC (History and Work of Committees II and III)" in the papers of Robert H. Jackson at the Library of Congress, Washington, DC, Box 118, Folder 8.

13 The Nuremberg Charter was signed at the end of the London Conference in August 1945.

14 On Vyshinsky's roles in Soviet law and foreign affairs, see Arkady Vaksberg, *Stalin's Prosecutor: The Life of Andrei Vyshinsky* (New York: Grove Weidenfeld, 1990); Peter H. Solomon, Jr., *Soviet Criminal Justice under Stalin* (Cambridge: Cambridge University Press, 1996); and Oleg Emil'ianovich Kutafin, ed., *Inkvizitor: Stalinskii prokuror Vyshinskii* (Moscow: Respublika, 1992). This charge against the "old Bolsheviks" was reiterated in slightly different forms at all three of the Moscow Trials. At the 1937 trial Vyshinsky accused Trotsky of conspiring "with one of the leaders of the German National-Socialist Party" to launch "a joint struggle against the Soviet Union." Andrei Y. Vyshinsky, *Traitors Accused: Indictment of the Piatakov-Radek Trotskyite Group* (New York: Workers Library Publishers, 1937), 6.

15 The Extraordinary State Commission was established in November 1942 to compile evidence about Nazi war crimes committed in the Soviet Union. See GARF f. 7445, op. 2, d. 391, ll. 49–56. It was also directed to calculate Soviet losses. For an outstanding account of the commission, see Marina Sorokina, "People and Procedures: Toward a History of the Investigation of Nazi Crimes in the USSR," *Kritika: Explorations in Russian and Eurasian History*, 6/4 (2005), 797–831. Also see Kiril Feferman, "Soviet Investigation of Nazi Crimes in the USSR: Documenting the Holocaust," *Journal of Genocide Research*, 5/4 (2003), 587–602.

16 This Moscow-based commission included in its ranks such highly placed figures as the new Procurator General of the USSR, Konstantin Gorshenin; the People's Commissar of Justice, Nikolai Rychkov; the President of the Supreme Soviet, Ivan Goliakov; the head of SMERSH Viktor Abakumov; and the head of the People's Commissariat of State Security (NKGB) Vsevolod Merkulov. It also included NKGB deputy Bogdan Kobulov; NKVD deputy Sergei Kruglov; and one of Vyshinsky's assistants in the People's Commissariat of Foreign Affairs, Ivan Lavrov. In addition it included Pavel Bogoiavlenskii from the Extraordinary State Commission. On SMERSH and its role in this commission, see Vadim J. Birstein's excellent *SMERSH: Stalin's Secret Weapon* (London: Biteback Publishing, 2011).

17 GARF f. 8131, op. 38, d. 238, ll. 158-159. Its full name was the Politburo Commission for Preparing to Conduct the Nuremberg Trials.

18 The trial of the leaders of Polish Underground State had been staged in Moscow over three days in June 1945 and had presented a damning narrative of Polish collaboration with the Nazis. On Rudenko's role, see Aleksandr Zviagintsev and Iurii Orlov, *Prokurory dvukh epokh: Andrei Vyshinskii i Roman Rudenko* (Moscow: OLMA-Press, 2001), 212–13.

19 Nikitchenko was approximately fifty years old in 1946; he had joined the Bolshevik Party in 1914 and had headed a military tribunal during the civil war. Arkadii Poltorak, *The Nuremberg Epilogue* (Moscow: Progress Publishers, 1971), 153–55. Rudenko was approximately forty years old and procurator of the Ukrainian SSR in 1946; he had been a party member for some twenty years. Hiroaki Kuromiya, *Freedom and Terror in the Donbas: A Ukrainian-Russian Borderland, 1870s–1990s* (Cambridge: Cambridge University Press, 1998), 223. On Rudenko's life and career, also see Aleksandr Zviagintsev, *Rudenko* (Moscow: Molodaia gvardiia, 2008).

20 AVPRF f. 082, op. 27, p. 122, d. 23, ll. 16–18. American and British officials shared this view of the Soviet translators. Telford Taylor, *The Anatomy of the Nuremberg Trials: A Personal Memoir* (Boston: Little, Brown, & Co., 1993), 100–01.

21 AVPRF f. 07, op. 13, p. 41, d. 4, ll. 5–6; d. 8, ll. 88–89. On the Stalinist Terror and the transformation of the Commissariat of Foreign Affairs, see Teddy J. Uldricks, "The Impact of the Great Purges on the People's Commissariat of Foreign Affairs," *Slavic Review*, 36/2 (1977), 187–204. Also see Albert Resis, "The Fall of Litvinov: Harbinger of the German-Soviet Non-Aggression Pact," *Europe-Asia Studies*, 52/1 (2000), 33–56.

22 For example, AVPRF f. 06, op. 7, p. 20, d. 208, l. 21.

23 GARF f. 8131, op. 38, d. 238, ll. 17–21.

24 For example Douglas, *Memory of Judgment*, 2.

25 One of Kempner's jobs as part of Jackson's team was to anticipate the arguments of the defense.

26 GARF f. 8131, op. 38, d. 238, l. 71. These Soviet leaders and heads of the security apparatus were members of a special Soviet Indictment Commission—which preceded the Nuremberg Commission and contained many of the same members.

27 GARF f. 8131, op. 38, d. 238, ll. 87–90.

28 AVPRF f. 07, op. 13, p. 41, d. 10, ll. 40–43.

29 GARF f. 8131, op. 38, d. 238, l. 89.

30 AVPRF f. 07, op. 13, p. 41, d. 10, l. 64.

31 "Indictment: Count Three," and "Indictment: Count One," *Nuremberg Trial Proceedings*, vol. 1, Avalon Project at Yale Law School, http://avalon.law.yale.edu/imt/count3.asp and http://avalon.law.yale.edu/imt/count1.asp (accessed June 10, 2018). On the evolving Soviet narrative of the war and its victims, see Karel C. Berkhoff, "Total Annihilation of the Jewish Population: The Holocaust in the Soviet Media, 1941-45," in Michael David-Fox, Peter Holquist, and Alexander M. Martin, eds., *The Holocaust in the East: Local Perpetrators and Soviet Responses* (Pittsburgh: University of Pittsburgh Press, 2014) and the excellent essays in Harriet Murav and Gennady Estraikh, eds., *Soviet Jews in World War II: Fighting, Witnessing, Remembering* (Boston: Academic Studies Press, 2014). It is not clear from the archival record why (or on whose initiative) "the Russians" was removed from the list. The Indictment Act calls particular attention to Nazi crimes in German-occupied Ukraine and Belorussia.

32 GARF f. 8131, op. 28, d. 238, l. 135.

33 The German accusation and Soviet response are reprinted in Anna M. Cienciala, Natalia S. Lebedeva, and Wojciech Materski, eds., *Katyn: A Crime without Punishment* (New Haven, CT: Yale University Press, 2007), 305–07. On the Burdenko Commission and the Soviet compilation of evidence on Katyn, see Sorokina, "People and Procedures." Also see I. S. Iazhborovskaia, A. Iu. Iablokov, and V. S. Parsadanova, *Katynskii sindrom v sovetsko-polskikh i rossiisko-pol'skikh otnosheniiakh* (Moscow: ROSSPEN, 2001).

34 AVPRF f. 07, op. 13, p. 41, d. 10, ll. 40–43, 50–51.

35 AVPRF f. 07, op. 13, p. 41, d. 10, ll. 62–65.
36 AVPRF f. 07, op. 13, p. 41, d. 10, ll. 40–68.
37 AVPRF f. 06, op. 7, p. 20, d. 208, l. 22.
38 *Nuremberg Trial Proceedings*, vol. 1, http://avalon.law.yale.edu/imt/count1.asp (accessed June 10, 2018).
39 Ibid.
40 GARF f. 7445, op. 2, d. 8, l. 394.
41 GARF f. 7445, op. 2, d. 391, l. 47. On this list also see Yuri Zorya and Natalia Lebedeva, "The Year 1939 in the Nuremberg Files," *International Affairs*, 10 (Moscow, October 1989), 117–29.
42 AVPRF f. 07, op. 13, p. 41, d. 8, l. 80.
43 AVPRF f. 07, op. 13, p. 41, d. 7, l. 1.
44 AVPRF f. 07, op. 13, p. 41, d. 4, l. 12.
45 "Third Day, Thursday, 22 November 1945," *Nuremberg Trial Proceedings*, vol. 2, http://avalon.law.yale.edu/imt/11-22-45.asp (accessed June 10, 2018).
46 AVPRF f. 07, op. 13, p. 41, d. 9, ll. 121–24. Also G. P. Kynin and I. Laufer, eds., *SSSR i germanskii vopros, 1941–1949: Dokumenty iz Arkhiva vneshnei politiki Rossiiskoi Federatsii*, vol. 2 (Moscow, 2000), 750–51 (footnote 140) and Vaksberg, *Stalin's Prosecutor*, 259.
47 GARF f. 7445, op. 2, d. 391, ll. 45–46.
48 Kynin and Laufer, eds., *SSSR i germanskii vopros*, vol. 2, 84, 750–51 (footnote 140).
49 RGASPI f. 558, op. 11, d. 99, ll. 111–12.
50 GARF f. 7445, op. 2, d. 373, ll. 83–85.
51 "Fifty-Fourth Day, Friday, 8 February 1946," *Nuremberg Trial Proceedings*, vol. 7, http://avalon.law.yale.edu/imt/02-08-46.asp (accessed June 10, 2018).
52 RGALI f. 2989, op. 1, d. 190, ll. 27–29. Karmen's studio in Moscow put together the Soviet evidentiary films. For more on Karmen's role in the trials, see Hirsch, *Soviet Judgment at Nuremberg* and Jeremy Hicks, *First Films of the Holocaust: Soviet Cinema and the Genocide of the Jews* (Pittsburgh: University of Pittsburgh Press, 2012).
53 "Fifty-Ninth Day, Thursday, 14 February 1946," *Nuremberg Trial Proceedings*, vol. 7, http://avalon.law.yale.edu/imt/02-14-46.asp (accessed June 10, 2018). On the fabrication of evidence, see Sorokina, "People and Procedures," 797–831; Iazhborovskaia, Iablokov, and Parsadanova, *Katynskii sindrom v sovetsko-polskikh i rossisko-pol'skikh otnosheniiakh*; Claudia Weber, "Stalin's Trap: The Katyn Forest Massacre Between Propaganda and Taboo," *Theatres of Violence: Maccacre, Mass Killing and Atrocity throughout History*, ed. Philip G. Dwyer and Lyndall Ryan (New York: Berghahn, 2015), 170-185; and Witold Wasilewski, "The Birth and Persistence of the Katyn Lie," *Case Western Reserve Journal of International Law* 45, no. 3 (2012): 671-693.
54 "Sixtieth Day, Friday, 15 February 1946," *Nuremberg Trial Proceedings*, vol. 7, http://avalon.law.yale.edu/imt/02-15-46.asp (accessed June 10, 2018).
55 GARF f. 7445, op. 2, d. 400, l. 30. Naville had served on the German-sponsored International Katyn Commission. See Cienciala, Lebedeva, and Materski, eds., *Katyn*.
56 Winston Churchill, "The Sinews of Peace," in Churchill, *Winston S. Churchill: His Complete Speeches, 1897–1963*, ed. Robert Rhodes James, 8 vols (New York, 1974), 7: 7285–93.
57 Poltorak, *Nuremberg Epilogue*, 90.
58 AVPRF f. 06, op. 8, p. 1, d. 8, ll. 29–34, in Kynin and Laufer, eds., *SSSR i germanskii vopros*, vol. 2, 475–79.

59 Poltorak, *Nuremberg Epilogue*, 90–93.
60 GARF f. 7445, op. 2, d. 8, ll. 47–48.
61 GARF f. 7445, op. 2, d. 8, l. 170.
62 GARF f. 7445, op. 1, d. 2625, ll. 166–76, in Lebedeva, *SSSR i Niurnbergskii protsess*, 412–18.
63 GARF f. 7445, op. 2, d. 400, l. 30.
64 GARF f. 7445, op. 2, d. 391, ll. 61–63. The letter was penned by the Nuremberg Commission.
65 On the falsification of the documents, also see Sorokina, "People and Procedures."
66 For example, GARF f. 7445, op. 2, d. 391, l. 49.
67 "Eighty-Seventh Day, Thursday, 21 March 1946," *Nuremberg Trial Proceedings*, vol. 9, http://avalon.law.yale.edu/imt/03-21-46.asp#Goering8 (accessed June 10, 2018).
68 "Eighty-Eighth Day, Friday, 22 March 1946," *Nuremberg Trial Proceedings*, vol. 9, http://avalon.law.yale.edu/imt/03-22-46.asp (accessed June 10, 2018).
69 "Ninetieth Day, Thursday, 25 March 1946," *Nuremberg Trial Proceedings*, vol. 10, http://avalon.law.yale.edu/imt/03-25-46.asp (accessed June 10, 2018).
70 Taylor, *Anatomy of the Nuremberg Trials*, 350.
71 "Ninety-Sixth Day, Monday, 1 April 1946," *Nuremberg Trial Proceedings*, vol. 10, http://avalon.law.yale.edu/imt/04-01-46.asp (accessed June 10, 2018).
72 AVPRF f. 07, op. 13, p. 41, d. 9, ll. 112–16. This report was forwarded to Vyshinsky and Molotov.
73 Ibid. For the article he is referencing, see "War Eve Pact Revealed at Hess Trial," *The Daily Mail*, March 26, 1946, 1.
74 AVPRF f. 07, op. 13, p. 41, d. 9, ll. 112–16.
75 The transcript included the secret protocols of August 23, 1939, and the secret additional protocols of September 28, 1939.
76 AVPRF f. 07, op. 13, p. 41, d. 9, l. 122. It's not clear who this informant was.
77 Ibid.
78 GARF f. 7445, op. 1, d. 2625, ll. 177–88, in Lebedeva, *SSSR i Niurnbergskii protsess*, 442–45.
79 Ibid.
80 GARF f. 7445, op. 2, d. 400, ll. 36–38 and "One Hundred and Twenty-Seventh Day, Saturday, 11 May 1946," *Nuremberg Trial Proceedings*, vol. 13, http://avalon.law.yale.edu/imt/05-11-46.asp (accessed June 10, 2018).
81 GARF f. 7445, op. 2, d. 400, ll. 36–38.
82 "One Hundred and Thirty-Fifth Day, Tuesday, 21 May 1946," *Nuremberg Trial Proceedings*, vol. 14, http://avalon.law.yale.edu/imt/05-21-46.asp (accessed June 10, 2018) and Richard L. Stokes, "Secret Soviet-Nazi Pacts on Eastern Europe Aired," *St. Louis Post-Dispatch*, May 22, 1946, 1, 6. Zorya and Lebedeva also discuss the details of Weizsaecker's testimony in "The Year 1939 in the Nuremberg Files."
83 Ibid.
84 Ibid.
85 Stokes, "Secret Soviet-Nazi Pacts on Eastern Europe Aired," *St. Louis Post-Dispatch*.
86 Christopher J. Dodd with Lary Bloom, *Letters from Nuremberg: My Father's Narrative of a Quest for Justice* (New York: Crown Publishing, 2007), 251.
87 On the politics of the moment, see John Lewis Gaddis, *Russia, the Soviet Union, and the United States: An Interpretive History* (New York: McGraw-Hill, 1990).
88 One of the Soviet assistant prosecutors Nikolai Zorya apparently took his life over the incident.
89 GARF f. 7445, op. 2, d. 400, ll. 59–61.

90   Taylor, *Anatomy of the Nuremberg Trials*, 469. Biddle was the most forceful in his opposition.
91   GARF f. 7445, op. 2, d. 391, ll. 50–51.
92   GARF f. 7445, op. 2, d. 8, ll. 18–20.
93   Ibid. It is unclear whether Rudenko knew at this point that Dodd had helped Seidl to place his copy of the secret protocols in the American press.
94   GARF f. 7445, op. 2, d. 6, ll. 9–10.
95   Zorya and Lebedeva, "The Year 1939 in the Nuremberg Files."
96   Lev Bezymensky, "The Secret Protocols of 1939 as a Problem of Soviet Historiography," in Gabriel Gorodetsky, ed., *Soviet Foreign Policy, 1917-1991: A Retrospective* (London: Frank Cass and Co., 1994), 75–85.
97   The classic work on the Soviet propaganda state is Peter Kenez, *The Birth of the Propaganda State: Soviet Methods of Mass Mobilization, 1917-1929* (Cambridge: Cambridge University Press, 1985).
98   I discuss these developments in detail in Hirsch, *Soviet Judgment at Nuremberg*. For a discussion of the witness testimony, see Taylor, *Anatomy of the Nuremberg Trials*, 466–72.
99   In April 2010, following the air crash that killed Polish president Lech Kaczynski, the Russian government posted on the internet documents showing once and for all that the Soviets were responsible for the 1940 Katyn massacre of Polish officers; and the Russian State Duma affirmed that the massacre "was committed on the direct orders of Stalin and other Soviet officials." The documents were available at http://www.rusarchives.ru/publication/katyn/spisok.shtml (accessed January 7, 2015).
100 AVPRF f. 012, op. 7, p. 106, d. 186, ll. 11–19, reprinted in Lebedeva, *SSSR i Niurnbergskii protsess*, 500–05. Also see Norman J. W. Goda, *Tales from Spandau: Nazi Criminals and the Cold War* (New York: Cambridge University Press, 2007), 34–45.
101 "Judgment: Dissenting Opinion," *Nuremberg Trial Proceedings*, http://avalon.law.yale.edu/imt/juddiss.asp (accessed June 10, 2018).
102 For example, AVPRF f. 012, op. 7, p. 106, d. 178, l. 49, in Kynin and Laufer, eds., *SSSR i germanskii vopros*, vol. 2, 712–13.
103 ARAN f. 499, op. 1, d. 71, ll. 74–99.
104 E. A. Korovin, *Mezhdunarodnoe pravo na sovremennom etape: Stenogramma publichnoi lektsii* (Moscow: Pravda, 1946).

7

Soviet Journalists at Nuremberg: Establishing the Soviet War Narrative

Jeremy Hicks

The Nuremberg IMT is usually thought to have performed a didactic function in part, as a kind of show trial.[1] Given that the world public could not be in the courtroom, journalism had a key role to play in drawing lessons from the evidence. The largest group of journalists and writers ever gathered in one place to cover one event: over 160 writers,[2] as well as the artists and filmmakers who represented what happened there, all had a crucial role to play in mediating and distilling the lessons to be drawn from the nine-month-long proceedings. While their interpretations have been supplemented and superseded by subsequent writings, memoirs, and histories, as well as films, these contemporary journalistic reports played a crucial role in the struggle between competing understandings of the trial and the war.

The tension was a confrontation not only between those on trial and those trying them but also between the victor nations administering justice. As discussed in Chapter 5, this contest encompassed many facets of the trial including the legal debates about what was or was not to be presented in the courtroom, and the roles of the various legal teams. The many conflicts beneath the surface impression of common endeavor undertaken by United Nations, anticipated the emerging Cold War.[3] Indeed, they may be seen as its opening battle, since the tribunal itself and the reporting of it became "the site and the subject of an immense propaganda struggle."[4]

In Western historiography, the United States is widely thought to have won the battle, so that the hegemonic view of the IMT may be summed up as "a tale of liberal triumph" and "a devastating propaganda failure" for the Soviets.[5] This view has prevailed to such an extent that Western accounts often sideline the Soviets, whose presence inconveniently undermined the legal value of the trial, also introducing hard to pronounce names and difficult to understand motives.[6] Such an approach distorts the picture by treating the Soviets' marginalization as a foregone conclusion, and largely silences the alternative Soviet account of the war and approach to the IMT that failed to gain hegemonic status. This simplification, in addition to reading the events through the distorting lens of their outcome, also underplays the Soviets' pivotal role in setting up the trial, and the significance of the evidence revealed by them, while simultaneously assuming the irrelevance of the Soviets' attempts to interpret the proceedings in line with their own emerging narrative of the war.[7]

Yet by defining and examining the evolution and distinct character of the Soviet account we can not only better understand why it failed and the Western account prevailed but also grasp the extent to which it had merits and emphases missing from the dominant view of the IMT, some of which remain relevant to understanding Nazism and the Holocaust.

In broad terms the contemporary Soviet account of the IMT followed the formula of "Russian exceptionalism, heroism and victimization" emphasizing the importance of the Soviet, and implicitly Russian, role in defeating the Nazis, of the suffering inflicted by the Nazis specifically on the Soviet people and talking up the Soviet role in the trial.[8] Yet, despite the fact that all Soviet journalism underwent a process of preliminary censor's scrutiny to ensure unanimity on the overall narrative, a key distinguishing feature of the Soviet coverage, when compared with that of the American or British journalists, is that those covering the trial had far more experience as eyewitnesses of the most brutal of Nazi atrocities. The result was that, despite Soviet attempts to vet, centralize, and standardize reporting, the conclusion of a number of recent accounts of Soviet wartime journalism taken as a whole, yet when we look at the detail of specific articles and personalities, we see there are instances where individual reporters strove to retain their distinct voices and echo their personal histories. They necessarily not only refracted their courtroom perceptions through the overarching Soviet template and conventions for understanding the Nazis and the war but also attempted to convey their own specific wartime positions as eyewitnesses to the immediate aftermath of Nazi mass murder, including the Holocaust.[9] Of particular interest here is the Soviet writer and journalist Boris Polevoi in part because he was one of the only two Soviet journalists to publish an eyewitness account of Auschwitz on its liberation, at least in the central press, but also because he reworked that account in his reporting of the trial and again in his subsequent diaries and memoirs. The shifting emphases between these accounts are evident from a comparison of the different pieces by the same author on the same subject.

A further factor counteracting the homogenizing thrust of the Soviet leadership was that their own views on many of the issues were changing fast. Thus, the place of the war in the Soviet imaginary was shifting from the wartime patterns of representation and still unclear: the war had unleashed a "plurality of narratives and actors" in the Soviet media, which could not be readjusted and standardized overnight.[10] Thus, journalists' personal investments and the not-yet-fixed Soviet narrative on the war and Holocaust make Soviet journalistic coverage of the Nuremberg tribunal distinct, heterogeneous, and a rewarding object for analysis.

Conveying the Soviet narrative

The American prosecution team set out to steal everyone else's thunder at the courtroom itself, and ensure they played the central role, achieving this through a broad interpretation of the "conspiracy" charge that meant using many of the documents supplied to them by the French, British, and Russians. This was part of a deliberate and largely successful attempt to keep "the bulk of the case in American hands."[11] Consequently, other teams had good reason to be worried that this would make their interventions less dramatic and less telling, and they ultimately ended up repeating some of what the Americans had done, rather than cut down their cases, and this prolonged the trial needlessly.[12] Necessarily, the first iteration of the Nazis' crimes was of greater interest than the subsequent ones, which presented the Soviet press with a difficult task: the Soviet narrative of the war cast the Soviet Union as the main character, and so Soviet coverage had to find a way to make the Soviets central, and overcome, at least to the satisfaction of domestic readers, the Americans' upstaging of them.[13]

First, however, Soviet journalists had to adapt their established wartime templates for understanding Nazism to the actual Nazi leaders physically present in front of them. In the first weeks of the trial particularly, it was the defendants themselves who attracted the most coverage, especially Göring, the "Nazi number two," and Hess, for his simulated memory loss. Even the American prison psychologist was writing a book intended from the outset as a scoop on the subject.[14]

The same fascination was evident in Soviet journalistic accounts. Yet, while they made some attempts to analyze the inner workings of the Nazi defendants, they were hampered by their established habits of representing the Nazi leaders in highly effective wartime caricatures. Seeing these people in the flesh forced a reappraisal of such portrayals: Polevoi was not alone in being struck by a sense that Göring was not like his caricatures.[15] As journalist and documentary filmmaker Roman Karmen commented, cartoonists Boris Efimov and the Kukryniksy triumvirate of artists now had an opportunity to revise their caricatures:

> For many years their sharp pencils and brushes have represented this band of Fascist leaders on caricatures and posters. Now for the first time they are drawing them from nature.[16]

Yet Efimov's cartoons continued the old habit of depicting the top Nazis as abnormal and monstrous. In a series entitled "The Fascist Menagerie" Göring is depicted as a snake, Keitel as a jackal followed by a whole series of bestialized defendants.[17] Likewise, the Kukryniksys's series of portraits of the defendants, used in pairs to accompany brief articles by writer Vsevolod Vishnevsky devoted to each of the defendants, emphasize Göring as cruel and greedy by showing him to be enormous and fleshy, in an echo of the classic early Bolshevik representations of capitalists as porcine. For grotesquely comic contrast, he is portrayed alongside an exaggeratedly skinny Hess.[18] The combination of the Kukryniksys's caricatures and Vishnevskys sketches do not always work well, since the grotesque mode is most effective when accompanied by a character sketch, but elsewhere Vishnevsky gives a biography and list of the crimes committed, which suggest these were the crimes of an inhuman system, rather than those of an exceptional individual.

One Soviet artist who attempted to depart from the established hyperbolic depictions was Nikolai Zhukov, whose sketches of the defendants strove to suggest moral corruption in a subtler, realist manner, as opposed to the Kukryniksy and Efimov:

> When I looked from the figure of the chair of the court to the dock, I particularly felt their insignificance. They were not wearing prison clothes, they sat in their suits and ties, and in this they differed little from other people, and yet their Fascist essence, despite this, was clearly evident. Maybe people will think I'm biased, but I'm convinced that a truthful, realistic, successful drawing can in this case be more expressive in its damning force than caricature, because caricature is the hyperbolic use of physical shortcomings, extending them to the point they become funny. In such cases you never know what percentage of truth there is in this and how much artistic transformation. The Fascist criminals' appearance is such that an accurate copy of them was also the essence of their most unpleasant and negative character traits, whereas any exaggeration would be too much and a deviation from artistic truth. I could feel this intensely when I looked at the likes of Kaltenbrunner, Streicher, Hess etc.[19]

Zhukov's more subtle pencil drawings add literal and figurative shades of grey, suggesting an attempt to turn away from exceptional and monstrous portrayals, and to come to a more rounded appraisal of what the Nazis were, and how they came to do the things they did. The trial itself, through the conspiracy charge in particular, suggested an understanding of the individuals on trial as representatives of various organizations, that is, of the Nazi state's component parts. Zhukov echoes the shift toward a sense of the unexceptional nature of the accused, which went together with an exploration of Nazism as a system.[20]

This reorientation had been present in Soviet coverage of the trial from the outset, that is, as early in proceedings as *Pravda*'s leading article on the day the indictment was published in October 1945, which argued that it was not just individuals on trial but Fascism itself, and that the crimes were committed by both individuals and organizations.[21] Influential Soviet legal expert Professor Aron Trainin had already written about the need for the trial as a means of achieving the "moral and political defeat of Fascism."[22] To this end, the format of the trial enabled a more sophisticated understanding of the machinery of Nazi crimes, and shifted attention onto criminal organizations. Trainin explained that it was not just a question of establishing the guilt of the major Nazis, but of the organizations that they lead, to enable national courts to prosecute those found guilty of membership of those organizations.[23] In a memorable turn of phrase, Lev Sheinin argued the trial was analogous to a "pathological-anatomical" clinical process—an autopsy on the corpse of Fascism attempting to find out how it functioned, and the reasons for its behavior. The verdict would also be a diagnosis.[24]

Yet, while Soviet commentators were willing to look at the systematic nature of the Nazi crimes, they were unwilling to do so, if this meant humanizing the defendants excessively, as, in contrast with the other Allied treatments, there was a greater distance to the defendants. Whereas a number of English-language publications included interviews with the accused, the Soviets condemned the practice.[25] Writer Leonid

Leonov in particular criticized the international press for their obsession with Göring, and their recounting details such as his staring at a female member of the court staff, when scribes should have been taking an interest in the documents.[26] Vishnevsky was angered by a comment made by an "Anglo-Saxon" neighbor that Göring resembled Falstaff. He reacted, that despite his human failings, Falstaff was actually a human being: "But Göring, the creator of German concentration camps . . . is he human at all?" For Vishnevsky, the answer is evidently, no.[27] Leonov drew a different literary analogy, from Dostoevskii's *Crime and Punishment* to stress the Nazis' careful premeditation rather than irrational atavism: "The clarity of thought of the murderer is striking: I doubt even Raskolnikov thought through his murder of the old woman so methodically."[28] For the Soviets, of course, Russian literature was a more appropriate frame of reference for understanding the Nazis than Shakespeare.

The emphasis on the analysis of systems and organizations rather than individuals enabled the Soviets to highlight the role of the German Army in carrying out Nazi policy, a connection the Western allies were reluctant to make.[29] Indeed, they widely employed a translation of the Nazi term describing the invasion of the Soviet Union as a "war of annihilation" (*Vernichtungskrieg*; *voina na unichtozhenie*), with its obvious parallels with extermination camps (*Vernichstungslager*). This has only recently been widely adopted by Western historians to describe the Eastern front.[30] Semen Krushinskii expanded, rejecting the distinction that Keitel made between the German military and German Fascism: he argued that the corpses left by *Einsatzgruppen* who accompanied the army's triumphant march across the Soviet Union are a clear illustration of this.[31]

While Soviet journalists' understandings of the Nazis evolved during the trial, they consistently viewed Nazism in such a way as to bolster the Soviet Union's own importance. One way of doing this was by stressing the anti-Communist component in National Socialism, and the Nazis' own use of the Bolshevik bugbear to distract democracies from their actions.[32] Leonov distilled the Nazis' racist and anti-communist message to the German population—go to sleep and do not worry: "Our long-range artillery and SS angels in azure raiments will guard your slumber from the Mongolo-Slavic-Jewish designs of Moscow."[33]

Throughout the presentation of the US, British, and French evidence, the Soviet press reworked material so as to stress the centrality of the Soviets' own contribution and sacrifice in the war. One way of doing this was by the paratextual strategy of arranging material on the newspaper page, such as *Pravda*'s setting of Vsevolod Vishnevsky's November piece on Germany's Anschluss, which makes no mention of the war on the Eastern front, alongside an article about Operation Barbarossa by David Zaslavskii which included the word "Barbarossa" prominently in its title.[34]

Soviet writers also shifted focus onto the Soviet experience by emphasizing the fate of Soviet victims and drawing comparisons from their own prior experience or other stories reported in the Soviet media: Erenberg, when commenting upon the Americans' detailed presentation of Nazi crimes, enumerates the earlier offenses inflicted on the Soviets and exposed by the Soviet press as far back as 1942—Volokalamsk, Istra, Kerch.[35] Vishnevsky recounts the witness testimony of those called by the French, such as Marie-Claude Vaillant-Couturier's testimony about Auschwitz, but his article ends with these witnesses' account of the crimes committed against Russian prisoners of war.[36] Roman Karmen does something similar when reporting the crimes committed at Dachau, concentrating on the Soviets killed there, going through the records to list their names. Having been part of the team filming Majdanek in autumn 1944, Karmen commented that Dachau differed little from Majdanek or Auschwitz, and that it was an extermination camp.[37]

Yet the most interesting and significant means whereby the Soviets insisted upon the centrality of their part in the war was through the supplementing of what was said or seen in the courthouse with personal memories summoned by the evidence. Thus, when watching footage of the American film *The Nazi Plan*, Vishnevsky describes the terrible scenes these images stir, the evidence of Germany's use of slave labor elicits Vishnevsky's reflection upon the devastation and depopulation of the Soviet Union, an evocation of the tears that lie behind the documents and causes Polevoi to address an article to the woman he met in Khar´kov in 1943, entreating her to stop crying now that her tormentors were facing justice.[38]

This sense of the Soviets as both the key participants and as crucial eyewitnesses was put forcefully by the leading article in *Izvestiia* on the day of the verdict:

> The Soviet people, that have borne on their shoulders the main weight of the war of liberation against Fascism, know the Fascists' barbarous crimes not from hearsay accounts, and not from newspaper reports alone. With their own eyes Soviet people have seen the ruins of towns and the ashes of villages, with their own hands they have buried the corpses of those tortured and murdered.[39]

The Soviet journalist as witness: Boris Polevoi

The Nuremberg IMT deliberately played down the role of witnesses in favor of documents so as to establish a firm evidential base for the prosecution, and for the future historical record.[40] This did little to enhance the drama and interest of the proceedings and was one reason why they were often perceived as boring at the time. Leonov commented that time at Nuremberg was measured in the number of documents presented by the prosecution, and it provided "food solely for the mind but not the heart."[41]

A distinct feature of the Soviet journalists' accounts of the trial is that they try to reinsert the personal and emotive dimension widely perceived to be lacking from proceedings, and they do so by drawing on their extensive experience of wartime reporting, recalling the victims of Nazism they had encountered earlier on in the conflict. In doing so they may be seen to mobilize an inherent possibility of the act of testimony that it involves the person listening to the testimony in the original traumatic experience.[42] While Lyndsey Stonebridge refers to the public intellectuals who were at the Nuremberg IMT as "secondary witnesses to Nazi crimes,"[43] the Soviet journalists were witnesses of a more direct kind than this implies, having often been on the scene to see the immediate aftermath of Nazi atrocities earlier in the war, since 1941; most had seen far more sites of this kind, were closely related by language and culture to those whose fates and stories they witnessed, and consequently, experienced a sense of co-owning the victims' testimony to their traumatic experiences at the hands of the Nazis.⁴⁴ This meant that Soviet journalists were able to supplement the often arid proceedings with corroborating and enriching supplementary accounts. Polevoi's coverage of the trial is especially interesting in this respect, because he recalls his personal experience of Auschwitz, notably in an April 1946 article entitled "The Smoke of Auschwitz," where he refers to his visit to the camp, a day he will never forget. "Auschwitz," stated Polevoi, "was the most monstrous of the Nazis' creations."⁴⁵

Few present at Nuremberg were able to grasp this fact, which has now become axiomatic to our understanding of the Holocaust.⁴⁶ Polevoi, however, was alive to the meaning of testimony given at the trial by Auschwitz commandant Rudolf Franz Ferdinand Höss, and gave full credence to his boastful claims that Auschwitz was the place where the Nazis perfected the technology of destruction because the Soviet journalist's experience at Auschwitz meant he was better able than almost anyone at the trial to make the distinction between labor and extermination camps, even if his article from Nuremberg, quoted below, mentioned Auschwitz and Mauthausen in the same breath. Indeed, this was a separation of functions he claims to have grasped already in his diary account of the original visit first to Auschwitz, when the Polish railway man with whom he was billeted explained that it was in fact Birkenau where the extermination function was conducted.⁴⁷

Yet Polevoi's personal experience does not just sharpen his conceptual grasp as to the function of Auschwitz, it also adds an emotional tenor born from a sense of his being an eyewitness, of visiting Höss's personal quarters, and of seeing the dying prisoners:

> I listen to the rustling of this calm and business-like voice [of Höss], and think what kind of system, environment, ideas there must be in which such monsters could be born, brought up and nurtured. I recalled the smoke of Auschwitz. I recalled its prisoners and their dying entreaties. And I wanted to say to those half-dead men in striped uniforms, who had been rescued from the fiery ovens by a miracle, that their murderer has not and will not escape punishment, and nor will all those who cultivated him, who directed his bloody hand who thought up all these Auschwitzes, Mauthausens, that there is no place for them on earth, there is none and will be none.⁴⁸

This ending of "The Smoke of Auschwitz" echoed Polevoi's original publication from February 1945, which concluded with praise for the Red Army, for liberating the camp. It was also preceded by precisely the same arresting image of the cadaverous survivors he encountered at Auschwitz:

> I saw those thousands of martyrs of Auschwitz—people exhausted to the point where they swayed like shadows in the wind, people whose age was impossible to guess.
>
> The Red Army saved them, tore them from hell. They praise the Red Army that has wrought vengeance on the Fascist executioners for Auschwitz, for Majdanek, and for all the pain and suffering they have caused the peoples of Europe.⁴⁹

In comparing the two articles we sense an evolution: in Polevoi's initial newspaper report he had stressed its provisional nature, the sense that his report would necessarily not be able to grasp the full picture, just as Simonov had at Majdanek, and the British and American reporters were later to do in the camps they discovered.[50] We might note here that Polevoi does not mention the Jewish identity of the overwhelming majority of the camp's victims.

However, Polevoi's original, unpublished January 29, 1945, report to the Army Political Directorate, who effectively exercised censorship, has now been released from the Russian Ministry of Defense archive to mark the 70th anniversary of the liberation of Auschwitz. Here he describes the systematic killing as a "death factory" and clearly articulates a sense that the Jews were murdered immediately on arrival, unlike others, who were worked to death.

In both his article at the time, and that published at Nuremberg, the image of the camp's inmates as a haunting presence dominates the conclusion, and it is these prisoners who are made to articulate its central message. A cynical attitude to Soviet propaganda might say that this exploits their image: the Soviets' shrill emotional pitch contrasts with the prevailing, drily legal tone of the tribunal, moreover it also harks back to the Moscow show trials, and both their hysteria and concomitant lack of concern for legal process.[51] But while that is part of what is happening, the image of camp survivors also seems to be one that truly haunted Polevoi, making his report so poignant: it was his burden as a witness to life in the camp in the aftermath of liberation. This same combination of propagandist motives and fresh firsthand experience was present in Soviet reporting of the Soviet prosecution case.

The Soviet prosecution

Soviet coverage of the trial was initially extensive, with a leading article on the front page of *Pravda* on the day the indictment was announced, a further two pages detailing it, and a laconic TASS report on the proceedings. Throughout the first months the Soviet press contained opinion pieces by author-journalists, sometimes as many as three or four on a single day. However, Soviet attention began to stray despite the efforts of reporters to inflect the other prosecution team's presentations so as to underscore the Soviet perspective: Vishnevsky even claims that when chief prosecutor for the Soviet Union, Roman Rudenko spoke in December to counter efforts made by the defense, "even the American guards put their headphones on."[52] As the Soviet press began to lose interest many reporters returned home at Christmas and the coverage began to dwindle to the telegraphic TASS summaries in January. This was interrupted on February 9, 1946, when once more there appeared a three-and-a-half-page verbatim report in *Pravda* and *Izvestiia*, this time of Rudenko's opening speech.

The remaining Soviet journalists now made a renewed effort to stimulate interest in the trial, stressing the vital importance and dramatic effect of the Soviet evidence. This was the opportunity they had been waiting for to articulate the Soviet perspective on events. They did this first of all by heralding Rudenko as expressing the "voice of the

Soviet people."⁵³ Polevoi argued that this intervention made the Soviet achievement in saving humanity from Nazism clearer to all than it had been previously:

> Although the court already possessed documents of extraordinary strength, until today, in the courtroom during the Soviet prosecutor's speech, never yet had the image of Fascism unfolded before it with such breadth, the blood-drenched designs of Fascism had never yet been exposed before it so fully, and those present at the trial had never yet grasped with such strength of conviction the mortal danger from which the Red Army and our Soviet state had saved humanity.⁵⁴

The Soviet prosecution then presented evidence including its own films of Nazi atrocities, and a series of witnesses to substantiate their narrative of the trial. The Soviet journalists present made sure that the emotional power and underlying political message of this testimony was spelled out to their readers.

The Soviet witnesses

Polevoi's articles stressed the impact on the trial of the Soviet witnesses' testimony, writing that "their strength and significance made a profound impression."⁵⁵ The Soviet journalists certainly did their best to ensure that this would be the case, and spent considerable energies recounting the experience of these witnesses: Russian peasant Iakov Grigoriev; academic Orbeli (director of the Hermitage museum in Leningrad, who was also a member of the Soviet war crimes commission); Evgenii Kivil´sha, a Ukrainian military doctor; Auschwitz eyewitness Severina Shmaglevskaia; and survivor of the Vilnius ghetto Abram Sutskever.⁵⁶ Nikolai Zhukov likewise drew portraits of these same witnesses.

Each of these people had suffered personally at the hands of the Nazis, and consequently the effect was to heighten the emotional atmosphere. As Soviet journalist Semen Krushinskii put it, the words of these witnesses, such as Shmaglevskaia's address to the accused: "Where are our children?" were not part of the legal process but nevertheless much needed simple and righteous words.⁵⁷

Along with intensifying the emotional pitch, the Soviets were also trying, in calling these witnesses, and especially Sutskever, to Sovietize the narrative of the trial, trying to do so by showing evidence of the crimes against the Jewish people, but presenting it in such a way as to emphasize the Soviets' role in ending this suffering, and play down independent Jewish resistance.⁵⁸

Jewish dimension

In view of the Soviet Union's later anti-Semitism, and near silence over the Holocaust, it may seem surprising that Soviet journalists such as Erenburg mentioned the figure of 6 million Jews killed by the Nazis and that both he and Vishnevsky refer to the Nazi description of this as the "solution of the Jewish question," a phrase here quoted by

Vishnevsky as being used by Göring in a personal letter to architect of the Holocaust, Reinhard Heydrich.[59] Yet, while the destruction of Europe's Jews was reported by the Soviet press covering the trial, the harrowing account of Sutskever, one of the only 600 Jews to have survived in Vilnius, from an original population of 80,000, is retold so as to stress that he was helped to escape by Soviet partisans.[60]

The same message is evident when Polevoi discusses the diary of Hans Frank, the governor general of occupied Poland. He mentions Jews far less but once again ends by emphazing the fact that it was the Red Army, with the help of the United Nations, that saved the world from the likes of Frank.[61]

And in a piece on the destruction of the Warsaw ghetto, which he incorrectly called the "Stumpf" report, Polevoi describes its annihilation in terrifying detail. He also writes about the photos from the report as well as the Nazi film on the SS's campaign to destroy it. On the other hand, he said nothing about the fate of the remaining Jews in the ghetto or the ragtag army of Jewish resisters who kept over 2,000 crack German troops from taking full control of the ghetto for over three weeks. Instead, Polevoi wrote that the remaining Jews either fled the Nazi assault or chose to burn to death in the ghetto. In the end, Polevoi did not consider the ghetto uprising, an independent Jewish operation with no link to the Red Army or the role of the Soviet Union in defeating Nazi Germany, important enough to mention in his article.[62]

Subsequently, Polevoi further "Sovietized" this evidence in his memoirs by moving the description of the Stroop report (now spelled correctly) to Soviet prosecutor Smirnov's evidence, and the opening of the Soviet prosecution, giving Smirnov some of the lines describing the elegantly bound volume that he used in the newspaper article in December 1945.[63] The effect of this rewriting of history is to undo some of the scene-stealing done by the Americans during the trial, by placing the evidence back in Soviet hands.

The Soviet films

A further tool the Soviet team used to convey a sense of their own narrative of the war was the screening of films compiled from Soviet newsreel footage of the aftermath of Nazi occupation. Strangely, however, these films attracted less attention, even from Soviet journalists than the earlier footage shown by the US prosecution, which had a sensational and much discussed impact. The problem seems to have been that by the time the Soviet films were shown, most of the Soviet journalists had lost interest in the trial, and there were few reports about it in the Soviet press. Indeed, the same is true of their coverage of the Soviet prosecution's production of star witness Field Marshall Von Paulus, who had surrendered to the Red Army at Stalingrad, an event that is treated in many accounts as the high point of the Soviet case, but not covered in *Pravda* or *Izvestiia* at the time.[64]

Izvestiia's report on the main film shown by the Soviets, *Film Documents of Atrocities Committed by the German-Fascist Invaders* (*Kinodukumenty o zverstvakh nemetsko-fashistskikh zakhvatchikov*), written by Roman Karmen, who had a hand in making the film itself, tended to rehash the film's content. However, it also stressed the Soviets' role in pushing for the trial, in collating film evidence since 1941, and in fulfilling their "great mission of liberation."⁶⁵ While the gruesome film with its catalogue of corpses, whom Karmen describes as "mute witnesses," does not itself directly articulate this message of the Soviet role, its timeframe, geographical emphasis, and the very fact that it was made and shown by the Soviets all draw attention to their role in the trial.⁶⁶ The conviction that this film footage too was a form of witness testimony was one deeply held by Karmen, who had not only overseen its compilation but also filmed some of the footage.

Echoing descriptions of the films screened by the US prosecution, which concentrated on the shocked reactions of the defendants, Karmen claims that the Soviet film distressed them more than at any previous point in the proceedings and turned their faces pale with fear. This is corroborated by Ann and John Tusa's history of the trial: "The film surpassed in horror anything yet shown, anything envisaged from the evidence which had yet been heard."⁶⁷

In addition to *Film Documents of Atrocities*, the Soviets showed a number of films at the trial, including a captured German film showing the destruction of the Czech town of Lidice, which Krushinskii describes, but the emphasis is upon the suffering inflicted by the Nazis upon the Soviet people, and the attempted destruction of the Russian nation in particular. This is the underlying message of the Soviet film showing Nazi destruction of sites of cultural value in the Soviet Union, and another one recording the destruction of Soviet towns. Krushinskii comments that, for all its importance, such film "is only able to represent the full extent of the Nazis' crimes in the way that a test-tube full of sea water represents the sea."⁶⁸ Yet while a case can be made for the importance of these Soviet films, they failed to attract the attention the films shown by the United States did.⁶⁹

The evolving political situation

Despite the impression created by Soviet journalists, the Soviet prosecution did not have much of an effect on a trial that was already regarded as at best tedious and at worst irrelevant, both in the Soviet Union and beyond. Tensions within the United Nations outside the courtroom were rising. Throughout the trial, Soviet journalists complained about the toleration of Nazi sympathizers in Britain, where Oswald Mosley was said to be on the march again, about former Nazis being still at liberty to sell pro-Nazi literature in British-controlled West Germany, and about the fact that the remnants of the German Army were under British jurisdiction in Schleswig-Holstein.⁷⁰

The implication was that Britain as a whole had pro-Hitler sympathies, and that the only true opponents of the Nazis were the Soviets. In a variation on this theme, Vishnevsky argued that the defense's interventions were an attempt to use the tribunal as a forum to inspire wider Fascist views and cited examples of these expressed in Britain.⁷¹

The simmering hostility boiled over when Winston Churchill made his March 5, 1946, speech in Fulton, Missouri, where he condemned the Soviet Union of crushing democracy in Eastern Europe.⁷² A front page editorial in *Pravda* described this as nothing other than the "liquidation" of the United Nations.⁷³ Later that year *Pravda* published an article entitled "The Kiss of Goebbels" written by David Zaslavskii, which argued that Churchill's Fulton speech was inspired by Goebbels.[74] The Cold War adversaries were beginning to see each other as similar to the Nazis.

If the participants did not previously understand that the Cold War was breaking out, then they began to now. With the Soviet Union realizing that it had effectively been outmaneuvered in legal, diplomatic, and propaganda terms, and therefore had little to gain from the trial any more, the journalistic coverage was allowed to dwindle to a minimum, with almost no cartoons and very few authored articles, including none at all in May and June. Polevoi began devoting his energies to the writing of a novel *The Story of a True Man*, which even took him back to Moscow for several months in spring.[75]

Only toward the very end of the trial did it become newsworthy once more, as in August when, after an absence of anything other than TASS reports for months, the Soviet press published a lengthy verbatim report of Chief Prosecutor for the USSR Rudenko's closing speech, covering most of a folio page.[76] There was further coverage at the end of August and beginning of September, concentrating on Rudenko's speeches, and on the day of the verdict, there was a leader and the verbatim reproduction of it, followed, on October 5, by a lengthy condemnation of the judgment, criticizing the innocent verdict on Papen, Schacht, and Frickk, and also on the imprisonment and not death sentence handed to Hess.[77]

The Cold War mood was signaled by the *Izvestiia* leader on the day of the verdict, which argued that the defense and defendants were aided by their supporters in the Vatican and the Hearst media empire.[78] Inside the Soviet Union, the final moments of the trial were accompanied by the ideological retrenchment led by Andrei Zhdanov and many of its targets related to the themes raised at Nuremberg. First of all, in August, prominent journals (*Zvezda*) and writers (Mikhail Zoshchenko and Anna Akhmatova) associated with Leningrad were criticized, implicitly for their independence of mind and their city's independence of action during the war. Then in September a film, *A Great Life, Part Two* (*Bol'shaia zhizn'*), was criticized for its unacceptably frank depiction of the occupation.[79] The ambiguities and deviations from the Stalinist norm during the war were now becoming a major source of embarrassment, and since the trial necessarily touched upon them, as well as showing the erstwhile Western allies in a good light, and unacceptably highlighting the fate of the Jews, it was becoming an ever more unwelcome and sensitive subject. The war was now to be remembered primarily as a glorious, unproblematic, overwhelmingly Soviet victory. Writers, journalists, and filmmakers unable to articulate that vision adequately were to be censured.

Conclusion

The Soviet press coverage at Nuremberg attempted to present the proceedings in such a way as to highlight Soviet wartime losses, their part in the victory, and their role as arbiters of the postwar order. However, the way in which Soviet reports of the trial ebbed away into near silence seems to corroborate accounts of the Soviets' participation in the trial as a failure. Hirsch sees Soviet failures as linked to the centralized nature of their propaganda and as a consequence of being institutionally and politically outmaneuvered.[80]

While it is hard to dispute that the Soviets were outmaneuvered or that their propaganda system's overall centralization was a hindrance, when we look at particular themes, such as the depiction of the Nazis or particular journalists' reworking of material they had already covered (e.g., Polevoi on Auschwitz), we see an illuminating picture of someone grappling with the problem of fitting their own experiences and thoughts into the emerging template for representation of the trial.

The result is that, while the Soviet reporting all served centralized propagandist aims, at its best it combined this overarching purpose with a poignant tone of emotional immediacy with the candor of the reporters' personal experiences and eyewitness accounts to the worst of the Nazi atrocities. Given that the trial more broadly sidelined witnesses in favor of documents, the Soviet accounts may be said to add something of a corrective to the dull prevailing course of the tribunal. These personal memories were the main reason of, in some instances, the Soviets anticipated modern views on the importance of Auschwitz as a site of the Holocaust, and on the nature of the Wehrmacht's complicity in the "war of annihilation" and hence the Holocaust in the Soviet Union.

But it is also true that the Soviets' failure to convey their narrative convincingly to the wider world, especially the Western powers present at Nuremberg, was due to the difficulties Soviet propaganda faced in adapting its domestic methods to the international sphere: what worked in the Soviet Union did not work so well at Nuremberg.[81] While the focus of this chapter has been Soviet journalism aimed at a domestic readership, it is evident that even in attempting to make the trial corroborate with the emerging Soviet narrative of the war to this constituency there were problems, since the trial's Western and American bias was hard to redress. This challenge for Soviet journalists at Nuremberg pointed to the wider problem for the Soviets in the postwar period, where their stressing of the price paid by the Soviets for victory was not properly recognized abroad, and Nuremberg was one of the first indications of the Soviets' impending defeat in the Cold War battle over the memory of the Second World War. Indeed, Geoffrey Roberts argues that one of the factors driving the anti-Western campaign and the initial stages of the Cold War was genuine indignation from Stalin that the West did not recognize sufficiently the Soviet contribution to the war with concrete diplomatic concessions.[82]

Ultimately, however, the trial itself was addressed, as Polevoi surmised, not to contemporaries, but to posterity.[83] If this is so, then we can productively revisit it and decide for ourselves what evidence, which documents, and what testimony was the most important. By doing so I believe we shall increasingly decide that the Soviet evidence and media presence has been undervalued.

Notes

1 Francine Hirsch, "The Soviets at Nuremberg: International Law, Propaganda, and the Making of the Postwar Order," *American Historical Review*, 113/3 (June 2008), 701–30 (713).
2 William J. Bosch, *Judgment on Nuremberg: American Attitudes toward the Major German War-Crime Trials* (Chapel Hill: University of North Carolina Press, 1970), 94.

3 Joseph E. Perisco, *Nuremberg: Infamy on Trial* (London: Penguin, 1995), x–xi.
4 Hirsch, "The Soviets at Nuremberg," 703, 722.
5 Ibid., 701, 703.
6 See, for example, Perisco, *Nuremberg: Infamy on Trial*: This account stresses the Soviet attitudes as simply to be overcome to achieve a just trial and uses no Russian-language sources.
7 On Soviets' legal input, see Hirsch, "The Soviets at Nuremberg," *passim*.
8 James V. Wertsch, *Voices of Collective Remembering* (Cambridge University Press, 2002), 106.
9 For an account of Soviet wartime reporting as overwhelmingly centralized, see Karel C. Berkhoff, *Motherland in Danger: Soviet Propaganda During World War II* (Cambridge, MA: Harvard University Press, 2012). Hirsch also argues this with regard to Nuremberg and sees this centralization as the reason for the Soviets' defeat in propaganda terms: (Hirsch, "The Soviets at Nuremberg," 728).
10 Jeffrey Brooks, *Thank You, Comrade Stalin: Soviet Public Culture from Revolution to Cold War* (Princeton, NJ: Princeton University Press, 2000), 193.
11 Chief prosecutor, Robert Jackson, quoted in Ann Tusa and John Tusa, *The Nuremberg Trial* (London and Basingstoke: Macmillan, 1983), 175.
12 Tusa and Tusa, *The Nuremberg Trial*, 175.
13 Wertsch compares Soviet and post-Soviet Russian textbooks' narratives of the war, stressing that they all place the Soviet Union at the center of their narratives. Wertsch, *Voices of Collective Remembering*, 106–12.
14 Persico, *Nuremberg: Infamy on Trial*, x.
15 Boris Polevoi, *Sobranie sochinenii*, 9 Vols, Commentary N. Zheleznova (Moscow: Khudozhestvennaia literatura, 1981), vol. 8, 448.
16 Roman Karmen, "Iz zala suda," *Izvestiia*, November 28, 1945, 3.
17 Boris Efimov, "Fashistskii zverinets. Iz zala suda," *Izvestiia*, December 5, 1945, 4.
18 Vsevolod Vishnevsky, Kukryniksy, "Na Niurembergskom protsesse. Ikh portety," *Pravda*, December 5, 1945, 4.
19 Nikolai Zhukov, "Niurnbergskii protsess. Reportazh khudozhnika N. Zhukova," in Boris Polevoi, ed., *V kontse kontsov. Niurnbergskie dnevniki. Zarisovki Nikolaia Zhukova*, 2nd edn (Moscow: Sovetskaia Rossiia, 1972), 247.
20 Anon., "Germanskii fashizm pered sudom narodov," *Pravda*, October 19, 1945, 1.
21 Ibid.
22 Aron Trainin, "Mezhdunarodnyi voennyi tribunal," *Pravda*, August 11, 1945, 4.
23 Aron Trainin, "Prestupnye organizatsii gitlerizma," *Pravda*, December 23, 1945, 3.
24 Lev Sheinin, "Nemye svideteli," *Izvestiia*, December 2, 1945, 3.
25 For an example of condemnation of the practice of interviewing the Nazis, see: Vsevolod Vishnevsky, "Nichego ne zabyto!" *Pravda*, December 17, 1945, 4.
26 Leonid Leonov, "Liudoed gotovit pishchu," in Leonid Leonov, *V nashi gody. Publitsistika 1941-1948* (Moscow: Sovetskii pisatel´, 1949) 175–85 (176) (Original: *Pravda*, December 10, 1945).
27 Vsevolod Vishnevsky, "Iz zala suda," *Pravda*, December 6, 1945, 3.
28 Leonov, "Liudoed gotovit pishchu," 177.
29 Sergei Krushinskii, "'Otkroveniia' bitogo polkovodtsa," *Izvestiia*, April 6, 1946, 4.
30 The term "war of annihilation" features as the title of a chapter, in, for example, Geoffrey Roberts, *Stalin's Wars: From World War to Cold War, 1939–1953*, New Haven, CT and London: Yale University Press, 2006.
31 Krushinskii, "'Otkroveniia' bitogo polkovodtsa," 4.

32 Vsevolod Vishnevsky, "V Niurnberge," *Pravda*, November 26, 1945, 4.
33 Leonov, "Liudoed gotovit pishchu," 180–81.
34 David Zaslavskii, "Razboinichnyi 'plan Barbarossa,'" *Pravda*, November 30, 1945, 3; Vsevolod Vishnevsky, "Terror i provokatsii—oruzhie gitlerizma," *Pravda*, November 30, 1945, 3.
35 Il'ia Erenburg, "Chas otveta," *Izvestiia*, December 4, 1945, 3.
36 Vsevolod Vishnevsky, "Govoriat svideteli, govoriat ochevidtsy…" *Pravda*, February 1, 1946, 5.
37 Karmen, "Palachi Dachau," 4. Curiously, this is not strictly true: for all its horrors, Dachau was never intended to exterminate inmates on arrival, a point that Polevoi made when he visited it. Whereas the US and British tendency was to downplay death camps by seeing them through the prism of concentration camps, the Soviets did precisely the opposite, and exaggerated the importance of the concentration camps by eliding them with the extermination function. Thus Karmen says that no one ever left Dachau: in fact they did. Polevoi, *Sobranie sochinenii*, vol. 8, 390.
38 Vsevolod Vishnevsky, "Gitlerovskii plan agressii na ekrane," *Pravda*, December 13, 1945, 3; Vsevolod Vishnevsky, "Na gitlerovskoi katorge," *Pravda*, December 15, 1945, 3; Boris Polevoi, "Ne plach'te bol'she, Mariia!," *Pravda*, December 13, 1945, 4.
39 Anon., "Prigovor gitlerizmu," *Izvestiia*, October 2, 1946, 1.
40 Persico, *Nuremberg: Infamy on Trial*, 43, 92; Annette Wieviorka, *The Era of the Witness*, translated from French by Jared Stark (Ithaca and London: Cornell University Press, 2006) [orig. L'Ère du témoin, 1998], 68. Donald Bloxham argues that this led to the trial failing to engage a wider public with the facts of the victims. Donald Bloxham, *Genocide on Trial: War Crimes Trials and the Formation of Holocaust History and Memory* (Oxford: Oxford University Press, 2001), 152.
41 Leonov, "Liudoed gotovit pishchu," 175. Curiously, very similar words were used by the chief prosecutor at the Adolf Eichmann trial. See: Wieviorka, *The Era of the Witness*, 83.
42 Dori Laub, "Bearing Witness of the Vicissitues of Listening," in Shoshana Felman and Dori Laub, eds., *Testimony: Crises of Witnessing in Literature, Psychoanalysis, and History* (New York and London: Routledge, 1992), 57–74 (57).
43 Lyndsey Stonebridge, *The Judicial Imagination: Writing after Nuremberg* (Edinburgh: Edinburgh University Press, 2001), 8.
44 Laub, "Bearing Witness of the Vicissitudes of Listening," 57. It should, however, be noted that Martha Gelhorn, who was also at Nuremberg, was one of the first journalists to enter Dachau: Stonebridge, *The Judicial Imagination*, 5. Although she does not refer to Soviet examples, Marilyn B. Meyers refers to the journalistic accounts written at the time of liberation as "acts of witnessing": Marilyn B. Meyers, "Historic and Psychic Timeline: Opening and Closing the Space for Witnessing," in Nancy R. Goodman and Marilyn B. Meyers, eds., *The Power of Witnessing: Reflections, Reverberations, and Traces of the Holocaust* (New York and London: Routledge, 2012), 27–43 (35).
45 Boris Polevoi, "Dym Osventsima," *Pravda*, April 19, 1946, 3.
46 Bloxham, *Genocide on Trial*, 103–04.
47 However, Polevoi's diary was only published years later, and we cannot be sure he did not rework it after the war. Likewise, when Polevoi recounts the testimony of Shmaglevskaia in his later published diary, he is able to contextualize it because he knows that the Birkenau camp was the epicenter of the killing, and the place where enormous numbers of children were murdered. Polevoi, *Sobranie sochinenii*, vol. 8, 130–31, 394.

48 Polevoi, "Dym Osventsima," 3.
49 Boris Polevoi, "Kombinat smerti v Osventsime," *Pravda*, February 2, 1945, 4.
50 Polevoi, "Kombinat smerti v Osventsime," 4. For a discussion of Simonov's use of this trope in the representation of Majdanek, see Jeremy Hicks, "'Too gruesome to be fully taken in': Konstantin Simonov's 'The Extermination Camp' as Holocaust Literature," *The Russian Review*, 72 (April 2013), 242–59.
51 There were a number of such echoes, such as poet Maksim Ryl´skii referring to the accused as "rabid dogs" and the sudden appearance at the tribunal of the Soviet prosecutor Andrei Vyshinsky. "Rabid dogs" was a phrase associated with Vyshinsky. Maksim Ryl´skii, "Sud," *Izvestiia*, October 20, 1945, 2; Tusa and Tusa, *The Nuremberg Trial*, 232.
52 Vishnevsky, "Nichego ne zabyto!" 4.
53 Boris Polevoi, "Pomni ob etom, izbiratel´," *Pravda*, February 9, 1946, 5.
54 Ibid.
55 Boris Polevoi, "Ot imeni chelovechestva," *Pravda*, March 4, 1946, 4.
56 Ibid.; Sergei Krushinskii, "Sud´ba tsivilizatsii," *Izvestiia*, February 24, 1946, 4; Sergei Krushinskii, "Prostye slova," *Izvestiia*, March 1, 1946, 3.
57 Krushinskii, "Prostye slova," 3.
58 For a discussion of Soviet wartime media representations of the Holocaust, see Berkhoff, *Motherland in Danger*, 134–66; Hicks, *First Films of the Holocaust*, passim.
59 Il´ia Erenburg, "Kontrataka nochi," *Izvestiia*, March 30, 1946, 3; Vsevolod Vishnevsky, "Podsudimye i svideteli," *Pravda*, January 7, 1946, 3.
60 Polevoi, "Ot imeni chelovechestva," 4; Krushinskii, "Prostye slova," 3.
61 Boris Polevoi, "Vot on, 'novyi poriadok!'" *Pravda*, February 18, 1946, 3.
62 Boris Polevoi, "Kniga v kozhe," *Pravda*, December 16, 1945, 3.
63 Polevoi, *Sobranie sochinenii*, vol. 8, 346.
64 However, Polevoi discusses the incident in his diary/memoir, subsequently translated into English. Polevoi, *Sobranie sochinenii*, vol. 8, 427–35.
65 Roman Karmen, "Mertvye obviniaiut," *Izvestiia*, February 20, 1946, 3.
66 Persico, *Nuremberg: Infamy on Trial*, 244–48. Polevoi writes no piece about it at the time but discusses it at length in his diary adding eyewitness details to substantiate and expand on the film. Polevoi, *Sobranie sochinenii*, vol. 8, 416–17.
67 Tusa and Tusa, *The Nuremberg Trial*, 198.
68 Krushinskii, "Sud´ba tsivilizatsii," 4.
69 For a more extended discussion of *Film Documents of Atrocities*, see Hicks, *First Films of the Holocaust*, 186–95.
70 Lev Sheinin, "Prizraki zagovorili…" *Izvestiia*, December 22, 1945, 3; Leonov, "Liudoed gotovit pishchu," 185; David Zaslavskii, "Pozemel´e fashistskikh prestupnikov," *Pravda*, December 31, 1945, 5; Erenburg, "Kontrataka nochi," 3; David Zaslavskii, "Volch´ia golova i volchii khvost," *Pravda*, December 1, 1945, 3.
71 Vsevolod Vishnevsky, "Vylazki gitlerovskikh posledyshei," *Pravda*, December 21, 1945, 4.
72 Hirsch discusses impact of Churchill's speech, presented during the Soviet prosecution, Hirsch, "The Soviets at Nuremberg," 719–21.
73 Anon., "Cherchill´ briatsaet oruzhiem," *Pravda*, March 11, 1946, 1.
74 David Zaslavskii, "Lobyzanie Gebbel´sa," *Pravda* August 1, 1946, 4.
75 Polevoi, *Sobranie sochinenii*, vol. 8, 455–58.

76 "Zakliuchitel′nnaia rech′ Glavnogo Obvinitelia ot SSSR tov. R. A. Rudenko," *Pravda*, August 1, 1946, 3; *Pravda* August 2, 1946, 2; *Pravda* August 3, 1946, 2; *Pravda* August 4, 1946, 3; *Pravda* August 5, 1946, 2–3.
77 "Osoboe mnenie chlena Mezhdunarodnogo Voennogo Tribunala ot SSSR t. Nikitchenko op povodu resheniia Tribunala," *Pravda* October 5, 1946. 3; October 6, 1946, 3.
78 Anon., "Prigovor gitlerizmu," 1.
79 B. Suchkov, "Protiv bezideinykh I falæ shivykh kinofil′mov," *Pravda* September 11, 1946, 2.
80 Hirsch, "The Soviets at Nuremberg," 726.
81 Ibid., 728.
82 Roberts, *Stalin's Wars: From World War to Cold War*, 331–32.
83 Polevoi, *Sobranie sochinenii*, vol. 8, 523.

8

From Geneva to Nuremberg to New York: Andrey Vyshinsky, Raphaël Lemkin, and the Struggle to Outlaw Revolutionary Violence, State Terror, and Genocide

Douglas Irvin-Erickson

Raphaël Lemkin, the originator of the concept of genocide and a leader of the movement to outlaw genocide at the United Nations after the Second World War, has become increasingly recognized as a human rights hero. Yet, Lemkin was all but a footnote in the history of international criminal justice and human rights in the twentieth century until the 1990s. The arc of Lemkin's rising fame contrasts with the arc of the notoriety of Andrey Vyshinsky. A towering jurist in the Soviet Union, Vyshinsky served as prosecutor of the Russian Soviet Socialist Republic, was the architect of Stalin's Great Purge between 1934 and 1938, and is forever a symbol of Stalinist manipulations of the law in the service of political struggle. Lemkin, on the other hand, was a minor figure in the Polish prosecutor's office, and a modest professor of international law whose career was cut short by the Soviet and German conquest of Poland. In the United States in the 1940s, Lemkin devoted himself single-mindedly to his campaign to outlaw genocide at the UN. He succeeded in guiding the convention into law, but at a sharp cost. Lemkin's efforts prevented him from fulfilling his teaching and research duties at Duke, Yale, and Rutgers universities. Each showed him a polite exit. In his last years of life, he was in debt to his friends, living in a cold-water flat in New York, and the US government was working to undermine the UN Genocide Convention in the practice of international affairs.[1] By the time he sat down to write his autobiography, Lemkin thought his life's work had been for naught.

As the authors in this volume demonstrate, the Soviets played an important role in the development of international criminal justice during and after the Second World War. Nevertheless, if the Soviet role in shaping international law has been overlooked, it is probably because of the contradiction between the goals of twentieth-century international criminal law to limit state brutality on the one hand and, on the other hand, the mass violence committed by the Soviet state, where terror and mass violence against ethnic and national minorities were tools of nation-building, state-building, or empire-building.[2] Nevertheless, the Soviets helped usher into existence the twentieth century's system of international criminal law. After the Second World

War, the Soviets and the victorious powers certainly had no interest in limiting their own state sovereignty at the Nuremberg tribunals, where a general coconscious emerged that the Allies would only prosecute crimes committed by Axis powers in connection to the war and thus would only hold defendants accountable for what they did to foreign populations. At the UN, after the Nuremberg tribunal, the Genocide Convention expanded international criminal law in two important ways. First, because genocide was defined as a crime of peace and war, a treaty outlawing genocide would expand humanitarian protections beyond the purview of war crimes. And, secondly, the Genocide Convention allowed for the prosecution of crimes committed by state leaders against their own state's citizens and became the cornerstone of international efforts to establish a system of international law to limit the killing and suffering a state could inflict upon its own population under the shield of state sovereignty.

During their lifetimes, Vyshinsky dismissed Lemkin as an insignificant figure, unimportant in world affairs because he did not speak on behalf of a government. In Vyshinsky's mind, Lemkin's words and ideas were not supported by the hard power of a state, so ignoring Lemkin carried no consequences.[3] By the time Lemkin and Vyshinsky arrived at the UN, Lemkin's tireless activism proved that civil society pressure could sway the foreign policy of democratic states, such as the United States and the United Kingdom. The Soviet delegation at the UN, however, was unmoved by Lemkin's appeals to outlaw genocide, yet they were still highly motivated to support the drafting of the Genocide Convention because they were concerned with the geopolitical consequences of what might happen if they withdrew from the drafting committees and United Nations still ended up passing the treaty anyway. This context—where the Soviet Union was a central geopolitical actor in efforts to create this system of international criminal law while simultaneously committing mass violence within its borders—put Lemkin and Vyshinsky on a collision course.

The relationship between these two jurists, Lemkin and Vyshinsky, and their personal disputes over the span of three decades, provides insights into the larger evolution of international criminal law before and after the Second World War. The portrait that emerges from their interactions, however, runs in contrast to much of the accepted wisdom presented in the scholarship of twentieth-century humanitarian law and international criminal law. As their ethical and humanitarian concerns could not have been more at odds, so too were their theories of the law and politics, and the relationship between the law and state power. As Valentyna Polunina argues in her chapter in this volume, Vyshinsky understood the law as a coercive instrument used by states to regulate human behavior. Lemkin, by contrast, saw the law not as a coercive instrument wielded by states but as a normative instrument enshrined into law through bottom-up social movements that could then be used to regulate human behavior—including the behavior of states themselves.[4]

Barbarism, vandalism, and capitalist intrigue

The occasion of Vyshinsky and Lemkin's first encounter was after Lemkin published his essay, "Akte der Barbarei und des Vandalismus als Delicate Juris Gentium."[5]

Lemkin intended to deliver the paper at the Fifth Conference for the Unification of Penal Law in Madrid in 1933, but the Polish government prohibited him from attending.⁶ The paper is now famous in the field of genocide studies for presenting the conceptual precursors of the word "genocide" that he would coin in the winter between 1941 and 1942. In his memoirs, Lemkin wrote that his colleagues at the Association Internationale de Droit Pénal, and many of his friends, discussed Hitler's *Mein Kampf* in the early 1930s and believed the German chancellor intended to carry out his promise to institute a regime of biological national purity. "Now was the time to outlaw the destruction of national, racial and religious groups," Lemkin wrote.⁷ Building on his works on the Soviet penal code, the proposal was Lemkin's first attempt to outlaw the destruction of nations.⁸ Lemkin's paper that he published in the conference proceedings listed five "new types of crimes" under the law of nations:

1. barbarity (*actes de barbarie*)
2. vandalism (*actes de vandalisme*)
3. provoking catastrophes in international communication (*provocation de catastrophes dans la communication internationale*)
4. disrupting international communication (*interruption intentionnelle de la communication internationale par Poste, Télégraphe, Téléphone, ou par la T.S.F.*)
5. spreading human, animal, or vegetable contagion (*propagation de la contamination humaine, animale, ou végétale*).⁹

In his text, Lemkin credited his colleague at the association, Vespasian Pella, with creating the concepts of barbarity and vandalism, and cited previous papers delivered by Pella and Henri Donnedieu de Vabres. Pella had used these concepts in his 1929 proposal to outlaw currency counterfeiting, to differentiate between modern crimes such as counterfeiting and fraud.¹⁰ Lemkin's writings gave the words their theoretical content.¹¹ Lemkin applied the principles of universal jurisdiction to these crimes that linked the legal concept of terrorism to the practice of state violence targeting national minorities. This was a direct response to the Nazi rise to power and terror against Jews in Germany, and a response to Soviet state terror.¹²

Lemkin defined barbarity as the attempt to destroy ethnic, religious, national, or other types of social collectivities. He included in this category brutalities that strike at the lives and dignity of individuals as part of a campaign to destroy the collectivity of which the victim is a member.¹³ A systematic and organized assault against whole populations, barbarity encompassed pogroms, massacres, mass rape, forced removal of populations, forced adoptions, and cruelties designed to humiliate the victims, or even attempts to destroy the economic existence of the members of a collectivity in order to destroy the collectivity. Vandalism, Lemkin wrote, was an attack targeting a collectivity taking the form of a systematic and organized assault against the heritage or unique genius and achievement of a collectivity. Vandalism was the crime of destroying a group's cultural works, including libraries and art, but also their unique rituals, ceremonies, and beliefs. The cultural creations, arts, and traditions of each nation contributed to the enrichment of all humanity, Lemkin reasoned, and therefore belonged rightfully to humanity.[14] Lemkin insisted the two crimes were intertwined in one process of attacking the physical and spiritual existence of nations.

In the existing laws of nations, Lemkin wrote, explaining his ideas on barbarity and vandalism, there were three categories of humanitarian protections under international law. The first category corresponded to attacks on individual rights and included "laws against slavery or the trade in women and children . . . to protect the freedom and dignity of individuals and prevent them from being treated as commodities." The second category of offenses "relates to the individual and the collectivity" and essentially amounted to minority rights treaties that he believed were inadequate. The third category concerned "the relationship between two or more collectivities" and encompassed "offenses against the laws of nations that seek to protect peaceful relations between collectivities, such as the outlawing of propaganda intended to incite wars of aggression, and have as their goal the maintenance of good economic and political relations between nations and groups."[15] In his proposal to outlaw barbarity and vandalism, Lemkin offered a fourth type of violation—one he believed was a hallmark of Soviet terror and the kinds of violence defining Nazi politics in Germany.[16] This fourth category was attacks committed against individuals with the intention of destroying a collectivity. In such cases, Lemkin wrote, "the goal of the perpetrator is to harm an individual while causing damage to the collectivity to which the individual belongs. These type of offenses bring harm not only to human rights, but also undermine the foundation of the society."[17] Yet, in these matters, international law was silent. Lemkin grouped barbarity and vandalism together with laws against state terrorism; piracy; slavery; pornography; narcotics trade; counterfeiting money; disrupting international communication; and spreading human, animal, and vegetable contagions.

Vyshinsky, who at the time was the procurator general of the Soviet Federative Socialist Republic (SFSR), believed this grouping was illogical and amounted to a ruse. He denounced Lemkin as proposing ideologically and politically motivated laws to target the Soviet Union under the pretense of creating a neutral, apolitical body of unified international laws. In the introduction to a book by Aron Trainin covering the international movement for the unification of penal law, Vyshinsky wrote that the unification movement never mentioned actual struggles "with international crooks and charlatans of any stripe, not the fight with the bandits like Al Capone," but instead focused on abstract concepts like "terrorism." The concept of terrorism these Western liberals claimed to be fighting, Vyshinsky continued, "turned into the central problem of the bourgeois unification movement" because it created the basis for limiting state sovereignty and "removing the state from its pedestal." Vyshinsky went on to add that "no evasions and intricacies of such unifiers as Lemkin, who tried again to disguise the true purpose of the criminal interventionists with references to 'vandalism' and 'barbarism,' can mislead anybody" because "the true meaning of the unifiers' efforts is to legally and politically justify the right of the counterrevolutionary bourgeoisie to intervene in the internal affairs of any state, under the pretext that they are concerned for the fate of 'culture and civilization.'"[18]

The unifiers at the League of Nations

Who were these "unifiers" Vyshinsky thought were trying to use international law to wage political struggle against the Soviet Union, and protect a capitalist and imperialist international system against a socialist revolution?

In 1932, Lemkin's law school mentor Emil Stanisław Rappaport brought Lemkin into the Association Internationale de Droit Pénal. The two collaborated to draft a new Polish criminal code in 1932. The code was highly unusual in that Article 113, which Lemkin wrote, criminalized the production and dissemination of propaganda intended to incite a domestic population toward aggressive war and violence.[19] Just a few years earlier, in 1927, Hersch Lauterpacht had published an influential essay with the Grotius Society, finding that prohibitions on propaganda to incite war were not violations of international law but could be enshrined in national laws, and even in municipal laws, through reciprocal treaties.[20] Lemkin followed Lauterpacht's ideas in drafting Article 113, and he claimed the Polish penal code was the first in the world to outlaw propaganda to incite violence.[21] In his commentary on the law, Lemkin argued that domestic laws could be instruments for international peace because war and political violence were aspects of state policy that had to first be legitimized domestically.

Lemkin's idea to criminalize hate speech and propaganda that incited violence drew on the works of Pella, who had authored a well-known book that argued that fanatical nationalists or religious groups were capable of seizing control of state institutions and directing state security forces to destroy internal opponents while moving the state toward aggressive war.[22] The challenge of international law, Pella argued, was that these groups were closed societies with their own internal symbols and shared language that forced people to follow a "spirit of the group," thinking and acting in unified ways that inherently rejected international law as legitimate. Pella argued that such groups—from religious movements, to paramilitaries, cliques within armies, to criminal rings—could seize control of state institutions and use threats of violent repression or promises of favor to bring other social groups into the fold who could bestow legitimacy on the movement while disseminating the movement's values, such as teachers, religious leaders, and artists.

Pella believed the only way under international law to handle these movements was to hold the groups—and the state they controlled—collectively responsible for international crimes.[23] Pella saw nations as a group of people joined by language or custom, and he defined nations as equivalent to races, Lewis writes, so that he ascribed to nations an atavistic and timeless essence.[24] Pella argued that international criminal law could be used to prosecute individuals and nations, in order to prevent these groups from taking control of state institutions and mobilizing the state toward war and violence. When a state fell under the control of such movements and began suppressing competing nations or races within its borders, or even massacring entire groups, internationally sanctioned military intervention to remove the national or religious group from power was justified.[25] As Vyshinsky complained, Pella's formulation legalized aggressive war so long as a humanitarian pretext could be invented.

De Vabres, meanwhile, had authored a study of the stranger in international law from antiquity to the present, arguing that the modern state needed to develop a type of criminal law that erased the distinction between citizens and foreigners and treated everyone who happened to pass within the state's borders equally under the law—regardless of their nationality, citizenship, or particular identity.[26] Pella, building on this work, pioneered the development of a new form of law for "collective state crimes," to create a criminal justice system that could regulate the relationship between states.[27] With Pella and de Vabres leading the way, the Association Internationale de Droit Pénal became one of the most important organizations at the League of Nations, working to establish an international criminal court and write an international criminal code.

Lemkin was not entirely unknown when he joined the association. In the 1920s, he developed a reputation as an expert on Soviet terror. Indeed, he was well on his way to being a widely recognized expert on the way ruling political parties in governments used domestic criminal codes to repress political opponents in the name of protecting society. In his 1928 book, *The 1927 Criminal Code of Soviet Russia*, Lemkin noted that the reforms made to the Soviet Russian penal code after Lenin's death marked no substantive difference from the laws Lenin's party enacted in 1922. The only difference was that the new code drew on nineteenth-century Italian positivist legal theory to explicitly codify "social protection" as the purpose of the law, he wrote. The Soviet system conceived of the law as a form of social protection and not simply a system to punish individual crimes, Lemkin wrote.[28] He added that this legitimized the arrest and killing of people who had a social consciousness considered criminal. The Soviet legal code was not merely a tool for maintaining the gains of the proletarian revolution, he argued; the law was a means for the education of the proletariat in the new social order, and therefore it actively helped create the new Communist system by providing the state violence necessary for the destruction and transformation of the bourgeoisie.[29] This small, but crucial, observation would remain a central component of his study of state violence against identity-based groups and the law: he saw such repression and violence (whether he called it barbarism and vandalism, or genocide) as legitimized through the law under slogans of social protection—to remove ethnic and national minorities from society to either protect society or create new societies built around new social identities.

In his 1929 book on the Italian penal code, Lemkin concluded his description of the law with the argument that the legal code extended Italian sovereignty beyond Italy's borders through laws such as the criminalization of "insults to Mussolini committed by foreigners abroad." This "exaggerated nationalism," Lemkin wrote, cannot contribute to world peace in any sense of the word.[30] In addition to writing about Soviet and Italian state terror—and the way the criminal codes of both states provided the violence necessary for securing political gains of the ruling party, while directing state violence against national cultural minorities—Lemkin was also paying close attention to the rise of Hitler and the National Socialist Party in Germany. For Lemkin, the fate of peoples could not be left to humanitarian movements, and the existing laws of war were inadequate to handle the new forms of political violence afflicting the world.

Lemkin's 1933 proposal to outlaw barbarism and vandalism at the League of Nations, therefore, drew on robust intellectual and legal traditions. Vyshinsky saw this movement to create an international, unified system of criminal law that Lemkin was a part of as nothing but an attempt by capitalist countries to coordinate international repression against economic and political adversaries. The keynote speaker on the Conference for the Unification of Penal Law in Madrid that Lemkin had wanted to attend, Vyshinsky wrote, proclaimed as the main objective "of the standardization" of international law the need to combat the communist movement. "And no evasions and intricacies of such unifiers as Lemkin," Vyshinsky continued, "who tried again to disguise the true purpose of the criminal interventionists with references to 'vandalism' and 'barbarism', can mislead anybody." The true meaning of unifiers' efforts, he continued, is to "legally and politically justify the right to counter-revolutionary bourgeoisie to intervene in the internal affairs of any state, which condition can cause 'concern' for the fate of 'culture and civilization.'"[31]

In the text, Trainin argued that Lemkin intended barbarity to also refer to the destruction and capture of railways, telegraphs, and the infrastructure of states, which were always tactics of revolution. The destruction of cultural artifacts entailed in Lemkin's idea of vandalism, Trainin continued, was a hallmark of revolution. Lemkin had thereby sought to collapse laws against terrorism into a law against barbarism and vandalism that was defined in such a way that the law encompassed revolutionary violence. Thus Lemkin, Trainin and Vyshinsky argued, was using the notion of barbarity and vandalism in order to outlaw revolutionary violence as a form of terrorism. The struggle against revolutionary violence was thereby given the label of "humanitarianism," revealing the true purpose of Lemkin's laws against barbarity and vandalism: they were preparations for attempts by imperialist governments to militarily intervene against revolutions that threatened their interests.[32] "In a nutshell," Weiss-Wendt argues, "Trainin was arguing that revolutionary violence could not be subject to international criminal law" while Lemkin was arguing that it could.

The effort to standardize international law, therefore, according to Vyshinsky, was nothing but an attempt to provide capitalist countries with a humanitarian excuse to militarily intervene in the affairs of other states to, ensure the domestic politics of those states progressed in a way that was advantageous to their own interests. Quoting Pella, Vyshinsky noted that "such intervention . . . denied state sovereignty under the slogan of 'We must remove the state from its pedestal.'"[33] Humanitarian intervention to save "cultures" and "innocent" civilians, Vyshinsky wrote, was nothing but "an example of hottentot morality," using humanitarian sentiments to conduct direct interference in the internal affairs of another state in the interests of the bourgeoisie.[34]

The unifiers at the United Nations

In the late 1930s, Lemkin pursued other academic and legal interests, researching and publishing scholarly works on a wide range of topics—from the regulation of international payments and methods of easing international conflicts through alignments of domestic penal codes, to a short thesis arguing that judges should receive consistent training in the latest developments in the criminological sciences. When Stalin and Hitler's armies converged on Poland in 1939, Lemkin fled to Sweden as a refugee, and took up a visiting position at Stockholm University, where he began his research for what would eventually become his magnum opus published in 1944,

Axis Rule in Occupied Europe—the text in which the word "genocide" first appears in print. This portion of Lemkin's life, from his flight from occupied Europe to his resettlement in the United States at Duke University, has been covered extensively in scholarship.[35] This research includes a growing body of work on Lemkin's time at the IMT in Nuremberg.[36] Though he was largely sidelined from much of the tribunal, Lemkin was deeply disappointed with the IMT not because his concept of genocide was not extensively employed, but because he believed the court was "timid" for limiting the reach of the laws of war only to times of formal war between states. Lemkin, instead, had advocated for a more sweeping vision of international law, to extend the laws of war so that they applied during times of formal peace, in order to bring the conduct of state security forces against their own civilian populations under the rule of international law. During his efforts at the United Nations in 1946, Lemkin was explicit in insisting that the UN should rectify the shortcomings of the Nuremberg precedent, and use a convention against genocide as a way of creating a form of international criminal law that could both apply to times of formal peace, and regulate the actions of state security forces against their own citizens.

Lemkin's vision of robust body of international law governing the way state security forces treated their own populations was completely at odds with almost every one of the UN member state delegations. The Soviet Union was no exception. But one area of convergence between the Soviet delegation and Lemkin's position was that they understood international law to be a fundamentally political undertaking—and not a neutral, moral structure that could be separated from the political realities that brought the law into existence. It was for this reason that Lemkin embarked on his famous worldwide campaign to mobilize civil society members from every country represented at the UN to lobby their governments in support of the UN Genocide Convention. This early form of a strategy human rights advocates refer to as "naming and shaming" was more or less effective in countries with democratically elected governments. But, Lemkin found, moving the delegations of UN member states such as China and the Soviet Union required a different kind of political struggle.

In July of 1938, Vyshinsky delivered his *Twelve Theses on International Law*. In his *Theses*, he argued that the Soviet Union could assent to international law and accept some of the principles of international law—even though international law was a bourgeois undertaking being advanced by imperialist states—when it served the interests of the state.[37] International law, for Vyshinsky, was therefore not a neutral undertaking or a moral undertaking. Rather, international law was an instrument of policy.[38] Under this principle, the Soviets approached the UN Genocide Convention and the Declaration of Human Rights with the utmost importance, as extensions of the Cold War, and a primary battle ground of international politics.[39] Lemkin's strategy for engaging the Soviets during the UN drafting process accepted this reality of the Soviet outlook on politics, and he would attempt to frame the UN Genocide Convention as something that could serve narrow Soviet geopolitical interests.

The Soviet delegation began the debates on the convention by noting that the Genocide Contention was not necessary, and that it would be more desirable to codify the Nuremberg principles. Indeed, at Nuremberg, Lemkin recalled the Soviet delegates arguing then that prosecuting German defendants for genocide was not necessary either. Lemkin wrote that he had heard rumors that the Soviets were executing German collaborators and sending political prisoners to labor camps in Siberia. "Was this the reason for the Russian delegation's opposition," Lemkin wondered, or was it simply their desire to oppose the interests of the United States?[40] At the United Nations drafting committees, the Soviet delegation followed a strategy of attempting to prevent the passage of the Genocide Convention first and, if this could not be achieved, to work to define genocide as closely to Nazism as possible.

In 1946, at the height of Soviet opposition in the first stage of the drafting processes, Lemkin called on the Czech minister of foreign affairs, Jan Masaryk, to discuss the Soviet opposition, pleading for help in lobbying the Soviets. "I have studied the writings of your father, Professor Tomáš Garrigue Masaryk, who devoted his life to explaining the cultural personality of nations. . . . If your father were alive, he would be fighting for the Genocide Convention. I appeal now to his son," Lemkin told Masaryk, and asked Masaryk to remind the Soviet minister of foreign affairs that Communists and Soviet prisoners of war died with Jews in the Nazi massacre of 100,000 people at Babi Yar in Kiev.[41] Vyshinsky was now opposing Lemkin's genocide convention on the same grounds as he had opposed Lemkin's ideas on barbarity and vandalism—that the goal of outlawing genocide was to provide a humanitarian pretext for allowing the United Nations and powerful states from interfering in the affairs of other states. Lemkin told Masaryk, "why not tell him that penicillin is not an intrigue against the Soviet Union." Taking out his schedule for the next day, Masaryk wrote "Vishinsky. Genocide. Penicillin." The next day the Czech foreign minister called to tell Lemkin that Vyshinsky promised the full cooperation of the Soviet Union. The Soviet delegation, however, never fully supported the genocide convention, and remained committed along with the United States and United Kingdom to ensuring that the eventual text of the convention could not be applied to the atrocities they were committing.[42]

During the drafting processes, the Soviet delegation sought to define genocide as the killing of individuals on national, racial, and religious grounds, and sought to tie the act as closely as possible to aggressive war. Race was outlawed in the Soviet Union, and racism was punishable as a counterrevolutionary crime, the Soviet delegates argued; thus genocide was impossible in the state. The position allowed the Soviet Union to point to the United States and its history of racial tension as a potentially genocidal society. The decision to eliminate references to genocide as a fascist or Nazi crime or racial hatred was therefore met with protestations by the Soviet delegation, who saw the move as an effort by Western states to attempt to criminalize communism, and secretly encourage the rehabilitation of fascism as a check against communism.[43] For Lemkin's own part, he described much of his lobbying efforts at the UN as a fight to prevent the Soviet and French delegations from defining genocide according to the "Hitler Case," to instead push the Genocide Convention drafting committees to define genocide in universal terms to prevent genocide in the future, in whatever form it might take. For Lemkin, the German genocide of the last war was one of many genocides that had occurred in history—different in form from those in the past, and from those in the future. To write a Genocide Convention that essentially described the crime according to the German case would outlaw a very specific historical event, not a crime he argued, thus ensuring that future genocides would not fall under the purview of the law.⁴⁴

Lemkin observed that the Soviet Union, the United Kingdom, and the United States, together with France and a host of other countries, collaborated to try and produce a convention that was "non-enforceable . . . with many loopholes" so that "they can manage life like currency in a bank."⁴⁵ The delegates at the United Nations who drafted the convention, indeed, were career diplomats whose first priority—above the humanitarian impulse that underscored the treaty against genocide and was used to legitimize the need for such a law—was to advance and protect the interests of their governments and states. It is not just that the Soviet Union's delegates who attempted to weaken the treaty and bend the text of the convention so that the law could be applied to their geopolitical adversaries but not themselves. The US delegates wanted to outlaw atrocities such as those unleashed by Nazi Germany, but they worried that the United States was also guilty of genocide against "red" and "negro" Americans, so they fought to weaken the treaty accordingly. Swedish diplomats were instructed to make sure the convention could not be applied to their country's treatment of the Sami, the Canadian delegation was under orders to ensure the convention would suffer death by committee if it seemed the law might criminalize massacres of native peoples and residential schools. The French government attempted to undermine the ability of the treaty to hold individual officials responsible for genocide and they fought to make the law non-applicable in colonial territories. The South African delegation generally felt that outlawing genocide would hinder their state's ability to deal with their problem of "backwards" peoples. Brazil's delegation believed that genocide against political opponents was part of Latin American culture, and that genocide should be preserved as a right for any government when it needed to deal with threats to the existence of the state. The paradox of this moment, which can seem incongruous at first glance, was that every delegation at the United Nations could agree that the horrors of genocide should be outlawed and atrocities such as the Holocaust should never be repeated—but they also wanted a law that could not be applied to their own grave actions, but still be applied to acts of mass murder that hurt their own national interests. In such a way, Pakistan and India, while accusing each other of genocide and trying to craft a law that could be applied to each other but not themselves, both worked together to support the UN Genocide Convention because they believed it would criminalize the kinds of horrors they suffered under the British.⁴⁶

The starting point for understanding the politics and history of the UN Genocide Convention is a recognition that the Soviet Union was a party to the drafting of the Convention, and that Joseph Stalin personally read and annotated every draft, as Anton Weiss-Wendt has made perfectly clear.⁴⁷ More broadly, Weiss-Wendt has shown that some of the most important authors of the law were the Soviet jurists who orchestrated Stalin's show trials and defended Soviet famine. The final wording of the convention carefully defined genocide so as to avoid criminalizing the kinds of mass violence that had been committed by the powers that won the Second World War—the United States and Canada ensured it could not be applied to native peoples, the United Kingdom and France ensured it could not be applied to the colonies, and the Soviet Union ensured that it could not be applied to political and class conflict and carefully expunged all allusions to starvation as an act of genocide. For this reason, and others, the Genocide Convention itself was very much a reflection of the emerging Cold War politics of the postwar world, where the United States and the Soviet Union could agree that the new institutions of the UN, such as the Genocide Convention, should be strong enough to constrain the kinds of atrocities that threatened the stability of the international order from which their power derived, but weak enough not to threaten their own sovereignty or jeopardize their national interests. For the Soviet Union, outlawing genocide at the United Nations was a good thing so long as it did not hurt them geopolitically. If the law could be used to hurt the United States, all the better. For the United States, the calculation was exactly the same.

In this sense, Vyshinsky was right about the law. International law was not a moral or neutral undertaking, but rather governments supported it when it served the interests of the state. International law, as the UN Genocide Convention drafting processes demonstrated, was an instrument of policy. Lemkin, for his part, understood this. He described the Paris Assembly in 1948, where the Genocide Convention was passed by the General Assembly, as "the end of the golden age for humanitarian treaties at the U.N."[48] When "the lights in Palais de Chaillot went out," Lemkin wrote, "the delegates shook hands hastily with one another and disappeared into the winter mists of Paris."[49] Although an act of government, the signatures of the UN delegates merely signified their state's intention to ratify the treaty in their own parliaments. The UN Genocide Convention was now in the hands of the world's politicians and statesmen—people "who lived in perpetual sin with history" and could hardly be trusted with "the lives of entire nations," Lemkin wrote.[50] "The fact is that the rain of my work fell on a fallow plain," Lemkin wrote describing his efforts to outlaw genocide, "only this rain was a mixture of the blood and tears of eight million innocent people throughout the world. Included also were the tears of my parents and my friends."[51]

The fault lines of the law: Legitimacy, grounding, and politics

Western liberal legal theory has been preoccupied with two intertwined questions: the question of the legitimacy of the law, and the question of how to ground the law. The question of legitimacy, broadly defined, sought to sort out exactly what criteria should be used to justify or sanction the law, and what criteria should be used to justify and sanction the authority that had the right to issue the law and enforce the law in the first place. In Kantian terms (more so with the Kantian tradition rather than Kant's writings) the legitimacy of the law follows from the norms and values of a given society, which are used to both posit and judge the law. For Weber, asserting perhaps the most famous theory of legal legitimacy, the law was a system of rules applied through bureaucratic and judicial institutions according to principles that are known prior to the application of the law, and applied through procedures that are themselves delineated through the law, so that those who applied the law were constrained by the law. In this Weberian view, the legitimacy of modern law is derived from the fact that the law could be rationalized based on general principles, applied equally and fairly, through principles that can be freely known. It is possible to argue these approaches reduce the values used to judge legitimacy to those same values (a neo-Kantian approach), or reduce the legitimacy of the law to the belief in legitimacy while removing values as a criteria of legitimacy (a Weberian approach).[52] Both approaches remove power as a criteria for judging the legitimacy of the law, and therefore make it difficult to assess the legitimacy of the law in terms of power.[53] This removal of power as a criteria of analysis and judgment occurs despite the fact the question of whether or not a system of laws is legitimate already implies that the law represents an "unequal distribution of power" and an "asymmetric relationship constituted by the command relations between the governors and the governed."[54]

What is striking about both Lemkin and Vyshinsky's views on the law—during the League of Nations years and during the United Nations—is how little they were concerned with any questions of legitimacy, even though they stood on opposing ends of the debates over international criminal law. In fact, the role of politics in the law was something that Lemkin and Vyshinsky understood intimately. For these two thinkers, in fact, politics was the guiding principle in all law—which meant that questions of legitimacy were irrelevant. The law, by its very existence, generated its own legitimacy. That is to say, there was no justification of the law necessary beyond the fact that the law had been brought into existence through political struggle.

How did the two thinkers arrive at such a position?

As Anton Weiss-Wendt has shown, Stalinist Soviet legal theory was based on communist assumptions about the relationship between the law and political power, that the state and the law were institutions that existed to protect, legitimize, and perpetuate class hierarchies.[55] The law emanated from the state and, as such, the law was never apolitical and therefore always an instrument of state policy.[56] International law, it followed, was likewise an instrument of policy wielded by the most powerful actors in international politics. Consequently, in the Soviet view, the law was at once a reflection of the political order and a buttress to it. This practical and political notion of international law flew in the face of liberal, or bourgeois, conceptions that saw the law as just only when it was politically neutral. Criminal law that was used as a political tool, in the liberal view, produced show trials—indeed, a term often applied to Soviet tribunals. Likewise, from a liberal perspective, international law that was seen as politically motivated was believed to provoke instability and threaten the foundation for peaceful international relations. That any liberal theory of law would see both criteria as eroding the legitimacy of the law is beyond doubt. Yet, in the Soviet conception, where all law was political, to worry about the legitimacy of law and courts was dangerous. The laws and courts were legitimate because the state existed and had come into existence through political struggle. The law and courts, therefore, were ultimately a product of the political struggle. To pretend otherwise was either delusional or hypocritical.

Lemkin believed this, too. Never in any of his writings did he waste words pondering the philosophical foundation of the law or worrying about how to create fair international trials. For Lemkin, international law was instead a pedagogical tool and a political project, brought into existence through political struggle.[57] Of course,

Lemkin's thinking on how the law was brought into existence also set him at odds with another core component of liberal legal theory, the question of how the law was grounded. What is striking about Lemkin's legal theory is that, for as much as he is taken as a liberal legal thinker,[58] he was completely unconcerned with questions of legitimacy and grounding. For Lemkin, the law was not a philosophical undertaking.[59] The law was a social and moral undertaking, with the potential to constrain human behavior, including political behavior. Remarkably, Lemkin furthermore did not restrict the value of international criminal law, nor the Genocide Convention, to legalism.[60] Justice and due process were important, he believed, but it was more important for the law to integrate the world in a cosmopolitan order.[61] Here, Lemkin was of like mind with Vyshinsky, his Soviet counterpart and political adversary, in that they both saw the law as a political tool. The task of the Genocide Convention, in Lemkin's mind, was to achieve what the Nuremberg tribunal could not: to serve as a normative and political buttress for efforts to prevent genocide and restructure an international political system accordingly. For Lemkin, like Vyshinsky, this meant there was nothing inherent in the law, or the process of the law, that could guarantee a desired outcome, or justice. The value of international law to the larger effort to prevent state repression and terror against identity-based groups, to prevent genocide, Lemkin believed, was the social, moral, and political struggle the law inspired and supported. In this regard, Vyshinsky might well have agreed with Lemkin that the purpose of the law was to inspire and bolster social and political struggles.

Notes

1   Anton Weiss-Wendt, *A Rhetorical Crime: Genocide in the Geopolitical Discourse of the Cold War* (New Brunswick: Rutgers University Press, 2018).
2   Whether one sees this violence as part of Soviet nation-, state-, or empire-building depends on one's perspective on the nature of the relationship between Moscow and the rest of the Soviet Union. See, Alexander J. Motyl, *Imperial Ends: The Decay, Collapse, and Revival of Empires* (New York: Columbia University Press, 2013).
3   Anton Weiss-Wendt, *The Soviet Union and the Gutting of the UN Genocide Convention* (Madison: University of Wisconsin Press, 2017).
4   Douglas Irvin-Erickson, *Raphaël Lemkin and the Concept of Genocide* (Philadelphia: University of Pennsylvania Press, 2017).
5   Raphaël Lemkin, "Akte der Barbarei und des Vandalismus als Delicate Juris Gentium." *Internationales Anwaltsblatt* 19 (1933): 117–19.
6   Why Lemkin was prevented from going to Madrid is disputed, with some suggesting anti-Semitism and others suggesting it was Poland's fear of provoking Germany or the Soviet Union. It seems both factors played a role. For varying accounts, see William Korey, *An Epitaph for Raphael Lemkin*; Samantha Power, *A Problem from Hell: America and the Age of Genocide* (New York: Basic Books, 2002); and Ryszard Szawłowski, "Raphael Lemkin's Life Journey: From Creative Legal Scholar and Well-to-Do Lawyer in Warsaw Until 1939 to Pinnacle of International Achievements During the 1940s in the States, Ending Penniless Crusader in New York in the 1950s," in Agnieszka Bienczyk-Missala and Slawomir Debski, eds., *Rafał Lemkin: A Hero of Humankind* (Warsaw: Polish Institute of International Affairs, 2010), 31–58.

7. Raphaël Lemkin, *Totally Unofficial: The Autobiography of Raphael Lemkin*, ed. Donna-Lee Frieze (New Haven, CT: Yale University Press, 2013), 22.
8. Daniel Marc Segesser and Myriam Gessler, "Raphael Lemkin and the International Debate on the Punishment of War Crimes (1919–1948)," *Journal of Genocide Research*, 7/4 (2005), 453–68.
9. Raphaël Lemkin, "Les Actes Constituant un Danger General (Interétatique) Considerés Comme Delits du Droit des Gens," in Jimenez de Asua, Vespasien Pella, and Manuel López-Rey, eds., *Actes de la Vème Conférence Internationale Pour l'Unification du Droit Pénal, Madrid 14–20 Octobre 1933* (Paris: A. Pedone, 1935), 48–56.
10. Mark Lewis, *The Birth of the New Justice: The Internationalization of Crime and Punishment, 1919-1950* (Oxford: Oxford University Press, 2014), 188.
11. See Jimenez de Asua, Vespasien Pella, and Manuel López-Rey, eds., *Actes de la Vème Conférence Internationale pour l'Unification du Droit Pénal (Madrid 14–20 Octobre 1933)* (Paris: A. Pedone, 1935).
12. Claudia Kraft, "Nationalisierende Transnationalisierung: (Inter)nationale Strafrechtswissenschaft in der Zwischenkriegszeit," in Dietmar Müller and Adamantios Skordos, eds., *Leipziger Zugänge zur Rechtlichen, Politischen und Kulturellen Verflechtungsgeschichte Ostmitteleuropas* (Leipzig: Leipziger Universitätsverlag, 2015), 15–26. And see Dietmar Müller, "Zu den Anfängen des Völkerstrafrechts: Vespasian Pella und Raphaël Lemkin," in Dietmar Müller and Adamantios Skordos, eds., *Leipziger Zugänge zur Rech- tlichen, Politischen und Kulturellen Verflechtungsgeschichte Ostmitteleuropas* (Leipzig: Leipziger Universitätsverlag, 2015), 27–40.
13. Lemkin, "Les Actes Constituant un Danger General."
14. Ibid.
15. Ibid.
16. Bartolomé Clavero, *Genocide or Ethnocide, 1933–2007: How to Make, Unmake and Remake Law with Words* (Milan: Giuffr´ Editore, 2008), 22–25.
17. Lemkin, "Les Actes Constituant un Danger General."
18. Andrey Y. Vyshinsky, foreword to *Criminal Intervention: The Movement for the Unification of the Criminal Law of the Capitalist Countries*, by Aron Trainin, ed. Andrey Y. Vyshinsky, 3–7 (Moscow: State Publishing House OGIZ, 1935). I thank Gennadi Poberezny for helping me translate this text.
19. Raphaël Lemkin, *The Polish Penal Code of Minor Offenses*, trans. Malcolm McDermott (Durham, NC: Duke University Press, 1939).
20. Hersch Lauterpacht, "Revolutionary Propaganda by Governments," in Elihu Lauterpacht, ed., *International Law: The Collected Papers of Hersch Lauterpacht*, vol. 3, *The Law of Peace* (Cambridge: Cambridge University Press, 1977), 279–96.
21. See Michael Kearney, *The Prohibition of Propaganda for War in International Law* (Oxford: Oxford University Press, 2007).
22. Vespasien V. Pella, *L'esprit de Corps et les Problèmes de la Responsabilité Pénale* (Paris: Ernest Sagot, 1920).
23. For an analysis of this argument and its influence, see Lewis, *The Birth of the New Justice*, 103.
24. Ibid., 104.
25. Vespasian V. Pella, *La Criminalité Collective des États et le Droit Pénal de l'Avenir* (Bucharest: Imprimerie de l'État, 1925).
26. Henri Donnedieu de Vabres, *Introduction á l'Étude du Droit Pénal International: Essai d'Histoire et de Critique sur la Compétence Criminelle dans les Rapports avec l'Étranger* (Paris: Recueil Sirey, 1922).

27 Pella, *La Criminalité Collective*.
28 Rafał Lemkin, "Dzieje I Charkter Reform Karnego we Włoszech," in *Kodeks Karny Faszystowski Włochy* (Warsaw: Nakladem Ksiegarni F. Hoesicka, 1929), 10.
29 Rafał Lemkin, "Ustawodawstwo Karne Rosji Sowieckiej, Kodeks Karny, Procedura Karna," in Waclaw Makowski, ed., *Encyklopedji Podrecznej Prawa Karnego, Volume 25* (Warsaw: War- zawiej, 1938), 7.
30 Rafał Lemkin, *Kodeks Karny Faszystowski Włochy* (Warsaw: Nakladem Ksiegarni F. Hoesicka, 1929).
31 Vyshinsky, foreword to *Criminal Intervention*, 4–5. The text in the original reads: Podlinnyj smysl usilij unifikatorov—juridicheski i politicheski obosnovat' pravo kontrrevoljucionnoj burzhuazii na vmeshatel'stvo vo vnutrennie dela vsjakogo gosudarstva, sostojanie kotorogo mozhet vnushat' "bespokojstvo" za sud'by "kul'tury i civilizacii."
32 Aron Trainin, *Ugolovnaia interventsiia* (Moscow: OGIZ, 1935), 42–48, 89. This reading of Trainin comes from Weiss-Wendt, *The Soviet Union and the Gutting of the UN Genocide Convention*, 13–14.
33 Vyshinsky, foreword to *Criminal Intervention*, 5–6. The text reads as: Takoe vmeshatel'stvo prjamo proklamiroval odin iz naibolee vidnyh dejatelej unifikacionnogo dvizhenija prof. Pella, otricavshij bezgranichnost' gosudarstvennogo suvereniteta, brosivshego otkryto lozung: "Nado snjat' gosudarstvo s p'edestala."
34 Ibid. The text reads as: Eshhjo otkrovennee v jetom smysle vystuplenie prof. Levita (SShA), proektirujushhego v svoem "Mezhdunarodnom ugolovnom kodekse" prjamoe vmeshatel'stvo vo vnutrennie dela drugogo gosudarstva v interesah burzhuazii, kvalificiruemoe prof. Trajninym kak "dvojnaja buhgalterija." Vprochem, pravil'nee, nam kazhetsja, bylo by jeto vystuplenie kvalificirovat' kak obrazec gottentotskoj morali.
35 See Irvin-Erickson, *Raphaël Lemkin and the Concept of Genocide*. And see John Cooper, *Raphael Lemkin and the Struggle for the Genocide Convention* (London: Palgrave, 2008). See Mark Klamberg, "Raphaël Lemkin in Stockholm: The Significance of his Work for Axis Rule in Occupied Europe," *Genocide Studies and Prevention: An International Journal*, forthcoming.
36 Irvin-Erickson, *Raphaël Lemkin and the Concept of Genocide*, especially chapters 5 and 6.
37 Weiss-Wendt, *A Rhetorical Crime*, 14.
38 Ibid.
39 Ibid.
40 Lemkin, *Totally Unofficial*, 126–27.
41 Ibid.
42 Lewis is correct that Lemkin was wrong in his memoirs, and that Masaryk had no lasting influence on the Soviet position. See Lewis, *The Birth of the New Justice*, 204.
43 United Nations Official Records of the Third Session of the General Assembly, Sixth Committee, 63rd Meeting (September 30, 1948). See Weiss-Wendt, *The Soviet Union and the Gutting of the UN Genocide Convention*.
44 Pearl Buck to Raphaël Lemkin, Correspondence and Proposed Manifesto, American Jewish Historical Society, New York, New York, Box 1, Folder 17, Dated Sunday (circa 1947).
45 Lemkin, *Totally Unofficial*, 217.
46 See Irvin-Erickson, *Raphaël Lemkin and the Concept of Genocide*.
47 Weiss-Wendt, *The Soviet Union and the Gutting of the UN Genocide Convention*.

48 Lemkin, *Totally Unofficial*, 173.
49 Ibid., 178.
50 Ibid., 115.
51 Ibid., 132.
52 For a discussion, see Jean-Marc Coicaud, *Legitimacy and Politics: A Contribution to the Study of Political Right and Political Responsibility*, trans. David Ames Curtis (Cambridge: Cambridge University Press, 1997).
53 Ibid., 155.
54 Ibid., 25.
55 Weiss-Wendt, *The Soviet Union and the Gutting of the UN Genocide Convention*.
56 Ibid.
57 Irvin-Erickson, *Raphaël Lemkin and the Concept of Genocide*, especially chapter 7.
58 For an important, more nuanced discussion, see Mark Mazower, *No Enchanted Palace: The End of Empire and the Ideological Origins of the United Nations* (Princeton: Princeton University Press, 2013), 104–48.
59 See Irvin-Erickson, *Raphaël Lemkin and the Concept of Genocide*, especially chapter 8.
60 Raphaël Lemkin, "Reflections on Cure and Treatment," n.d., New York Public Library, New York, New York, Reel 3, Box 2, Folder 3/4.
61 Raphaël Lemkin, "The Concept of Law in Genocide," in *Introduction to the Study of Genocide*, n.d., New York Public Library, New York, Reel 3, Box 2, Folders 1–4.

Bibliography

Primary Sources

The Case of the Trotskyite-Zinovievite Terrorist Centre. Heard before the Military Collegium of the Supreme Court of the U.S.S.R., Moscow, August 19–24, 1936. New York: Howard Fertig, 1967.

Constitution (Fundamental Law) of the Union of Soviet Socialist Republics: Adopted at the Extraordinary Eighth Congress of Soviets of the U.S.S.R., December 5, 1936. Karagah: H. Dawson, 1937.

Davies, Joseph E. Mission *to Moscow*. Garden City, NY: Garden City Publishing, 1943.

Documents on the Tokyo International Military Tribunal: Charter, Indictment and Judgments. Ed. by Neil Boister and Robert Cryer. Oxford: Oxford University Press, 2008.

The Genocide Convention: The Travaux Préparatories. Ed. by Hirad Abtahi and Philippa Webb. Leiden: Martinus Nijhoff, 2008.

Getty, J. Arch and Oleg V. Naumov. *The Road to Terror: Stalin and the Self-destruction of the Bolsheviks, 1932-1939*. New Haven, CT: Yale University Press, 1999.

Iampol'skii, V. P., et al. *Organy gosudarstvennoi bezopasnosti SSSR v Velikoi Otechestvennoi voinie: sbornik dokumentov* [The Soviet Security Services in the Great Patriotic War: Collection of Documents]. 6 vols. Moscow: Izdatel'stvo "Rus," 2008.

Istoriia gosudarstva i prava Rossii v dokumentakh i materialakh 1930-1990-e gg. [History of State and Law of Russia in Documents and Materials]. Ed. by I. N. Kuznetsov. Minsk: Amalfeia, 2003.

Khruschchev, Nikita. *The Crimes of the Stalin Era: Special Report to the 20th Congress of the Communist Party of the Soviet Union*. Annotated by Boris I. Nicolaevsky. New York: The New Leader, 1956.

Lebedeva, N. S., ed. *SSSR i Niurnbergskii protsess. Neizvestnye i maloizvestnye stranitsy istorii: Sbornik dokumentov* [The USSR and the Nuremberg Trials.: An Unknown and Little Known History: Document Collection]. Moscow: Mezhdunarodnyi fond Demokratiia, 2012.

Lenin on Politics and Revolution: Selected Writings. Ed. by James E. Connor. New York: Pegasus, 1968.

Lubianka: Stalin i NKVD-NKGB-GUKR 'Smersh' 1939-March 1946 [Lubianka: Stalin and NKVD-NKGB-GUKR 'Smersh' 1939-March 1946]. Ed. by V. N. Khaustov, V. P. Naumov, and N. S. Plotnikova. Moscow: Mezhdunarodnyi Fond "Demokratiia," 2006.

Lyons, Eugene. *Assignment in Utopia*. New York: Harcourt, Brace, 1937.

Office of United States Chief of Counsel for Prosecution of Axis Criminality. *Nazi Conspiracy and Aggression*, Vol. I. Washington, DC: United States Government Printing Office, 1946.

Office of United States Chief of Counsel for Prosecution of Axis Criminality. *Nazi Conspiracy and Aggression: Opinion and Judgment*. Washington, DC: United States Government Printing Office, 1947.

Organy bezopasnosti SSSR v 1941-1945 gg. [The Soviet Security Services in 1941-1945]. Ed. by V. S. Khristoforov. Moscow: Izdatel'stvo Glavnogo arkhivnogo upravleniia Moskvy, 2011.

Preliminary Commission of Inquiry. *The Case of Leon Trotsky: Report of Hearings on the Charges Made against Him in the Moscow Trials*. New York: Harper & Brothers, 1937.

Protsess Bukharina 1938 g.[The Bukharin Process 1938]. Ed. by Zh. B. Artamonova and N. B. Petrov. Moscow: Mezhdunarodnyi Fond "Demokratiya," 2013.

Report of Court Proceedings in the Case of the Anti-Soviet Trotskyite Centre. Heard before the Military Collegium of the Supreme Court of the U.S.S.R., Moscow, January 23–30, 1937. Verbatim Report. New York: Howard Fertig, 1967.

Report of Court Proceedings in the Case of the Anti-Soviet 'Bloc of Rights and Trotskyites.' Heard before the Military Collegium of the Supreme Court of the U.S.S.R., Moscow, March 2–13, 1938. Verbatim Report. Moscow: People's Commissariat of Justice of the U.S.S.R., 1938.

Report of Robert H. Jackson, United States Representative to the International Conference on Military Trials. London, 1945. Washington, DC: Department of State, 1949.

"Shvernik Report on the Trial against Tukachevsky and Other Members of the RKKA [*Raboche-krest'yanskaya Krasnaya armiya*; Workers' and Peasants' Red Army], II," April 28, 2009, 3. Accessed September 20, 2016. http://skoblin. blogspot.com/2009/04/shvernik-report-on-trial-against_28...

Smith, Bradley. *The American Road to Nuremberg: The Documentary Record, 1944-1945*. Stanford, CA: Stanford University Press, 1982.

Soobshchenia Chrezvychainoi Gosudarstvennoi Kommissii po Ustanovleniiu i Rasledovaniiu Zlodeianii Nemetsko-Fashistikh Okkupantov i ikh posobnikov na Vremenno Okkupirovannoi Territorii SSSR [Communications of the Extraordinary State Commission on the Establishment and Investigation of the Evildoings of the German-Fascist Occupiers and Their Accomplices on the Temporarily Occupied Territory of the USSR]. Moscow: ChGK, 1944.

SSSR I Niurnbergsxkii protsess: Neizvestnye I Maloizvestnye Stanitsy Istorii: Sbornik dokumentov [The USSR and the Nuremberg Trial: Unknown and Little Known Pages from a Collection of Historical Documents]. Ed. by N.S. Lebedeva. Moscow: Mezhdunarodnyi Fond "Demokratiya," 2012.

Taylor, Telford. *The Anatomy of the Nuremberg Trials: A Personal Memoir*. New York: Alfred A. Knopf, 1992.

Taylor, Telford. *Die Nürnberger Prozesse*. Munich: Heyne, 1994.

Trotsky, Leon. *My Life*. New York: Pathfinder Press, 1970.

Die UdSSR und die deutsche Frage 1941-1949: Dokumente aus dem Archiv für Außenpolitik der Russichen Föderation. Ed. by Jochen P. Laufer and Georgij P. Kynin. Bd. 2:9. Mai 1945 bis 3 Oktober 1946. Berlin: Duncker & Humblot, 2004.

United States Holocaust Memorial Museum, Washington, DC.

RG-06.027. Latvian State Archives of the Former Latvian KGB (State Security Committee) records from Fond 1986 relating to war crimes investigations and trials in Latvia, 1941-1995 (bulk 1944-1966).

RG-26.004M. War crimes investigations and trial records from the former Lithuanian KGB archives, 1944-1992.

RG-31.018M. Post-war crimes trials related to the Holocaust, 1937-1943, from the archives of the Security Service of Ukraine.

RG-38.001. Post-war crimes trials from the archives of the Ministry of the Interior of the Georgia SSR (ex-KGB archives).

Secondary Sources

Articles

Borisova, Tatiana. "Public Meaning of the Zasulich Trial 1878: Law, Politics, and Gender." *Russian History*, 43 (2016), 221–44.
Burakovskiy, Aleksandr. "Holocaust Remembrance in Ukraine: Memorialization of the Jewish Tragedy at Babi Yar." *Nationalities Papers*, 39, 3 (May 2011), 371–89.
Exeler, Franziska. "The Ambivalent State: Determining Guilt in the Post-World War II Soviet Union." *Slavic Review*, 75, 3 (2016), 606–29.
Ginsburgs, George. "Laws of War and War Crimes on the Russian Front during World War II: The Soviet View." *Soviet Studies*, 11, 3 (January 1960), 253–85.
Hicks, Jeremy. "'Too Gruesome to Be Fully Taken in': Konstantin Simonov's 'The Extermination Camp' as Holocaust Literature." *The Russian Review*, 72 (April 2013), 242–59.
Hirsch, Francine. "The Soviets at Nuremberg: International Law, Propaganda, and the Making of the Postwar Order." *American Historical Review*, 113, 3 (2008), 701–30.
Penter, Tanja. "Collaboration on Trial: New Source Material on Soviet Postwar Trials against Collaborators." *Slavic Review*, 64, 4 (2005), 782–90.
Pipes, Richard. "The Trial of Vera Z." *Russian History*, 37, 1 (2010), v, vii–x, 1–3, 5–31, 33–49, 51–82.
Sorokina, Marina. "People and Procedures: Toward a History of the Investigation of Nazi Crimes in the USSR." *Kritika*, 6, 4 (2005), 797–831.
Turetskii, M. V. *Osobo opasnye gosudarstvennye voiny* [The Military Tribunals in the Conditions of the Great Patriotic War]. *Sotsialisticheskaia zakonnost'*, 7 (1942), 1–3.
Zorya, Yuri and Natalia Lebdeva. "The Year 1939 in the Nuremberg Files." *International Affairs*, 10 (October 1939), 117–29.

Books

Alderman, Sidney. "Negotiating the Nuremberg Trial Agreements, 1945." In Raymond Dennet and Joseph E. Johnson, eds. *Negotiating with the Russians*. Boston, MA: World Peace Foundation, 1951, 49–100.
Arad, Yitzhak. *The Holocaust in the Soviet Union*. Lincoln, NE: University Nebraska Press, 2009.
Autin-Perrault, Annabelle. *Conspiracy and Paranoia at Shakhty: The First Stalinist Show Trial, May-June 1928*. Lexington, KY: CreateSpace Independent Publishing Platform, 2014.
Ball, Howard. "The Path to Nuremberg, 1941-1945." In Samuel Totten, ed. *The Genocide Studies Reader*. London: Taylor and Francis, 2009.
Believ, A. M. *Kuban' v gody Velikoï Otechestvennoi Voĭny, 1941-1945: khronika sobytiĭ* [Kuban' during the Great Patriotic War 1941-1945: The Chronicle of Events]. 3 vols. Krasnodar: Sov. Kuban', 2000–2003.

Berkhoff, Karel. *Motherland in Danger: Soviet Propaganda during World War II.* Cambridge, MA: Harvard University Press, 2012.

Berman, Harold J. *Soviet Criminal Law and Procedure: The RSFSR Codes.* Cambridge, MA: Harvard University Press, 1972.

Birstein, Vadim J. *SMERSH: Stalin's Secret Weapon.* London: Biteback Publishing, 2011.

Bloxham, Donald. "Milestones and Mythologies: The Impact of Nuremberg." In Patricia Hdeberer and Jürgen Matthäus, eds. *Atrocities on Trial: Historical Perspectives on the Politics of Prosecuting War Crimes.* Lincoln, NE: University of Nebraska Press, 2008, 263–82.

Brooks, Jeffrey. *Thank You, Comrade Stalin: Soviet Public Culture from Revolution to Cold War.* Princeton, NJ: Princeton University Press, 2000.

Brown, Raymond W. "The American Perspective on Nuremberg: A Case of Cascading Ironies." In Herbert R. Reginbogin and Christopher J. M. Safferling, eds. *The Nuremberg Trials: International Criminal Law since 1945.* München: De Gruyter Saur, 2006, 21–29.

Burnham, James. *Why Did They "Confess?": A Study of the Radek-Piatakov Trial.* New York: Pioneer Publishers, 1937.

Cassiday, Julie. *The Enemy on Trial: Early Soviet Courts on Stage and Screen.* Dekalb, IL: Northern Illinois University Press, 2000.

Chebrikov, V. M., G. F. Grigorenko, N. A. Dushin, and F. D. Bobkov. *Istoriia sovetskikh organov osbezopasnosti* [History of the Soviet Security Services]. Moscow: Vysshaia Krasnoznamennaia shkola KGB pri Sovetie Ministrov SSSR imeni F.E. Dzerzhinskogo, 1977.

Cienciala, Anna M., Natalia S. Lebedeva, and Wojciech Materski, eds. *Katyn: A Crime without Punishment.* New Haven, CT: Yale University Press, 2007.

Conquest, Robert. *The Great Terror: Stalin's Purge of the Thirties.* Harmondsworth: Penguin Press, 1971.

Conquest, Robert. *Harvest of Sorrow: Soviet Collectivization and the Terror-Famine.* New York: Oxford University Press, 1986.

Crowe, David M. *The Holocaust: Roots, History, and Aftermath.* Boulder, CO: Westview, 2012.

Crowe, David M. *War Crimes, Genocide, and Justice: A Global History.* New York: Palgrave Macmillan, 2014.

Epifanov, A. E. *Otvetstvenost' za voennye prestupleniia, sovershennye na territorii SSSR v gody Velikoi Otechestvennoi voiny* [Responsibility for War Crimes Committed on the Territory of the USSR during the Great Patriotic War]. Volvograd: Volgogradskaia akademiia MVD Rossii, 2005.

Felman, Shoshana and Dori Laub. *Testimony: Crises of Witnessing Literature, Psychoanalysis, and History.* New York: Routledge, 1992.

Ginsburgs, George. *Moscow's Road to Nuremberg: The Soviet Background to the Trial.* The Hague: Martinus Nijhoff, 1996.

Ginsburgs, George and V. N. Kudriavtsev, eds. *The Nuremberg Trial and International Law.* Dordrecht: Martinus Nijhoff, 1990.

Harris, James. *The Great Fear: Stalin's Terror of the 1930s.* Oxford: Oxford University Press, 2016.

Hicks, Jeremy. *First Films of the Holocaust: Soviet Cinema and the Genocide of the Jews.* Pittsburgh, PA: University of Pittsburg Press, 2012.

Iablokov, A. Iu., V. S. Parsadanova, and I. S. Iazhborovskaia. *Katynskii sindrom v sovetsko-pol'skikh i Rossiisko-Pol'skikh otnosheniiakh* [The Katyn Syndrome in Soviet-Polish and Russian-Polish Relations]. Moscow: ROSSPEN, 2001.

Iazhnorovskaiia, Inessa, Anatolii Iablokov, and Valentna Parsadanova. *Katynskii sindrom v Sovetsko-Pol'skikh i Rossiisko-Pol'skikh otnosheniiakh* [The Katyn Syndrome in Soviet-Polish and Russian-Polish Relations]. Moscow: ROSSPEN, 2009.

Irvin-Erickson, Douglas. *Raphaël Lemkin and the Concept of Genocide*. Philadelphia, PA: University of Pennsylvania Press, 2017.

Jensen, Mark. *A Show Trial under Lenin: The Trial of the Socialist Revolutionaries, Moscow, 1922*. Trans. by Jean Sanders. The Hague: Martinus Nijhoff, 1982.

Kochavi, Arieh. *Prelude to Nuremberg: Allied War Crimes Policy and the Question of Punishment*. Chapel Hill, NC: University of North Carolina Press, 1998.

Kotkin, Stephen. *Stalin, I: Paradoxes of Power, 1878-1928*. New York: Penguin Press, 2014.

Kudriavtsev, V. N. and M. E. Karyshev, eds. *Politicheskaia iustitsiia v SSSR* [Political Justice in the USSR]. St. Petersburg: Iuridicheskii tsentr Press, 2002.

Kuznetsova, N. F. *Trainin, Izbrannie proizvenedia [Selected Works]*. St. Petersburg: Yuridichesky Center Press, 2004.

Lebedeva, N. S., V. V. Ishenko, and I. Iu Korschunov, eds. *Niurbergskii protsess: uroki istorii: Materialy mezhdunarodnoi nauchnoi konferentsii* [The Nuremberg Trials. Lesson of History: Proceedings from an International Conference]. Moscow: Institut vseobshchei istorii RAN, 2007.

Lebedeva, N. S. *Podgotokva Niurnberskogo protsessa* [The Preparation of the Nuremberg Trials]. Moscow; Izdatel'stvo Nauka, 1975.

Lemkin, Raphaël. *Axis Rule in Occupied Europe: Laws of Occupation, Analysis of Government Proposals for Redress*, 2nd edition. Clark, NJ: The Lawbook Exchange, 2008.

Maksimov, S. S. and M. E. Karyshev, eds. *Neotvratimoe vozmezdie: po materialam sudebnykh protsessov nad izmennikami rodiny, fashistskimi palachami I agentami imperialisticheskikh razvedok* [Inevitable Retribution: On the Records of the Trials of the Traitors of the Motherland, Fascist Henchmen and Agents of the Imperialist Intelligence Services]. Moscow: Voennoe izdatel'stvo, 1987.

Marrus, Michael R. *The Nuremberg War Crimes Trial, 1945-1946: A Documentary History*. Boston, MA: St. Martin's Press, 1997.

Medvedev, Roy A. *Let History Judge*. New York: Vintage Books, 1971.

Medvedev, Roy A. *Nikolai Bukharin: The Last Years*. Trans. by A. D. P. Briggs. New York: W.W. Norton, 1980.

Minear, Richard. *Victor's Justice: The Tokyo War Crimes Trial*. Princeton, NJ: Princeton University Press, 1971.

Penn, Michelle Jean. *The Extermination of Peaceful Soviet Citizens: Aron Trainin and International Law*. Dissertation. Boulder, CO: Department of History, University of Colorado, 2017.

Persico, Joseph. *Nuremberg: Infamy on Trial*. New York: Viking, 1994.

Pikhoia, R. G. and V. P. Kozlov, eds. *Katyn'*. Moscow: ROSSPEN, 1997.

Poltorak, A. *The Nuremberg Epilogue*. Moscow: Progress Publishers, 1971.

Pomorski, Stansław. "Conspiracy and Criminal Organizations." In George Ginsburgs and V. N. Kudriavtsev, eds. *The Nuremberg Trial and International Law*. Dordrecht: Martinus Nijhoff, 1990, 213–48.

Pompe, Cornelius A. *Aggressive War and International Crime*. Berlin: Springer, 1953.

Pomper, Philip. *Lenin's Brother: The Origins of the October Revolution*. New York: W.W. Norton, 2010.

Priemel, Kim Christian. *The Betrayal: The Nuremberg Trials and German Divergence*. Oxford: Oxford University Press, 2016.

Rakhemetov, S. M., S. A. Krementsov, and M. O. Kolkobaev. *Prestupleniia protiv osnov konstitutsionogo stroia i bezopasnosti gosudarstva* [Crimes against the Fundamentals of the Constitutional Order and State Security]. Almaty: TOO "Baspa," 1998.

Rauschenbach, Gerhard. *Der Nürnberger Prozeß gegen die Organisationen The Nuremberger Case against [Nazi Organizations]: Basic Facts, Problems, Impact, and Criminal Results]. Grundlagen, Probleme, Auswirken auf die Mitglieder und strafrechtliche Ergebnisse.* Bonn: Röhrschied, 1954.

Riabchuk, V. N. *Gosudarstvennaia izmena I shpionazh: ugolovno-pravovoe I kriminologicheskoe issledovanie* [High Treason and Espionage: Criminal-Legal and Criminological Research]. Sankt-Petersburg: Isdatel'stvo R. Aslanova "Iuridicheskii tsentr Press," 2007.

Riggs, Robert. *Sofia Perovskaya. Terrorist Princess: The Plot to Kill Tsar Alexander II and the Woman Who Led It.* Berkeley, CA: Global Harmony Press, 2017–2018.

Rogovin, Vadim Z. *Stalin's Terror of 1937-1938: Political Genocide in the USSR.* Trans. by Frederick S. Choate. Oak Park, MI: Mehring Books, 2009.

Rogovin, Vadim Z. *1937: Stalin's Year of Terror.* Trans. by Frederick S. Choate. Oak Park, MI: Mehring Books, 1998.

Schlesinger, Rudolf. *Soviet Legal Theory: Its Social Background and Development.* London: Kegan Paul, Trench, Trubner & Co., Ltd, 1945.

Schulmeister-André, Irina. *Internationale Strafgerichtsbarkeit unter sowjetischen Einfluss; Der Beitrag der UdSSR zum Nürnberger Hauptkriegsverbrechersprozess* [Soviet Influence on International Criminal Justice: The Contribution of the USSR on the Principal Nuremberg War Crimes Trial]. Berlin: Duncker & Humblot, 2016.

Segesser, Daniel Marc. *Recht statt Rache oder Rache durch Recht? Die Ahndung von Kriegsvervbrechen in der internationalen wissenschaftli chen Debatte, 1872–1945* [Right Instead of Revenge or Revenge by Right?: The International Debate about the Punishment of War Crimes, 1872-1945]. Paderborn: Verlag Ferdinand Schönigh, 2007.

Sellars, Kirsten. *"Crimes against Peace" and International Law.* Cambridge: Cambridge University Press, 2013.

Sellars, Kirsten. *Trials for International Crimes in Asia.* Cambridge: Cambridge University Press, 2013.

Service, Robert. *Lenin A Biography.* Cambridge, MA: Belknap Press, 2000.

Sharlet, Robert and Piers Beirne. "In Search of Vyshinsky: The Paradox of Law and Terror." In Piers Beirne, ed. *Revolution in Law: Contributions to the Development of Soviet Legal Theory, 1917-1938.* Armonk: M.E. Sharpe, 2015.

Snow, Edgar. *The Pattern of Soviet Power.* New York: Random House. 1945.

Solomon, Peter H. *Soviet Criminal Justice under Stalin.* Cambridge: Cambridge University Press, 1996.

Stalin. J. V. *On the Opposition (1917-27).* Peking: Foreign Languages Press, 1974.

Stonebridge, Lyndsey. *The Judicial Imagination: Writing after Nuremberg.* Edinburgh: Edinburgh University Press, 2001.

Trainin, Aron. *Ucheniye o souchastii* [The Doctrine of Complicity]. Moscow: Yuridicheskoye izdatel'stvo NKU SSSR, 1941.

Trainin, Aron. *Ugolovnaia otvetsvennost' gitlerovtsev* [Criminal Responsibility of the Hitlerites]. Ed. by A. Ia. Vyshinskii. Moscow: Iurid. Izdatel'stvo NKIU Soiuza SSR, 1944.

Trainin, Aron. *Zashchita mira i ugolovnyy zakon* [The Defense of Peace and Criminal Law]. Ed. and Forward by Andrei Vyshinsky. Moscow: Yuridicheskoye izdatel'stvo NKU SSSR, 1937.

Tumarkin, Nina. *The Living and the Dead: The Rise and Fall of the Cult of World War II in Russia.* New York: Basic Books, 1995.

Tusa, Ann and John Tusa. *The Nuremberg Trial.* London: Atheneum, 1983.

Vaksberg, Arkady. *Stalin's Prosecutor: The Life of Andrei Vyshinsky*. New York: Grove Weidenfeld, 1990.

Vneshnaia politika Sovetskogo Soiuza v period otechestvennoi voiny [Foreign Policy of the Soviet Union in the Period of the Fatherland War]. I. Moscow, Gospolitizdat, 1946.

Vyshinsky, Andrei Y. *The Law of the Soviet State*. Trans. by Hugh W. Babb. New York: Macmillan, 1948.

Voisin, Vanessa. "*Au nom des vivants*, de Léon Mazroukho: rencontre entre denunciation officielle et homage personnel" [In Memory of Leon Mazroukho's Life: Between Official Denunciation and Homage]. In Valérie Posner and Natacha Laurent, eds. *Kinojudaica. Les representations des Juifs dans le cinema russe et soviétique des années 1910 aux années 1980*. [Kinojudaica: The Representations of Jews in Russia and Soviet Cinema From 1910 to 1981]. Paris: Noveau Monde éditions, 2012, 365–407.

Voisin, Vanessa. *L'URSS contre ses traîtres Épuration soviétique (1941-1955) [The USSR and Its Traitors: The Soviet Purge]*. Paris: Publications de la Sorbonne, 2015.

Volkogonov, Dmitri. *Stalin: Triumph & Tragedy*. Trans. by Harold Shukman. New York: Grove Weidenfeld, 1988.

Weiss-Wendt, Anton. *A Rhetorical Crime: Genocide in the Geopolitical Discourse of the Cold War*. New Brunswick, NJ: Rutgers University Press, 2018.

Weiss-Wendt, Anton. *The Soviet Union and the Gutting of the UN Genocide Convention*. Madison, WI: University of Wisconsin Press, 2017.

Wieviorka, Annette. *The Era of the Witness*. Trans. by Jared Stark. Ithaca, NY: Cornell University Press, 2006.

Wood, Elizabeth. *Performing Justice Agitation Trials in Early Soviet Russia*. Ithaca, NY: Cornell University Press, 2005.

Zorin, P. *Soviet Military Tribunals*. New York: Research Program on the U.S.S.R., 1954.

Zviagintsev, Aleksandr. *Glavnyi protsess cheovechestva: Reportazh iz proshlogo obrashchenie k budushchemu* [The Major Trial of Humanity: Reporting from the Past, Addressing the Future]. Moscow: OLMA Media Group, 2011.

Zviagintsev, Aleksandr and Iurii Orlov. *Prokurory dvukh epoch: Andrei Vushinskii i Roman Rudenko* [Prosecutors of Two Eras: Andrei Vyshinsky and Roman Rudenko]. Moscow: OLMA-Press, 2001.

Zviagintsev, Aleksandr. *Rudenko*. Moscow: Molodaia gvardiia, 2008.

Zviagintsev, Viacheslav. *Voina na vesakh Femidy: voina 1941-1945 gg. v materialakh sudebnosledstvennykh del* [War on the Scale of Lady Justice: The War of 1941-1945 in Judicial-Investigative Cases]. Moscow: Terra, 2006.

Index

aggression (in war and international law) 7, 9, 10, 14, 127, 130, 132, 133, 134, 135, 137, 138
agitation trials. *See* Bolshevik trials
Akhmatova, Anna 210
Alexander II 34
Alexander III 2, 35, 36
Alexandrov, Georgii 114, 120
Anti-Right Bloc of Rights and Trotyskites trial (March 1938) 60–5. *See also* Moscow "show" trials; Vyshinsky, Andrei
anti-Semitism. *See* Holocaust; Jews
Anti-Soviet Trotskyite Center trial (January 1937) 52, 53, 55–6, 57
Arajs commando. *See* trials, postwar Soviet
Article 58. *See* Soviet criminal code (1926)
Association Internationale de Droit Pénal (International Association of Penal Law) 7, 9, 219, 221
Auschwitz 21, 119, 200, 203, 204, 205, 207, 211
Axis 7, 85, 90, 91
Azat Krym (Liberated Crimea). *See* Crimean Tatars

Babi Yar 225
Ball, Howard 111
Belzec 120
Beria, Lavrentii 84. *See also* NKVD
Bernays, Murray 112, 113, 151
Biddle, Francis 113
Bochkov, Viktor (Prosecutor General, 1940–1943) 6, 84, 85, 86, 92
Bolsheviks 3, 37, 47, 51
Bolshevik trials 38
Buck, Pearl S. 24
Budenko Commission 182, 183, 184, 187, 189

Bukharin, Nikolai 5, 6, 7, 9–10, 39, 54, 55, 58, 60, 61, 62. *See also* Anti-Soviet Trotskyite Center trial; Moscow "show" trials; Trotskyite-Zinovievite Terrorist Centre trial; Vyshinsky, Andrei, Anti-Soviet Bloc of Rights and Trotskyites trial

Cassiday, Julie 1, 2, 3
Central Committee 5, 6, 50, 51, 54, 58, 61
Cheka 37, 40, 68 n.48
Chelmno 120
ChGK. *See* Extraordinary State Commission for Ascertaining and Investigating Crimes Perpetrated by the German-Fascist Invaders and their Accomplices
Churchill, Winston 18, 21, 105, 109, 110, 111, 113, 114, 209
Cold War 199, 210
Comintern (Communist International) 42, 47, 50, 54, 55
complicity, theory of 7, 9, 10, 64, 131–2, 133, 134, 138. *See also* Trainin, Aron; Vyshinsky, Andrei
Conquest, Robert 48, 59, 66. *See also* Great Purges (Great Terror)
conspiracy, theory of. *See* complicity, theory of
Council of People's Commissars 42, 54
Crimean Tatars 7, 89–91
crimes against humanity 10, 128, 135, 137
crimes against peace. *See* International Military Tribunal, Nuremberg
Criminal Code of the Ukrainian SSR
  Article 54 94–5
  trial of members of member of the organization of Ukrainian Nationalists (OUN) (1945) 94–5

Dachau   204
Davies, Joseph E.   56, 57, 59, 60
decree (*Ukaz*) 39 (April 19, 1943)   85–6, 89, 96
Dewey Commission report (1937)   56–7
    See also Trotsky, Leon
Dondua, Mikhail   93–4
Dostoevsky, Fyodor   35
Duranty, Walter   43, 56

Ečer, Bohuslav   134, 135
Efimov, Boris   201
Einsatzgruppen   83, 203
Erenburg, Il'ia (Ehrenburg, Ilya)   21, 207
Extraordinary State Commission for Ascertaining and Investigating Crimes Perpetrated by the German-Fascist Invaders and their Accomplices (ChGK)   8, 16, 72 n.129, 114, 115, 173, 174, 176, 177, 182

Falco, Robert   13, 14
field courts martials. *See* military tribunals
Film Documents of Atrocities Committed by the German-Fascist Invaders (Soviet film, Nuremberg)   21, 208–9
First Five Year Plan (1928–1932)   42, 47, 51
Four Power Agreement (1945).
    See London Conference
Frank, Hans   208
Fyfe, Maxwell D.   133, 134, 146

General Plan for the East   105
genocide. *See also* Genocide Convention, United Nations (1948); Holocaust; Lemkin, Raphaël   128, 137, 139, 217–229 *passim*
Genocide Convention, United Nations (1948)   10–11, 23, 24, 217, 128, 137, 139, 217–29
Germany, Nazi   5, 6, 9, 55, 56, 60, 66
Gestapo   61, 89
Ginsburgs, George   8, 11, 105
GLAVPURKKA (Main Political Administration of the Workers and peasants' Red Army)   116–17

Goebbels, Joseph   209–10
Göring, Hermann   179, 183, 184, 185, 201, 203
Gorky, Maxim   61, 65, 76 n.248
Gorshenin, Konstantin   177, 179
GPU. *See* OGPU
Great Fatherland War   8, 20, 21–2, 72 n.129, 88, 92
    Soviet narrative of   199–200
Great Patriotic War. *See* Great Fatherland War
Great Purges (Great Terror)   83, 173, 175. *See also* Conquest, Robert

Hague Conventions (1899, 1907)   107, 115
Harriman, Averell   146
Hess, Rudolf   19, 105, 110, 180, 185, 201
Heydrich, Reinhard   207–8
Himmler, Heinrich   105, 115
Hirsch, Francine   8, 11, 19, 106, 107, 113, 121
Hitler, Adolf   17, 20, 50, 51, 60, 155.
    See also Germany, Nazi
Holocaust (Shoah)   96, 97, 200, 205, 211, 226. *See also* genocide
Höss, Rudolf   205. *See also* Auschwitz

industrialization campaign. *See* Stalin, Joseph
Industrial Party trial (1930)   4, 45–6
International Military Tribunal, Nuremberg (1945–1946)   7, 12, 14, 22, 23, 107, 112, 113, 114, 115, 120–1, 119, 135
    Charter   128, 134
    Articles   12, 13, 14, 19, 21, 150–1, 155
    Counts   1–4, 16, 17
    crimes against peace   172, 173, 190, 191
    Nuremberg Commission (Soviet)   14
    Nuremberg principles   14, 224
    witnesses   200, 204, 207
Izvestia   21

Jackson, Robert   10, 18
    IMT Nuremberg trial   17, 18, 112, 178, 179, 180, 183, 184, 185
    London Conference   12, 13, 14, 133–4
Japan   4, 9, 50, 51, 55, 56, 66
Jews   8, 9, 17, 20. *See also* Holocaust

anti-Semitism 8, 9, 17, 20
  genocide and 7, 8, 9, 21
Jowitt, Sir William 14

Kaganovich, Lazar 50, 54
Kamenev, Lev 50, 51, 55, 60. *See also*
    Moscow "show" trials
Karelin, Vladimir 63, 64, 76 n.264
Karmen, Roman 182, 201, 204, 208–9
Katyn massacre (1940) 12, 16, 18, 19,
    172, 177, 182–3, 184, 186, 187,
    189, 190
Keitel, Wilhelm 181, 201
Kellogg-Briand Pact (1928) 6
Kerensky, Alexander 38
Kharkov trial (1943) 6, 8
Khrushchev, Nikita 52, 59
Kirov, Sergei 5, 65
  murder of 50, 51, 65
Koni, Anatoly 2, 31, 32, 33
Krasdonar trial (1943) 6. *See also*
    military tribunals
Krasnodon trial (1943) 6. *See also*
    military tribunals
Krestinsky, Nikolai 5, 61, 62, 65
Krushinskii, Semen 203, 207, 209
Krylenko, Nikolai 4, 39, 49, 71 n.120
  early career 43
  Industrial Party trial 46
  Shakhty trial 43
  SR trial (1931) 46–7
Kukryniksy (name for trio of caricaturists
    Mikhail Kuprianov, Porfiri
    Krylov, and Nikolai
    Sokolov) 201
Kursky, Dmitri 4, 38, 40

Lauterpacht, Hersch 221
*Leading Principles of the Criminal Law of
    the R.F.S.F.R.* (1919) 41
League of Nations 106, 107, 120, 221
Lebensraum 105–6
Lemkin, Raphaël 9, 22, 23, 24, 217–29
    passim. *See also* genocide;
    Genocide Convention
  Axis Rule in Occupied Europe
    (1944) 23, 24
Lenin, Vladimir Ilyich 1, 3, 4, 8, 35, 36–7,
    38, 39, 40, 41, 61, 65, 69 n.53
Leonov, Leonid 20, 202–3, 204

Lewis, Mark 7
London Conference (1945) 11–14, 18,
    133, 134, 145–62 *passim*. *See
    also* International Military
    Tribunal, Nuremberg
  Articles, discussion of 150–8
  Falco, Robert 148, 161
  Four Power Agreement 145
  Fyfe, David Maxwell and 146, 148,
    155, 156, 159, 161
  Jackson, Robert and 145, 146, 148,
    149, 152, 154, 155, 157, 158–9,
    160, 161, 165 n.49
    Report of Robert H. Jackson
      (June 1945) 145, 161 n.49,
      166 nn.54, 59, 62, 167 nn.63, 65,
      66, 67, 169 n.94
  Jowitt, William 160–1
  Molotov, Vyacheslav and 147, 149
  Nikitchenko, Ion and 146–7, 148,
    149, 150, 152, 153, 154, 155,
    156, 157, 159, 161, 164 n.37,
    166 n.54
  Postdam conference and (1945)
    158–61
  Soviet delegation 13–14, 146–9
  Stalin, Joseph and 147
  Trainin, Aron and 146, 148, 149,
    152, 153, 154, 157–8, 161,
    164 n.37
  Vyshinsky, Andrei and 146, 147, 149,
    153
Lyons, Eugene 43, 45, 48

Majdanek 120, 204, 206
Masaryk, Tomáš 225
Mauthausen 205
Medvedev, Roy 59
Mein Kampf 105–6. *See also* Hitler,
    Adolf
Mensheviks 46–7, 59
  trial of (1931) 46–7
Metro-Vickers trial (1933) 4, 47–8
MGB (Ministry of State Security;
    1946–1953) 93
Military Collegium of the Supreme Soviet
    of the USSR 5, 52, 54, 57,
    81, 92
Military Council of the Commissariat of
    Defense 58

military tribunals (Soviet)   83, 84–7, 89
    Kharkov (1943)   88
    Krasdonar (1943)   87–8
    Krasnodon (1943)   88
    Kuban (1946)   88
    southern Russia   87
Molotov, Vyacheslav   11, 18, 50, 106, 107, 109, 148, 172, 174, 177, 179, 181, 185. *See also* International Military Tribunal, Nuremberg; London Conference; Molotov-Ribbentrop Pact
Molotov-Ribbentrop Pact (Soviet-German Nonaggression Pact, 23 August 1939)   16, 19, 178, 179, 185, 187, 188, 189
Moscow Declaration (30 October 1943)   10
    London Conference   13, 14
Moscow "show" trials (1936–1938)   5, 33, 50, 173, 174, 179. *See also* Anti-Soviet Bloc of Rights Trotskyites trial (March 1938); Anti-Soviet Trotskyite Centre trial (January 1937); Trotyskite-Zinovievite Terrorist Centre trial (August 1936)
Moscow State University   9, 11. *See also* Vyshinsky, Andrei
Muslim Committee   93. *See also* Crimean Tatars

Nazi Party   219. *See also* Hitler, Adolf
The Nazi Plan (Soviet film, Nuremberg)   21, 204
NEP (New Economic Policy)   3, 37, 40, 41, 42, 44, 45, 47
Nikitchenko, Iona T.   11, 12, 14, 19, 22, 23 *See also* International Military Tribunal, Nuremberg; London Conference
Nikolayev, Leonid   50
NKVB (People's Commissariat for State Security; 1943–1946)   90–7
NKVD (People's Commissariat for Internal Affairs, 1934–1943)   5, 6, 51, 52, 53, 54, 55, 58, 59, 60, 76 n.248, 82, 84, 90, 91, 92, 94, 95, 97
    Special Section or Commission   84, 86, 91, 92

Nuremberg. *See* International Military Tribunal, Nuremberg
Nuriev, Izet   91. *See also* Azat Krym; Crimean Tatars

OGPU   4, 40, 43
Old Bolsheviks   5, 60, 173
OUN (Organization of Ukrainian Nationalists). *See* Criminal Code of the Ukrainian SSR

Pal, Radhabinod   10, 135–6
Panina, Sophie   38
Pashukanis, Evgeny   45, 71 n.112, 127
Paulus, Friedrich von   18, 208
Pella, Vespasian   9, 22, 23, 219, 222
Penn, Michelle Jean   9
The People's Will (*Narodnaya volya*)   34
Perovskaya, Sophia   2
Poland   61, 63, 177, 182, 184. *See also* Katyn massacre (1940)
    Soviet invasion of (1939)   12, 16, 171, 176, 178, 185, 186
Polevoi, Boris   21, 22, 200, 201, 204, 205, 206, 210
Politburo   61, 85
Potsdam Conference (1945)   159–60
    Potsdam Protocol   14
Pravda   3, 9, 20, 21, 115, 118
Pyatakov, Georgii   55, 56

Radek, Karl   48, 54, 55, 56, 57
Rakovsky, Khristian   61, 62, 65, 66
Ramazanov, Miknil   90
Rappaport, Emil   9, 221
Red Army   8, 85
red terror   37, 38
Ribbentrop, Joachim von   179, 185, 186
Riutin Platform   50
Roosevelt, Franklin   105, 110, 111, 113, 160
Rudenko, Roman. *See* International Military Tribunal, Nuremberg
Russian Civil War (1918–1921)   3, 57, 58
Rykov, Alexei   54, 58, 60, 62, 63, 65

St. James Declaration (13 January 1942)   8, 109, 110
San Francisco Conference (1945)   11–12

SD (*Sicherheitsdienst*; Security Service of the SS) 90, 91, 96. *See also* Crimean Tatars
Second World War. *See* World War II
Seidl, Dr. Alfred 19
Service, Robert 3, 4
Shakhty trial (1928) 4, 42–3
"show" trials 1, 2, 3
   Soviet era 33–4, 36–7. *See also* individual Moscow "show" trials
   Tsarist era 31, 36–7
Simon, John 110
Skaiskalns, Adolf 95–6. *See also* trials, postwar Soviet
Socialist Revolutionaries 3–4, 37, 59–60, 67 n.6
Socialist Revolutionary trial (1922) 38–40, 43, 55
Solomon, Peter 4, 48
Soviet narrative of World War II. *See* Great Fatherland War
Soviet criminal code (1922) 39, 40, 41, 81
Soviet criminal code (1926) 6, 81, 86, 88, 89, 95, 96
   Article 58 64, 71 n.98, 82, 84–5, 94. *See also* complicity, theory of
   Basic Principles of Criminal Legislation of the USSR (1924) 80
   Crimean Tatars 89–90, 91
   counterrevolutionary crimes 32
   high treason 80–1
   Statute of Criminal Responsibility for High Treason 81–2
   Statute of State Crimes (1927) 81
Sovnarkom. *See* Council of People's Commissars
Stalin, Joseph 1, 4, 5, 6, 7, 8, 9, 11, 12, 14, 16, 18, 23, 24, 42, 46, 47, 50, 51, 52, 53, 54, 58, 66, 105, 106, 111, 112, 113, 118, 171, 172, 173, 174, 179, 181, 188, 191, 226
   Andrei Vyshinsky relationship with 32
   collectivization and industrialization campaigns 42
   Leon Trotsky and 42

Moscow "show" trials 53, 54, 55, 58, 59, 60, 62
Stalin Constitution (1936) 49. *See also* Vyshinsky, Andrei
Steinberg, Isaac 37
Stimson, Henry 112
Stroop report 208. *See also* Warsaw ghetto
Stuchka, Piotr 37
Supreme Court of the USSR 6
Sutskever, Avram 207

Taylor, Telford 12, 121
"Terror Economics". *See* Service, Robert
Trainin (Trajnin), Aron 8, 9, 112, 115, 172, 191, 202, 220, 223. *See also* Vyshinsky, Andrei
   Criminal Intervention: The Movement towards the Unification of Criminal Law in Capitalist Countries (1935) 9, 23, 128, 130
   The Defense of Peace and Criminal Law (1937) 7, 9, 106, 107, 130–1
   The Doctrine of Complicity (1941) 9
   London Conference 11, 13, 14, 131, 146
   Nuremberg IMT trial 11, 14, 19, 20, 22, 112–13, 128, 179, 189
   On the Criminal Responsibility of the Hitlerites (1944) 7, 107, 132, 152, 161, 173
   Protection of Peace and the Fights against Crimes against Mankind (1956) 10–11
Treblinka 119
Trepov, Dmitri 2, 31–2, 33
trials, postwar Soviet 92–3. *See also* criminal code of the Ukrainian SSR
   Arajs commando 95
   Transcaucasia military district 93–4
Trotsky, Leon 40, 47, 55, 56, 57, 58, 60, 61, 62. *See also* Dewey Commission report; "show" trials
Trotskyist Anti-Soviet Military Organization trial (1937) 52, 57, 58, 59

Trotyskite-Zinovievite Terrorist Centre trial (August 1936)   51, 52, 53, 54, 56, 58, 60
Troyanovsky, Oleg   146
Truman, Harry   160
Tukachevsky, Marshal Mikhail   5, 57, 58, 59, 60. *See also* Trotskyist Anti-Soviet Military Organization trial

Ulrikh, Vasili   5, 52, 53, 55, 56, 58, 59, 61, 62, 63, 64, 65
Ulyanov, Alexander   2, 3, 35, 36. *See also* Lenin, Vladimir Ilyich
United Nations   217, 223, 224–7. *See also* Genocide Convention
United Nations War Crimes Commission (UNWCC)   10, 16, 110, 122, 134, 151, 173
Universal Declaration of Human Rights (1948)   224
UNWCC. *See* United Nations War Crimes Commission

de Vabres, Henri Donnedieu   22, 23, 219
Valliant-Couturier, Marie-Claude   203–4
Vernichtungskrieg (war of annihilation)   203
Vernichtungslager (extermination camps)   203
Vishnevsky, Vsevolod   21, 201, 203–4, 207–8
Vyshinsky, Andrei   4, 5, 7, 8, 9, 22, 23, 24, 66, 106, 127, 128, 217
    Anti-Right Bloc of Rights and Trotskyites trial   60–5
    Aspects and Lessons of the Shakhty Trial   45
    Criminal Trials; A Textbook for Law Schools and Judicial Courses (1936)   57
    Deputy Procurator General   48
    early career   43–4
    Essays on the History of Communism (1924–1925)   44

Genocide Convention   224–7
Industrial Party trial (1930)   45–6
The Law of the Soviet State (1938)   5, 49, 50
Lemkin and   218–21, 228–9
London Conference   11, 14, 146
    as a Menshevik   43–4
Metro-Vickers trial (1933)   47–8
Moscow "show" trials (1936–1938)   52, 53, 54, 55, 56, 173, 177, 178, 179, 180, 181, 184, 186
Moscow State University   44
Nuremberg IMT trial   16, 17, 18, 19, 22, 128, 174
Procurator General   49, 52, 53
publications (general)   44, 45
Shakhty trial   43
Stalin and   43, 45, 48, 49, 53
Theory of Court Evidence in Soviet Law (1946)   44
Trotskyist Anti-Soviet Military Organizational trial (1937)   57–8
Twelve Theses on International Law (1938)   224

Warsaw ghetto   208. *See also* Stroop report
Wood, Elizabeth   3
World War II (Second World War)   79–80, 82–3, 217. *See also* Great Fatherland War; Great Patriotic War

Yagoda, Genrikh   5, 54, 61
Yalta Conference   113
Yezhov, Nikolai   5, 54, 55, 60, 65

Zaslauskii, David   203, 209–10
Zasulich, Vera   2, 31–2, 34, 35, 37, 38
Zhukov, Nikolai   201–2, 207
Zinoviev, Gregory   50, 51, 55, 61
Zoshchenko, Mikhail   210

www.ingramcontent.com/pod-product-compliance
Lightning Source LLC
Chambersburg PA
CBHW050325020526
44117CB00031B/1788